Advancing Practice in Academic Development

Within the field of academic development, the last twenty years have seen a great expansion of published research into practice and the further development of theoretical approaches. This growth in the scholarship of academic development matches a growth in the scholarship of teaching and learning. *Advancing Practice in Academic Development* draws on these evolving scholarships to advance professional practice in academic development, addressing questions such as:

- How have global academic developers and their units developed and changed over recent decades?
- How has the context in which academic development work is done altered?
- What have academic developers and their professional associations learnt?

Case studies and examples are used throughout the text to illustrate development scenarios and methods. Academic development is considered as, among others, a critical, a scholarly, a principled, a pragmatic, a supporting and a leadership role. This book is ideal for use on academic development courses run by SEDA and other international organisations as well as by those who have responsibility for leading the improvement of educational practice. Written in a scholarly, accessible, stimulating and practical style, this book acknowledges difficulties and offers ways forward. As well as analysing problems, it offers solutions.

Links to web sources referenced in this book can be found at www.seda.ac.uk/apad.

David Baume is an independent international higher education researcher, evaluator, consultant, staff and educational developer and writer.

Celia Popovic is Director of Teaching Commons at York University, Toronto, Canada.

The Staff and Educational Development Series
Series Editor: James Wisdom

Advancing Practice in Academic Development
edited by David Baume and Celia Popovic, 2016

Academic and Educational Development: Research, Evaluation and Changing Practice in Higher Education
edited by Ranald Macdonald and James Wisdom, 2002

Assessment for Learning in Higher Education
edited by Peter Knight, 1995

Benchmarking and Threshold Standards in Higher Education
edited by Helen Smith, Michael Armstrong and Sally Brown, 1999

Changing Higher Education: The Development of Learning and Teaching
edited by Paul Ashwin, 2006

Computer-Assisted Assessment in Higher Education
edited by Sally Brown, Phil Race and Joanna Bull, 1999

Developing Effective Part-time Teachers in Higher Education
edited by Fran Beaton and Amanda Gilbert, 2013

Education Development and Leadership in Higher Education: Implementing an Institutional Strategy
edited by Kym Fraser, 2004

Educational Development Through Information and Communications Technology
edited by Stephen Fallows and Rakesh Bhanot, 2007

Enabling Student Learning; Systems and Strategies
edited by Gina Wisker and Sally Brown, 1996

Enhancing Staff and Educational Development
edited by David Baume and Peter Kahn, 2004

Facing Up to Radical Change in Universities and Colleges
edited by Steve Armstrong and Gail Thompson, 1997

SEDA is the professional association for staff and educational developers in the UK, promoting innovation and good practice in higher education. SEDA offers services to its institutional and individual members through its Fellowship scheme, its Professional Development Framework and its conferences, events, publications and projects. SEDA is a member of the International Consortium for Educational Development.

SEDA
Woburn House
20 - 24 Tavistock Square
London
WC1H 9HF
Tel: 020 7380 6767
www.seda.ac.uk

Advancing Practice in Academic Development

Edited by David Baume and Celia Popovic

Routledge
Taylor & Francis Group

LONDON AND NEW YORK

First published 2016
by Routledge
2 Park Square, Milton Park, Abingdon, Oxon OX14 4RN

and by Routledge
711 Third Avenue, New York, NY 10017

Routledge is an imprint of the Taylor & Francis Group, an informa business

© 2016 David Baume and Celia Popovic

The right of David Baume and Celia Popovic to be identified as the authors of the editorial material, and of the authors for their individual chapters, has been asserted in accordance with sections 77 and 78 of the Copyright, Designs and Patents Act 1988.

British Library Cataloguing in Publication Data
A catalogue record for this book is available from the British Library

Library of Congress Cataloging in Publication Data
Names: Baume, David, 1943- editor. | Popovic, Celia, editor.
Title: Advancing practice in academic development / edited by David Baume and Celia Popovic.
Description: New York, NY : Routledge, 2016.
Series: SEDA Series | Includes bibliographical references and index.
Identifiers: LCCN 2015029394 | ISBN 9781138854703 (hardback) | ISBN 9781138854710 (pbk.) | ISBN 9781315720890 (e-book)
Subjects: LCSH: Universities and colleges—Administration. | Universities and colleges—Planning. | Education, Higher—Aims and objectives
Classification: LCC LB2341 .A359 2016 | DDC 378.1/25—dc23LC record available at http://lccn.loc.gov/2015029394

ISBN: 978-1-138-85470-3 (hbk)
ISBN: 978-1-138-85471-0 (pbk)
ISBN: 978-1-315-72089-0 (ebk)

Typeset in Galliard
by diacriTech, Chennai

For Millie, Bianca and George
—*Celia Popovic*

For Carole
—*David Baume*

Contents

A full set of references and URLs for this book is available from www.seda.ac.uk/apad.

List of figures

List of tables

Notes on contributors

David Baume PhD SFSEDA SFHEA is an independent international higher education researcher, evaluator, consultant, staff and educational developer and writer. He was founding chair of the UK Staff and Educational Development Association (SEDA); a founder of the Heads of Educational Development Group (HEDG); a founding council member of the International Consortium for Educational Development (ICED); and founding co-editor of the *International Journal for Academic Development (IJAD)*. His contributions to academic development have been acknowledged by awards from SEDA and ICED. David was previously a Director of the Centre for Higher Education Practice at the UK Open University. He has published over 60 papers, articles and reports on higher education teaching, assessment, evaluation, learning outcomes, course design, portfolios and personal development planning. He reviews papers for higher education journals, and blogs on higher education and technology topics. He has co-edited three previous books on academic development.

Fran Beaton is a Senior Lecturer in Higher Education and Academic Practice at the University of Kent, UK, which she joined in 2004. She is also the PGCHE Programme Director in the Unit for the Enhancement of Learning and Teaching (UELT). Prior to that she was Programme Co-ordinator for Modern Languages courses for part-time students at Goldsmiths, University of London, UK, where her work included professional development for the part-time staff teaching these programmes. Fran has worked as a teacher educator since the early 1990. Her current research focuses on the impact of different kinds of interventions and experiences on early career academics' conception of their identity.

Stephen Bostock started his academic career as a biologist but strayed into computing and psychology, teaching at every level of higher education. In 1996 he discovered SEDA, and became a (Senior) Fellow in 1998. He became a full-time academic staff developer and then founded the educational development unit at Keele University, UK, and then another at Glyndŵr University, UK. In both cases he was responsible for academic professional development and accreditation.

Within SEDA he has been on the executive committee for 15 years, chair of the professional development framework (accreditation) committee, and co-chair of SEDA. He is now retired.

Sally Brown is an Independent Consultant and Emerita Professor at Leeds Beckett University, UK, where she was, until July 2010, Pro Vice Chancellor (Academic). She is Visiting Professor at the University of Plymouth, UK, and at Liverpool John Moores University, UK, and works in around 30 universities a year in the UK and internationally. In 2012 she was awarded an Honorary Doctorate from Plymouth University for Services to Teaching and Learning in Higher Education and in 2015 an Honorary D Litt from Kingston University, UK. She is Principal Fellow of the Higher Education Academy, SEDA Senior Fellow and a UK National Teaching Fellow. Widely published in the field of teaching, learning and particularly assessment, her latest book (2015) is *Learning, Teaching and Assessment: Global Perspectives* (Palgrave).

Diana Eastcott is a higher education consultant and coach/mentor. An academic developer with many years' experience at a senior management level at Birmingham City University, UK, Diana was awarded an Emeritus Professorship for leadership in learning and teaching. She has worked at a national level with the Higher Education Funding Council for England, the Higher Education Academy and SEDA. Now an HE consultant, Diana holds a Postgraduate Diploma in Coaching and Mentoring and works with a number of universities on policy and evaluation projects and specific coaching/mentoring initiatives, including establishing awards and recognition and one to one work with staff.

Rachel Forsyth is a developer at the Centre for Excellence in Learning and Teaching at Manchester Metropolitan University, UK. Rachel's responsibilities include curriculum development and enhancement, assessment in HE, and staff development for link tutors and programme leaders. Her most recent projects include Transforming Assessment for Institutional Change (TRAFFIC), Students as Partners for the HEA, and Supporting Responsive Curricula. She was the recipient of MMU's MMUnion Teaching Award for Outstanding Achievement in 2014. She has published on a range of subjects including games for learning, identity in HE, delivery systems and the phenomenon of lurking.

Barbara Grant is an Associate Professor in the School of Critical Studies in Education at the University of Auckland, New Zealand. Before taking up that position in late 2011, she worked in academic development for almost 20 years, addressing many aspects of academic work but with a particular interest in the professional development of graduate research supervisors. Based on largely empirical research, Barbara writes post-critical accounts of higher education with a particular focus on the supervision of graduate research students, academic identities, academic development and research methodologies. Barbara is also the executive editor for the journal *Higher Education Research and Development*.

David A. Green is Director of Seattle University's (US) Center for Faculty Development, which supports academics in their learning and teaching, research practice and professional development. He also continues to teach undergraduates in International Studies. Prior to moving to the US, David was Head of Educational Staff Development at Birmingham City University in the UK. His recent research focuses on the locations and identities of educational developers and on academics' preconceptions of their students. David is a board member of the International Consortium for Educational Development and is a former co-editor of the *International Journal for Academic Development*.

Julie Hall is Deputy Provost Academic Development at the University of Roehampton, UK. She is a National Teaching Fellow and Principal Fellow of the Higher Education Academy, as well as being a former co-chair of SEDA for three years and is an active member of the academic development community. At Roehampton she has responsibility for all academic departments and the continued focus on excellent academic experiences for students. Previously she held posts including interim director of the university's business school, and Director of Learning and Teaching Enhancement.

Peter Hartley is now Higher Education Consultant and Visiting Professor at Edge Hill University, UK, following previous roles as Professor of Education Development at the University of Bradford, UK, and Professor of Communication at Sheffield Hallam University, UK. As National Teaching Fellow since 2000, he has promoted new technology in education and developed software, including 'The Interviewer' simulations (now online at Edge Hill) and 'Making Groupwork Work' (with the LearnHigher CETL). His current interests also include assessment strategies (e.g. from the PASS project at Bradford), concept mapping and visual thinking, and developments in human communication (e.g. second edition of *Business Communication*, Routledge, 2015).

Sheila MacNeill is a Senior Lecturer in Blended Learning at Glasgow Caledonian University, UK. This team provides strategic direction, pedagogic guidance and practical support to staff in embedding blended and online learning across the curriculum. Developing meaningful understandings of concept of the digital university is an increasingly important part of Sheila's research and practice. A self-identifying open practitioner, Sheila blogs regularly and is active on many social networks. Before working at GCU, Sheila was an assistant director at Jisc Cetis, a national innovation support centre for the UK HE Sector. She was the ALT Learning Technologist of the Year 2013.

Katarina Mårtensson is an academic developer at the Centre for Educational Development, Lund University, Sweden. Her work includes running pedagogical courses as well as supporting organisational development through academic development, scholarship of teaching and learning, and leadership. Her research focuses on social networks, academic microcultures and academic leadership. She is regional vice-president Europe in ISSOTL, the International Society for Scholarship of Teaching and Learning.

Charles Neame has been a teacher and educational developer since 1991, moving gradually from an Environmental Business Management specialism into educational development. He worked at Cranfield University, UK, for 18 years, at Glasgow School of Art, UK, for five, and at Manchester Metropolitan University, UK, since 2014. His doctoral study investigated the adoption of new practices in higher education, including an investigation of the professional relationships between educational developers and different academic communities. He has designed and delivered programmes for academic staff development, and now has a specific role supporting those new to pedagogic research. His current research focuses on values-based higher education.

Rowena Pelik is Director of the Quality Assurance Agency Scotland (QAA Scotland). She has extensive experience with intuitional-level review in the UK. Prior to taking up her current post in 2014 she was a Senior Academic Reviewer for QAA Scotland, participating in three Enhancement-led Institutional Reviews. Between 2003 and 2009 she participated in eight QAA Institutional Audits to English HEIs and three Collaborative Provision Audits. She recently chaired a university audit for the quality assurance agency in Finland. She was a member of the Scottish Higher Education Enhancement Committee from 2009 until taking up her present post and was involved more widely with the QAA's enhancement work in Scotland, most recently with updating the sector's Descriptors of Enhancement.

Ruth Pilkington (NTF, SFSEDA) is employed by the HE Academy as Academic Lead (CPD), and by Liverpool Hope University, UK, as Professorial Fellow in Learning and Teaching. She also contributes to a number of UK institutions' CPD Frameworks as reviewer and assessor. These roles reflect her profile within academic development nationally in the UK. She has held a number of committee roles in SEDA, and continues to work actively as a member of SEDA PDF Committee. She received National Teaching Fellowship for her work in using dialogic assessment for professional recognition in HE, and supporting lecturers' professional learning from entry through to professional doctoral level. Her publications address professional learning, CPD, dialogic assessment and employability.

Kathryn M. Plank, Ph.D. is Director of the Center for Teaching and Learning and Associate Professor of Education at Otterbein University in Westerville, Ohio, USA. She has been an educational developer for almost 25 years. Her current scholarship focuses on implementing change in STEM teaching, and she has published on a variety of educational development topics, such as program assessment and inclusive teaching. In 2011, she edited the book *Team Teaching: Across the Disciplines, Across the Academy.* She is a past president of the POD Network in Higher Education and is currently vice-president of the International Consortium for Educational Development.

Celia Popovic is the Director of the Teaching Commons at York University in Toronto, Canada. Before moving to Canada in 2011, Celia had an extensive career in educational development in the UK including at the University of Birmingham, UK, De Montfort, UK, The Open University, UK, and most recently Birmingham City University, UK, where she was Head of Educational Staff Development. She holds a Masters and Doctorate in Education from Birmingham University, SFSEDA, and Fellowship of the Higher Education Academy, having been a founder member of the Institute for Learning and Teaching in Higher Education. She is the co-editor for *Innovations in Education and Teaching International,* and teaches the SEDA online course 'Supporting and Leading Educational Change', which is the required course for SEDA Fellowship. She has published 15 articles in peer reviewed journals, presented at dozens of conferences, and with David Green authored *Understanding Undergraduates* (2012), published by Routledge as part of the SEDA series.

Torgny Roxå works at Lund University, Sweden, Faculty of Engineering with a research focus on organisational change in higher education through a sociocultural perspective. He has organised and taught pedagogical courses for academic teachers since 1988, and has initiated several institutional and national development programs. He is honorary fellow at the University of Ulster, UK, and has previously for three years served as regional vice-president Europe in ISSOTL, the International Society for Scholarship of Teaching and Learning.

Ellen Sims is Head of Learning and Teaching at Plymouth College of Art, UK, having many years as an Educational Developer and lecturer in HE. Previously she was a Senior Educational Developer at York University, Toronto, and Program Director for Academic Practice at the University of the Arts, London. Ellen's professional raison d'etre is creating space for engaging staff in collaboration, reflective practice and creative approaches to teaching. She has worked successfully with staff/faculty in developing scholarly approaches and outputs. Research interests include teaching in the disciplines and interdisciplinarity, retention and attainment and inclusive curriculum design. She has published widely in topics related to scholarship of teaching in HE and in practice-based/experiential learning.

Keith Smyth is Professor of Pedagogy and Head of the Learning and Teaching Academy at the University of the Highlands and Islands, UK. He works across the UHI partnership to lead strategic learning and teaching developments, educational research projects, and to support staff engagement in educational scholarship and research. In his previous role as Senior Lecturer in Higher Education at Edinburgh Napier University, UK, Keith was Programme Leader for the award-winning MSc Blended and Online Education. Keith also developed the openly-licensed 3E Framework for technology-enhanced learning, which since publication has been implemented within over 40 educational institutions across and beyond the UK.

Ian Solonomides is Director of the Learning and Teaching Centre at Macquarie University in Sydney, Australia. Solonomides and his team are responsible for a wide range of operational and strategic activities supporting teaching and learning. He completed a Bachelor of Education (Hons) as a mature student, entering higher education in the UK in 1992. Initially working with engineers, Ian then taught extensively in art and design and was Program Leader for Furniture and Product Design, and Learning and Teaching Coordinator, at Nottingham Trent University, UK, before moving to Australia in 2006. He is President of the Council of Australian Directors of Academic Development.

Lorraine Stefani is Professor of Higher Education Strategic Engagement at the University of Auckland, New Zealand. She has over 20 years' experience of leading educational and organisational change through contextualised facilitation processes and leadership capacity building. She is currently President of HETL, the Higher Education Teaching and Learning Association, and has had extensive governance experience in national and international higher education organisations including Ako Aotearoa (New Zealand National Centre for Tertiary Teaching Excellence). She has published widely on a range of contemporary topics relevant to a learning organisation. Her current research interests include evidencing the value of academic development, academic leadership and managing change in complex organisations.

Kathryn Sutherland is Associate Dean (Students, Learning and Teaching) in the Faculty of Humanities and Social Sciences at Victoria University of Wellington in Aotearoa New Zealand. Prior to becoming Associate Dean, she worked in the academic development centre for 11 years. She has served on the editorial team for the *International Journal for Academic Development* since 2010, and has been co-editor since 2012. Her research interests range from the experiences of early career academics, to the use of students as teachers, to the history and nature of the field of academic development.

Sue Thompson is an independent higher education consultant, National Teaching Fellow, and Emeritus Professor of Academic Development in Higher Education at Liverpool John Moores University, UK. She has over 25 years' experience in academic development, as a teacher trainer, staff developer and senior manager with an institutional remit for learning, teaching and assessment. Using consultancy has been a key feature of Thompson's professional practice, in leading an academic development unit, directing a nationally funded Centre for Excellence in Teaching and Learning and two National Teaching Fellowship projects, and chairing the Heads of Educational Development Group.

Nancy Turner is Director of the Gwenna Moss Centre for Teaching Effectiveness, University of Saskatchewan, Canada. Nancy took up this role in 2013 after a decade working in the UK, most recently as Associate Dean of Learning, Teaching and Enhancement at the University of the Arts London, UK, and prior to that, Director of Educational Development at Royal Holloway, University of London, UK. She provides strategic leadership of learning and teaching enhancement including professional development for instructors, curriculum development, technology enhanced learning, reward and recognition for teaching, and indigenisation of the academy. Her main area of research is change in higher education institutions.

Shân Wareing is Pro Vice-Chancellor Education and Student Experience at London South Bank University, UK. She is a Professor of Teaching in Higher Education, a National Teaching Fellow, a Principal Fellow of the Higher Education Academy, Fellow of the Leadership Foundation for Higher Education, Senior Fellow of the Staff and Educational Development Association, and has held educational development roles at four universities, and senior manager roles at three. Earlier in her career, she taught English language, linguistics and literature, English as a foreign language, and study skills, and has enjoyed all of it.

And finally.... We would like to especially thank Joelle Adams for her valuable input in planning the early stages of this book, and the many colleagues who offered comments on the manuscript at different stages from inception through to production. Without their thoughtful comments and suggestions this book would not have seen the light of day.

Series editor's foreword

In 2013 the Staff and Educational Development Association (SEDA) celebrated its twentieth year, and one of the most significant outcomes of that year's activities was the determination to create this volume. We took the opportunity to reflect on the work we had been doing, what we as a community had learnt, and how we could continue to serve our members and the world of higher education in the future. This book has been written in that spirit, and we thank David Baume and Celia Popovic for their work in creating it.

SEDA is the association through which the UK's educational and academic developers advance their knowledge, skills, scholarship and professionalism. Routledge's SEDA Series has played a major role in this work. This present volume brings us chapters by 26 leading academic developers to stand beside the contributions in David Baume and Peter Kahn's earlier books in the SEDA Series: *A Guide to Staff and Educational Development* (2003) and *Enhancing Educational Development* (2004).

The course 'Supporting and Leading Educational Change' is another aspect of SEDA's work to support the professional development of its members. It serves as the route to SEDA Fellowship. Celia Popovic is the course leader, and this present volume will become an essential element for the online community formed by the participants and tutors.

SEDA was one of the eight founding associations of the International Consortium for Educational Development. This is now a network of 24 national bodies, and it has supported the growth of the international community of academic developers. One of the pleasures I have in writing this preface is noting the contributions from academic colleagues in Canada, New Zealand, Australia, Sweden and the US and the strength of the international relationships within this community.

Teaching and learning are so basic to the human condition that we sometimes take their significance for granted. As more citizens in so many countries are benefiting from increasing opportunities to study at a university or college, we should remember how honourable it is to be a teacher, and how satisfying it is to teach well. Academic and educational developers are hugely privileged to be able to follow a profession devoted to good teaching and meaningful learning, and that is celebrated by the authors and editors of this volume.

James Wisdom
Visiting Professor in Educational Development
Middlesex University, UK

Chapter 1

Introduction

Some issues in academic development

Celia Popovic and David Baume

Summary

We suggest an overall purpose for academic development – to lead and support the improvement of student learning. We explore issues including becoming and then developing as an academic developer; working with regional and national associations; relationships between academic development and scholarship; the developer's orientation to problems and solutions; some of the responses developers are likely to encounter to development initiatives; the huge range of neighbouring development activities in higher education, and the need for developers to cooperate with them; approaches taken in the book to maintaining the currency of its content; and a comment on language, humour and seriousness.

Links to web sources referenced in this chapter can be found at www.seda .ac.uk/apad.

Academic development in support of good student learning

<u>Note on terminology</u>. We generally use UK terms throughout the book, although sometimes modified by chapter authorship. In particular, in the UK, *staff* is a term applied to all employees in a university, including academics and administrators. In North America and elsewhere, *staff* may mean only non-academics – academic staff are generally called *faculty*. We recognise that teaching and teaching support may be performed by those who are not academics, and we include anyone who teaches or supports teaching in this broad definition. (In many countries, a Faculty can also be a large unit of a university, often a cluster of departments.)

Academic development is taken to include both staff/faculty development – that is, work to enhance the capabilities of academic staff/faculty; and educational development – that is, work to improve educational methods and processes. There is, of course, always overlap between these functions. Also, some authors use 'educational development' in the more inclusive way that we use 'academic development'.

Academic development remains a topic of lively and complex debate, even as we academic developers worldwide go about our mysterious contested lively challenging and sometimes immensely rewarding work. In this chapter we explore some of these issues, acknowledging but hopefully not glorying in the complexity (see *Problems and solutions* below), and always looking for principled and practical ways forward.

Forward, we suggest, generally means in the direction of improved student learning. Improved student learning will carry different meanings in different settings. We may feel that students are learning well when, among other virtues, they are:

- Often working hard and appropriately at their studies, although enjoying the whole student experience;
- Both collaborating and working alone;
- Working towards goals that they, their teachers, their intended profession(s), employer(s) or role(s), and some at least of the wider world, value;
- Clear about the progress they are making and clear what progress they wish and need to make next;
- Aware of and extending their capabilities as learners;
- Taking seriously ethical as well as academic and technical dimensions of their studies;
- Negotiating their way through the complexities of their lives as students as well as the rest of their lives;
- Hopefully enjoying at least some of the process; and
- Leaving as capable and enthusiastic independent and collaborative learners.

Beyond that, institutions and departments and programmes and teachers and learners will need to produce their own accounts of good learning, and work towards these, reviewing and modifying as they go.

Uncertainty and debate about the nature, indeed the legitimacy, of academic development permeate the literature of our field (including the *International Journal for Academic Development, IJAD*) and find their way into this book. A few examples:

- Is academic development a field, a discipline, a profession, a subject, something else?
- Should academic developers be academic, or should they be support/administrative?
- How can developers be appropriately scholarly?
- How can academic development face both ways – to senior university staff, serving them as a tool for implementing university policy and strategy in relation to teaching and learning (and hopefully also contributing to such policy and strategy), whilst at the same time meeting the needs of individual and groups of frontline teaching and learning support staff?
- How do academic developers maintain their integrity in the face of these not always fully aligned sets of needs and values?

- And the very idea and nature of development are themselves contested – what gives us the right to seek to develop other people?
- How do developers become, improve as and maybe move on from being developers?
- What are some key elements of our craft?
- How can we support others to become developers?

Not necessarily under these headings, we explore these and other issues in this introduction and throughout the book.

Becoming an academic developer

If there is a consistent characteristic among a group of educational developers it is the diversity of routes into the profession (McDonald and Stockley, 2010; Little and Green, 2012). Many have questioned whether educational development is a profession at all; Chapter 3 explores the notion of professionalism in relation to educational development. Some of the apparent dilemmas around identity and legitimacy – for example, are we able to pass judgement on the professionalism of others (teachers in HE) if we aren't members of a legitimate profession ourselves? – may stem from the comparative youthfulness of the field.

The field has grown, and continues to grow. Some countries have more developers per institution than others, as Chris Knapper has observed (McDonald and Stockley, 2010). However, overall more people are identifying themselves as developers now than 20 or even ten years ago. Some who find the label of developer to be problematic may nonetheless be willing to say that they do development work.

Developers may be engaged in full-time educational development activities, others are seconded full time for a limited period or work part-time in a faculty and part-time in a centre. Previously it was common to start in a teaching and or research role and then over time discover an interest in the field. Happenstance played a large part in many developers' stories. For a useful overview see McDonald and Stockley (2008).

With the increase in masters in education and professional doctorates (e.g. EdD) it is becoming more common for someone to start their career in academic development. This trend may continue to expand, particularly if the number of jobs in the field also expands. However it is also likely that we will continue to see academics moving from a particular discipline into academic development, whilst retaining membership of the original discipline, often as a result of a growing fascination with learning and its facilitation. This parallels, indeed often follows, other forms of professional engagement in HE where, for example doctors, artists, lawyers or engineers first have a career in their profession, then move into teaching as a second career. These transitions are considered further in Chapter 3 on professions and professionalism.

Being and improving as an academic developer

How do developers develop themselves? Or are we destined for a fate much like that of the shoemaker's children, running barefoot whilst everyone else benefits from our nurturing natures? There is not a consensus in the community regarding the benefit or need for developers to formally develop themselves or be developed by others. Most would agree on the benefits of professional development for developers, but not necessarily on a formal centralised approach. In the UK the Staff and Educational Development Association (SEDA) provides a structured approach to initial and continuing development, with the Fellowship scheme. So far this is the only jurisdiction to do so, and even here the majority of developers are not Fellows of SEDA, nor is this a requirement in many, if any, hiring processes.

We would argue that we have a duty as individuals to attend to our own professional proficiency, and that ongoing professional development is necessary. We would encourage readers to consider the SEDA Fellowship scheme, perhaps with a view to developing nationally or locally appropriate qualifications processes.

Aside from the formal SEDA Fellowship scheme, what are the most common means for developers to develop? Later in this chapter we discuss the role of developer organisations in this process. Aside from organisations, we would encourage developers at all stages of their career to consider mentoring, both as a mentor for someone else and being mentored by another developer, perhaps via co-mentoring. Chapter 6 discusses mentoring mainly in the context of academic activity in general, but the principles apply with equal validity to mentoring for academic development. Participating in the online forum for your professional association can also be very developmental and informative.

Groups of developers have had success in forming informal reading groups. Grant and Knowles (2000) describe the use of writing groups for academics. Technology, as discussed in Chapter 8, provides multiple opportunities for colleagues to share ideas and discuss their thoughts regardless of geographic constraints. In some cases a reading group has led to two or three members identifying a common interest which in turn has led to a publication and a wider sharing of ideas with the community. A developer who is new to field may want to consider reviewing for journals such as *IJAD* (the *International Journal for Academic Development*) and *IETI* (*Innovations in Education and Teaching International*), the journals for ICED and SEDA respectively, or for their local/national equivalent. This is a voluntary task which can become time-consuming but which offers multiple benefits. A reviewer will see articles well before they are published, and can engage in the community through scholarly practice. As writers are often advised: if you want to improve your writing, start reading – this is true in a scholarly context as well as with fiction.

Educational developers in North America have begun to make use of portfolios both as a way of documenting and organising their professional development. This reflects the practice in the US and Canada for lecturers to create teaching portfolios – see for example Seldin (2010).

Working with regional and national associations

Where do developers get their professional support, create networks, find their identity and keep abreast of changes in the sector? The answer may be different for different people but educational development associations figure high for most practitioners.

In the UK the Staff and Educational Development Association (SEDA) is the obvious meeting point for those involved in academic development. However, even SEDA does not attract all those engaged in the field. The All Ireland Society for Higher Education, (AISHE) caters for both developers and teachers, as does HERDSA in Australasia. Becoming more specialised, the UK has had since 1995 a Heads of Educational Development Group (HEDG) and Australia since 2005 the Council of Australian Directors of Academic Development (CADAD). In the US the professional organisation (the Professional and Organizational Development Network [POD]) offers a broader church in that practitioners include but are not restricted to academic development. The Educational Developers' Caucus in Canada is an offshoot of the larger Society for Teaching and Learning in Higher Education (STLHE). All of these organisations can readily be found online. Regardless of the history of the development of the various associations, these groups are important to developers for several reasons. In summary they provide what is described in Chapter 3 as an academic and professional infrastructure of events, courses, conferences, online forums, publications, professional relationships and sometimes qualifications and accredited continuing professional development.

In some countries, such as the UK, the density of populations in general and universities in particular has led to the emergence of regional organisations, operating independently of a national organisation while often attracting the same members.

Many educational developers value collegial approaches to work, and thrive on contact with others. Centres are often small, perhaps consisting of just one person; this may be one reason for the attraction of organisations. However attendance and engagement in organisations is not restricted to members of small centres.

Bodies such as SEDA, POD, EDC or HERDSA offer developers the opportunity to meet with others engaged in similar activities and facing similar challenges and constraints – a place to 'huddle together for warmth', as we used to say in the early days (the early 1990s). Sharing of thoughts can help at least to dispel feelings of isolation, and on a more practical level provide possible solutions and ideas. Most conference attendees state this as one of the key reasons for attending. However, such organisations offer more than this. A developing developer may not have many opportunities to engage in formal service-related activities – activities that are important in their development but which also develop skills that are valued in academia in general. Engagement in a development organisation can provide the opportunity to improve these skills: for example, chairing a committee or work group, contributing to a research project, organising a conference or workshop, editing or reviewing for a scholarly journal.

Organisations are usually run on a voluntary, not-for-profit basis. This may be seen as a weakness, through lack of funds, long-term planning or ownership. But in practice it is often a source of strength – external funding is very attractive, but it can breed dependence, and can quickly dry up. Developers are often passionate about their field, and willing to offer hours of unpaid work to ensure the organisation thrives. They do this because they are committed, but also because they see the benefit to themselves and the field.

On a personal note, I (CP) can trace the trajectory of my own career very closely to my involvement in SEDA in the UK and more latterly with EDC in Canada and my local organisation COED (Council of Ontario Educational Developers). It was SEDA that gave me multiple opportunities to network and learn in the form of two conferences each year. I wasn't always able to attend, but when I could I came away energised and brim-full of ideas. I was also better informed about the context in which I was working. I became involved with the conference committee – and then as chair of the conference committee I became a member of the executive. These experiences enabled me to hone my skills in chairing and taking part in committees, as well as the more obvious lessons in planning and running conferences. It was through a chance conversation at a SEDA conference that I learnt of a forthcoming conference that EDC was holding that related to some work I was involved with at the time. Attendance at the EDC conference led directly to hearing about a vacancy at a Canadian university – so, between them, SEDA and EDC literally changed my life!

Scholarship and academic development: being scholarly

In pursuit of a practical scholarship/scholarly practice of academic development, we need to say a little more about scholarship. Whether academic development is a field, a subject, a profession, a discipline or something else, it is certainly an area of practice. So, rather than considering scholarship as a noun, a thing, we ask – what is involved in being scholarly?

As well as considering being scholarly in academic development, what follows also suggests approaches to developing a scholarship of teaching and learning which academic developers may wish to encourage those with whom they work, both colleagues and clients, to adopt.

There may be three principal ways of being scholarly:

- Reflecting critically on practice
- Using ideas from the literature
- Contributing to the literature

These do not necessarily form a developmental sequence – although they do involve an increase in sophistication. One can start anywhere, although Chapter 12 on research suggests strongly that reading the literature is a necessary precondition for undertaking research. However, the three ways of being scholarly suggested here certainly support and enrich each other.

Being scholarly as reflecting critically on practice

There is a valuable literature on reflection and professional practice, including Bolton (2014), and Moon (2013). These books suggest how reflection can provide a powerful and rich approach to making sense of and improving both practice and understanding.

Critical reflection, at its core, means asking and striving to answer questions about the nature and effectiveness of one's practice, and the reasons for its effectiveness. It thus has links to, indeed can be a precursor to, both research and evaluation, considered respectively in Chapters 12 and 10. Critical reflection can be applied at any level, from strategic to immediate.

Of a particular teaching or development intervention, one might ask, preferably beforehand, 'What am I (or, what are we) trying to achieve here?' During the intervention, 'How is it going?' And afterwards, 'Did I/we achieve what was intended?' and 'What else happened and was achieved that was not planned for?' And, moving beyond simple audit and towards a search for understanding, 'Why?' and 'What factors (may) account for what was achieved? What wasn't achieved?' Through addressing these latter questions, explanations or even hypotheses are beginning to be generated. It may be possible to test these, perhaps by doing something different next time, or digging deeper. Or this process can suggest questions to be asked, topics to search out, in the literature.

Being scholarly as using ideas from the literature

The literature about teaching and learning higher education ranges from hints and tips, including the 53 (e.g. Gibbs, Habeshaw and Habeshaw, 1984) and 500 (e.g. Race, Smith and Brown, 2005) series, through explicitly scholarly books (e.g. Beard, 1979; Bligh, 2000; Pascarella, Terenzini and Feldman, 1991 and subsequent editions; Ramsden, 2003; Biggs and Tang, 2011; Cannon and Newble, 2000; Knight, 2002; Cowan et al., 2007), to research articles in academic journals including *Studies in Higher Education, Higher Education Research and Development, Teaching in Higher Education, Assessment and Evaluation in Higher Education, To Improve The Academy* and *Innovations in Education and Teaching International.* The online world, not to mention the library, mean that we are no longer gatekeepers standing between academics and this vast literature. On the other hand we still have the responsibility and the opportunity to select what we feel may be helpful to individual and groups of academics as they face teaching questions and make teaching decisions. How to undertake this role?

We know that, if you give someone a fish, you feed them today, whereas if you teach them to fish you enable them to feed themselves for life, assuming of course a thriving population of fish. But we should be wary of our learners starving during their fishing lesson. A useful first response to a question is often simply to answer the question, or to point the questioner at a source of good answers. This engenders trust, and makes us immediately useful. Of course we shall also say why we have made the particular suggestion, hopefully referring to evidence and theory. We may also explore how we may help further. But sometimes a reasoned answer is enough. Experienced developers, like all experienced teachers, know when not to teach too much, and when simply to tell and explain.

Which literature? As suggested above, we face choices. Gibbs (2013) says

> Most teachers in the universities I have worked in have never read any of my refereed journal articles, though many thousands have read my practical manuals and guides come up to me when I give talks in out of the way places to tell me how important these pragmatic publications have been in their teaching lives.

Courses on teaching in higher education typically use a range of literature, from scholarly monographs to hints and tips. The hints and tips of course make extensive if implicit use of published research. Gibbs may be underestimating the influence of his scholarly output. Gibbs' (2015) '53 powerful ideas...' are being published.

But there is another layer to this problem. However valuable they have been, the titles, the very existence, of the hints and tips literature also carry the message that teaching and learning in higher education is, at least in part, a matter of hints and tips. We have not seen books called *53 Interesting Things for Property Lawyers To Do*, or *500 Tips for Brain Surgeons*, although such books could be written. Full disclosure - one of the authors has made a small contribution to the hints and tips literature (Baume, 1996).

This is partly unfair. The 53 and the 500 series of books are written by people who know, indeed have contributed to, the research literature. Many of the hints and tips have a strong basis in experience, research and scholarship. But, for the most part, the authors made the decision to keep this scholarship away from view. As Gibbs, author and co-author of many of the 53 series, acknowledges:

> The '53 Interesting Ways To Teach' books … were underpinned by the authors' shared conceptions, but these conceptions were deliberately hidden from view and they looked theory-free so as to avoid frightening the horses. (Gibbs, 2013)

But, sometimes, in accepting the status quo, in this case the perceived need to describe pedagogy without theory, one inadvertently reinforces it. Gibbs goes on to say:

> Today, educational developers are much more likely to be explicit about the theoretical underpinnings of attempts to change teaching. (ibid.)

If we want to, in a scholarly and sustainable way, continue to lead and support the improvement of teaching and learning, we are probably right to turn the attention of academics and universities to the research literature on teaching and learning, and especially to any literature on teaching and learning in particular disciplines, and to the scholarly monographs derived from this research. We need to be appropriately confident (as well as critical) in our expertise.

Another powerful reason for explicitly using theory is provided by Angela Ho's work (Ho, 1998 and 2000), which reports that changes in practice are more likely to happen, to stick, when they are accompanied by cognate changes in thinking about, and models and theories about, teaching and learning. Many new teachers, intent on surviving, welcome hints and tips. But we should offer them the 'why' as well as the 'what' and the 'how'.

There is a distinct literature about academic development, including Brew (1995), Fraser (2004), Baume, Edwards and Webb (2003), Kahn and Baume (2003), Baume and Kahn (2004), and the *International Journal for Academic Development* (*IJAD*). At the time of writing *IJAD* is in its twentieth year, and continues to provide research, support and challenge for developers and development.

Once the use of research literature, and of sources explicitly derived from research, becomes a leading part of the repertoire of any academic or developer as they seek to improve their practice, developers become more likely to contribute to the literature, as we consider in the next section.

Being scholarly as contributing to the literature

Not all academics and developers will want to take this step. The first two steps described above are very likely to lead to good and improving teaching and development. However, for some academics and developers, this will not be enough. They may become intrigued by particular questions, in learning and teaching, in assessment, in the design of learning, in uses of technology to support learning, or in other topics. The typology of approaches to investigating one's practice offered by Ashwin and Trigwell (2004), described in Chapter 10 on outcomes and evaluation, will be valuable. The academic who is investigating their own practice, and perhaps the practice of their colleagues, is a natural ally for the academic developer, worthy of support and encouragement.

Chapter 12 describes researching academic development. And there is a literature on researching teaching and learning, notably Cousin (2009).

Problems and solutions

Being critical and analytical is an important element of being scholarly. Ideas, data, conclusions and recommendations are to be teased apart, checked, deconstructed, contextualised, problematised. To the extent that the academic development is a discipline, seeking to advance understanding and practice, a critical approach is important.

However, academic development is also a field of practice, with a mission to lead and support improvement. (We know that many of the words in the previous sentence, and indeed throughout the book, could be put between quotation marks, acknowledging their problematic nature. We choose not to do this, mainly on the grounds of readability.) We may feel that, once we have been analytic and critical, we should also suggest – of course with appropriate cautions – potentially useful ways forward. Having analysed and critiqued and deconstructed, we should also be willing to answer the harried academic's or manager's question 'Yes, but what should I do?', albeit hedged about with such reservations as we feel to be necessary. Being scholarly is compatible with being useful.

'And', not 'or'

The literature frequently offers 'or' statements, e.g. 'development may be either transformative or compliant', which is as far as we know a made up, but nonetheless hopefully representative, formulation. Such polarisation can lead us astray. It can restrict our view of what goals we can set and achieve. There is generally more value in considering when and how one or the other of a pair of suggested opposites applies.

It is usually more useful still to consider how the two approaches may be combined. For example, from the suggested transformative/compliant dichotomy about development mentioned above, we may establish goals for work that will simultaneously comply with current institutional policy and use the policy to transform thinking and practice, as well perhaps as seeking an evidence base on which to transform the policy into something more productive. Chapter 17 considers developers' work with policy and strategy. The world may be digital, but that does not mean that it is binary. The world is best approached as a set of 'ands', rather than as a set of 'ors'.

This substitution of 'or' with 'and' goes well beyond a potentially rather wishy-washy 'everyone is right' stance, again in two main ways. First, moving towards the use of 'and' encourages us to be clear who we are, how we are acting and thinking, what role or roles we are taking, now. For example:

- In conducting or leading or supporting research into some teaching and learning or academic development topic, or in editing a book, we are hopefully being academic and scholarly, although we should still have an eye to the potential usability of our research and publication.
- When we are contributing to the formulation of university policy and strategy on or around learning and teaching, we are probably being professional; necessarily to some extent also political, in that we are concerned with what is possible; and having due regard to the culture and contexts in which the policy and strategy are being developed and will need to be implemented. But we should remain in part as scholars, feeding in, hopefully increasingly explicitly, ideas and findings from the literature which are relevant to the policy.
- And when we are planning and undertaking an academic development intervention of some kind, we are hopefully again being both professional and

scholarly, seeking to identify and meet the needs of the people with whom we are working, but also being to some extent political in the sense of being informed by, indeed referring to, relevant university goals and priorities, and acknowledging any relevant power relationships.

Second, the use of 'and' encourages us to seek synthesis and integration, of ideas and practices.

Responses to development initiatives

Alongside enthusiastic embrace and acceptance, academic developers also experience a range of other responses to initiatives, particularly to initiatives which are, or are perceived as, coming from outside, that is, from anywhere other than from those who are the intended subjects of the initiative. These responses – from individual, groups or indeed the institution as a whole – may include:

Rejection – 'That will never work here (because, generically, here is different)'
No need – 'We are already doing that (in the following respects...)'
Suffocation – 'We will give it serious consideration (and let it slowly die, perhaps in and between committees)'
Absorption – The idea is taken, adapted and adopted
Subversion – The idea is taken, apparently adapted and adopted, but in fact quietly and gently strangled or abandoned, perhaps with a few traces remaining

These and other responses to academic development are considered in a special issue of *IJAD* (2014).

The developer's realistic ideal is probably absorption. Academics probably invented the not invented here syndrome – in many places and on many occasions, of course. Academics and universities will be much more committed to implementing an idea which they perceive as their own, whether by origination or by heavy modification. And this perception must be substantially real – academics are bright people, and developers have to stay honest.

This all points to a view of development as a process of doing with rather than doing to. Those senior managers, mostly new in post, who briefly believe in what we may call Star Trek management – 'Make it so' – will benefit from a gentle but clear introduction to the realities of educational change. Academic developers are well placed to provide this. Chapter 16 says much more about working with senior managers.

Neighbours

Not all problems, opportunities or possible sites for action in higher education fall tidily under the heading of teaching, learning, assessment, course design, educational development, staff/faculty development, student development, advice and guidance, personal tutoring, language development, numeracy development, learning technology, management, researcher development, research supervision development, administration, support for students with specific learning difficulties, international education, support for students from overseas, equality of opportunity, graduate careers education and advice, employability, community links, open and distance learning, learning resources, estate planning, designing and equipping teaching and learning spaces, learning analytics, organisational development, library and information services, human resources, etc. (building on Chalmers and Solomonides, 2015). This suggests, if it were not already obvious, the great need for the various university development functions, including but not limited to those above, to cooperate.

Frequent reorganisations, sometimes driven by the optimistic management view that the crucial thing is to get the structures right, may aid this process, if only because many of the players may already know each other from previous formations.

However, whatever the current and future structures of and formal links between the services, it is vital that the units and the individuals know each other well, know their capabilities and enthusiasms, and are prepared from the earliest moment to share intelligence and to devise joint courses of action. This can be difficult in a climate of competition for resources and attention within a university. But, perhaps a little below the radar, cooperation can normally be achieved.

Also, and occasionally despite appearances, it is unusual for universities to actively seek to prevent or discourage good things from happening. Developers should work on this basis, anyway.

A similar case for cooperation, this time among national academic and professional development associations, is made in Chapter 18.

Variety, its sources and uses, in academic development

In this edited book, many flowers bloom, many different views are presented, and sometimes compared and contrasted. At this splendid moment in the life of book editors, when the chapters are clear in outline and moving steadily towards their negotiated final form, and the introduction is to be written, it is tempting to seek the grand synthesis, to try to give definitive answers to some at least of the questions indicated above.

We mostly resist this temptation. Not on any particular ideological or academic grounds, but rather on pragmatic grounds, concerned with the aim of the book to offer practical scholarships – we could equally have said scholarly practices – of academic development. Reading the chapters, we see both splendour and utility in the variety of views expressed about the nature and function and indeed legitimacy of academic development. The splendour lies in the continued creation and testing of models, ideas and practices. The utility of course lies in having a wide range of models, approaches etc. to adopt and adapt to particular settings.

What has generated this rich variety of models and approaches?

One factor is simply the demands of the job, the need to meet, or at any rate address, a spectacular range of requirements, interests and priorities across, to mention the two key variables: institutions and disciplines.

Another source of this variety is the range of disciplines and professions from which academic developers come (Little and Green, 2012). When we developers work effectively together, we can undertake academic development work in and across the many subjects and professions taught in the university. But beyond that, and perhaps even more important, this variety also gives us a spectacular range of conceptual approaches and practical tools for undertaking our development work.

This disciplinary promiscuity – versatility may be a more acceptable term – gives us the intellectual and practical tools to be very effective across the range of challenges we tackle.

However, this versatility does not automatically increase our credibility with our academic colleagues. They may be more comfortable with the narrower range of ways of thinking and acting within the own discipline or profession.

This difficulty is likely to fade, for at least two reasons.

The first is the increasing fragmentation of the world of academia into smaller subspecialties, with a corresponding increase in the number of academics who are working at the productive boundaries between these sub-specialisms. This is out of our hands, but it is still there for us to enjoy and, in a good way, exploit.

The second reason why any difficulties caused by our disciplinary and professional versatility as developers may fade is the demonstrable effectiveness of our work in bringing multiple approaches to bear. And that of course is mostly in our own hands.

Timescales

Apart from a short initial print run – to meet prepublication orders, provide review, author and archive copies, and supply copies to selected bookshops – most copies of this book will be printed on demand. A copy is ordered, it is manufactured and dispatched. No capital is tied up in as yet unsold copies, no expensive warehouse space is occupied.

Print on demand is both a blessing and a curse for authors and editors. This book is potentially immortal – why withdraw it from the catalogue when even a few copies are being sold each year? Only because it has become hopelessly out of date and redundant, an object of embarrassment rather than pride.

Intellectual immortality of course has some appeal. But it is also a load. How to write and edit for an audience five, 10, 15, 20 or more years into the future?

One possible approach would be to strip out the contemporary references that will rapidly date the book. But this could leave it dry and dull, missing the examples which bring theories and models to life.

We have tried to address the challenge of remaining current in three main ways.

First, we have tried, as our math teachers used to say, to 'show our working', to give some rationale for suggestions and propositions. The scholarly and evidence base for academic development work will of course extend and change. Current popular theories and models and concerns will fall out of fashion – perhaps through refutation (new evidence or a huge change in context shows them no longer to be valid); or boredom (the idea has just been around too long); or a sense of completion (the feeling that we have done pretty much everything we can usefully do with that idea); or embedding (the idea is now such an automatic part of our practice and thinking that we no longer give it explicit consideration). Some will survive and thrive. Some will be supplanted by new ones. For example, when we all are immersed in the digital sea, the digital water may become unproblematic, unconsidered. Foci of concern will shift – we identify some possible changes of focus in Chapter 18. But, if we are successful in showing our working, readers can adjust the recommendations and suggestions on the basis of new evidence, new scholarship, indeed revised goals and priorities for academic development. Although we suggest that the core goal will not change.

Second, we have tried where possible to be clear about the contexts in which the academic development we describe is being undertaken. To the extent that the context is explicit, readers should be able to make accommodations to different contexts.

Third, we have tried to stay true to the mission of academic development. We have taken this mission to be the systematic, scholarly and practical enhancement of teaching and learning (in their broadest and most encompassing senses) in higher education, with the direct goal, considered at the start of this chapter, of improving student learning. However the world of higher education turns, this goal, or something like it, will remain a valid and important goal for decades to come.

Language and tone

Ingrid Moses (2012:277), a developer turned vice-chancellor, challenges us on our language:

> To judge from the tenor of some of the articles [in *IJAD* 17:3], it seems to me [from the different languages that they use] that the academic developers and the senior academics responsible for teaching and learning do not share concepts of academic development work.

She concludes:

> The jargon, the reflection or agonising about identity, status and locus are for the insiders, the academic developers.

Language, jargon, and the ways of thinking that jargon tries to express to insiders – and, maybe, to hide from, to exclude, outsiders – have a way of bleeding across from one audience to another. This book is written by and largely for insiders, academic developers current and future. Nonetheless, we have tried, albeit with only partial success, to say things and to say them in a way which both new and established insiders can use, and which any outsiders who stray into the book would generally find clear and useful, although perhaps would not in every case accept or employ.

You may notice occasional attempts at humour, occasional flashes of cynicism, in this chapter and elsewhere in the book. Decades spent working in higher education can occasionally make humour and cynicism appropriate, and indeed sometimes necessary, responses. And humour, playfulness – not the telling of jokes, but the identification and analysis of strangeness and inconsistency, of unexpected juxtapositions, in the practices of teachers and universities and academic developers – can be a creative and productive act, a useful part of the developer's repertoire.

But, to make it explicit – the editors believe passionately in the central importance of higher education. Not just to disciplinary or professional interests, nor even just to national and global economic development. We believe that a good and improving education system, including of course higher education, is essential for a civilised society, indeed essential for anything recognisable as society:

> If you think education is expensive, try ignorance. (attributed to Derek Bok, President of Harvard University, n.d., and applicable much beyond financial cost)

And because we value higher education, we believe in the importance of the academic development function, of working in scholarly, pragmatic, collaborative, professional and values-led ways to support and lead the improvement of higher education, and thereby the improvement of student learning.

References

Ashwin, P. and Trigwell, K. (2004). 'Investigating staff and educational development'. In D. Baume and P. Kahn (Eds.), *Enhancing Staff and Educational Development* (pp. 117–131). London: RoutledgeFalmer.

Baume, D. (1996). *First Words on Teaching and Learning* [E-Book]. Retrieved 28 October 2015 from http://shop.brookes.ac.uk/browse/extra_info.asp?prodid=948.

Baume, D. and Kahn, P. (2004). *Enhancing Staff and Educational Development*. New York: Taylor & Francis.

Bolton, G. E. J. (2014). *Reflective Practice: Writing and Professional Development*. United Kingdom: SAGE Publications.

Brew, A., ed. (1995). *Directions in Staff Development*. Bristol, PA: Society for Research into Higher Education and Open University Press.

Cannon, R. and Newble, D. (2000). *Handbook for Teachers in Universities and Colleges* (4th ed.). London: Kogan Page.

Cousin, G. (2009). *Researching Learning in Higher Education: An Introduction to Contemporary Methods and Approaches*. New York: Routledge.

Cowan, J. (2007). *On Becoming an Innovative University Teacher* (2nd ed.). Maidenhead, UK: McGraw-Hill International.

Edwards, H., Baume, D., & Webb, G. (Eds.). (2003). *Staff and educational development: case studies, experience, and practice from higher education*. London: Kogan Page.

Fraser, K. (2004). *Education Development and Leadership in Higher Education: Implementing an Institutional Strategy*. New York: RoutledgeFalmer.

Gibbs, G. (2013). 'Reflections on the changing nature of educational development'. *International Journal for Academic Development*, 18(1): 4–14.

Gibbs, G. (2015). '*53 Powerful Ideas*'. Retrieved 26 November 2015 from http://www.seda.ac.uk/53-powerful-ideas

Gibbs, G., Habeshaw, S. and Habeshaw, T. (1984). *53 Interesting Things To Do in Your Lectures*. Bristol: Technical and Educational Services.

Grant, B. and Knowles, S. (2000). 'Flights of imagination: Academic women be(com)ing writers'. *International Journal for Academic Development*, 5(1): 6–19.

Ho, A. (1998). 'A conceptual change staff development programme: effects as perceived by the participants'. *International Journal for Academic Development*, 3(1): 24–38.

Ho, A. (2000). 'A conceptual change approach to staff development: a model for programme design'. *International Journal for Academic Development*, 5(1): 30–41.

IJAD – *International Journal for Academic Development*, 19(1), 2014, Special Issue: The agency game in academic development: compliance and resistance.

Kahn, P. and Baume, D. (2003). *A Guide to Staff and Educational Development (Staff and Educational Development Series)*. London: Taylor & Francis, Inc.

Knight, P. (2002). *Being A Teacher in Higher Education*. Philadelphia, PA: Society for Research into Higher Education and Open University Press.

Little, D and D. A. Green (2012). 'Betwixt and between: academic developers in the margins', *International Journal of Academic Development*, 17(3): 203–215.

McDonald, J. and Stockley, D. (2008). 'Pathways to the profession of educational development: an international perspective', *International Journal for Academic Development*, 13(3): 213–218.

McDonald, J. and Stockley, D. (2010) (eds.). 'Pathways to the profession of educational development', *New Directions for Teaching and Learning*, no. 122, Wiley Periodicals.

Moon, J. A. (2013). *Reflection in Learning and Professional Development Theory and Practice*. United Kingdom: Taylor & Francis.

Moses, I. (2012). 'Views from a former vice-chancellor', *International Journal for Academic Development*, 17(3): 275–277.

Pascarella, E. T., Terenzini, P. T. and Feldman, K. A. (1991). *How College Affects Students: Findings and Insights from Twenty Years of Research* (1st ed.). San Francisco: Jossey-Bass.

Ramsden, P. (2003). *Learning To Teach in Higher Education* (2nd ed.). London: RoutledgeFalmer.

Seldin, P. (2010). *The Teaching Portfolio: A Practical Guide to Improved Performance and Promotion/Tenure Decisions*. Bolton, MA: Anker Publishing Co.

Solomonides, I., and Chalmers, D. (2015). Private communications, providing information on development functions and associations in Australia, complementing information from the UK.

Chapter 2

Identifying needs and opportunities for academic development

Charles Neame and Rachel Forsyth

Summary

This chapter examines the role and responsibilities of the individual academic developer and how these reflect the context of the engagement. It considers how different responses to the development context can be identified – not as a prescription designed to treat each individual case, but as a framework for evaluating the need and creating an environment for meeting it successfully. It will make clear the distinctions between the kind of individual intervention being discussed in this chapter and the institutional overview reflected elsewhere in this book.

Links to web sources referenced in this chapter can be found at www.seda .ac.uk/apad.

How do academic developers come to intervene and engage?

The role and status of academic development may lack clear definition; academic development is directed by a wide variety of drivers. Academic developers need to be in a position to find out about these factors, to contextualise them in relation to disciplinary, institutional and national expectations, and prioritise their responses so that action can be taken according to available resources.

Responding to individual aspirations

One of the most obvious drivers for academic development occurs in response to requests from individual members of teaching staff. They may see support in addressing a specific issue, or to carry out a project; they may see engagement with academic development as an important strand in developing their careers. The further development of an individual's academic identity is one of the strongest drivers of such requests (Brew et al., 2014; McLean, 2012), fuelled by a desire to perform more effectively in a particular aspect of professional activity, such as lecturing, or giving feedback, and so to see themselves as a 'better' teacher. Other individuals may seek support to cope with the demands of a highly institutionalised academic regime. Requests to academic developers frequently come from academic or other staff who find themselves beleaguered by detailed process requirements. The anxieties engendered by such situations should not be underestimated; nor should the complexities of a professional relationship which requires the academic developer to recognise and respond professionally to these anxieties.

Whilst the individual may seek out the support of an academic developer, the approach may not always be entirely voluntary: an issue may have been raised by a manager, or in response to metrics with which the individual may not entirely agree. It is important for the academic developer to get a sense of the context for the request so that the response can be appropriately framed.

At the same time, an individual's particular challenge may, on investigation, be shared by many others, so what starts out as an individual issue may require a response that is addressed or taken up by a wider group.

The question of the individual relative to the group is important: we have already suggested that academic identity is one of the strongest drivers of academic development, and this chapter considers how it can have an impact on the management and effectiveness of particular academic development activities. There is a dynamic relationship between the individuals or the group who are the subjects of the development process and the academic developers and the development system charged with facilitating or supporting that development. This relationship is discussed in more detail later, and is outlined in Figure 2.1.

Responding to institutional priorities

The institutional priorities which concern academic developers express aspirations or intentions to take the organisation in a particular direction in relation to its learning, teaching and assessment policy. This might be achieved through targeted projects or by more open-ended changes in operational practice. Examples might include embedding global citizenship in the curriculum, increasing graduate employability, working towards improved student partnership, curriculum review, more or better online learning, or increasing the number of staff holding recognised teaching qualifications. Chapter 17 examines such policies as drivers of change in more detail.

Institutional priorities as drivers for educational development can be deceptively attractive. On the one hand, they make the need for academic development intervention clear: it is mandated by policy, with no need to 'sell' the intervention to colleagues. On the other hand, a top-down requirement for change may be considered pointless by academic staff, or even threatening, and the educational developer may be seen as the unwelcome face of management intrusion in academic freedom. The phenomenon of CAVES: 'Colleagues Against Virtually Everything' (Chelte and Coulter, 2008) may be more strongly pronounced in response to a mandated requirement for educational development.

Bamber and Anderson (2012) point out that institutional priorities have seen Quality Assurance become increasingly associated with the implementation of 'top-down' requirements. They say that 'the challenge for educational developers is to mediate between the institutional requirements for QA and academic norms'. The relationship between Quality Assurance and Quality Enhancement is central to the nature and impact of academic development and is expanded in Chapter 9. For now, it is important to remember that the academic developer often stands at a place where institutional requirements and expectations regarding educational practice meet the everyday perspectives of educational practitioners themselves. The developer's role in identifying needs and opportunities includes the necessity of responding to both these sets of influences. The position is an interesting one. Academic developers may be seen as the instruments of this kind of top-down policy: the mandarin, tasked with chivvying the academic staff who manage and teach programmes into compliance. At the same time they represent resources in the form of guidance, advice, support and problem-solving in relation to the same policy; the latter image being a much more constructive one, of course.

Responding to problems and external agendas

Educational developers may find themselves being drawn in to 'fix things' which are not working well. Usually, these problems will have been identified from data such as recruitment figures, numbers of students progressing to the next stage of study or student satisfaction surveys.

As with the institutional priorities, this top-down driver may represent both opportunities and difficulties. There will almost certainly also be an added defensiveness in response to the idea that something has gone wrong and that the professionalism of those 'responsible' is being questioned.

Vignette 1

Senior managers in the Faculty of Law in the University of Western Trombolia have approached the academic development unit (ADU) with concerns that undergraduate student progression rates from first to second year are unacceptably low. They want to know why, and how to improve the situation.

Colleagues in the ADU review the progression statistics with undergraduate programme leaders from across the faculty, and agree that certain courses or modules appear to be linked with the overall problem. The ADU proposes a scheme whereby module leaders are asked to review their module specifications and assessment strategies with an ADU liaison member, and to identify weak spots, including inconsistencies of constructive alignment (Biggs and Tang, 2011), and a lack of clarity in communication to students about such alignment. Together they will plan and propose amendments to the specifications and strategies concerned, along with a scheme of work for implementing such amendments to an agreed timeline.

This is both a strategic and a managerial approach: prompted by senior management, the process is a strategic intervention designed to analyse and solve a particular problem. It involves planned and scheduled activities, designed to achieve specified milestones.

Within this context, however, there is scope for some variation in the 'mode of engagement'. One member of the ADU team, Dr Zonk, is quite at ease with the strategic line. She sets her faculty-based module leader 'client', Mark, a 'task and finish' plan, whereby he has to do some analysis and report back with it at regular intervals, whereupon Dr Zonk gives him feedback and refines the next stage of the task for him. Fortunately Mark is quite happy to go along with this approach, as he feels insufficiently confident to devise the necessary unit amendments without such structured guidance.

In contrast, Dr Zonk's academic development colleague, Dr Fowler, takes a different approach. He suggests to his Law Faculty 'client', Maria, that they start the process with as many of the teaching team as possible, lured to a workshop on the promise of cakes and iced tea (it's warm in Western Trombolia at this time of year). Dr Fowler facilitates the workshop, but invites Maria to take notes and to sum up at the end, including an action plan that the whole group has agreed. Despite the managerial/strategic impetus behind this intervention, Dr Fowler is showing a preference for various other orientations: perhaps also emphasising the notions of the reflective practitioner, the modeler-broker, and the interpretive-hermeneutic orientation (Land, 2004: see Table 2.1).

External agendas may also lead to major changes in the design and delivery of higher education. Individual faculty members may be wanting to demonstrate their competence and professionalism within a recognised framework; the changing demographics of higher education participation may demand changes in skills or attitudes from faculty members; there is more use of technology to mediate learning; campus buildings may be changing in design; employers may be more involved in the design and delivery of courses. The academic developer needs to be aware of this broader context as they identify needs and opportunities.

The process of identifying needs and opportunities: establishing a way of working

A second major factor in identifying needs and opportunities is the preferred approach and experience of the individual academic developer. David Green (2012) talks of academic developers 'focus[ing] their lenses on different scales, from the big picture to the fine detail'. This section gives some examples and proposes a simple process for structuring the developmental approach, whether bigger picture or finer detail. The academic development that takes place in the middle (or around the edges) of the complex of drivers and motivations may be formulaic, or it may be organic and responsive. To some extent there is a place for both.

Ray Land (2004) identified a framework of 'orientations to development', which he developed from an analysis of interviews with 32 very different educational developers, working in a range of different working environments. This framework (see Table 2.1) presented 12 such orientations, as a blend of educational developers' working preferences and deliberate responses to context or need. For example, one developer might take a very deliberate strategic approach to addressing an academic development challenge, either because that was her preferred way of working, or because her analysis of the nature of the challenge and the institutional context both called for such an approach (see Vignette 1 above).

Land's 12 categories (and in principle we could devise vignettes to illustrate all of them, and hybrid variations) are listed and summarised in Table 2.1.

Table 2.1 Orientations to educational development (Neame, 2013; adapted from Land, 2004)

Orientation
Managerial (Development as an institutionally mandated process of transition from one state of staff competence to another)
Political – strategic (Pragmatic: using networks to achieve a balance between 'presence' across the institution and 'impact' in policy delivery)
Opportunist (Change agent, exploiting shifts, cracks, or uncertainty in the organisation)
Entrepreneurial (Emphasis on achieving innovation, employability targets, etc. Less focused on community building)
Researcher (Educational development mobilised as an integrated part of the academic community's disciplinary development)
Romantic (Ecological humanist) (Emphasis on development of the individual)
Reflective Practitioner 'Emphasis is not on competence but on the process of becoming more competent' (Gibbs, 1996). Development as experiential learning for developers and their colleagues.

(continued)

Table 2.1 Orientations to Educational Development (Neame, 2013; adapted from Land, 2004) *(continued)*

Orientation
Professional Competence (Combines an 'apprenticeship' notion which aligns with 'training' to serve learner needs)
Internal consultant (Support for client-specified development, not externally instigated intervention)
Modeller-broker (Good practice identified by developer, then 'promoted' within a community of practice)
Interpretive-hermeneutic (Development as dialogue: interpretation and re-interpretation by mutually respectful colleagues)
Provocateur (Emphasis on change agents – typically drawn from within an academic community itself)

As Vignette 1 shows, analysing the different approaches to addressing the academic development problem can paint a subtle and complex picture of forms of engagement. A simplification of Land's framework (Neame, 2011, 2013) is intended to offer a more practical, dichotomous model of interventionist versus democratic approaches to development.

This simpler framework starts with the premise that the orientations outlined above are primarily either interventionist or democratic in character. Interventions tend towards a problem-solving approach. They typically have the transactional characteristics of: 'task and finish'; achieving institutionally defined goals; training staff and developing specific competences.

More democratic approaches tend to focus on principles of collaboration. They typically have the characteristics of: trust-based relationship building, a focus on empowering staff rather than completing tasks, a mediating role for the educational developer, reflective engagement with practice; development by conversation. If the opportunity has arisen in response to individual aspiration or institutional or course priorities, then this may be a more natural approach.

The two approaches do not have to be mutually exclusive; a development relationship may start out along interventionist lines and become more democratic as the parties involved come to know each other better, or gain in confidence. The democratic approach tends to work in communities of what Fielding et al. (2005) called 'joint practice development'. They set this concept out in contrast to models of transferring knowledge and practice from an expert to an initiate. They found that teachers best develop professionally through the 'extension and refinement of their existing repertoire of practices, through collaborative and affirming work with other teachers'. This idea of development through supportive engagement with peers is an important one for academic developers, and underpins much of the character of their work.

A model of how these two broad approaches to academic development may work is shown at Figure 2.1.

The figure shows how members of a given academic community, such as a particular academic department, may be located at different points on a forked continuum of engagement. At one end are those characterised as 'traditionalists', who are less open to working towards changes in practice than others. This is not to denigrate tradition or traditionalism. It reflects the spectrum of responsiveness to innovation that Rogers identified (2003), demonstrating a tendency for any particular population's responsiveness to innovation to be distributed normally across a dimension from 'innovators' and 'early adopters' at one end, to 'laggards' at the other, with the 'early or late majority' clustered around the mean. It is unreasonable to expect all members of an academic community to adopt change at the same rate, so we have to adapt our forms of engagement according to the different expectations of different group members. Those who are, for the time being at least, completely averse to change, are likely to be hard to reach, regardless of the approach adopted by an academic developer.

Further towards the engagement end of the continuum (to the right in the figure) there is a separation: one line tending towards more transactional forms

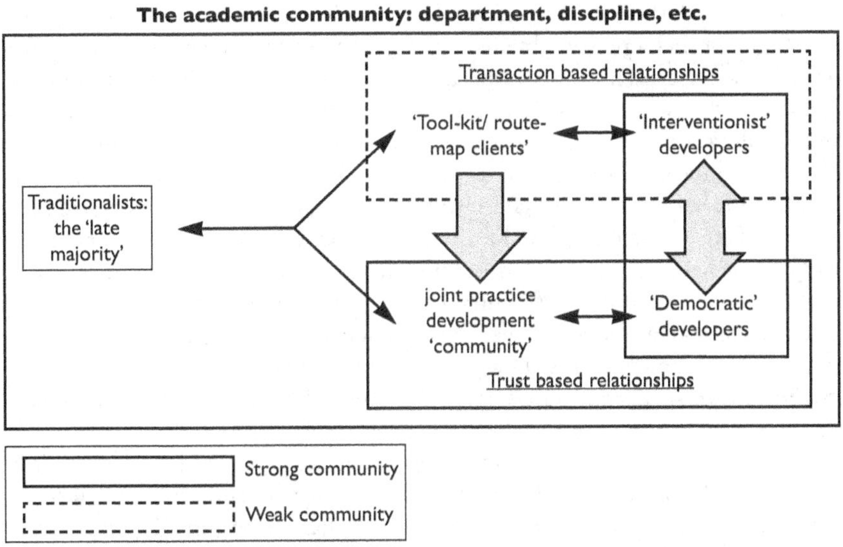

The academic community: department, discipline, etc.

Transaction based relationships

'Tool-kit/ route-map clients' → 'Interventionist' developers

Traditionalists: the 'late majority'

joint practice development 'community' → 'Democratic' developers

Trust based relationships

☐ Strong community

┆ Weak community

Figure 2.1 Moving from an interventionist to democratic approach to academic development (Neame 2013).

of engagement, and the other towards trust based forms. These are where interventionist and democratic development approaches may be seen to best fit, respectively. Whilst the figure illustrates 'interventionist' and 'democratic' developers as sitting within each of these two sites of engagement, the double-headed vertical arrow indicates that academic developers may move between these contrasting modes, according to the needs and perspectives of each client group with whom they are working. In metaphorical terms, the transaction-based groups tend to be seeking toolkits or road maps as devices to address their developmental needs. An objective for educational developers may be to get these groups to move towards the joint practice development model over time. That's not to say that a toolkit or a road map will never be needed again, but once a group of colleagues learns to work with academic developers within a trust based relationship and in a democratic mode, their horizons for action (Hodkinson, 2008: 4) are increased:

> The term horizon is a metaphor taken from vision. What we can see is limited by the position we stand in, and the horizons that are visible from that position…. The horizons for action are influenced by a person's position, by the nature of the field or fields within which they are positioned, and the embodied dispositions of the person him/herself.

The notion of 'horizons for action' was particularly developed by Hodkinson, Sparkes and Hodkinson (1996) in their study of how young people develop strategies and skills of careership, but it is a useful idea for supporting people of any stage of career or professional development.

The view of the horizon, of the possible futures within their professional development that a person obtains, can be influenced by an academic developer. The developer can encourage colleagues to adopt different viewpoints and perspectives, from which those horizons are extended. The 'toolkit clients' are not necessarily intrinsically resistant to the trust-based model, but they may have a technical-rational perspective of development by default. If academic development is understood as a mechanism for correcting deficiencies, or for extending pre-specified competences, the idea of a relational element to development may simply not have presented itself before. In such cases, the transactional mode is the only available mode of entry into a relationship, but it does not mean that the colleagues in question are fundamentally opposed to the notion of joint practice development through democratic engagement. The academic developer can introduce such possibilities as part of the technical rational programme of engagement that characterises the initial relationship.

An anecdote from an academic development colleague told of a meeting he had held with a programme leader whose course performance metrics left something to be desired. The meeting began somewhat uncomfortably, but an hour and a half later, both colleagues had discovered a number of things about each other: first, they found that they were able to agree surprisingly swiftly on an appropriate course of action to try and improve the underlying situation; second, they had experienced some comparable and significant developmental incidents during their respective careers, which gave them some important shared reference points for their discussion; and finally, they shared a number of research interests. As the developer left the meeting the two of them agreed to work together on some of the latter.

'*And I thought you were coming to wag your finger at me*', said the programme leader, laughing, and pleasantly surprised at how events had turned out.

Vignette 2

Josie, a newly appointed lecturer, was studying for her institution's Postgraduate Teaching and Learning Certificate. Owing to an unavoidable hospital appointment she had to miss an important workshop session on assessment, and arranged with the tutor to meet in the Academic Development Unit offices to discuss her strategy for catching up on the learning she had missed. Sitting in the unit's meeting room, the tutor, Ali, talked her through the resources on the unit's website: papers, 'toolkits', videos, links to other sites, handbooks, checklists, guidelines to the institution's regulations, and more.

'And what's here, under "Events"?' Josie asked.

'This is where you can find information about our conference, and the CPD workshops we run, as well as links to external events which we think may be useful', replied Ali.

'Goodness! I didn't realize you did all this other stuff... I thought you just taught this course, and that was it. You've got a whole consultancy service going on here!'

'Well, yes, I suppose you could put it that way', Ali laughed. Inside he was just a little annoyed to think that his team's extensive programme of work could be quite so invisible to colleagues across the university.

They explored the website some more, until Josie was happy about how she was going to make up for the lost workshop study time. By then she had also invited Ali to come to her department for coffee to meet her colleagues and talk about the revisions to a first year module they had been arguing about.

'We could do with an independent third party to help resolve some of our disagreements', said Josie.

'It will be a pleasure', replied Ali. 'I'll look forward to it!'

The process of identifying needs is closely related to the identification of the intended outcomes of any development plan. At the same time it is essential to consider how to develop and articulate relationships between academic developers and other functions and departments in their institutions, such as e-learning support, student services, academic staff in the disciplines with quality enhancement responsibilities, and student representatives.

A consequence of characterising the academic development field of operation as a dichotomous set of either interventionist or democratic interactions is that it highlights the question of the purpose and outcomes of academic relationships. It's not enough to realise, as Josie does in Vignette 2, that academic development work consists of (a) 'teacher training' and (b) 'all sorts of other stuff'. From an operational perspective there is never simply a generic academic development outcome that developers are always intuitively pursuing; there has to be a rationale to each engagement which shapes its nature. The careful identification of needs and opportunities is important to the overall process because it allows the rationale to be articulated, and begins the development of a relationship of trust and confidence with the other participants.

An idea which illustrates this never-take-it-for-granted-ness is the issue of academic leadership and its relationship to academic development. Marshall et al. (2000) summarised this issue thus:

> While mainstream academic staff conceive of academic leadership as being strictly associated with teaching, research and community outreach, university administrators and policy makers conceptualize it more broadly. Their definitions often include the management of change, quality, information, finance, and physical and human resources – functions that many mainstream academics perceive as being the responsibility of departmental/institutional administrative or support staff. Such differences create major challenges for academic development units. What type of training should they provide? Should they embrace activities that support these new conceptions of leadership and management?

Leadership as contested territory means that academic developers first have a job to do in defining academic leadership in ways which make sense to the colleagues with whom they work. Imagine, for example, a lecturer in the UK applying for recognition as a Senior Fellow under a scheme such as the UK Professional Standards Framework (HEA, 2011). The descriptor of the Senior Fellow as a professional includes this:

> Individuals should be able to provide evidence of: ... Successful co-ordination, support, supervision, management and/or mentoring of others (whether individuals and/or teams) in relation to teaching and learning.

An academic developer supporting this colleague as they try to interpret the expectations of Senior Fellowship has to help them unpick various descriptions around the construct of academic leadership.

This quotation does not actually mention or define leadership, but it seems to imply some similarities in terms of types of function and/or relationship. Supervision and management are about performance and accountability, whereas mentoring is about support and development. However, the descriptor continues to indicate that typical roles held by Senior Fellows would include:

> Individuals able to provide evidence of a sustained record of effectiveness in relation to teaching and learning, incorporating for example, the organisation, leadership and/or management of specific aspects of teaching and learning provision.

It continues by suggesting that:

> such individuals are likely to lead or be members of established academic teams.

It is perhaps understandable that there has been much anxious discussion with prospective Senior Fellows about whether they do leadership, and if they do, whether it's enough, or indeed someone's idea of the right kind of leadership. The expectation of leading or being members of established teams doesn't help in many of these conversations: how these two different relationships with one's team can refer to the same category of contribution confuses many. The academic developer, in supporting a colleague working towards recognition in this way, will have to balance the objectives generated by individual aspiration but also the context of institutional priorities.

Vignette 3 illustrates some of these dilemmas.

Vignette 3

Lily, Michael and Anastasia are discussing academic leadership over tea.

Lily: 'Well, I can see that you tick the "leadership" box straight away, Michael. You're programme leader, after all: your job "does what it says on the tin". The word "leader" has never shown its face in my job description – not in 20 years in post in this place! But you can point to all sorts of leadership functions – allocating staff teaching and assessment responsibilities, approving timetables, signing off a whole host of decisions; all that sort of thing'.

Michael: 'I suppose so – but I don't formally manage anyone on the teaching team... that clouds the issue for me. Does the academic development unit have a line on this, Anastasia? What's the definition of "academic leadership"?'

Anastasia: 'I don't think we have one – not like a dictionary definition. There's a huge literature on it and people have made careers out of researching and writing about it! But as far as we are concerned – we, that is, in the sense of those of us working at the coal-face of teaching and student support – leadership doesn't have to have anything hierarchical about it in organisational terms. So I partly agree with Lily – your programme leadership role is very definitely leadership in my book, Michael. The direction and success of the programme is hugely influenced by your role and your work. But I know from seeing your work that the same is true for you, Lily. Not so obviously, perhaps, but what about this: at last month's departmental curriculum review event you made a presentation about the assessment strategy and steered the subsequent discussion through the various options. You were asked to do that because of your experience, and because of your respected position in the department. And afterwards I saw you talking earnestly to that new young colleague of yours who was asking for advice. It may not be in your job description, but if all that isn't leadership I don't know what is!'

Achieving buy-in

Having planned an academic development activity, it is almost always essential to include other participants for the activity to be successful. This section briefly considers some of the prerequisites for engaging members of academic staff, students, senior managers and other professional staff. The management implications of this idea are developed in Chapter 16.

Think as widely as possible about the range of stakeholders who may be affected by the activity. If you aren't sure whether a particular group may need to be included, it's usually better to ask them than to make assumptions that they won't find it relevant. For instance, a change to assessment planning may affect professional staff who deal with coursework submission, as well as a different group who prepare data for a board of examiners. A move to problem-based learning may offer opportunities to colleagues in the library to provide access to a wider range of databases. Reorganising groupwork might have a particular impact on students with caring responsibilities, or who commute to university from a considerable distance. Making a comprehensive list of stakeholders at the needs identification stage will help you to get sustained engagement with them as the project develops.

The two essential components of successful buy-in are action planning and communications planning. Clear objectives, regular reporting and judicious use of institutional governance structures and mechanisms can all make for a more successful environment for academic development; the more so if they are addressed at the needs analysis stage.

When all stakeholders agree and understand the necessary milestones and how they will be measured and reported, they will be more likely to engage. Knight and Trowler (2000) indicate that 'it is the role of departmental leaders to act in a way that is sensitised to current practices, discourses and meaning construction'. This applies equally to academic developers working with teams or individuals. Whilst the academic developer may need to take a lead on proposing an action plan, it is important that people feel able to contribute to its final version. The plan needs to include a clear indication of responsibilities for deliverables and outputs, and for recording and reporting. If all this is clearly documented and shared at the outset, everyone's enthusiasm will be reinforced, and later amendments to the plan will be more easily negotiated.

Institutional governance structures can work as both carrot and stick when it comes to buy-in. The academic developer can point out where regulations require certain responses or changes, because to ignore them would lead to adverse consequences; but they can also be used, on many occasions, as guidelines and resources, designed to make life easier by providing templates for action, for instance, or straightforward principles and standards. The use of formal committee structures can be a requirement for implementation of change which may seem onerous; but careful contributions to committee agendas can speed the passage of your proposals and get them disseminated more widely, more quickly.

Opportunities

Golding (2014) calls for 'a broader conception of academic development'. He cautions against the constraints academic developers impose on themselves by focusing on means rather than ends. If we define our academic identities too exclusively in terms of what we *do* (support the professional development of staff, advise on teaching and assessment methods and so on), we limit our ability to promote development more broadly. He says, 'If we define ourselves in … broader terms we can develop a larger and more innovative repertoire of means for achieving our goals, and thus will be more likely to achieve them'.

Chapters 13 and 17 address the strategic and change management aspects of academic development, but Golding calls for all academic developers, regardless of their specific role, to think in terms of ends as well as means, in order to extend their capacity to innovate. The determination and use of goals and outcomes are considered in detail in Chapter 10. We do well to remember that academic developers may also be resistant to change (Thomas and Cordiner, 2014). Academic developers are change recipients as well as change agents (ibid.) and tend to behave in many respects just as the academics with whom we work tend to do. This presents an interesting perspective on the issue of identifying needs and opportunities which is the subject of this chapter. The technical rational approach to academic development needs assumes a world in which solutions to identifiable problems can be designed and implemented. In reality, the world is not so straightforward: if a colleague resists a change which we propose, who is to say that such resistance is inappropriate and something to be overcome? A question for academic developers to ask themselves repeatedly, therefore, is not only 'what is the need, and where is the opportunity', but 'who has a say in defining the needs and opportunities'? If we are to identify needs and opportunities effectively, we must first listen, empathise, and then work collectively to act. As Nel Noddings says (2012) in her discussion of the caring relation in teaching: 'We must listen, not just tell'.

References

Bamber, V. and Anderson, S. (2012). 'Evaluating learning and teaching: institutional needs and individual practices'. *International Journal for Academic Development*, *17*(1): 5–18.

Biggs, J. and Tang, C. (2011). *Teaching for Quality Learning at University*, 4th Edition. Milton Keynes, UK: Open University Press.

Brew, A., Boud, D., Crawford, K. and Lucas, L. (2014). 'The powerful and the powerless: academics' identities in a time of change'. Academic Identities Conference. Durham University, UK, 8–9 July 2014.

Chelte, A. F. and Coulter, J. M. (2008). 'You don't need a title to be a leader', *Journal of Business and Behavioral Sciences*, *19*(2): 4–10.

Fielding, M., Bragg, S., Craig, J., Cunningham, I., Eraut, M., Gillinson, S., Horne, M., Robinson, C. and Thorp, J. (2005). *Factors Influencing the Transfer of Good Practice*. Nottingham, UK: DfES.

Gibbs, G. (1996). 'Supporting educational development within departments', *International Journal for Academic Development*, *1*(1): 27–37.

Golding, C. (2014). 'Blinkered conceptions of academic development', *International Journal for Academic Development*, *19*(2): 150–152.

Green, D. A. (2012). 'The shifting lenses of academic development: on identities, careers, and programmes'. *International Journal for Academic Development*, *17*(2): 93–95.

HEA (The Higher Education Academy) (2011). UK Professional Standards Framework for teaching and supporting learning in higher education (UKPSF). Retrieved from: www.heacademy.ac.uk/sites/default/files/downloads/UKPSF_2011_English.pdf (Accessed February 2015).

Hodkinson, P., Sparkes, A. C. and Hodkinson, H. (1996). *Triumphs and Tears: Young People, Markets and the Transition from School to Work*. London: David Fulton.

Hodkinson, P. (2008). 'Understanding career decision-making and progression: careership revisited'. John Killeen Memorial Lecture. Woburn House, London. Retrieved from: www.crac.org.uk/CMS/files/upload/fifth_johnkilleenlecturenotes.pdf (Accessed February 2015).

Knight, P. T. and Trowler, P. R. (2000). 'Department-level cultures and the improvement of learning and teaching', *Studies in Higher Education* 25(1): 69–83. http://dx.doi.org/10.1080/030750700116028.

Land, R. (2004). *Educational Development: Discourse, Identity and Practice*. Maidenhead, UK: Society for Research into Higher Education and Open University Press.

Marshall, S. J., Adams, M. J., Cameron, A., and Sullivan, G. (2000). 'Academics' perceptions of their professional development needs related to leadership and management: What can we learn?', *International Journal for Academic Development*, *5*(1): 42–53.

McLean, N. (2012). 'Researching academic identity: using discursive psychology as an approach', *International Journal for Academic Development*, *17*(2): 97–108.

Neame, C. (2011). 'Exploring models of development of professional practice in learning and teaching in higher education: What can we learn from biology and marketing?', *Educate~*, *11*(*1*): 9–19. Retrieved from www.educatejournal.org/index.php/educate/article/view/242 (February 2015).

Neame, C. (2013). 'Democracy or intervention? Adapting orientations to development', *International Journal for Academic Development*, *18*(*4*): 331–343.

Noddings, N. (2012). 'The caring relation in teaching'. *Oxford Review of Education*, *38*(*6*): 771–781.

Rogers, E. M. (2003). *Diffusion of Innovations* (5th Ed.). London: Simon & Schuster.

Thomas, S. and Cordiner, M. (2014). 'The 'messy' business of academic developers leading other academic developers: critical reflection on a curriculum realignment exercise'. *International Journal for Academic Development*, *19*(*4*): 293–304.

Chapter 3

Professions and professionalism in teaching and development

Stephen Bostock and David Baume

Summary

The chapter explores the ideas of professions and professionalism. We suggest that teaching may be considered either as additional to the original profession or discipline of an academic, or, perhaps more usefully, as part of this original profession or discipline. We seek to resolve whether pedagogies are most usefully considered as generic or discipline-specific. We explore how various suggested elements of professionalism may be relevant to teaching and to development. We review the development of professional standards for teaching and development, and consider the professional bodies and associations through which these standards have been developed and implemented, in both cases drawing mainly from UK experience but hopefully with international implications. We consider some of the uses of teaching standards, and the training and accreditation of academic developers.

Links to web sources referenced in this chapter can be found at www.seda.ac .uk/apad.

Teaching, development and profession

The biggest difficulty that the idea of profession brings for teaching and for academic development in higher education may be that most academics, including academic developers, already have a profession, or a discipline (an adjacent concept). This profession or discipline may be one or more of:

- The profession or discipline in which they first qualified;
- The profession or discipline associated with their highest academic or professional qualification;
- The profession or discipline that they currently (or most recently) teach/ taught/research(ed) or practise(d).

Most academics can very readily identify their profession or discipline. At this level, the nature of profession or discipline is unproblematic.

So why do we refer to this first profession or discipline as a difficulty? Disciplines and professions, for their members, may be more than what they do, more than which groups they associate with, more even than what, for them, constitutes valid ways of knowing, thinking and acting. Their profession or discipline may well be a major element of who they feel they are, of their identity. And identities are resistant to change, sometimes even to questioning.

Most academics probably identify strongly with just one discipline or profession, and then probably with one or more subdivisions thereof. And this singularity of affiliation can lead to difficulty with regard to teaching, and a further difficulty with regard to academic development. To guide our work as academic developers, how can we most usefully conceptualise teaching or development in relation to a person's primary profession or discipline?

There are two obvious approaches, described in the following sections.

Teaching as an additional profession or discipline

We could describe teaching as a further, probably a second, profession. Similarly, we could describe academic development as a third profession, for those many academic developers who once taught in a discipline. (We acknowledge the growing number of academic developers who come direct from a background such as educational research or learning technology, and have not spent time as a teacher.)

This second or third profession – teaching or development – has many of the same elements as a person's primary profession or discipline. These elements might include a more-or-less explicit account of and examples of what comprises valid knowledge in teaching or development, a range of ways of thinking and acting and contesting, some common language, perhaps some common values. Also present are some elements of the usual infrastructure, including an extensive literature; in some countries a professional or scholarly association and professional standards; some form of initial training and qualification in higher education teaching or academic development, and then support and recognition for continuing professional development, in teaching or academic development, alongside any development they may continue to undertake in their original discipline or profession; conferences and events, both in person and online; and jobs, roles, websites, journals and other information sources.

One justification for considering teaching and then development in higher education as further professions is precisely the existence of this scholarly and professional infrastructure for teaching and development. So it is relatively easy and at least partially valid to talk about teaching and development as professions.

The main difficulty with considering teaching as a second profession can be just that; the suggestion that an academic should adopt an additional profession – that of teacher. An additional profession means an additional identity. 'I am a [insert name of discipline expert or professional here], not a teacher' is a sentence most developers have heard – often more than once. Another difficulty is that much of the scholarly infrastructure and literature on higher education teaching is generic, that is, outside the academic's primary profession or discipline. This literature from what may be seen as another discipline or profession – teaching or education – may seem alien, and less than relevant to the teaching of their specific discipline. In particular, education is probably a social science. Of course most academics are not social scientists. For example, those who consider themselves hard scientists bring different disciplinary assumptions, outlooks, concerns, ways of thinking and standards of proof.

More discipline-specific material on teaching is being produced, and we should try to be familiar with it, or at least aware of its existence. And there can be difficulties with such material. It may be very relevant to the discipline, but pedagogically less sophisticated and less research-informed than we would wish, sometimes because there is little good research into the pedagogy of the discipline. We may decide to use such literature anyway, sacrificing some rigour for enhanced credibility and effectiveness with members of the discipline.

However, in response to some teaching suggestion or pedagogic research finding from us, 'That's all very good, but [insert name of discipline expert or professional here], is different' is another oft-heard view. And there is often some truth in it. In these circumstances, the skill of the developer includes working with the teacher to seek to translate the idea for the particular discipline and setting. We consider this further below.

Teaching as part of the primary profession or discipline

The other main approach is to describe teaching (ignoring development for now), not as a further profession or discipline to be learned and adopted, but rather as part of an academic's current or primary profession or discipline. Most members of disciplines and professions acknowledge their responsibility to the future of their discipline or profession, as well as respect for its past. However, this responsibility to the future of the discipline or profession is most widely manifested through a commitment to research, scholarship, service, or otherwise undertaking and enhancing practice in the discipline or profession. Not only must the academic be expert in the profession's knowledge base, they must also contribute to it. The aspiration at least is that these forms of contribution to the future are undertaken to the highest academic and professional standards. The same is not always true of contributing to the future of the discipline or profession through teaching.

There is at least one exception. Chapter 7 on supporting part-time teachers quotes Gunderman's (2006:8) view that being an educator is 'built into the very essence of what it means to be a doctor'.

There is no need to rehearse here the factors that usually lead to the frequent prioritisation of, the rewards for and status of, research over teaching. Nonetheless, it remains mysterious why even the few things confidently known, sometimes for several decades, about the conditions for good teaching and good student learning have so often been ignored – in the learning and teaching strategies which should frame and guide educational practice, in the design and approval and quality assurance of programmes, in the implementation of teaching and feedback and assessment, and indeed in the design of educational buildings. At worst, effective teaching is seen as unproblematic for anyone who has the subject knowledge, some communication skills and some enthusiasm for the subject. Teaching can be seen as a minor part of the profession, even if takes up a good deal of time, and brings a substantial proportion of the institution's income.

The main advantage of this second approach (considering teaching as an essential component of the profession) is that it accepts and values the primary disciplinary or professional identity of the academic. It simply invites academics to broaden a little their view of what it means to be a member of the discipline or profession to include learning and teaching in the discipline, and then to act on this broader view. No change of identity; just a modest and reasonable accommodation to the changed circumstances of the disciplinary or professional specialist who works in higher education.

Lord Dearing's comments, reported in Chapter 17 in the section headed *Academic development as an agent for professionalism*, are worth reading at this point. Baume (2006) provides a short polemical overview of some of these issues.

Generic or discipline-specific?

The issue of generic vs. discipline specific pedagogic knowledge and practice is important in the nature of teaching as a profession, whether as a second profession or as part of the first profession. It is fundamental to the work of developers. The last chapter of the book gives it further consideration. However, for now, let's consider briefly how much of what we know about teaching and learning in higher education is true and applicable across the many disciplines taught, and how much is discipline-specific.

Our view is that much knowledge about pedagogical principles – for example, learning as an active process, the importance of rapid and usable feedback, learning as a collaborative as well as an individual activity – is very widely true and applicable. Of course, a generic account of learning and how to facilitate it needs to be translated into local practice – or, the other way round, these pedagogic principles need to be sought in current discipline-specific practice. And such translation and identification are often not trivial tasks. For example, active learning or individualised learning need to be enacted very differently in different disciplines, and may be found in unexpected places and forms in disciplinary pedagogic practices.

Our view is also that good and effective teaching is inevitably discipline-specific. Fine art and accountancy are different, with different structures of knowledge and practice and hence different ways of learning and teaching. But underpinning, or explaining, these different teaching methods are some of the same common principles of learning, some general theories and models.

We are saying more than that teaching is different in every discipline. We are saying that theory is of little value until it is applied to and tested against practice; that this application is not simple; and that practice carries embedded, sometimes unarticulated, theories and models and beliefs, which it is useful to surface and then test. Our professionalism as developers needs to include, among many other strands, the ability to facilitate conversations about theory and practice and their interrelationships, among ourselves and with academics of all disciplines and professions. These conversations will, in the short term, keep us engaged with academics. In the longer term, if we conduct the conversations well, these conversations will support and challenge academics to extend the conversations for themselves, interrogating their practice from theory, and finding, and then testing, theory in their practice; becoming, not in most cases educational researchers, but hopefully scholars and investigators of their disciplinary pedagogies, with the usual academic intentions to understand and to improve practice.

In both the short and medium term, we developers may take the view that the underlying pedagogic theories are mostly the same across the disciplines, although there is much to learn in the emergent pedagogy of the disciplines. However, we may also take the view that whether or not we are right about this isn't the main point. We may feel that we would be advised, as any teacher is (and we are among other things teachers), to start where the learner (who in our case is a teacher) is, and work with their beliefs. These beliefs, usually, and deserving shared investigation, include 'teaching my subject is different'. During a programme, relationships between generic and discipline specific pedagogies, and the possible relevance of pedagogies from other disciplines, can usefully be explored. This is an example of the principled pragmatism that characterises much academic development work.

Issues of professionalism and professional accreditation are also considered in Chapter 18.

Being appropriately professional in teaching and development

For each suggested element of professionalism below, selected and adapted from sources including Eraut (1994), Freidson (1994) and the older but still valuable Johnson (1972): what can we say about how professional teaching in UK higher education is? Table 3.1 offers some suggested elements of professionalism.

Table 3.1 Some suggested elements of professionalism

	Element, with some indicative examples
1	**Being scholarly, using scholarship** Seeking out and using public knowledge of different sorts. Sharing, researching and contributing to the knowledge base. (Ashwin and Trigwell, 2004)
2	**Being critical and reflective** Analysing own and institutional policy and practice with a view to maintain and improve them

3	**Using an explicit set of values, ethics, principles or codes of practice** Perhaps expressed in the form of professional standards
4	**Requiring a qualification or accreditation, a licence to practice** In relation to any relevant professional standards
5	**Doing continuing professional development and staying in good standing with a professional body** In relation to the professional standards, with regard to all professional roles and identities, again with the intention to maintain and improve
6	**Having autonomy, independence, academic freedom** These are rights and obligations, earned through being professional in the other ways suggested here. They do not include the right to practice badly, or in ignorance of what is known.

How might we adapt, extend and apply the ideas above and related ideas to professionalism in our work as developers? Some suggestions:

1 Where there are professional qualifications for teachers, develop and/or support the policy and practice at institutional and local level to encourage and support the development of staff to obtain these qualifications. The qualifications might be generic, such as a postgraduate certificate, or specific to a discipline and bestowed by a professional body such as the Royal College of Nursing.

2 Where there aren't such professional qualifications for teachers, work with professional and disciplinary associations, or within your university, to help create them. (More on this in the following section.)

3 Again where there aren't such professional qualifications, work with, for example, local concerns about ethical issues in teaching ('Ethical Principles in University Teaching', 1996), or try to make sure that any course in teaching and learning have clear and explicit intended learning outcomes that area at least compatible with possible standards. Always seek connections to possible areas for professionalising.

4 Work with teaching enthusiasts in particular disciplines and professions to explore any statements in their own professional standards and practices about teaching and about preparing future members of the profession or discipline. Build on these statements with courses or events or publications or awards about teaching in the discipline or profession.

5 Take or make opportunities to observe teaching in different disciplines and professions, to help you understand their goals, methods and problems better. You are not an expert in the teaching of every discipline, but you can engage in useful conversations about the teaching and learning of any discipline. You can also disseminate to the department or Faculty existing pedagogical materials that they may not be aware of, or offer to bring in external experts on the teaching of the discipline or profession.

6 Ensure that courses and processes to support initial and continuing professional development include discussions and comparisons of good teaching in different disciplines and professions, while making explicit links to any national standards. Respect differences between disciplines and encourage the making of comparisons across disciplines and finding commonalities across them.

7 Ensure that all the courses and processes that you run continue to be superb examples of professional teaching and development practice. As a developer you must be – you cannot avoid being – a role model. It comes with the territory. You will be judged much more by what you do and how you are than by what you say. This a great load, and a great opportunity.

8 In all your work as a developer, be explicitly scholarly, and encourage and support those with whom you work to do the same, using and contributing to knowledge about what works, and why.

9 Have the relevant academic and professional qualifications for your role as a developer, or make a plan to obtain them soon.

10 If there are no relevant professional qualifications for a developer in your setting, then work with your national association to develop one. Look at the SEDA Fellowships scheme described later in the chapter; not because it is the right scheme for you, but because it may provide you with a starting point, with some ideas to adopt and adapt and some prompts for what you may do differently, better.

11 Career planning is difficult in turbulent times and contexts. But you can be prepared: take opportunities to develop the experience, profile and qualifications you may need for future roles you want to take. Chapter 16 explores a route for developers into senior university management.

12 Be a principled opportunist. With a clear view of, and staying true to, what good professional thought and action look like, exploit any passing fad, policy or movement that you can. And you nearly always can.

13 An important part of professionalism is some degree of autonomy or independence of thought and action. This requires that your clients and managers trust you. Earn that trust; deliver as promised, and to a high standard.

14 Exercising independence of action can be problematic. Academic developers can be seen as, and in some cases may actually be, meddlers in the middle, with stakeholders all over an institution: students, student representatives, academics, senior managers, and non-academic professionals and managers. Working with senior managers is explored in much more detail, again in Chapter 16. You will not always be able to pursue what you believe is the best course of action; compromise is often necessary. Sometimes you may have to take actions you don't believe in, and sometimes you must say 'I really don't think we should be doing this, and here's why'. Occasionally you must make a stand. Choose your battles carefully. The occasional principled loss is OK.

15 Be tactful with your stakeholders. They don't necessarily understand learning and teaching issues and practices in the same way you do, any more than you fully understand their world.

16 Respect and learn from your stakeholders. You don't necessarily understand their learning and teaching issues and practices in the same way they do, any more than they fully understand your world.

17 Be proactively ethical. At the slightest hint of anything potentially untoward or dishonest, flag it up and/or get a second opinion, confidentially if necessary.

18 Professionals are part of a professional body and community. Be an active member of yours. Academic developers may have several relevant communities – some of these are described below and in Chapter 1 – but don't spread yourself too thinly.

19 Use the word 'professional' frequently and appropriately, in your work and materials.

Developing professional standards

The Staff and Educational Development Association

SEDA developed and implemented professional standards for teaching in higher education in the early 1990s. The story is told in detail elsewhere (Baume, 2003). But even a brief summary here can show the mixture of creativity, ambition and luck that characterises much successful academic development work:

An attempt in the early 1990s to design a course in teaching in higher education to be offered across universities and polytechnics in London had failed. The logistics of a shared course proved impossible – this was before online teaching. But one of the steps in devising the course had been to identify the intended learning outcomes of such a course, and also what necessary principles and values characterised a good higher education teacher:

In the absence of a course, how could we use the statement of outcomes and values? We realised that we could use it to accredit other, existing and new, courses. SEDA had no mandate to do this, no official status. But we devised a very simple course recognition process. Essentially, any course that could demonstrate that, in order to pass it, participants had achieved the outcomes and values that we had specified would be recognised by SEDA, and anyone successfully completing such a course would be accredited by SEDA as a higher education teacher. There were also requirements about the external examining, quality assurance and appeals. The standard is summarised in Table 3.2.

To our astonishment, over the next five years, some 60 higher education institutions – in UK and also in Australia, Aotearoa, New Zealand, Hong Kong, Singapore and Sri Lanka – sought SEDA recognition for their courses, and over 2,000 teachers were accredited. The Sri Lankan experience is summarised in Ekaratne (2003, p. 166). These courses were usually postgraduate certificates in teaching and learning in higher education. Thus far, a story of creativity and ambition, and some measure of success.

Table 3.2 The original 1993 SEDA Teacher Accreditation Scheme standard (summary)

Original 1993 SEDA Teacher Accreditation Scheme standard

Outcomes: The accredited teacher has shown how they have, in a way that is informed by the principles and values of the scheme:
  1 Designed a teaching programme or scheme of work from a course outline, document or syllabus
  2 Used a wide and appropriate range of teaching and learning methods effectively and efficiently in order to work with large groups, small groups and one-to-one
  3 Provided support to students on academic and pastoral issues in a way which is acceptable to a wide range of students
  4 Used a wide and appropriate range of assessment techniques to support student learning and to record achievement
  5 Evaluated their own work with a range of self, peer and student monitoring and evaluation techniques
  6 Performed effectively their teaching support and academic administrative tasks
  7 Developed personal and professional strategies appropriate to the constraints and opportunities of their institutional setting

Principles and Values: The accredited teacher has shown how these principles and values underpin their work and their attainment of the outcomes:
  8 An understanding of how students learn
  9 A concern for students' development
  10 A commitment to scholarship
  11 A commitment to work with and learn from colleagues
  12 The practising of equal opportunities
  13 Continuing reflection on professional practice

The luck came in the form the National Commission of Inquiry into Higher Education, chaired by Sir Ron (later, Lord) Dearing (Dearing, 2007). SEDA proposed to the Commission that teaching in higher education could be improved by requiring university teachers to gain a teaching qualification through successfully completing formally recognised course. We used the argument that 'all students have the right to be taught well'. Dearing applauded, and the Commission accepted our argument.

The Institute for Learning and Teaching in Higher Education

The Institute for Learning and Teaching in Higher Education (ILTHE) was established to implement the Dearing recommendations on teacher accreditation. This marked an important stage in the development of teaching as a professional activity in higher education (HE) in the UK (Bucklow and Clark, 2003). The ILTHE had wide support from sector bodies, and aimed to raise the status of teaching, which had suffered relative to research, and to address the challenges to teaching created by what was becoming a mass HE system. Bucklow and Clark admitted that teaching had none of the characteristics of traditional professions, and that the ILTHE would be a rather special professional body, for three reasons:

- It had been brought into existence, not by its putative membership, but by government agency, with the support from other sector bodies including trade unions. (The intention was to pass control to the membership within a reasonable time.)
- Secondly, it addressed only part of the role of its intended membership; teaching, but not research.
- Thirdly, its purpose was not to solidify current practice but to change and improve practice across the sector.

These were significant challenges for what aspired to be a new professional body.

The ILTHE's approach to professionalism centred on establishing an explicit standard of teaching, broadly understood. This had many similarities with that developed by SEDA. ILTHE organised the recognition of individuals as ILTHE members against that standard. This was achieved through individuals completing institutional staff development programmes, typically for the postgraduate certificates that were to be accredited by the ILTHE (following SEDA's practice of teacher accreditation since 1993) and also through a direct application route supported with a journal, website, conference, regional events, publications, book series and fortnightly email updates to foster engagement. Whichever route was taken to membership, an annual membership fee was payable. The employing university sometimes paid this fee. SEDA-recognised programmes were accredited by ILTHE en bloc based on the similarity of the standards. As well as providing support for evidence-based practice, ILTHE would also establish standards for continuing professional development, but there was no immediate intention of requiring regular evidence to retain 'good standing'.

A major difficulty for the ILTHE was the dual nature of the academic role, explored earlier in this chapter. Academics already regarded themselves as professionals in their discipline (Bucklow and Clark, 2003, p. 85). Nonetheless, by July 2002 the ILTHE had accredited 127 programmes at 106 UK universities and colleges. It had received over 16,000 individual applications for recognition and had already 12,000 members. Given the context, this was impressive.

The Higher Education Academy and the United Kingdom Professional Standards Framework

However, 'In January 2003, a committee established by HEFCE, Universities UK and the Standing Conference of Principals recommended the establishment of a single central body responsible for standards of teaching in higher education'

(Wikipedia, 2015). The government White Paper (DES, 2003) required 'new professional standards for teaching and a new national body to develop and promote good teaching' (p. 7). As part of a reorganisation of national bodies, the ILTHE with two associated organisations was replaced in 2004 by the Higher Education Academy (HEA), initially with government funding. The HEA is owned by Universities UK and GuildHE, representing respectively universities and those colleges which undertake substantial higher education teaching, the organisations which now largely fund the HEA.

The new professional standard was the UK Professional Standards Framework (UKPSF), managed by the HEA but created after wide consultation and 'owned by the sector' (UK Professional Standards Framework (UKPSF) | The Higher Education Academy, 2011). The first version of the UKPSF was reviewed after five years and the current version was published in 2011. It has three dimensions: Areas of Activity, Core Knowledge, and Professional Values (Table 3.3), each with statements in terms wide enough that they can be interpreted for local conditions in institutions and programmes.

Table 3.3 The HEA UK Professional Standards Framework (summary)

The Higher Education Academy UK Professional Standards Framework (summary)
Areas of activity undertaken by teachers and support staff: A1 Design and plan learning activities and/or programmes of study A2 Teach and/or support learning A3 Assess and give feedback to learners A4 Develop effective learning environments and approaches to student support and guidance A5 Engage in continuing professional development in subjects/disciplines and their pedagogy, incorporating research, scholarship and the evaluation of professional practices
Core knowledge needed to carry out those activities at the appropriate level K1 The subject material K2 Appropriate methods for teaching, learning and assessing in the subject area and at the level of the academic programme K3 How students learn, both generally and within their subject/ disciplinary area(s) K4 The use and value of appropriate learning technologies K5 Methods for evaluating the effectiveness of teaching K6 The implications of quality assurance and quality enhancement for academic and professional practice with a particular focus on teaching
Professional values that individuals performing these activities should exemplify V1 Respect individual learners and diverse learning communities V2 Promote participation in higher education and equality of opportunity for learners V3 Use evidence-informed approaches and the outcomes from research, scholarship and continuing professional development V4 Acknowledge the wider context in which higher education operates recognising the implications for professional practice
Four qualifications are available – Associate Fellow, Fellow, Senior Fellow and Principal Fellow – associated with different roles, responsibilities and stages of career.

Cutting across the three dimensions in Table 3.3 are four descriptors, each associated with a particular career stage. The HEA uses the UKPSF as the basis of its accreditation of institutional programmes and Continuing Professional Development (CPD) schemes, resulting in the recognition of individuals with an HEA Fellowship, a professional accreditation. (CPD as an area of activity for academic developers is considered in more detail in Chapter 4.) The four descriptors are used as the basis of the four levels of HEA Fellowships: Associate Fellow, Fellow, Senior Fellow and Principal Fellow. Fellow (FHEA) is the standard for new lecturers, requiring evidence in practice of all the 15 elements of the UKPSF (descriptor 2). There was a good deal of continuity between the UKPSF and the ILTHE standard, and indeed with the earlier SEDA accreditation standard. Members of the ILTHE on its demise were given a Fellowship of the HEA, which has since become the commonest professional accreditation for university teachers, with over 60,000 Fellows.

What impact has this had on the sector? In 2012 the HEA commissioned SEDA to conduct an evaluation of the awareness, understanding and use of the UKPSF at individual and institutional levels ('Measuring the impact of the UK Professional Standards Framework for Teaching and Supporting Learning (UKPSF) | The Higher Education Academy', 2013)

It showed that the UKPSF has been influential across the sector in changing institutional practice and that for some individuals it had had a 'profound impact' on how they undertake and think about learning, teaching and assessment (p. 6). The overwhelming majority of respondents to a survey reported the UKPSF had led to changed practice.

So, the UKPSF standard for teaching has been established and is now widely used as the basis for initial and continuing professional development. Alongside traditional academic qualifications like a PG Certificate, it provides professional accreditation, usually as an HEA Fellowship. A Code of Practice ('Code of Practice | The Higher Education Academy', n.d.) has also been established for HEA Fellows: ten statements of ethical practice, such as 'we will be fair and impartial in our engagement with learners'. Furthermore, for HEA Fellows a good standing requirement has been introduced. From 2013/14 it has been required as part of accredited institutional CPD schemes, while Fellows not in institutions are expected to maintain a record of CPD activity and 'evidence from a small sample of Fellows will be taken each year' (p. 3). Thus, in principle, a teacher might lose their Fellowship. What impact this might have on their career or current role will depend upon their institution's policies, but at the moment the possession of accreditation against UKPSF is some way short of the 'licence to practice' that traditional professions require.

The SEDA Professional Development Framework (SEDA-PDF)

In 2000 SEDA created a Professional Development Framework (SEDA-PDF) within which it has developed a total of (currently) 19 different awards for staff in HE (SEDA-PDF, n.d.). The values – it is stressed, 'values demonstrably informing practice' (authors' emphasis) – are maintained. SEDA-PDF distinguishes two kinds of outcomes – outcomes to do with professional development, common to all awards; and specialist outcomes related to particular roles. The two awards aimed at teachers, *Supporting Learning*, and *Learning, Teaching and Assessing* (based on SEDA's Teacher Accreditation Scheme from 1993), are accredited against UKPSF descriptors 1 and 2 (ACTCHQUAL, n.d.). (This is quite separate from SEDA's Fellowships for academic developers, discussed below.) The SEDA Professional Development Framework is summarised in Table 3.4.

Observations on professional standards

Each of these professional standards is very short – around a couple of hundred words. This is mainly because the professional standards do not prescribe how the outcomes should be achieved and how the values and knowledge should inform practice. Detailed implementation of standards is left to the individual professional. It may be thought that a longer, more detailed standard would better assure quality. The evidence suggests otherwise. Proposed standards for further education (college) teachers in the UK, published by the Further Educational National Training Organisation (FENTO, 1999), were some 10,000 words long, and were not well received. Less can be more, as long as it is the right less!

Also, there is considerable similarity between the various sets of professional standards. There are several reasons for this. First, each standard to some extent at least builds on what has gone before. Second, there is some common authorship.

Table 3.4 SEDA Professional Development Framework (summary)

SEDA Professional Development Framework (SEDA-PDF)
Those successfully undertaking and completing any SEDA-PDF accredited programme will be able to:
1 Identify their own professional development goals, directions or priorities
2 Plan for their initial and/or continuing professional development
3 Undertake appropriate development activities
4 Review their development and their practice, and the relations between them.
Values demonstrably informing practice:
1 Developing understanding of how people learn
2 Practising in ways that are scholarly, professional and ethical
3 Working with and developing learning communities
4 Valuing diversity and promoting inclusivity
5 Continually reflecting on practice to develop ourselves, others and processes
Sample specialist outcomes: these from the named award Enhancing Academic Practice In Disciplines
1 Apply a wide range of appropriate learning, teaching and assessing approaches in the discipline,
2 Contribute to enhancing the student experience of the subject discipline,
3 Demonstrate how their professional role is informed by relevant discipline-based centres and organisations,
4 Engage with a discipline-based community to enhance professional practice.

And third, at this very general level, there are perhaps only a few ways of describing the essentials of the work of the teacher in higher education.

This last point should not be overstated. A very simple standards framework was proposed for European work on teaching qualifications (Baume, 2008). This described five core activities – Planning (what is to be learned and hence taught), Teaching (and otherwise supporting learning), Assessing (and ensuring that students receive feedback on their work), Reviewing (the effectiveness of the teaching) and Developing (the capabilities and the practices of the teacher and the institution). The origins of this in Kolb's (1983) learning cycle can clearly be seen. Other models of the learning process, and other models of the process of supporting learning, can, and hopefully will, lead to other teaching qualification frameworks.

Professional bodies and associations

Roles of professional bodies and associations

A traditional profession such as law or medicine depends perhaps above all upon its expert base of knowledge, capability and values, and on it associated claim to merit the trust of those who engage with a member of the profession. Its members are experts who provide services to clients who, lacking this expertise, cannot be in a position fully to evaluate the services of an expert. Hence, society must trust professions to control themselves, and a client must trust the individual professional to exercise their power in the client's interests. This gives rise, firstly to the need for professions to assure the expertise of those in the profession, by initial and continuing training, development and assessment. It also leads to the need for professional probity and codes of conduct to clarify the proper exercise of that expertise in a position of trust. In return for freedom from interference, the professions maintain their expertise and exercise it with moral integrity and client confidence and confidentiality (Eraut, 1994, p. 2). That is the social contract between the professional body and society.

A growing number of occupations have wholly or partially established themselves as professions, and more are attempting to do so. For example, medical laboratory scientific officers are regarded as a profession, albeit one with lower status than medicine (Eraut, 1994, p. 3). Schoolteachers and social workers, on the other hand, continue to be troubled semi-professions, partly through difficulties in articulating their knowledge base, and partly through their lack of autonomy in the public sector. They aspire to be professions, but are often not treated as such by the public or government.

Academics *as teachers* (or as academic developers) may be in this limbo between the traditional professions and non-professional occupations, while academics as *discipline experts* or indeed as members of established professions have been regarded as, and have acted as, professionals, with their own discipline-specific professional bodies. While there have been a succession of developments promoting the professionalisation of university teaching in the UK, described above, there are also factors *deprofessionalising* academic life in a university sector where institutions are increasingly managed as businesses by CEOs. The traditional independence of academics as professionals has been constrained by managerialism in a sector increasingly dominated by the logic of the market, and more so in teaching than in research. This problem is not unique to academics – the role of the 'employed professional' is always somewhat problematic, principally with respect to their reduced autonomy.

The ILTHE and HEA compared to traditional professional bodies

In this context, the current HEA is not a traditional professional body, for the reasons given by Bucklow and Clark, above, in particular that it is not a membership organisation. To the extent that the prior ILTHE had individual fee-paying members, ILTHE was more a professional body. Progress towards professional status is not always linear. Options for the HEA include seeking to become an association with individual membership. This may transform Fellows into chartered members, who would pay an individual membership fee. This could increase the status of the accreditation. It could also bring a requirement or individuals to maintain good standing. Chartered status is an important, but probably not a sufficient, indication of the emergence of a profession.

Training and qualification for teachers

Increasingly, then, there are clear standards for teaching qualifications in UK universities. While most career-young staff are appointed as lecturers on the basis of their primary, disciplinary, expertise, they are usually expected to gain a teaching qualification before long. While before the 2003 White Paper this was normally a postgraduate academic qualification, accreditation against the UKPSF has rapidly incorporated these and also provided other routes to professional accreditation through institutional schemes and programmes without associated academic awards – a rare example of a move towards professionalisation not being accompanied by a demand for academic qualifications. More and more promotion procedures use teaching as part of the criteria, and more and more of these refer to national standards of teaching qualifications.

Since 2012–13 information on the teaching qualifications of all individual staff in UK universities has been collected as part of the annual data collection from institutions by HESA (ACTCHQUAL, n.d.). Ten categories of teaching qualifications are possible, including all four HEA Fellowship levels, those SEDA qualifications accredited against UKPSF, and academic qualifications. These data have yet to be published in detail but, when they are, it will undoubtedly begin to be incorporated into national league tables of institutions. This has incentivised institutions to support internal schemes and indicate a greater priority for teachers to have a teaching qualification or accreditation. In some cases institutions have targets of 100 per cent of teaching staff with teaching qualifications, but such targets are usually not public. The national figure for qualified teachers is currently about one quarter.

This is inevitably a political issue. A research-led university might consider it inappropriate to require its world-leading researchers, who may do little or no teaching, to take time to gain a teaching qualification. A bridge here may be a move to qualifications in research supervision, which has some but not complete similarity with teaching.

Training and qualification for developers

Academic developers as professionals share much of the situation of university teachers; hardly surprising, as they are among their other roles, as noted above, university teachers, of other teachers. One difference is that what they teach is not a primary discipline such as forms the basis of undergraduate courses, so they may appear to have no primary profession, with consequent loss of status. Again as discussed above, individual academic developers often have a career history of academic research and teaching before becoming an academic developer. While front-line teaching experience with real students gains some credibility, their claimed expertise as developers is usually generic and somewhat distant from that. Others may have a background in education as their discipline. Again their expertise is seen as mostly generic in a world where most if not all teaching is discipline-specific. Also, academics sometimes question, sometimes vigorously, the relevance of school, or even college education to higher education. This credibility gap can be partly addressed by scholarship and research in the discipline of academic development, and by credibility as a practitioner in the classroom or online space.

Qualifications in academic development have not followed the path of those for teachers. Few practicing developers have a higher degree in academic development, although many have higher degrees in other subjects. On the other hand, since 1993 in the UK there has been professional accreditation by a traditional professional association: Fellowships of SEDA.

The SEDA Fellowships scheme began in 1993, soon after the organisation was formed, to provide a qualification for the teachers of teachers. This qualification for developers was promptly in part by developers' realisation that we were accrediting university teachers whilst having no appropriate official qualification of our own. The current, revised scheme was launched in November 2010. The qualifications FSEDA and SFSEDA are both based on demonstrating a set of level-specific outcomes plus the SEDA professional values. The FSEDA qualification is currently gained through an online course. The Associate Fellowship is designed as a step towards full Fellowship. SEDA Fellowships are managed and awarded directly by the organisation, through an appointed part-time Fellowships coordinator. Table 3.5 summarises the SEDA Fellowships framework.

Table 3.5 SEDA Fellowships framework for academic developers (summary)

The SEDA Fellowship qualifications – Values, Development Outcomes and Specialist Outcomes
SEDA Values (all Fellowship awards) Recipients of the Fellowship will have shown how their work is informed by each of the SEDA values, namely commitments to: – Developing understanding of how people learn – Practicing in ways that are scholarly, professional and ethical – Working with and developing learning communities – Valuing diversity and promoting inclusivity – Continually reflecting on practice to develop ourselves, others and processes.
Core Development Outcomes (all Fellowship awards) Recipients of the Fellowship are required to demonstrate how they have, within their particular context(s): – Identified their own professional development goals, directions and/or priorities – Planned for their initial and/or continuing professional development – Undertaken appropriate development activities – Reviewed their development and their practice, and the relations between them.
Specialist Outcomes - Fellowship – Identified goals for academic development processes and activities – Planned and led academic development processes and activities towards achievement of these goals – Facilitated and led processes and activities to achieve the agreed goals – Monitored and evaluated the effectiveness and the acceptability of the development processes and activities – Identified any appropriate follow-up development process or activity
Specialist Outcomes – Senior Fellowship – Provided a sustained contribution to the improvement of education through academic development – Given service to the community of developers – Contributed to the body of professional knowledge and practice in academic development.

In February 2015 there are 105 current SEDA Fellows (of all types). Ten to 20 Fellowships are awarded annually. In addition there are 44 former Fellows (lapsed mostly through retirement or losing good standing). Is this significant penetration of the potential audience of developers? How many academic developers are there in the UK? It is hard to know exactly. There are about 1,000 subscribers to the free SEDA email list, including some overseas, so this may be the upper estimate. In about 150 UK universities, the number of academics for whom a SEDA Fellowship is appropriate varies from zero or one to several. The total number is therefore probably in the high hundreds and approaching a thousand. So SEDA Fellowships are probably held by a small minority of the potential audience.

This is lower than the penetration of the UKPSF with teachers. On 1 December 2013 there were about 194,000 academic staff in the UK, and in

2015 about 50,000 HEA Fellows (discussed in Bostock and Bradley, 2014); about one quarter but a proportion that is rising. In addition, many developers have teaching qualifications pre-dating the UKPSF. The higher proportion of teaching staff with a teaching qualification or accreditation than developers with a SEDA Fellowship is undoubtedly due to national and institutional policies focussing on the professionalism of teaching and student experience, as opposed to the professionalism of educational and staff development. Perhaps this has been assumed to be high and in no need of policies; SEDA has been the professional body since 1993. A SEDA Fellowship is not a licence to practice, but it is a significant item on the CV of those seeking employment as developers in the UK.

SEDA Fellowships have always required annual reporting, reflecting on and planning our professional development. For many years, these reports have been peer-reviewed, in triads of critical friends, whose discussions (face-to-face or virtual) are reported overwhelmingly as positive and supportive. The need for good standing is a reality: failure to report professional development for two years triggers a withdrawal of the Fellowship; Fellows are listed on the SEDA website.

The structures of UKPSF and that of SEDA Fellowships are different. UKPSF has five areas of activity, six core knowledge areas, and four professional values. SEDA Fellowships have specialist (learning) outcomes, generic outcomes of reflecting on practice, and five values. The two sets of values overlap, as do the SEDA outcomes and the UKPSF areas of activity. SEDA's outcomes incorporate knowledge rather than specify it separately. So the structures of what SEDA and HEA Fellows must demonstrate are different, but some of the content is similar. This is to be expected, as professionalism as a developer shares much with professionalism as a teacher: for example, continuing reflection on practice, scholarship, and a concern for learners as individuals and communities.

Conclusion

Contestable though it clearly is, the idea that teaching and academic development can usefully be considered and treated as professions can be very productive. The idea of profession raises questions that might otherwise not be raised: about the obligations and rights of academics and developers; about the preparation, qualification and continuing development of academics and developers; and about the nature of our practices.

Given the contested nature of profession, and the lack of a coherent and unified account of professionalism, academics and developers can adopt those elements that are appropriate and productive, modify those that don't quite work for us, and reject those which are inappropriate. This selective approach to the idea of the profession provides another conceptual framework or scaffolding around which to construct and describe our work, and, to the extent that we are our work, construct and describe ourselves.

References

ACTCHQUAL. (n.d.). Retrieved 10 June 2015 from www.hesa.ac.uk/component/studrec/show_file/14025/a%5E_%5EACTCHQUAL.html.

Ashwin, P. and Trigwell K. (2004). 'Investigating staff and educational development', Ch.7, pp. 117–131 in Baume, D. and Kahn, P. (eds.). *Enhancing Staff and Educational Development.* London: RoutledgeFalmer.

Baume, D. (2003). 'Far too successful', Ch .17, pp. 153–161 in Baume, D., Edwards, H. and Webb, G. (Eds.). *Staff and Educational Development: Case Studies, Experience and Practice.* London: RoutledgeFalmer.

Baume, D. (2006). 'Towards the end of the last non-professions?', *International Journal for Academic Development*, 11(1): 57–60.

Baume, D. (2008). *A Reference Framework for Teaching in Higher Education.* Available at www.edshare.soton.ac.uk/7337/1/32360_NETTLE_English.pdf.

Bostock, S. and Bradley, S. (2014). 'SEDA and HEA Fellowships – What's the difference?', *Educational Developments* 15(2): 6–7, London: SEDA.

Bucklow, C. and Clark, P. (2003). 'A new approach to professionalising teaching and accrediting training: The institute for learning and teaching in higher education', Chapter 7 in Blackwell, R. and Blackmore, P. (eds.). *Towards Strategic Staff Development in Higher Education.* London: SRHE.

Code of Practice | The Higher Education Academy. (n.d.). Retrieved 13 May 2015 from www.heacademy.ac.uk/professional-recognition/hea-fellowships/code-practice.

Dearing, R. (2007). 'Higher education in the learning society'. The report of the National Committee of Inquiry into Higher Education (NCIHE), 1997.

DES (Department for Education and Skills) (2003). White Paper: The Future of Higher Education. Retrieved 8 March 2015 from http://webarchive.nationalarchives.gov.uk/20040117001247/dfes.gov.uk/highereducation/hestrategy/.

Ekaratne, S. (2003). 'Take one country ...' Edwards, H., Webb, G. and Baume, D. (Eds.). *Staff and Educational Development: Case Studies, Experience and Practice.* London: RoutledgeFalmer.

Eraut, M. (1994). *Developing Professional Knowledge and Competence.* London: The Falmer Press.

Ethical Principles in University Teaching. (1996). Retrieved 10 June 2015 from http://www.stlhe.ca/awards/3m-national-teaching-fellowships/initiatives/ethical-principles-in-university-teaching.

FENTO (1999). Standards for teaching and supporting learning in further education in England and Wales. Retrieved 10 June 2015 from http://dera.ioe.ac.uk/4191/1/Standards%2520for%2520teaching%2520and%2520supporting%2520learning%2520in%2520%2520FE.pdf.

Freidson, E. (1994). *Professionalism Reborn: Theory, Prophecy and Policy.* Cambridge: Polity Press.

Gunderman, R.B. (2006). *Achieving Excellence in Medical Education.* London: Springer Verlag.

HEA (2014). The Higher Education Academy UK Professional Standards Framework. Retrieved 8 March 2015 from www.heacademy.ac.uk/sites/default/files/downloads/UKPSF_2011_English.pdf.

Johnson, T. J. (1972). *Professions and Power.* London: Macmillan.

Kolb, D. A. (1983). *Experiential Learning: Experience as the Source of Learning and Development,* 1st ed. Englewood Cliffs, NJ: Prentice Hall.

Measuring the impact of the UK Professional Standards Framework for Teaching and Supporting Learning (UKPSF) | The Higher Education Academy. (2013). Retrieved 10 June 2015 from www.heacademy.ac.uk/ukpsf-impact-study.

SEDA-PDF. (n.d.). Retrieved 23 May 2015 from www.seda.ac.uk/pdf.

UK Professional Standards Framework (UKPSF) | The Higher Education Academy. (2011). Retrieved 23 May 2015 from www.heacademy.ac.uk/professional-recognition/uk-professional-standards-framework-ukpsf.

Wikipedia (2015). Higher Education Academy. Retrieved 23 May 2015 from http://en.wikipedia.org/wiki/Higher_Education_Academy.

Chapter 4

Supporting continuing professional development (CPD) for lecturers

Ruth Pilkington

Summary

This chapter explores challenges and solutions for academic development when supporting the continuing professional development (CPD) of lecturers and teachers. This is important, as broader participation, marketisation and consumerist expectations are changing the nature of HE teaching and learning practice and environments. The chapter comprises three sections:

1 Why the lecturing role is a particular focus for academic development
2 Selected models and theory influencing lecturers' CPD
3 Options and approaches for CPD introduced by institutions and by academic developers

The chapter uses examples and relates theory and practice throughout. It encourages developers to consider implications for their future practice.

Links to web sources referenced in this chapter can be found at www.seda. ac.uk/apad.

Lecturers and CPD: a complex field

CPD is here taken to mean development that encompasses all aspects of academic and educational work associated with the lecturer role. The complexity of lecturing is increasing, leading to greater diversity of career and activities associated with lecturing. This diversity is causing an increase in the CPD needs for lecturers, and is thus making greater demands on the capabilities of academic developers. As well as a personal and professional development activity that should be undertaken purposefully by individual lecturers, CPD is increasingly an organisational priority.

Why have academic developers become linked particularly with the work of lecturers? I suggest that the work and practice of the lecturer has often been positioned outside the usual systems and processes of HE organisational human resource services (HR). When considering the development of lecturers, HR normally focus on the training needs for this group with respect to administration, work systems and processes, and managerial functions. The core work of a lecturer has for a long time resided primarily in their particular subject expertise and their research. CPD, if the term was used, and it rarely was, often meant going to a conference in the discipline. Over several decades, however, lecturing has extended beyond being identified predominantly with subject expertise. The professional craft of teaching and facilitation of learning has steadily acquired greater importance. This duality is now a core characteristic of the work of the lecturer, as is also explored, along with other issues raised throughout this section, in Chapter 3 on professionalism.

The professional function of teaching, or the facilitation of learning, in HE has evolved in parallel to shifts in nature of the student body and the growing role HE now plays in ensuring a skilled professional workforce. The causal factors have been amply discussed elsewhere (Ball, 2008; Evans, 2008). They include:

- Marketisation of HE
- Widening participation
- Alignment of HE graduateness with the productive capacity-building of society
- Technology and a growth in the demand for high-level technical skills as a response to the knowledge economy
- Globalisation and internationalisation.

As this shift has progressed, the lecturer role has become a site of tension between research, teaching work, administration and management. It has acquired a profile of dual professionalism (Robson, 2006; Peel, 2005) too, or even multiple professionalism, which has been explicitly acknowledged within several recent attempts to define lecturing by national and professional bodies in the UK, Australia and US. There has also been a shift in the relationship between lecturer and student, with increased emphasis on collaborative approaches, and a move from teaching as a teacher-centred activity towards facilitation of learning and learner-centred approaches. This change in the relationship between HE lecturer and student–client intensifies the demands on lecturers' CPD. Neither HR nor academic development alone can carry the task of CPD. This chapter argues that CPD should be a joint and organisationally constructed activity.

A recent EU illustration in the *Times Higher Education* (Grove, 2015) represents student to staff ratios as ranging widely, between 42:1 in Greece and 11:1 in the Netherlands. Student numbers make demands upon how students are supported to learn. The purpose of HE has also changed (Barnett, 2008; Ball, 2008). How lecturing is viewed is especially critical where students see themselves as carrying much of the cost of their education. Expectations of lecturing staff, on what they do and on their accountability, have changed. Finally, there has been a growth in the requirement for lecturing staff to hold a qualification to teach. This qualification might be aligned to an initial standard, framework or benchmark set by a professional group, body or by government intervention.

The UK Professional Standards Framework has further influenced the landscape of lecturers' CPD since its revision in 2011. Four Descriptors now differentiate roles and relationships for teaching and learning, accompanied by a drive to accredit institutions' CPD frameworks for awarding and recognising professional status in teaching and learning. More on this in Chapter 3.

The role of lecturer is thus becoming broader and more complex. It appears to be reframing itself, culminating in the disaggregation of component elements of the classic role of lecturer into discrete parts, duties and functions (Cashmore *et al.*, 2013; Locke, 2014). Disaggregation of functions at university level is considered briefly in Chapter 18. This further causes difficulty in role definition and in identifying career pathways. In the UK, this has been particularly strong, and resulted in a variety of options for the career routes of academic faculty and for the way in which the lecturer role is being configured. A series of funded studies into the academic role (Cashmore *et al.*, 2013; Locke, 2014) suggest that academic practice itself is becoming divided into roles and functions that no longer reflect the three main areas of research, teaching and administration (management), but divide responsibilities and practice across processes within each area.

- Lecturing may be broken into design, various teaching roles (e.g. seminar tutor, teaching assistant, learning technologist, online moderator), management of courses, modules, year groups, teaching at postgraduate and undergraduate, placement tuition, etc.
- Support components of administration may become more specialised with the rise of skills tutors, advisors and library staff having greater input into learning, and administrators having a more central role in supporting the learning experience of students overall. Locke (2014) for example speaks of para-academics (12). A further range of support roles is suggested in Chapter 1.
- Research, with its greater demands of funding, profiling and management, is changing, with specialisms divided across processes and functions: bid writing, management, analysis, leadership.

This complexity means professional development as a whole, and possible career routes for lecturers, are no longer straightforward and defined along subject, research or teaching management lines; but may involve amorphous role and career development with individuals moving in and out of roles as funding, institutional priorities, and teaching and programme demands, wax and wane. The result is corresponding demands upon HE organisational systems, which I would argue are still in their infancy with respect to lecturer CPD. There is also an increasing trend for some HEIs to employ staff on teaching only contracts (BLASST, n.d.). This raises issues when planning career progression opportunities for these employees, and also when considering the reward and recognition of staff in this capacity.

Ideally, as Peters suggests (2009), CPD for lecturers should unify academic development provision; personal and professional development review; probation, acclimatisation and mentoring to address needs across career paths; and reward. This suggests a holistic approach, with stronger communication between HR systems and how CPD is conceived from the lecturer and academic developer perspective. CPD from the academic developer standpoint consequently becomes a complex activity, undertaken as part of a broader set of organisational priorities and processes. The professional development of lecturers also sits in wider debates around how organisations themselves are managing and directing teaching and learning. As a consequence, questions arise for the appraisal and HR management tools which audit and record lecturer CPD. Lecturer CPD has broadened significantly in how it is positioned: it is now more about how HE institutions are developing transparency, and about local systems and processes lining up with wider industrial and professional norms. Some HE institutions are consequently designing mechanisms that can bring lecturer CPD into organisational management and monitoring systems. This also requires an understanding of how lecturers learn, to enable the development of appropriate CPD.

The main focus of the academic development support function itself lay originally with the initial professional training of lecturers. The increasing number of drivers surrounding HE have required attention to, for example, employability and entrepreneurial activity, academic skills and, increasingly, learning technologies and social media. More recently, this development work has extended to include the need for academic developers to know about research, not only for their own practice, but also for supporting lecturers' CPD. Alongside this, the shifts in the landscape of lecturing mean that academic developers have to think more creatively than ever about how they support lecturers across their career development and as HE lecturers. This demands greater sensitivity and appreciation for roles and functions across the organisation, across levels of responsibility, and across formal and informally constituted roles of academic leadership (Bolden, Petrov and Gosling, 2008). It also means supporting professional development that may cross systems and teaching and learning processes encompassing the whole student study life cycle. CPD is no longer a purely academic development issue, and academic developers need to support HE institutions to understand how lecturers learn most effectively in order to influence CPD design and planning.

Enabling CPD for lecturers – national issues

There is a particular interest in how the UK has addressed the professionalising of the lecturer role using a national framework, and the influence of marketisation and audit in framing the way HE organisations are providing CPD for lecturer roles. Australia has explored the use of a national framework (Ingvarson, 2007) in setting standards and as a means of supporting a promotion and career structure, and more recently targeted at sessional faculty (BLASST, n.d.) framework for sessional staff. However, national attempts to unite career progression and professional standards for lecturers can lack the flexibility to respond to the complex landscape associated with how lecturing work is evolving. Others – predominantly within the African continent and Middle East – are adopting government-led initiatives to introduce common teaching standards for HE. These are often undertaken in partnership with English-speaking partner-HEIs and hence draw on the experience of frameworks such as the UKPSF. In the EU, the position of HE quality and standards for HE teaching is still being debated, although the general trend is towards national benchmarks. It is likely that the impact of their introduction will be equivalent to that experienced in the UK. The requirement for HEIs in the UK to have their own CPD frameworks for recognising and awarding professional status to staff in learning and teaching roles was a significant step forward in changing how lecturers will be supported in HE. For example, most UK institutions are now paying more attention to how the academic development of lecturers is structured and profiled as an outcome of the introduction and wider adoption of UKPSF since 2011.

One of the benefits of benchmarks is that they encourage debate on how to frame careers, and therefore direct CPD processes. It is well accepted that quality in teaching for HE is a complex concept, as explored in Chapter 9 on QA and QE. The concept of quality incorporates discussion of, and potentially defining, what contributes to good teaching and 'excellence' (Skelton, 2005, 2007; Gunn and Fisk, 2013). This in turn is shaped by subject interests. The debate on CPD however is shaped by dialectic between three groups:

- The national or professional body;
- The HE institution and its priorities and vision of what teaching and learning should be; and
- The individual's own position and perspective.

The individual is ultimately responsible for managing and directing his or her efforts and CPD, taking account of these three perspectives. CPD for lecturers is often conceptualised therefore as a contingent, situated, and culturally framed activity undertaken within organisational systems and processes, with support from academic developers. The academic developer role may take the form of provider, designer, facilitator and mediator, or may adopt a form of brokering between stakeholders. The developer has therefore to operate within a complex network of forces, to accommodate and respond to the different ways the support of teaching may be enacted and understood at different levels and across roles. At the same time, the demands on academic development are significant, because academic development is often politically vulnerable within the organisational structure and has to align several stakeholder interests in planning, designing and delivering CPD. For this reason, national organisations for academic development such as SEDA (UK), HERDSA (Australasia), POD (US) etc. are valuable because they offer support and tools as well as development opportunities for the academic developers themselves. National organisations and their support roles are considered further in Chapters 1 and 18.

For example, the SEDA Professional Development Framework (PDF) (Named Awards, n.d.) offers a valuable resource to academic developers in its (currently) 19 awards. The awards have been designed to frame professional development in such a way that they accommodate some of the emerging complexity around lecturing. An academic developer might therefore draw on a selection of the PDF awards to meet the demands of a lecturer for professional development: upon entry, as course deliverer and designer, as researcher, as leader, and as mature professional; and as lecturers require development for new career or role functions. In other words, SEDA PDF enables a life cycle approach to respond to the needs of lecturers. Table 4.1 lists a selection of possible awards that might suit career development for the lecturer life cycle at each career stage:

Table 4.1 SEDA PDF awards mapped to career progression

Career stage & Commentary	Core award examples from SEDA PDF	Skills development examples from SEDA PDF
Entry / early career: Focuses on entry qualifications and skills development across all aspects of lecturer role	Supporting learning; Learning, teaching and assessing	Enhancing research practice; Supporting learning with technology; Supervising postgraduate research
Mid-career: Development of lecturer role and key functions around curriculum development and how to enhance practice	Enhancing academic practice in the disciplines; Leading programmes; External examining	Action research; Responding to change in HE
Mature / leadership: Sharing expertise, and/ or building programme teams, also reinvigoration of practice	Leading and developing academic practice; Leading programmes	Developing leaders; Mentoring and coaching

Table 4.1 shows how the awards can be used to meet the career and role needs of a lecturer and provides suggestions for appropriate awards at each stage. The awards themselves are non-credit-bearing, and so they can be used to structure a wide range of academic development activity. They can also be used to frame workshops, individual development facilitated through academic development, practitioner research, events participation, reflective practice-based activity, etc.

Three examples show how institutions have successfully adopted SEDA PDF for this purpose.

• Birmingham City University has used seven awards to create an extensive framework for lecturer CPD that is tightly linked to institutional goals.

Potential participants for awards might be identified in appraisal or may self identify. Awards are also used to help drive specific initiatives such as internationalisation and the use of students as mentors.

- Liverpool John Moores University designed its early CPD framework around the awards. Awards were used for lecturers and other staff to develop their practice across the organisation (Pilkington, 2007).
- The University of Central Lancashire (UCLan) drew on six SEDA awards to meet lecturers' development needs and university priorities with respect variously to early teaching development, mature professionals, action research, technology, student support and guidance and research supervision. (Pilkington, 2007).

As the academic development community and function has matured, a very clear picture of how to address the learning needs of lecturers has emerged (Laycock and Shrives, 2009; Appleby and Pilkington, 2014).

How do lecturers learn?

An answer to this question lies within wider theories of how professionals learn. Many of the characteristics of broader professional learning conditions are common, and the learning requirements of educators have been highly researched with respect to compulsory education sectors. A considerable amount of work has already been reported elsewhere (Eraut, 1994; Boud, Keogh and Walker, 1985; Appleby and Pilkington, 2014). This section first identifies key factors in lecturers' approaches to learning, and then explores examples of how this has been addressed within the academic development community.

One starting point for considering lecturer CPD is the nature of the knowledge base. This is a complex issue: the complexity is seen in Shulman's (1987) definition of teaching as having seven areas of knowledge and expertise:

- Content knowledge
- General pedagogic knowledge
- Curriculum knowledge
- Pedagogical content knowledge
- Knowledge about learners and their characteristics
- Knowledge of educational contexts
- Knowledge of educational purposes

These imply a demanding range of activities, skills and knowledge. We can combine and summarise these to say that a lecturer must know about:

- The subject and how to learn it;
- Teaching learners and supporting their learning;
- The educational environment and setting (organisational systems and processes) and the purpose of education.

Lecturers may feel they are rooted in the subject and their expertise as subject specialists. However, increasingly the other two fields of knowledge listed immediately above play a crucial role in making what they do effective.

Running tangentially to the issue of a complex knowledge base, there are career aspects of lecturer learning. These are often reflected in the organisational structures that frame CPD, and as we saw from the SEDA example have become complex in recent times.

Finally, the research emphasises again and again that the vast majority of practice learning occurs in and around the doing of the role (Barnett, 2008; Eraut, 1994; Wenger, 2008) and with peers through processes of deliberation and informed critical reflection (Brookfield, 1995; Moon, 1999). In a recent discussion of the literature on these issues, it was argued that the professional learning of lecturers could be founded on five premises (Appleby and Pilkington, 2014). These are:

- The belief that the professional learns best through social, discursive and reflective processes structured in and around practice.
- Recognition that there is a need for progressive structures to support identity creation in a way that reflects role, career stage, and personal and professional need.
- A need to question what educational knowledge is, who owns it and how it is acquired and developed.
- An acknowledgement that professional learning is contingent and situated within organisations, and contextualised practices and processes.
- Finally, the need to design purposeful and embedded approaches to professional learning that maximise critical learning opportunities.

The discursive and situated progression of professional educational learning is evident in the work of academic developers. Initial lecturing qualifications for learning and teaching as a formal learning programme are connected to progression routes such as further masters awards addressing teaching and learning. However, credit-bearing programmes form the least-preferred continuing professional development for HE lecturers (Laycock and Shrives, 2009). In fact, as emerges very clearly from Laycock and Shrives' edited discussion of CPD, the preferred approaches to CPD for teaching and learning practice lie with networks, peers, reading and scholarship, and curriculum development.

This highlights a widely shared view of how professionals (education practitioners) learn, and has led to considerable variety in academic development, with many informal ways of learning framed within a wider CPD and networked environment. The chapter now moves to explore examples of how academic developers are supporting lecturer CPD.

Structuring lecturer CPD

This involves four steps:

1   Identification of learning need.
2   Identifying and undertaking action to meet learning need.
3   Review and reflection on learning achieved.
4   Repositioning and revised assessment of goals and learning needs leading to new cycle.

Identification of learning need

For the lecturer, step one may involve self-identification as a result of wanting to develop or <u>having</u> to develop. It may also be directed by appraisal activity. CPD needs may emerge from work-related lecturer activity, e.g. subject and programme review, quality assurance mechanisms or processes of peer review, such as observation of teaching. These development needs may be communicated at a department level to academic development units. Alternatively, a need may be identified through a process of consultancy and brokering which mediates between teaching and learning development priorities coming down from strategic decision-making, or emerging up and out from departments and review processes. Chapter 2 considers needs analysis in some detail.

Identifying and undertaking action to meet learning need

In step 2 various development activities can be used to respond to lecturers' needs ranging from formal courses to conversations in and around practice. In response to the observation that lecturers' preferred CPD is often constructed by the individual and is practice-based, several innovative approaches are emerging, such as:

- Collectivities of practice. These differ from the more widely accepted communities of practice. They emerge around initiatives and projects for example, meet a professional need, and then fade. In this they respond to needs of the practitioner rather than of the managers (Lindkvist, 2005).
- There is a growing interest in dialogic ways of developing lecturers, especially since these can encourage practice-based reflection. Peer mentoring is attractive in this context.
- The Scholarship of Teaching and Learning (SoTL) is a powerful means for HE lecturers to develop practice (see Chapter 12). It complements the strong growth in disciplinary approaches to lecturer learning, embracing the dual professionalism and expertise of lecturers.
- Kreber has strongly argued for authenticity (2013) in the enhancement of teaching practice, because it specifically combines values, the integrity of the lecturer and the subject, professional identity and educational purpose.

These approaches counter the impacts of managerialism (Ball, 2008; Sachs 2001; Evans, 2008), which some argue is on the increase, and place the practitioner as owner of their CPD. The next section explores some of these approaches: courses, communities of practice, the Scholarship of Teaching and Learning (SoTL), dialogue, and systematised learning spaces. Together, they can be structured across organisations in enabling ways that meet the needs of lecturers across career spans and career transitions, and also share ownership for CPD between employer and employee. Such developments direct increased attention beyond completion of the initial stage of teacher development.

Formal courses are often seen as an appropriate starting point for CPD particularly for new lecturers, hence the numbers of postgraduate certificates catering for their early career needs. Formal courses are also useful to support the needs of academics around the development of deeper subject and pedagogic knowledge, where individual need or desire exists for higher qualifications, such as masters awards.

In recent years in the UK, both initial and continuing teacher development courses have been a major element in academic development for lecturing staff. However, this is changing, with growing importance attached to ongoing CPD. Masters courses for example can be explicitly designed to support practice-based development needs. At UCLan, course modules were designed to specifically address the mid-career needs of lecturers in relation to pedagogic research confidence, action research and writing; course and programme design through curriculum development; and the use of innovative approaches to education. Masters programmes have the advantage of being credit-bearing with strong theoretical underpinnings. They also provide opportunities for lecturers from different subjects to come together in a safe community for sharing and mutually supported learning. Courses, especially when run face-to-face, may be limited by accessibility and the availability of resources. Masters awards can focus on practitioner research-based approaches, allowing flexible enhancement of practice through practitioner-based evaluation, action research and similar evidence-based research work. There are examples at the University of Auckland (Stefani, 2011), Liverpool Hope University and Edinburgh Napier. An interesting development has been a shift to smaller bite-sized chunks of study that more closely align to institutional priorities. Examples of this are Edinburgh Napier (Gray, 2013) which developed a programme of bite-sized online CPD modules, and the Australian National University whose bite-sized programme of professional development both awards and supports teaching development. These are described in more detail in Chapter 17.

ANU Centre for Higher Education, Learning & Teaching (CHELT) has developed a themed set of ten modules (a decamod) within its Academic

> Professional Development program. All modules include time for writing and/or peer engagement..... Modules provide resources, personal writing and reflection time, and support as needed: they are offered in online, blended or face-to-face modes as appropriate. (ANU, n.d.)

The decamod has been framed around progression using UKPSF. Modules embrace reflection on practice, and ultimately leadership and mentoring of peers. Academic developers have a mechanism in such courses for meeting development priorities, certifying learning and teaching, as well as meeting individual CPD needs. The environments emphasise peer communication and practice-based learning. Although courses are limited with respect to where professional learning and development actually takes place, namely within the practice setting and doing of work, curriculum design and practitioner-research focused modules provide a means whereby subject expertise and pedagogic and curriculum understandings come together (Kreber, 2009).

Review and reflection on learning achieved

Some of the less formal structures that are widely in use by academic developers include forums, networks, communities of practice and conferences. These may be used to complement masters programmes and tend to flourish because they generate space and time for reflection and wider learning and exchange. Conferences are particularly powerful as a way of sharing teaching and learning practice. Some conferences that start out as institutional events become regional, disciplinary and national in focus. An example is the teaching and learning conference at Liverpool Hope University, which was established as a biennial event around national projects undertaken at the institution and using action research (Norton, 2014). Similar forums for exchange have emerged around the academic units at Plymouth University and at the Universities of Auckland and Ulster. At Plymouth University, their conference has become a significant event with a journal and book associated with the conference which is supported by the centre of research-informed academic practice (PedRIO, n.d.; Turner, Schoenborn and Wyness, 2013). At UCLan, a teaching and learning conference bridged a number of communities bringing together lecturers engaged in an institution-wide Pedagogic Research Forum, including a forum journal and linked to a funded Centre (Centre for Research Informed Teaching, n.d.), and lecturers on a teaching and learning masters in education and a professional doctorate. This community of lecturers latterly included FE college-based HE lecturers as well as UCLan faculty, resulting in a rich and vibrant network.

Such rich communities of practice allow HE lecturers to engage safely in the debate and discussion of practice, to encounter new ideas and theoretically informed innovation, and to hear about innovative and interesting practice across disciplines and even institutions. They encourage dialogue, networking and exchange, and hence reflect and support how lecturers learn. Within Canada and the US, such communities of practice have been formalised in 'Teaching Commons' and SoTL communities, which offer semi-formal space for learning and development informed by scholarship. An example is York University in Canada, whose mission states

> The Teaching Commons brings together like-minded individuals who are interested in exploring and sharing teaching and learning innovation across York University. The Teaching Commons team is based in ... and maintains a virtual presence via our website and Moodle courses. More than a presence, we are a network of colleagues, collaborations and projects, working across and within Faculties and Support Services. (York University, n.d.)

This type of initiative characterises the growing movement around SoTL, and is contributing to the development of teaching practice worldwide through conferences and online forums such as ISSOTL, NAIRTL, etc. The rationale behind this growth is the belief that university teaching is problematic, can be problematised and is researchable (Norton, 2014; Cousin, 2009). It is also founded on a belief in the enhancement of teaching through scholarship and an evidence base. This is strengthened by being articulated within criteria and statements associated with national frameworks. Scholarship and research into learning and teaching are, for example, highlighted within criteria drafted as part of the Australian University Teaching Criteria and Standards Project, the German Charta der Guten Lehre, and the UKPSF, all of which relate to professional development of HE lecturers (Courtney, 2014).

These initiatives comply with the principles listed at the start of this section on how lecturers engage in CPD. They also help to raise the status of teaching and learning practice to parallel the status of subject specialist research. Mårtensson, Roxå and Olsson (2011) identify the scholarship of learning and teaching and pedagogic research as crucial to culture change for HE teaching.

Repositioning and revised assessment of goals and learning needs leading to new cycle

Leeds Beckett University (Carauna, 2012) adopted research tools drawn from Appreciative Inquiry (appreciative conversations) in academic development work around teaching and learning. In pursuing this approach, the academic developers involved were also embedding discursive approaches to professional development. This fundamental need for dialogue around work has been promoted by, for example:

- Brookfield in his use of highly structured conversations to develop academic faculty (1995);
- Barnett (2008) in his view of lecturers as engaging in a discursive relationship with peers and practice as part of a developmental process that involves identity creation and reconstitution;

- Ho (2000), Mårtensson, Roxå and Olsson (2011) in the use of dialogue for changing cultures of teaching and learning;
- Pilkington (2013) in the use of dialogue to support and assess professional learning.

Teaching commons, conferences and networking events all create semi-formal spaces in which such dialogue can take place around practice. In these safe environments, discursive learning is promoted, encouraged and purposeful, consequently satisfying Eraut's idea of a deliberative process around practice (2004).

Dialogue is a powerful mechanism, in the development of lecturers and as a reflective tool for making learning meaningful. Dialogic learning around practice takes place within significant peer networks (Mårtensson, Roxå and Olsson, 2011) and in mentored and critical conversations with peers (expert others) (Brockbank and McGill, 1998) at key stages in career or role transition. It is often facilitated through the formal task of Peer Observation of Teaching (PoT), and through mentoring approaches (Laurillard, 1999), which have grown in use as HE institutions adopt techniques to strengthen practice-based CPD and leadership amongst academic staff. A number of institutions actively promote dialogue for CPD around curriculum activity, for example,

- Indiana University (2003) where course portfolios are being used to prompt critical dialogue and development of practice;
- Sheffield Hallam University adopted scaffolded conversations, and the University of Roehampton (Hall and Peat, 2012) uses dialogue between peers – both use dialogue to support professional learning in CPD frameworks;
- York St John, Ulster, Liverpool John Moores, Exeter, and a number of other UK institutions are actively using professional dialogue (Pilkington, 2013) to support and recognise lecturing staff in achieving professional status.

Such initiatives can become part of wider embedded approaches that formalise dialogue as a tool for CPD around curriculum and the enhancement of teaching and learning practice. Such dialogue is strengthened further when it also involves students as partners.

Concluding thoughts

Experience and evidence-based research have established a body of knowledge amongst academic developers concerning the best way to support lecturers' CPD. However, a challenge for academic developers remains in how they influence systems and processes effectively to build in the space and time for peer-supported dialogue and for learning to occur around practice. From an organisational perspective, another challenge is the overlap between academic development and HR management and how their respective reporting systems may be made compatible to record progress and show achievements. Further tensions may be caused by the shift in the nature of HE, leading to a growth in managerialism, emphasis on productivity, and rationalised delivery with shorter development cycles for curricula, producing pressures upon the established cycle of the academic year. Furthermore, an increased use of year-round teaching to extend delivery and international or income generating opportunities means that both space and time are under threat (Ball, 2008). The most frequently cited hurdles to development activity are pleas about lack of time or excessive workload by lecturers, or the desire to balance research with teaching and assessing students.

Responding to this requires effort from academic developers, but in the UK the introduction of UKPSF to the HE sector has raised the profile of teaching development in the face of reduced funding. Such national initiatives can be exploited by academic developers, and with reduced resources, academic developers have to be creative. One solution involves adopting integrated approaches to CPD, by taking a university-wide approach that builds on ideas of process enhancement around work, and building in space and time for dialogue. CPD for lecturers should draw on all the services involved, and make use of external drivers including standards in directing appraisal and professional development reporting.

A model for how this can be done emerged from work by a group of academic developers in the North West of England. It combined organisational thinking and consideration of how lecturers learn. The model emerged from over a decade of work, and, whilst simple, it reflects some of the approaches that are becoming commonplace across the sector. It involves the integration of national drivers, understandings of organisational learning and professional development, a responsiveness to local learning and teaching priorities, and an appreciation for how the processes of learning and teaching development can be expanded to build in time and space for reflection. It also involves combining institutional perspectives on CPD and what needs to be done by lecturing faculty with a more proactive stance by lecturers on their career and practice development. In the complex dynamic HE environment, the individual **must** be encouraged to take a more empowered position in relation to his or her CPD. A national driver towards professional status is a useful stimulus to this. The resulting model involves generating space and time for learning within systems and processes, and employs CPD activities such as those described above. The model proposes mechanisms whereby CPD can be supported as part of a unified and organisationally framed model. It includes:

- Space for reflection on practice – within appraisal and by developing practitioner-led reflection in spaces constructed around peer observation, course development and review, peer discussion, team learning and reflection.
- Communities of practice to support exchange and peer learning at local, team and department level, creating communities of 'champions' to support lecturers in subjects and teams, and the use of cross-institution networks, e.g. forums, groups and networks.

- Opportunities for dialogue around practice through mentoring, buddy pairings, learning sets, peer review, and practitioner-based conversations.

And uses;

- Research and scholarship that are relevant, supported by action research and SoTL communities and by journals and events for sharing outcomes of research.
- Education courses, formally designed to generate safe spaces for learning and exchange, and for deepening and extending the knowledge base. This includes ITE (initial teacher education), CPD courses and modules structured flexibly as free-standing learning opportunities. They can create academic credibility and are transferable by being aligned to national standards.
- Wider organisational opportunities such as projects, which generate resources and stimulate scholarship, and research that is relevant and rewarded.

By approaching CPD in a way that is organisationally responsive, and sensitive to potential career paths and demands in a dynamic practice context, academic developers can design a sympathetic, flexible and engaging means of supporting lecturer CPD that is structured around the doing and enhancement of practice.

References

ANU (n.d.). http://chelt.anu.edu.au/staff-education/anu-educational-fellowship-scheme, accessed 14 May 2015.

Appleby, Y. and Pilkington, R. (2014). *Developing Critical Professional Practice in Education*. NIACE.

Ball, S. (2008). *The Education Debate*. Bristol: Policy Press.

Barnett, R. (2008). 'Critical professionalism in an age of supercomplexity', in Cunningham, B. (2008) (Ed.), *Exploring Professionalism*. London: Bedford Way Papers, Institute of Education, 190–209.

BLASST (n.d.). Benchmarking Leadership and Advancement of Standards for Sessional Teaching, http://blasst.edu.au/index.html, downloaded 5 January 2015.

Bolden, R., Petrov, G. and Gosling, D. (2008). *Developing Collective Leadership in Education*. Centre for Leadership Studies, University of Exeter: LFHE.

Boud, D., Keogh, R. and Walker, D. (eds.) (1985). *Reflection: Turning Experience into Learning*. London: Kogan Page.

Brockbank, A. and McGill, I. (1998). *Facilitating Reflective Learning in Higher Education*. SRHE and Open University, Buckingham.

Brookfield, S. (1995). *Becoming a Critically Reflective Teacher*. San Francisco: Jossey Bass.

Carauna, V. (2012). 'Appreciatively inquiring into the internationalised curriculum – a model for CPD'. In *Educational Developments* 13(2): 11–17, SEDA.

Cashmore, A., Cane, C. and Cane, R. (2013). *Rebalancing Promotion in the HE Sector: Is Teaching Excellence Being Rewarded?* York, UK: Higher Education Academy.

Centre for Research Informed Teaching (n.d.). www.uclan.ac.uk/students/research/crit/index.php, accessed 12 May 2015.

Courtney, S. (2014). *Global Approaches to Developing Teaching Excellence Frameworks.* UK: Higher Education Academy/Manchester Metropolitan University.

Cousin, G. (2009). *Researching Learning in HE: An Introduction to Contemporary Methods and Approaches.* Abingdon, UK: Routledge.

Eraut, M. (1994). *Developing Professional Knowledge and Competence.* Abingdon, UK: Falmer Press.

Eraut, M. (2004). 'Informal learning in the workplace', *Studies in Continuing Education* 26(2): 247–273.

Evans, L. (2008). 'Professionalism, professionality and the development of education professionals', *British Journal of Educational Studies*, 56(1): 28–38.

Gray, C. (2013). 'Flexible accessible professional development: try bite-sized!', *Educational Developments*, 14(4): 14–17, SEDA.

Grove, J. (2015, January 22). 'Analysis: are EU students feeling the squeeze?' Retrieved 12 May 2015 from www.timeshighereducation.co.uk/news/analysis-are-eu-students-feeling-the-squeeze/2018090.article.

Gunn, V. and Fisk, A. (2013). *Teaching Excellence 2007–2013: a literature review since the CHERI Report 2007.* York, UK: Higher Education Academy.

Hall, J., and Peat, J. (2012). 'Using students' conversations about learning and teaching to surface troublesome knowledge about the HE classroom', *Educational Developments*, 13(3): 15–17, SEDA.

Ho, A. (2000). 'A conceptual change approach to staff development: a model for professional design', *International Journal of Academic Development*, 5(1): 30–41.

Indiana University (2003). Course Portfolio Initiative in *Peer Review of Teaching*, Spring 2003, 2(1), www.indiana.edu/~g131/CPS03nl.pdf, downloaded 12 December 2014.

Ingvarson, L. (2007). 'Conceptualising and evaluating teacher quality: substantive and methodological issues'. Australian Council for Educational Research, downloaded from ACEReSearch, http:///research.acer.edu.au/learning-processes/8, March 2015.

Kreber, C. (ed.) (2009). *The University and its Disciplines: Teaching and Learning Within and Beyond Discipline Boundaries.* Abingdon, UK: Routledge.

Kreber, C. (2013). *Authenticity In and Through Teaching in HE: The Transformative Potential of the Scholarship of Teaching.* Abingdon, UK: Routledge.

Laurillard, D. A. (1999). 'Conversational framework for individual learning applied to the "Learning Organisation" and the "Learning Society"', *Systems Research and Behavioral Science System Research* 16: 113–122.

Laycock, M. and Shrives, L. (eds.) (2009). *SEDA Paper 123: Embedding CPD in HE.* SEDA.

Lindkvist, L. (2005). 'Knowledge communities and knowledge collectivities: a typology of knowledge work in groups', *Journal of Management Studies* 42(6): 189–210.

Locke, W. (2014). *Shifting Academic Careers: Implications for Enhancing Professionalism in Teaching and Supporting Learning.* York, UK: Higher Education Academy.

Mårtensson, K., Roxå, T. and Olsson, T. (2011). 'Developing a quality culture through the scholarship of T&L', *Higher Education Research and Development* 30(1): 51–62.

Moon, J. A. (1999). *Reflection in Learning and Professional Development: Theory and Practice.* Abingdon, UK: RoutledgeFalmer.

Named Awards. (n.d.). Retrieved 12 May 2015 from www.seda.ac.uk/named-awards.

Norton, L. (2014). 'Chapter 4: Pedagogical action research: Research and teaching intertwined'. In McEwen, L. and Mason O'Connor, K., *SEDA Special 37: Developing Pedagogic Research in Higher Education*, SEDA.

PedRIO   (n.d.).   www1.plymouth.ac.uk/research/pedrio/Pages/default.aspx, accessed 12 May 2015.

Peel, D. (2005). 'Dual professionalism: facing the challenges of continuing professional development in the workplace?', *Reflective Practice* 6(1): 123–140.

Peters, J. (2009). 'What is the purpose of a CPD Framework'? Chapter 5. In Laycock, M. and Shrives, L. (eds.), *Embedding CPD in HE*. SEDA Paper 23, 45–50.

Pilkington, R. (2007). *SEDA Special 21: SEDA PDF as a tool for structuring and supporting CPD*. SEDA.

Pilkington, R. (2013). 'Professional dialogues: exploring an alternative means of assessing the professional learning of experienced HE academics', *International Journal of Academic Development*, 18(3): 251–263. http://dx.doi.org/10.1080/1360144X.2012.717225.

Robson, J. (2006). *Teacher Professionalism in Further and Higher Education: Challenges to Culture and Practice*. Abingdon, UK: Routledge.

Sachs, J. (2001). 'Teacher professional identity: competing discourses, competing outcomes', *Journal of Educational Policy*, 16(2): 149–16.

Shulman, L. S. (1987). 'Knowledge and teaching: foundations of the new reform', *Harvard Education Review* 57(1): 1–22.

Skelton, A. (2005). *Understanding Teaching Excellence in Higher Education: Towards a Critical Approach*. Abingdon: Routledge.

Skelton, A. (2007) (Ed.). *International Perspectives on Teaching Excellence in Higher Education*. Abingdon: Routledge.

Stefani, L. (2011). 'How does academic development make a difference in the twenty-first century university?', *Educational Developments* 12(3):1–5, SEDA.

Turner, R., Schoenborn, P. and Wyness, L. (2013). 'Evaluation of a university teaching fellowship scheme as a tool to promote PR and development', *Educational Developments* 14(2): 5–9, SEDA.

Wenger, E. (2008). *Communities of Practice: Learning, Meaning and Identity*. CUP.

York University (n.d.). http://teachingcommons.yorku.ca, accessed 3 March 2015.

Chapter 5

Consultancy in academic development

Sue Thompson

Summary

This chapter explores the roles of consultancy in academic development. Drawing on exemplar cameos and stories from within the sector to describe a range of internal and external consultancy approaches, the chapter considers how consultancy can form a valuable part of the academic developer's toolkit. Particular attention is given to how consultancy can be most effectively used as part of a planned change process, and the practical implications for the developer's role.

Links to web sources referenced in this chapter can be found at www.seda.ac.uk/apad.

An introduction to the why, what, who and how of consultancy

As Shrives and Bond (2003) observe, a large part of the day-to-day work of an educational development unit involves consultancy. Land (2004) identified the role of internal consultant as one of the key orientations of academic development (see Chapter 2). Indeed it has been suggested that most people in staff and support roles in organisations are really consultants (Block, 2011). As well as having a consultancy focus to their own role, however, academic developers may themselves draw on the expertise and knowledge of both external and internal consultants.

Two points of terminology about consultancy used in this chapter:

Internal and external mean internal and external to the organisation.

The client may be a single individual, a work group, department or the whole organisation. The client here is not necessarily the person who commissions the work. The client is the person that the consultant seeks to influence. 'Who is the client/who are the clients?' are important questions, to which the chapter returns.

The why of consultancy

There are several sources of need for the use of consultancy. These include:

- Access to particular expertise and knowledge
- Support for strategic change initiatives such as review, development and implementation support

- Support for staff development – to work with people on an institutional, team and individual basis
- To help deliver a project
- To evaluate and review specific activity

Using consultants can be a cost-effective means of realising objectives in a climate of limited and diminishing resource. For example:

> My unit was restructured and we lost six staff. I was given a pot of money to buy people in. I've used that to buy in external consultants who have worked with us on a number of strategic initiatives over a sustained period.

> I have a small team of four people working across the university. It's important to manage expectations as they can only do so much as a team. Their time is pretty much taken up by our everyday business. There is little time for bespoke work and I buy in consultants to help with this.

External consultants may be brought in for their expert knowledge, reputation and track record:

> I think it's about 'paying talent', not fiddling about with things you are not an expert on, thereby using extra time, with the likelihood of a lower-quality result, risking frustration and stress. I think the strength and wisdom of using consultants is employing the appropriate expert for the part of the task you need expertise on to add to your own.

Discipline teams and staff working in a range of teaching and learning roles across the institution may work in an internal consultancy capacity, as part of a deliberate strategy to widen the reach of academic development, as a means of engaging staff and in supporting implementation of change initiatives.

The what of consultancy

Academic development is concerned with improving teaching, learning and assessment across the institution. Academic developers need to be skilled in the technical aspects of these topics. They also need to be skilled in what are sometimes and misleadingly called the softer skills. These include knowing when to ask, when to suggest and when to tell; making connections between strategy, policy and practice, as explored in Chapter 17; and facilitating and empowering. For those in leadership roles, development has another dimension. Development also means knowing how to manage and provide leadership, how to act strategically in an organisational context and in a climate of rapid and continual change. Chapter 15 considers leadership in academic development. The work of academic development is often, by its very nature, concerned with bringing about cultural change. Academic developers need to work as effective agents for change within the organisational culture.

The use of consultancy in academic development can support work concerned with improvement and change. The goal or end product in any consulting activity is fundamentally about change (see Chapter 13), about helping another person, team or an organisation make a transformation from one state to another.

Change comes in two varieties. At one level it is about creating change of a structural, policy or procedural nature. The second kind of change is the end result that people in the organisation have learnt something new and act in new and different ways:

> The consultant's objective is to engage in successful actions that result in people or organizations managing themselves differently. (Block, 2011, p. 4)

Much has been written about the purpose and nature of the consultant role (Lippitt and Lippitt, 1986; Schein, 1987; Block, 2011; Cockman et al., 1992). The consultant role is typically defined through its separation from the system it serves; the consultant holds neither line responsibility nor budget, though may often have status and recognition:

> [A consultant is] in a position to have some influence over an individual, group or organisation, but has no direct power to make changes or implement programs. (Block, 2011, p. 1)

The process of consultation can be seen as a dynamic, within which there are negotiated and defined roles (the client and the consultant), where the client experiences dissatisfaction with the current state, and where there is an understanding that the consultant is there to provide some sort of help:

> A 2-way interaction – a process of seeking, giving and receiving help. (Lippitt and Lippitt, 1986)

Given their externality to the client system and their lack of formal power to impose change, the most that a consultant can hope for is to influence the client, through the consultant's credibility, expertise, skills, knowledge and understanding, to change something. They do this through their intervention, coming into the client system and leaving once the client has been helped (Kenton and Moody, 2003).

Consultants, whether external or internal, may adopt different roles. Schein (1998) identified three ways that consultants work:

- *Expert* – the consultant identifies the problem and suggests a solution
- *Extra pair of hands* – the client defines the task and the goals and the consultant is expected to carry it out

- *Participant in a more collaborative effort* – client and consultant work together to solve the problem.

Schein's (1998) model of process consultancy is focused on helping people in organisations to help themselves. It is a facilitative or empowering model. The consultant's role again is to help clients to solve their problems, as these comments from consultants suggest:

> As a consultant my role is not to solve their problems but to deliberately do myself out of a job.

> It's easy to say 'in my experience', but people need to work through things themselves, doing things they believe are right in their particular context.

> Good consultancy works with people on what they need, asking critical questions, working with them to help them achieve their own goals.

Lippitt and Lippitt (1986) developed a model that identifies eight roles that may be considered consulting styles. Raelin (2003) considers these consultant roles in the context of leaderful practice and as eight possible roles for change consultants, ordered from a directive to a nondirective style of intervention:

1 Advocate
2 Information specialist
3 Trainer/educator
4 Joint problem solver
5 Identifier of alternatives and linker
6 Fact finder
7 Process counsellor
8 Objective observer

The choice of role(s) depends on a number of contingencies, such as the kind of contract that has been arranged, the goals of the intervention, the norms and standards of both the client system and the consultant, past practices, and whether the consultant is internal or external to the system. The key is that the consultant should display flexibility and versatility based upon the readiness level of both the system and the individuals committed to the change process.

The who of consultancy: External consultants

Conversations with academic developers reveal a degree of commonality in the reasons for employing external consultants:

- A consultant may have particular expertise/technical knowledge.
- A consultant may have reputation and track record, be well known in the sector, have credibility.

- External consultants are perceived as having outsider objectivity, as not being from here, bringing fresh perspectives, uninfluenced by institutional history or baggage.
- An important influence of external consultants is their ability to say the things that staff of the institution cannot say, to speak truth to power, to ask the questions that others cannot on behalf of staff who may feel that asking the difficult questions would make them vulnerable.
- External consultants, because of their reputation and credibility, can also be in a position to exert more influence and secure buy-in at a senior level.
- They can provide benchmarking and examples of best practices, as well as insights into potential pitfalls learned from other clients, bringing a wider knowledge of the sector.
- They can act as knowledge brokers, linking to other work going on in the sector, distilling information.
- Working with external consultants can also be seen as making efficient use of finite resources, providing a degree of flexibility in being able to respond quickly to identified needs.

The who of consultancy: Internal consultancy

Internal consultants could be those working in a designated academic development role, seconded staff, staff from within discipline teams working with other teams, staff with a variety of teaching and learning roles, not all of whom would see themselves as educational developers (Shrives and Bond, 2003).

Reasons for using internal consultants include:

- They have in-depth knowledge of the organisation.
- They understand the language and culture of the wider institution and know the issues.
- Their use enables the institution to share and hence maximise use of knowledge and skills currently existing in pockets within the institution.
- The need to sustain a long-term initiative where internal ownership is important and follow-up and quick access are needed.

While internal consultants may be seen as authentic and relevant, they are not necessarily independent, perhaps holding preconceptions because they know the people and institution so well. Colleagues may perceive them as organisational agents. There may be tensions for the internal consultant in how to help the client when the best help might not align with the organisation's goals. Their client may also be their line manager. Internal consultants are less able to influence senior staff. While internal consultants may have competence and personal skills, they may lack consultancy expertise and are perhaps less likely to fulfil the aspirational challenges of process consultancy (Kenton and Moody, 2003).

Table 5.1 Inside or outside: internal and external consultants, from Scott and Hascall (2006)

When to Use External Consultants	When to Use Internal Consultants
To support development of strategy or facilitate corporate-wide initiatives or key priorities	To support implementation of strategic priority, or intervention as an operational focus
Do not have internal expertise	Have the internal expertise
Deep expertise is needed	Broad generalist knowledge is needed
An outside, neutral perspective is important	Knowledge of the organisation and business is critical
New, risky alternatives need validation from an outside expert	Speaking the jargon or the language of the organisation and the culture is important
Internal does not have status, power or authority to influence senior management or the culture	A sensitive insider who knows the issues is needed
CEO, president or senior leaders need coach, guide or objective sounding board	Need to sustain a long-term initiative where internal ownership is important
Initiative justifies the expense	Cost is a factor
Project has defined boundaries or limits	Follow-up and quick access is needed

The how of consultancy

The judicious use of consultancy, both external and external, can be a powerful addition to the educational developer's toolkit. Determining what sorts of interventions are needed, by whom, and when is a demanding process that requires academic developers to be well versed in the nature of consultancy skills and processes.

The following section draws on cameos of practice to illustrate the range of roles that consultants can play and approaches they might use in supporting the work of academic development.

Consultancy as part of the educational developer's toolkit: roles and approaches

Context is critical to deciding the role and type of consultancy to adopt:

It's tricky working out the best way to do it. Situational framing is really crucial.... You can have a general framework but it's important to know what that means for individuals... A really good consultant knows their constituency, can provide a tailored, focused service.

Increasingly, the expectation is that academic developers are able to operate strategically in a climate of rapid and continual change and can work as an effective agent for change within the organisational culture (see Chapter 2). This is a complex role and task. There are key challenges here in determining how best to achieve results in a climate of limited/diminishing resources and who and what approaches can help. Academic developers need to have a sophisticated understanding of change and how it works in a complex organisation. In the example that follows, a head of learning and teaching in a large metropolitan university describes the use of consultancy within the context of a change model that is used to frame and maximise the deployment of a blend of both external and internal consultants:

The why, what, who and how of consultancy – an educational developer's perspective

The role of an educational developer can be a challenging one. The task of initiating and facilitating institution-wide change can be daunting, and consultancy, external or internal, is an important part of the developer's toolkit. As with any other task, using the wrong tool can set a project back, causing, at best, a loss of momentum, and possibly much worse. This case study will explore the why, what, who and how of consultancy from the perspective of an institution-wide change initiative at a large post-1992 metropolitan university.

Faced with the task of bringing about cultural change in assessment practice, and new to the world of educational development, I was uncertain of which way to turn. Yes, of course I knew my stuff about assessment practice, and had bundles of experience. But how could I influence and bring about lasting institution-wide change?

My starting point was not to think of which expert I should bring in, but rather to have a clear change model within which to develop the project and its interventions. Change in large institutions involves understanding a highly complex system where the responsibility for changing academic practice lies with different groups of stakeholders. The approach I adopted therefore was to recognise the complex nature of academic practice and to understand how change happens in organisations, particularly with regard to the notion of emergent change and the need for connectivity across the institution (Seel, 2000). This sets a context for the role of the consultant – an external consultant would struggle to engender emergent change, given the nature of their intervention and their outsider role.

The result was a model for an integrated approach to change (adapted from Joughin and Macdonald, 2004). This provided a clear framework within which the culture of academic practice can be understood and influenced. The model comprises five principal levels of the organisation (Module, Course, Faculty, Institutional and External), with the introduction of the student voice as an additional level. Different activities at each level result in a multiplier effect resulting (in theory) in long-lasting change:

Student Level: The student experience of assessment and feedback
Module Level: Where assessment happens
Course/Programme Level: Supporting good practice
Faculty Level: The faculty context
Institutional Level: The institutional context for good practice
Wider Level: The external context

This model provided a structure in which to consider how best to use interventions such as consultancy to influence change. The model also enabled informed judgements over the nature of the intervention from the consultant to maximise impact (the why of consultancy).

The project used three different types of consultants (the who of consultancy): external subject expert, internal subject experts working alongside academics from other subject disciplines and students acting as consultants. Consultancy was then used in different ways at different levels depending on the phase of the project and the desired outcome (the what of consultancy), for example:

Students acted as consultants in the early stages of the project to provide the context for change (the student experience) and to facilitate the development of practical and engaging interventions for staff and students – e.g. the Feedback for Learning Campaign. Students also acted as agents of change (a form of consultancy) at a number of institution-wide events, providing the authentic voice of the student.

A network of temporary Faculty-based Teaching Fellows positions and/or secondments was created to support change at all levels of the model. The Teaching Fellows/secondees acted as authentic practitioner voices, working in consultancy mode and encouraging dialogue between all stakeholders within the faculties in the context of their own subject or profession. In this way the Teaching Fellows/secondees fulfilled a key role as change agents, by taking a top-down directive and making it work at the local level through a bottom-up approach based on dialogue at the subject level.

External consultants of course played a key role, and a number of experts were brought in at different stages within the project, to inform debate, to share practice from outside the university and to facilitate dialogue between stakeholders.

Interestingly I chose not to use external consultants to inform the development of the project or to act as a critical friend throughout the lifetime of the project. This decision was based on the level of expertise within the institution around project management, change management and assessment practice. Had we been less well versed in these areas, we would have chosen a different path.

How well did it work? The project received positive feedback from across the institution and received the following comments from an external consultant brought in to review the impact of the initiative and that of the university's Centres for Excellence in Teaching and Learning:

> The Assessment for Learning Initiative (TALI) was the initiative held up by all to be the most effective in supporting change and innovation. The characteristics recognised as attributing to the success of this project were the involvement of a wide range of staff across levels and structures of the University, the way that project had built capability of individuals and capacity within teams/groups, and the direct involvement and impact of students. The 'Hub and Spokes' Model was recognised as an effective way of enabling change within the institution and of gaining a multiplier effect. (Extract from External Consultant Report)

So, in summary, having a clear change model helped provide an important context for the use of consultancy and enables a clearer understanding of the purpose of the intervention and its desired impact.

Graham Holden, Director of Innovation in Learning and Teaching, Sheffield Hallam University

The next example describes how external consultants were employed in different capacities over a sustained period to support implementation of strategic change:

Using external consultants for strategic change

Experienced consultants with national reputations were used to support institutional work on assessment and feedback. Key interventions such as a review of assessment practices, a conference keynote and a seminar on improving student learning through assessment and feedback stimulated discussion and thinking. In this first phase, institutional priorities for development and strategies to take forward were identified. The next phase of the project then involved working on these key priority areas with faculties and course leaders.

Critical success factors were that consultants had credibility with staff. It was a whole-institution initiative, backed by the deputy vice chancellor and with the support of the university registrar. An added benefit was that the work on assessment and feedback highlighted the importance of the course leader role and has fed into other capacity-building work to enhance and relaunch this role across the university. In terms of embedding the outcomes of the work, it is now built into National Student Survey action plans and the university's teaching and learning strategy.

From a consultant perspective, the advantages of working across a whole institution in this way over a sustained period included being able to:

- Tune into a context thoroughly and get to know the organisational imperatives and constraints
- Work with large numbers of people across the whole institution, and work with the same people on a number of occasions, building deeper relationships with colleagues
- Work at all levels within the hierarchy, including lecturing staff, senior managers, registry staff and students
- Feel as if the consultants made a difference, contributing to and supporting work that had led to a measurable improvement in NSS scores
- Build a strong working relationship with the project sponsor, and to feel well supported

Working with internal consultants

The following example of the use of Teaching Fellows as internal consultants illustrates benefits and challenges:

Teaching Fellows as internal consultants

The Edinburgh Napier Teaching Fellowship Scheme is an excellence recognition mechanism that offers a three-year, renewable appointment to a leadership role in teaching or supporting learning within a discipline area, or possibly also across the university. Together with Senior Teaching Fellows, a Senior Lecturer role in the promotions structure from 2008, they have been used in a consultancy capacity as a means of widening the reach of academic development activity and supporting local learning and teaching initiatives through, for example:

- Supporting pedagogic development of technology enhanced learning across a faculty;
- Starting off the process of taking forward work from the National Teaching Fellowship project on programme assessment, Transforming the Experience of Students through Assessment (TESTA); and
- Individual input and work within the context of special interest groups led by Teaching Fellows, helping set institutional direction for areas such as internationalisation or academic practice mentoring.

Success factors include:

- Buy-in from senior managers, including heads of department, to ensure that the purpose of the intervention was understood and supported, with outputs that were measureable or at any rate demonstrable;
- Recognition of Teaching Fellow and Senior Teaching Fellow as academic leadership roles within the institution with status and credibility; and
- Linking Teaching Fellow interventions to the strategic objectives of the university's learning and teaching strategy, as well as to the UK Professional Standards Framework.

Consultant as critical friend

The role of external consultant as critical friend can be an important use of consultants in an educational development context. A critical friend has been defined as:

> ... a trusted person who asks provocative questions, provides data to be examined through another lens, and offers critique of a person's work as a friend. (Costa and Kallick, 1993)

Working with individuals, teams and project groups, the critical friend provides a new lens through which to examine and refocus. A critical friend takes time to understand the context of the work and the outcomes that the group or person are working towards, and is an advocate for the success of the work. In an educational development context, a critical friend approach might be taken to evaluation and to supporting projects and other initiatives. The critical friend role has been extensively used by Jisc for its funded projects ('Critical Friends', 2011).

Consultant as coach

The following example describes how an external consultant, brought in to support the delivery of specific strategic targets, worked in a coaching capacity with an academic developer who herself needed to operate as an internal consultant in her own role as professional developer officer. This is also an example of the consultant working in a capacity building context. Chapter 6 says much more about coaching and mentoring.

Consultancy and coaching to support the development of new staff

Help was needed to develop a coherent, formalised strategy to support new staff. The driver for this work was delivering strategic plan targets. As well as specific 'subject' expertise in mentoring and coaching, the consultant's own professional networks and previous senior educational development role in another institution brought a level of strategic oversight and a good understanding of the challenges of developing and embedding strategy, as well as wide experience of the sector. Working with the client in her professional role as an educational developer supporting others, the consultant used her coaching/mentoring skills to provide support, to be a critical friend and offer a listening ear. The openness and trust of this relationship were important. The external consultant helped the client to develop the structure of the programme of support for staff (an accredited mentoring programme), develop materials, undertake direct work with other colleagues and review the scheme. The client saw the consultant as providing an objective view and affirmation.

Being outside the university the consultant was able to be objective, but at the same time understood the issues. She helped the client clarify her thinking, and home in on what was important. She was instrumental in helping the client develop her own influencing skills. This was particularly important as at the time the internal team were working 'from the bottom up' at grassroots level.

Implications for the academic developer's role of using consultancy

In designing interventions to ensure maximum impact, academic developers must consider multiple factors. They need to be able to understand change, how change happens and why it fails (Fullan and Scott, 2009) and to be able to operate as effective change agents (Buchanan and Boddy, 1992). The use of consultancy, as one approach among many in academic development, needs to be located in a model and context. Having determined what interventions are needed, by whom and at what point, the use of consultancy has to be managed and supported.

Academic developers need to have an understanding of the nature of consultancy, of consultancy roles and skills. For each moment of consulting, three kinds of skills may be needed to do a good job:

- Technical skills (some area of expertise),
- Interpersonal skills (communication skills, maintaining a relationship) and
- Consulting skills.

Academic developers need to be familiar with the processes worked through by consultants and the consultancy cycle, described in various models. Block (2011), for example, describes each consultancy project, 'whether it lasts ten minutes or ten months' as having five sequential stages:

1 Entry and Contracting
2 Discovery and Dialogue
3 Analysis and the Decision to Act
4 Engagement and Implementation
5 Extension, Recycle or Termination

Shrives and Bond (2003) used a simpler account of the consultancy process:

1 Getting in
2 Getting on
3 Getting out

Getting things right at the contracting stage is crucial. When consultants talk about their disasters, their conclusion is usually that the project was faulty in the initial contracting stage (Block, 2011).

> The business of contracting is the hardest part of all, getting clarity in what's wanted. You almost need a pre-contract stage for this, to give everyone involved time to sort out what is needed.

> It's important to set out expectations clearly for the consultant's input and manner of engagement, including reporting, and work to these.

> Consider carefully what the consultant is contributing to the short, medium and long-term future of the work/project and specify engagement in writing with that in mind.

> At the beginning it's important to clarify whether the consultant's role is to make the project the best it can be or whether it is to build capacity.

Contracting is obviously important when engaging external consultants. To what extent are contracts also required for internal consultants? Contracting on an internal basis may be more likely to take place on an informal basis, with little attention paid to defining the time and resources needed for the work (including access to people). While there are difficulties with a too tightly defined contract, leaving little flexibility, some defined parameters are essential for helping people establish roles and responsibilities for both client and consultant (Kenton and Moody 2003):

> As well as seeking clarity of the brief at the outset, it is also important to keep the brief under review. The presenting problem may not turn out to be the actual problem:

> You often find that what people thought they needed is not what they actually need.

> It's important to have clarity and focus. You need to change the goals if necessary ... there needs to be clarity about goals, milestones and review points.

Conversations with academic developers working as consultants stressed the important of determining who is the client. Any helping or change process always has a target or client/client group. In most discussions of consultation, clients are referred to as if they were always clearly identifiable but, in reality, the question of who is actually the client can be ambiguous and problematical. Consultants can find themselves not knowing who they are working for, or working with several clients whose goals are in conflict with each other:

> It's important to bottom out who the client is at the beginning, otherwise you get into trouble.

> There is the client who asks you in, and the real client, the people who turn up.

> Quite often you can walk into a hostile environment, the three-line whip scenario where people have been told to turn up.

> Even when working at the front line I always try to understand the strategic policy context in which this work is being done.

Supporting consultants and managing the relationship

Working as a consultant, internal or external, can be a challenging and lonely process. Experienced external consultants are used to dealing with the challenges. When things don't work out, they can move on, albeit possibly with some damage to their confidence or reputation. Internal consultants may have more to lose when things go wrong.

Logistical issues can be complex and time-consuming, including dealing with university contracting policies and procedures.

It is important to be clear about intellectual property rights; what clients will get in the way of resources from the work and what use they can make of those resources. Such legal aspects can seem secondary and frustrating, but they are important to clarify and they safeguard the right of the contracting parties.

Conversations with academic developers and consultants highlighted some key guidelines in supporting the consultancy role:

- Establish and revisit/review the definition of the task
- Be clear about the consultant role and role boundaries (consultant as expert, extra pair of hands, collaborator ...)
- Negotiate consultant access to the necessary individuals, groups, documentation
- Identify a primary point of contact
- Identify outputs, outcomes, timescales, review points
- Recognise and deal with client resistance, the not invented here syndrom
- Promote a culture of empowerment, not dependency
- Secure buy-in at all levels, before the consultant is hired or at a very early stage of the project
- Negotiate the politics
- Manage and maintain the relationship, build trust

Realising the benefits: Closing and embedding

> As an educational developer engaging in consultancy, you should be working to do yourself out of a job.

Most consultancies are finite. They have an end point; for example, when the project is over, the consultancy ends. (There is much more on projects in Chapter 14.) Given the finite nature of consultancies, how can the benefits of consultancy be sustained and realised over the longer term?

Consultants do not have the power to make things happen, or to implement recommendations; they can only hope to inform and influence outcomes. The 'now what?' or 'what next?' questions are for the institution to answer. The answer depends on the nature of the consultancy and on the change process of which it is a part. For example, if the objective is to improve assessment and feedback, then outcomes may be measureable through, for example, indicators such as improved National Student Survey results. Outcomes may be built into departmental action plans and institutional learning and teaching strategies. Chapter 10 suggests approaches to defining intended outcomes and then monitoring and evaluating their attainment.

The role of the consultancy may have been particularly focused on capacity building and engagement:

> It's not just about measureable impact but also about keeping people happy, keeping going, securing people's goodwill and being enthused about what they are doing. It's about a culture of continuous improvement, about engaging people in the process, how to do things differently, about effective practice, thinking about are there other ways we could do this.

The end point of a consultancy may be the final report, with recommendations. The likelihood of take up and adoption will depend on how well the consultancy has been managed on both sides:

> I always suggest future actions in my report, but I have to leave it at that. It always helps when the client organises a meeting with key stakeholders to discuss the final report and its actions.

> The final report and recommendations should contain few if any surprises for the stakeholder group and the client.

The recommendations of external consultants can carry weight with senior managers simply because of who the consultants are. Often, though, the impact of consultancy may not have to do with a final report with case studies that busy people do not have the time to read. What consultants can do is synthesise, help people make sense of what is out there, pull things together, giving people the confidence and understanding to do it for themselves:

> Consultancy is not necessarily about bringing in a set of solutions, but rather about also engaging people in critical conversations, about asking the right questions, nudging and elbow jogging.

In conversation with academic developers, a recurrent theme was the relationship between consultancy and the development of the learning organisation. Consultancy was seen as an empowering process, helping to remove inhibitors and leaving people in a better place to do things for themselves.

Further implications for the academic developer's role

Much of what academic developers do is concerned with managing change. Academic developers need to be able to operate as skilled change agents, and support others. The use of consultancy can support that work. Whether acting in a consultancy capacity, using external consultants or supporting internal colleagues operating in a consultancy role, academic developers need to:

- Situate the need for consultancy, for example, within the context of a change model and the role of a change agent
- Determine what interventions are needed and at what point
- Identify appropriate roles for the consultant – external and internal – and the nature and sequence of the consultancy process
- Be clear about the roles that consultants can play and provide support for people in those roles.

Acknowledgements

The chapter was informed by conversations with many academic developers and consultants, to whom I am very grateful.

References

Block, P. (2011). *Flawless Consulting A Guide to Getting Your Expertise Used*, 3rd Edition. San Francisco: Wiley.

Buchanan, D. A. and Boddy, D. (1992). *The Expertise of the Change Agent: Public Performance and Backstage Activity*. Hemel Hempstead, UK: Prentice Hall.

Cockman, P, Evans, B. and Reynolds, P. (1992). *Client-Centred Consulting – A Practical Guide for Internal Advisers and Trainers*. London: McGraw-Hill.

Costa, A. L. and Kallick, B. (1993). 'Through the lens of a critical friend', in *Educational Leadership: New Roles, New Relationships* 51(2): 49–51.

'Critical friends' (2011). Retrieved 19 April 2015 from www.jiscinfonet.ac.uk/infokits/critical-friends/.

Fullan, M and Scott, G. (2009). *Turnaround Leadership for Higher Education*. San Francisco: Jossey-Bass/Wiley.

Joughin, G. and Macdonald, R. (2004). *A Model of Assessment in Higher Education Institutions*. York, UK: Higher Education Academy.

Kenton, B. and Moody, D. (2003). *The Role of the Internal Consultant*. Horsham, UK: Roffey Park Institute.

Land, R. (2004). *Educational Development Discourse, Identity and Practice*. Maidenhead, UK: Open University Press.

Lippitt, G. and Lippitt, R. (1986). *The Consulting Process in Action*, 2nd Edition. San Francisco: Jossey-Bass/Pfeiffer.

Raelin, Joseph, A. (2003). *Creating Leaderful Organizations How to Bring Out Leadership in Everyone*. San Francisco: Berrett-Koehler.

Schein, Edgar H. (1987). *Process Consultation Vol. 11*. Cambridge, MA: Addison-Wesley.

Schein, Edgar H. (1998). *Process Consultation Revisited: Building the Helping Relationship*. Reading, MA: Addison-Wesley.

Scott, B. and Hascall, J. (2006). 'Insider or outside: the partnerships of internal and external consultants', in Biech, E. (Ed.) *The 2006 Pfeiffer Annual Consulting*, pp. 209–222. San Francisco: Pfeiffer.

Seel, R. (2000). 'Culture and Complexity: New insights on organisational change', in *Organisations and People* 7(2): 2–9.

Shrives, L., & Bond, C. (2003). 'Consultancy in educational development', in P. Kahn & D. Baume (Eds.), *A Guide to Staff & Educational Development* (pp. 61–75). London: Routledge.

Chapter 6

Coaching and mentoring in academic development

Diana Eastcott

Summary

This chapter offers definitions and contexts of use for mentoring and coaching, and suggests their relations to training. The core idea of coaching and mentoring as 'conversations for learning' is explained and illustrated. Skills, processes and methods which are crucial in effective coaching and mentoring are described, and examples given. Accounts are given of coaching and mentoring as part of academic development. The idea of a formal contract for coaching and mentoring initiatives is explored, as is the use of coaching for staff taking on new roles. Examples are given of university-wide initiatives and recognition for coaching and mentoring. The chapter concludes with a summary of the benefits of coaching and mentoring and an overview of strategies for success.

Links to web sources referenced in this chapter can be found at www.seda. ac.uk/apad.

Introduction

Coaching and mentoring skills, processes and strategies are used in a range of contexts and have a variety of definitions and meanings in higher education.

The first core idea of both mentoring and coaching is a one-to-one learning relationship – that is, a relationship that has the explicit intention of facilitating learning. This learning is usually associated with the intention to support the enhancement of professional capability and performance. It will typically include conceptual and theoretical learning, as well as practical, professional and sometimes personal learning. Such learning relationships are usually conducted at least in part through learning conversations, using appropriate media and technologies.

The second core idea is that the coachee/mentee, not the coach/mentor, decides on the agenda for the learning.

Some specific examples are:

- Mentoring of new staff
- Mentoring as part of Postgraduate Certificate in Education Courses

- Mentoring for Higher Education Academy accreditation
- Mentoring/coaching of staff taking on new roles
- The use of coaching/mentoring skills and processes as part of consultancy and facilitation

This chapter will assist academic developers to select, use appropriately and review the use of a range of coaching and mentoring skills, strategies and processes in academic development. The focus will be on coaching and mentoring for and by staff in an academic context. It will include all professional groups engaged in enhancing the student learning experience. Work with students will not be included.

What is mentoring and what is coaching? How do they relate to training and to counselling?

Connor and Pakora (2007) describe both coaching and mentoring as learning relationships which help people to take charge of their own development, to release their potential and achieve results which they value. Coaching and mentoring draw on a similar range of skills, and the key to success is a shared, relevant and appropriate understanding between the partners on goals, methods and outcomes.

The word *mentor* comes from the Greek myth of the king, Odysseus, who asked Mentor, an older and wiser man, to look after his son during his absence. Over time the word has become synonymous with trusted adviser, teacher and wise person. Two principal, albeit overlapping, types of mentoring are currently used in higher education; they are often called 'sponsorship mentoring' and 'developmental mentoring'.

In sponsorship mentoring, the learner is guided by a more senior and powerful individual, an acknowledged expert, who often acts as a role model and provides sponsorship, information and advice, for example, on making career choices. Typically such a mentor works in the same or a parallel organisation.

Developmental mentoring by contrast places more emphasis on self-managed learning. A mentor may, for example, be working with a member of staff who is new to the university, or who has changed roles within the institution. In these contexts, the role of the mentor is to assist the mentee in finding their own effective means of working in the new role, rather than to advocate a particular approach. Developmental mentoring is help by one person to another in making significant transitions in knowledge, work or thinking. Importantly, this help is off-line; that is, not help from a direct manager. (Megginson and Clutterbuck, 1995, p.35).

The word *coach* is used to mean many different things. In some organisations, coaching is seen as a process for people with performance problems, implying a deficit model. A simple and positive definition of *coaching*, which can be used effectively in many contexts, is:

> Coaching is partnering with clients in a thought-provoking and creative process that inspires them to maximise their personal and professional potential. (International Coach Federation, 2008)

The word *partnering* is of importance here. In higher education, it may be appropriate to replace the word *client* with *coachee* or *mentee*.

An individual requesting assistance may not use the term *coaching*. Requests for coaching, or more generally for assistance, may be triggered by a need to accomplish tasks more effectively. For example:

- 'Please help me to find ways to perform better when working with large groups of students'.
- 'Please show me how to run that board of studies more efficiently'.
- 'Please help me to have more confidence in using the assessment criteria when marking the final dissertations'.

A request for assistance, or coaching, may also be triggered by organisational and/or personal change – a change in role through promotion or restructuring, or a change in manager who demands a different kind of performance.

Effective coaching/mentoring support learning, development and enhanced professional practice. Whatever the process is called, the core relationship must be based on objectivity, honesty, trustworthiness and confidentiality. Effective coaches and mentors are skilled in working from these foundation values, and use active listening, appropriate questioning and reflective feedback with their learners.

Thus far, I have emphasised the similarities between coaching and mentoring. One difference may be that a mentor may be expected to give more direct information and advice than a coach. But the effective coach or mentor generally only gives such advice in response to an expressed wish or question. The coach/mentor then supports and encourages the coachee/mentee, either to make the idea their own by planning how they might use it, or to reject it without any difficulty.

Training by contrast is usually one-to-many, with common assumed training and development needs, and hence largely predetermined outcomes and processes. Good training can embody some of the elements of coaching and mentoring – attention to individual goals, and support for individual work and learning conversations by participants. But the responsibility lies mainly with the trainer.

What of the relations between coaching/mentoring and counselling? The emphasis in *counselling* tends to be on the power of non-judgemental listening, which, by contrast to coaching/mentoring, may or may not lead to action, in the short term at least. Counselling is usually more appropriate for people who are distressed. One useful skill for an academic developer is to know their own capabilities and limitations in the counselling role. A few minutes of non-judgemental listening can sometimes be very helpful for issues on that permeable boundary between the professional and the personal. Another useful skill for an academic developer is to judge when to refer elsewhere for appropriate help.

Coaching and mentoring as conversations for learning

A key principle underpinning this chapter is that coaching and mentoring in academic development can be viewed as an extension of the concept of developmental conversations for learning. A starting point is the work of Neil Haigh (2005), an academic developer in New Zealand. Haigh suggests that 'learning conversations' constitute an important aspect of day-to-day work in an academic staff development role.

The theoretical base for learning conversations includes the insights of Senge (1994), who devised the term 'learningful conversation' to describe conversation that evokes reflection, in particular reflection on the mental models which are a foundation for personal action. Senge describes mental models as 'deeply ingrained assumptions, generalisations, or even pictures or images that influence how we understand the world and how we take action.' (Senge, 1990, p. 8). Senge believes that the willingness to engage in a 'learningful conversation' is a prerequisite for professional learning.

> The discipline of working with mental models starts with turning the mirror inward; learning to unearth our internal pictures of the world, to bring them to the surface and hold them rigorously to scrutiny. It also includes the ability to carry on 'learningful conversations' that balance inquiry and advocacy, where people expose their own thinking effectively and make that thinking open to the influence of others. (Senge, 1990, p. 9)

Spiller (2002), an academic staff developer, gives an account of the place that a learning conversation has in a mentoring relationship with new teachers. A regular professional conversation can provide space and a safe environment for the new teacher, not only to do the job of a teacher but also to engage with the complexities of being a teacher. Spiller (2002) proposes four ways in which such a conversation for learning can be important for the new teacher:

- For exploration and reflection
- For emotional expression
- As a safe and hospitable place
- As a rehearsal for performances

A further example of the power of developmental dialogue, or conversation for learning, comes from Lumsden and Eagle (2014). In 'Dialogue as a developmental tool', they describe how an ongoing dialogue over a period of two years between staff with shared academic identities can have unexpected benefits in their roles as academic developers. The authors argue that their shared academic identity/ culture enabled them to communicate quickly using common language. An initial discussion about audio feedback extended to a wider conversation on their roles as academic developers, and helped them make sense of their new academic identity. Both authors cite a number of constructive developments in their own practice as academic developers which arose directly or indirectly from their dialogue. An example was making changes in the culture of the PG Certificate programme to enhance the student experience, which led to an improved achievement rate.

The idea of a developmental conversation for learning as extended to academic coaching/mentoring can be summarised as follows:

One-to-one academic coaching/mentoring is a process of professional learning and development, which can be described as a learning alliance or learning conversation. The coach/mentor acts as an enabler, providing space for the client to explore their own concerns. The coaching/mentoring conversation aims to provide:

- Help with identifying and planning goals
- Help with strategies for achieving individual and collective goals
- A safe, objective, non-judgemental and confidential reflective space
- The stimulation of insight and identification of learning opportunities
- Encouragement in self-directed reflection and the provision of appropriate challenge

One-to-one academic coaching/mentoring does not involve the coachee/ mentee being told what to do. Nor is it a therapy session, or a cosy chat that will be gossiped about with other colleagues. The discoveries that the coachee/ mentee makes during the learning conversations, and the approaches that they devise, facilitated but not led by the coach/mentor, will be more effective and far more likely to be adopted than a long list of advice from the coach/mentor, however excellent. Kamvounias, McGrath–Champ and Yip, (2008) give a fascinating account of mentees' perspective on mentoring.

Coaching and mentoring skills, processes and methods

Coaching and mentoring skills and processes are used in much academic development work. In this chapter, a distinction is made between formal coaching/ mentoring, as a distinct process with a clear contract, and instances where a range of coaching/mentoring approaches and skills are used along with other academic development processes, for example consultancy. (Consultancy in academic development is the subject of Chapter 5.) Here the terms *coaching* and *mentoring* tend to be used more loosely than in the formal context. The contract typically addresses confidentiality, a code of ethics (see for example International Coach Federation, 2008), frequency, purpose and location of or media for meetings, and methods of record keeping.

The skills described below are crucial in effective coaching and mentoring with a clear contract. Versions of these skills, processes and methods also underpin other developmental learning processes.

Active and authentic listening is fundamental in effective coaching/mentoring. Connor and Pokora (2007) distinguish between diagnostic listening and active listening. Diagnostic listening is useful in problem solving, where it is important to selectively listen to the facts and make decisions about relevant and irrelevant data. The listener drives the conversation and narrows options until the problem is solved. In active listening, the coach/mentor concentrates on the coachee/mentee in a holistic way, seeking to understand what the individual is trying to say, including being aware of any underlying issues. The aim is to explore, be open to all information and find out more, and in this way enable the coachee/mentee to expand their own understanding of an issue. The practice of active listening also includes clarifying, reflecting back, paraphrasing and summarising in order to assist the coach/mentor in grasping the story and its meaning for the coachee/mentee. Active listening also helps the coachee/mentee to clarify and deepen their own understanding, for example, through interventions that begin with 'If I've understood ...', or 'You seem to be saying ...'. These can be cliché questions. But they work, if asked sincerely.

Described by Rogers (2004) as 'the skilled language of coaching', asking the right questions at the appropriate time is a key coaching/mentoring skill. Effective questions are generally open questions that broaden the awareness of the coachee/mentee by provoking thinking and challenge. Similarly, they go beyond asking for factual information and lead to the opening up of options, through discovery and learning. For example, 'What are your responsibilities here?' 'What do you want the outcome to be?'

Trust is central to effective coaching and mentoring. Creating and sustaining an environment of confidentiality and trust often requires the coach/mentor to abandon many of the normal conventions of conversation, and replace them with skills and behaviours which communicate acceptance and respect. These include building rapport through authentic listening and questioning which convey acceptance of the coachee/mentee, a genuine concern for their well-being, and commitment to their development. Implicit in this process is that the agenda of the coachee/mentee is important, and also that confidentiality will be maintained at all times.

Effective feedback is important in building and maintaining rapport and trust. For example, a coachee/mentee may ask for comment or judgement on an aspect of their thinking or actions to inform their future actions. Here feedback may reflect back in order to help the coachee/mentee evaluate the event being discussed for themselves and also their behaviours and intentions. The coach/mentor does not articulate judgement, either negative or positive, but clarity is achieved by assistance in thinking the events through. Feedback, in this sense of providing clarity for the coachee/mentee, lies at the heart of developmental learning.

Sometimes, however, with the process described above exhausted, it is appropriate for the coach/mentor to provide comments and judgements from their own experience.

Several models of coaching and mentoring relationships can be used effectively in higher education. The best-known model is one-to-one and face-to-face, whether in person or online. This can be extended to team or group coaching/ mentoring, where in instances of limited time and resources a coach/mentor works with a group on similar issues. Peer coaching/mentoring can be very beneficial, and often takes place on an informal basis, for example between colleagues who are working on similar issues. The work of Lumsden and Eagle (2014) cited earlier in this chapter is a good example of peer coaching.

Online coaching/mentoring and e-coaching/mentoring methods include the use of telephone, audio and video over Internet (for example Skype) and email. These approaches can be cheaper and easier to schedule, and provide benefits of increased flexibility and overcoming geographical constraints and travel time and cost. Challenges include potential difficulties in picking up emotional clues. Also, in email coaching/mentoring, there is scope for misunderstandings in the use of language to arise.

Coaching and mentoring as part of academic development

How can coaching/mentoring skills be used, often informally, as part of the toolkit of academic developers? Their formal use will be considered later.

The term *academic development* covers a wide range of practice. Land (2004) identifies 12 orientations to educational development. The 'Internal Consultant', 'Ecological Humanist' orientation, and the 'Interpretive–Hermeneutic' orientations are all processes which use coaching and mentoring approaches and skills.

The 'Internal Consultant' (Land, 2004) orientation is used by many academic developers. It includes working with specific departments or course teams, and also working on a more individual basis. In both instances there is a need for credibility and for offering practical and relevant solutions. But effective consultancy is not simply a matter of telling people what to do (any more than effective teaching is). Consultancy draws on coaching and mentoring skills of listening, collaborative dialogue and reflecting back before offering ways forward. Caplan (2003) makes the point that there are distinct differences between consulting and coaching/mentoring, but sometimes it is helpful to combine the two approaches:

> The coach does not need to be a consultant, but the consultant who coaches the client when this is appropriate will provide a far better service. (Caplan, 2003, p. 80)

Schein (2000) regards coaching as a subset of consultancy, and believes that the consultant needs to establish this helping relationship in order to determine the nature of the consultancy that will be offered. A respondent in Land (2004) from a large traditional Scottish university illustrates these points by describing how an important part of consultancy is being able to contextualise the issues:

> A good example is architecture. They ring you up and they say 'Can you come and train our tutors, who come from practice, to be able to teach architectural design?' … Yes, it's all about situated cognition so you go in and you listen and you watch and you say very little at first. And you talk to people and you say 'Mmmh ….' (Land, 2004, p. 101)

Relations between consultancy and coaching/mentoring are explored further in Chapter 5.

The 'Ecological Humanist' orientation (Land, 2004) is principally concerned with working with the academic as an individual practitioner, for example in this quotation from an academic developer:

> I think staff development is about supporting staff … to develop as professionals. I am delighted when I hear someone say 'I write so much better now as a result of our work together'. (Land, 2004, p. 53)

The 'Interpretive–Hermeneutic' orientation to academic development (Land, 2004) involves a 'conversational kind of process in which the interpreter learns by adjusting his or her perspective'. (Webb, 1996, p. 66). For example, in the words of one academic developer:

> For me the key issue is about how educators come to judgements … We need to try to understand what shared judgemental processes might involve in academic life. (Land, 2004, p. 109)

The two orientations described immediately above highlight the processes of supporting individual development and participating in learning conversations. These processes are part of the day-to-day work of many academic developers, and using a version of coaching/mentoring skills as part of the work will be implicit. However, consciously incorporating these skills can lead to enhanced effectiveness.

Coaching and mentoring initiatives where a formal contract is used

This section describes three substantial projects where a formal coaching and mentoring contract was used. The projects are:

* Professional learning and development for staff taking on new roles
* Mentoring of new staff
* The development and expansion of an existing successful mentoring initiative

Recognition for mentors/coaches is also considered.

These examples are written in some detail in order to make both specific and generic points about strategies for effective coaching and mentoring.

Academic coaching for staff taking on new roles

Blackmore (2008) recommends induction and continuing mentoring/coaching for staff taking on new roles in higher education, to alleviate the stress often experienced when embarking on additional and unfamiliar work.

An example of a positive use of coaching in academic development is a three-year faculty-wide professional development project in a post-1992 university. One-to-one coaching by an external consultant was provided for 18 staff recently appointed to part-time academic development roles. (Working with part-time staff is discussed in Chapter 7.) The purpose of the initiative was to build capacity in staff with learning, teaching and assessment roles. Teaching Fellows in the Faculty had a range of responsibilities for leading change in learning, teaching and assessment in addition to their teaching, course leadership and research roles in their departments. The academic development roles were complex, often requiring political sensitivity, strategic alignment and responsibility for the development of colleagues.

Attendance at the one-to-one sessions was 100 per cent and an evaluation of the initiative showed that the academic coaching sessions had a positive impact on the ability of the Teaching Fellows to perform their roles effectively. The main success factors identified were:

- Many staff commented that the coaching sessions enhanced their understanding of a complex and often diverse role. For some this involved working on a change in their academic identity.
- All those involved commented that the sessions had improved their confidence and enhanced their ability to perform tasks and complete projects. The opportunity to talk through scenarios and open up a range of possibilities and solutions with a coach was seen as very valuable in decision making and focusing on projects.
- The coaching helped individuals to take a more strategic and holistic view of their work by providing external assistance with ways of balancing different commitments and seeing the overlap and connections between competing priorities.

Participants in the initiative commented that this was the first time that one-to-one development of this nature had been provided for them at the university. Some examples of positive comments on the process of academic coaching:

> Coaching is so different from a conversation with a line manager – more focused on me as an individual.

The coaching conversations helped me to make informed decisions.

It was great to have time and space to think and stand back from day to day pressures.

Two different approaches to university-wide initiatives are described in the following two sections. The first emphasises mentoring of new staff. The second describes mentoring for University Teaching Fellows and outlines strategies for extending this across the university. In both examples the strategic aims include influencing university policy and working to create a mentoring/coaching culture, including the provision of accredited courses as a means of recognition for mentors and coaches.

Mentoring for new staff

When people become academics, especially if they are doing so after working in industry, government or the professions, they often mistakenly believe that knowledge of their subject is all that is required to be a successful academic. In fact they are taking on the mantle of an entire profession, replete with its own vocabulary, its own research traditions and its own scholarly literature. (Candy, 1996, p. 1)

Barkham (2005) uses personal autobiographical data collected over an academic year to write about her experiences as a new member of staff in higher education. She describes her initial feelings of bewilderment and vulnerability, not even knowing what questions to ask. An effective mentoring relationship assisted Barkham through this disorientating process when, as a mid-career professional, she had changed career and found herself asking questions about survival which she felt to be very foolish.

Studies by Knight and Trowler (1999) and Knight, Tait and Yorke (2006) show the importance of mentoring alongside formal courses in the effective professional learning of new academic staff in higher education. In the more recent study, based on a sample of nearly 3,000 tutors at the Open University, Knight, Tait and Yorke (ibid.) argue that non-formal learning approaches for new academics in the context of the school/department are gaining recognition. Nearly half of those surveyed said that they would like more support and guidance from a mentor. Knight, Tait and Yorke's (ibid.) view of professional learning for new academics is that it is both systemic and situated, with the development of abilities occurring as a result of situated social practices. In this context, a mentor has an important part to play in assisting in the development of relevant values and competencies.

Mentoring for new members of staff takes place in a range of contexts and with varying degrees of formality across higher education. In some institutions, mentoring of new academic staff through Post Graduate Certificate programmes is prioritised and in others mentoring takes place through schools and departments.

An initiative at Liverpool John Moores University is an example of moving beyond small scale, local initiatives to the promotion of a mentoring culture across the university. A Mentoring Working Group, with membership from a range of staff from across the university, provided impetus and focus. (Boulter and Eastcott, 2009). As well as bringing advantages for mentees, the Working Group was keen to disseminate the potential benefits for the organisation. Mentoring, as part of a system of effective support for new staff, aimed to have a positive impact on the university goal of increasing staff satisfaction. This strategic focus on mentoring was also a core element of the Liverpool John Moores approach to professional standards, using the standards as a process by which staff can plan their development through the set of Standard Descriptors ('UK Professional Standards Framework (UKPSF)', n.d.)

The Mentoring Group used the outcomes of research into existing development routes at the university and literature on the benefits of mentoring and coaching in professional development as the context for discussion on benefits to the organisation. Four key objectives for a university-wide mentoring scheme were identified:

- To improve the induction experience of full and part time staff new to the university
- To provide professional development for established staff in identifying promotional or career opportunities
- To assist programme leaders in preparing for the role and to provide ongoing support for this and similar roles in managing teaching and learning
- To support and recognise the contribution of mentors and mentees to continuous professional development and to the achievement of the strategic objectives of the university. (Boulter and Eastcott, 2009, p. 11)

The Working Group prioritised mentoring for new full time academic staff and a scheme was started. Crucially, a definition and a framework for mentoring were selected from the considerable range available, using the criteria of relevance for the higher education context. Discussions in the Working Group concluded that the key to the framework was flexibility, so a semi-formal mentoring framework was chosen, together with a definition of mentoring which focused on the development of knowledge. The time spent in determining the form of mentoring to be used at the university and agreeing expectations was vital to the success of the scheme. Mentoring for new staff was defined as:

Off-line help by one person to another in making significant transitions in knowledge, work or thinking. (Megginson and Clutterbuck, 1995, p. 35)

The key components of the semi-formal framework chosen were:

- Measurement for the benefit of the programme and the individuals
- Recording by means of notes kept by the mentee

- An agenda which is determined by the mentee
- Programme management through the scheme coordinator and peer support. (adapted from Klasen and Clutterbuck, 2002)

More than 20 staff from around the university initially volunteered to be mentors. They were not required to have any previous mentoring experience or training, but had to attend a half day briefing session, the aim of which was to '... direct, support and enhance the potential for positive mentoring experiences' (Klasen and Clutterbuck, 2002, p. 254). Central coordination of the matching of mentors and mentees was a crucial ingredient in the success of the scheme and, where possible, mentors were matched with mentees from their own subject discipline. Evaluation of the scheme showed benefits for both mentees and mentors. For example:

From a mentee:

> Being mentored was the quickest way to get up to speed with the way the systems worked. You've got no idea of the importance of timings when you are new; you are quite reliant on having someone else there to help you with that ....

From a mentor:

> Ultimately it makes our job easier because it's a really efficient way of working ... you are supporting, you are there as a motivator and sounding board.

Mentoring for University Teaching Fellows extended across the university to support academic practice

Another example of a university-wide initiative, aiming to build a coaching/mentoring culture, started with the mentors who are an important part of the Teaching Fellowship scheme at Edinburgh Napier University. A key aspect of the application process is working with a mentor on portfolio development over a period of several months. The mentor works with potential Teaching Fellows to explore achievements and specialist areas of interest against the criteria.

See also Chapter 5 on consultancy for more information on this work.

This well-established process has been expanded to stimulate and support academic practice development more widely across the university by means of a Mentoring and Coaching Special Interest Group and the establishment of a Mentoring/Coaching Award. The award (ENMCA – Edinburgh Napier Mentoring and Coaching Award) contributes to increased professionalism in mentoring and coaching, and encourages staff to actively seek out new opportunities and areas of work where they can use their skills. The SIG (Special Interest Group) links colleagues working on mentoring and coaching initiatives across the university.

Recognition for mentoring and coaching

A key part of the university-wide mentoring initiative at Liverpool John Moores University was the development of an accredited programme to provide those staff acting as mentors with a means of increasing their knowledge of the process of mentoring and recognising and formalising their experience. The award, 'Mentoring: Theory and Practice', was accredited through the Staff and Educational Development Association (SEDA) Professional Development Framework ('SEDA-PDF', n.d.) as an Action Research Award. One of the key aims of the programme was to create, develop and support a community of mentors in the university through a cycle of action research.

The Edinburgh Napier Mentoring and Coaching Award was developed with similar aims to the programme at Liverpool John Moores. The programme is also recognised by SEDA through the Professional Development Framework and is the pioneer of the SEDA Coaching and Mentoring Award.

Participants have positively evaluated the programmes at both universities. Participants reported an increase in confidence and enthusiasm, learning about a different model for working with staff, gaining a clearer understanding of the skills required and how to use them, and appreciation of the recognition which the award provides.

Benefits of coaching and mentoring

This chapter has considered coaching/mentoring interventions at both the individual and at the university-wide level. Potential benefits can be summarised as follows:

For mentees/coachees

- Information, support and development in the context of personal and/or organisational change
- Improvement of competence in taking on a new role, through assistance in developing knowledge, skills and attitudes which are directly relevant
- Enhancement of motivation and satisfaction, for example in aspects of developing learning and teaching

For mentors/coaches

- Value and satisfaction. Those who mentor/coach others report gaining personal satisfaction from knowing that they have contributed to the growth and development of others
- Learning and self-development. Coaches/mentors can develop new skills, abilities and insights. Clutterbuck (2004) argues that becoming involved

in coaching/mentoring can be 'a valuable means of delaying plateauing' (Clutterbuck, 2004, p. 32) by providing fresh challenges
- Recognition. Acting as a mentor/coach can help in gaining credibility for professional progression.

For the organisation

- Contributing to staff satisfaction through the process of staff feeling valued and informed
- Contributing to organisational learning and enhanced communication
- Contributing to professional standards and professional learning.

Strategies for success

The idea that coaching and mentoring processes build on the concept of developmental conversations for learning is fundamental to this chapter. Key strategies for success include spending time determining the form of coaching/mentoring that is relevant for a particular context, and agreeing expectations at a local level rather than debating the definitions of coaching and mentoring in an abstract sense and discovering that there is limited consensus. This quotation provides a clear starting point:

> Practitioners draw on similar traditions of one-to-one developmental dialogue ... both traditions draw on a similar range of skill sets and adapt them to the particular form of the dialogue in use within the particular environmental setting. (Garvey, Stokes and Megginson, 2009, p. 86).

The following examples demonstrate that a clear focus for an intervention can lead to positive outcomes and in each case the process could be labelled as 'coaching' or 'mentoring'.

Piccinin (1999), an academic developer in a large Canadian university, reports that holding focused individual conversations with academic staff about their teaching formed a large part of his work. He was interested to know if these coaching/mentoring conversations made any difference. A detailed study found significant improvements in teaching, as measured by student ratings before and after the conversations. Interestingly, improvements were found even after quite brief consultations.

Two further examples of focused coaching/mentoring interventions which can be important in the work of academic developers are supporting staff in obtaining HEA Accreditation and supporting staff as part of Postgraduate Certificate and Masters Programmes in teaching and learning in higher education. Both processes have clearly-defined outcomes and expectations, and may use both coaching and mentoring approaches.

At an organisational level, the following are important success factors:

- In successful initiatives, resources are allocated to the careful selection and matching of mentors/coaches with mentees/coachees. Waugh (2014), Human Resources Director at University College London, writes of the success of coaching and mentoring initiatives in the organisation. Twenty externally accredited internal coaches work throughout the organisation. They are described as 'the jewel in the crown' of the professional development strategy. The coaches are complemented by a number of mentoring schemes: 'In my personal experience, mentoring has been hit and miss, but it does work' (Waugh, 2014, p. 42). An online matching service which puts mentor and mentee together based on their profile contributes to the success of the scheme.
- The provision of appropriate briefing and training for mentors/coaches is an important factor in the success of university-wide schemes; for example, the training for mentors provided in the scheme for mentoring new staff at Liverpool John Moores University.
- There is unlikely to be a widespread consensus about the meaning of coaching and mentoring in any particular context. It is important that some common understanding of meaning within that setting is established.

At an individual level, it is important to have clear ground rules and systems in place to manage relationships that come to an end. Some mentoring/coaching relationships do not work out. Possible reasons include failure to build rapport, limited commitment by either party, or a mentee/coachee feeling that their particular coach/mentor is unable to meet their needs. It is important that the ending of the relationship is handled in a way which will not cause personal hurt or offence. Breaches of confidentiality can, indeed probably should, lead to the ending of a mentoring or coaching relationship.

Coaching/mentoring relationships also come to a natural or contractual end. Exit procedures are needed, including debriefing, review, and the defining of next steps for learning for the coachee/mentee. Where the coaching/mentoring has taken place as part of a large-scale initiative, recruiting coachees/mentees as future coaches or mentors can be a useful next step.

The examples provided in this chapter have demonstrated some ways in which coaching and mentoring approaches can have an important place in the toolkit available to academic developers. Klasen and Clutterbuck (2002) argue that mentoring/coaching can have an impact and effectiveness that goes beyond that of other one-to-one development methods. The two factors which provide the advantage are the integrated approach, which can be adapted to individual needs and contexts, and the development of the capacity in the learner for continuous self-managed learning.

Coaching and mentoring have been variously described as a 'learning alliance' (Brockbank and McGill, 2012) and a 'developmental alliance' (Hay, 1995).

The core relevance of these approaches and skills for academic developers can be found in the words *learning* and *development*, as both of these processes are fundamental in our work.

References

Barkham, J. (2005). 'Reflections and interpretations on life in academia: a mentee speaks', *Mentoring and Tutoring*, 13(3): 331–345.

Blackmore, P. et al. (2008). *Investigating the Capabilities of Course and Module Leaders in Departments*. York, UK: Higher Education Academy.

Boulter, R. and Eastcott, D. (2009). 'From research to recognition: mentoring for staff at Liverpool John Moores University', *Educational Developments*, 10(3): 10–12.

Brockbank, A. and McGill, I. (2012). *Facilitating Reflective Learning: Coaching, Mentoring and Supervision*. London: Kogan Page.

Candy, P. (1996). 'Promoting lifelong learning: Academic developers and the university as a learning organisation', *International Journal for Academic Development*, 1(1): 7–18.

Caplan, J. (2003). *Coaching for the Future: How Smart Companies Use Coaching and Mentoring*. London: Chartered Institute of Personnel and Development.

Clutterbuck, D. (2004). *Everyone Needs a Mentor: Fostering Talent in Your Organisation* (4th ed.). London: Chartered Institute of Personnel and Development.

Connor, M. and Pakora, J. (2007). *Coaching and Mentoring at Work: Developing Effective Practice*. Maidenhead, UK: Open University Press.

Garvey, R., Stokes, P. and Megginson, D. (2009). *Coaching and Mentoring: Theory and Practice*. London: Sage.

Haigh, N. (2005). 'Everyday conversation as a context for professional learning and development', *International Journal for Academic Development*, 10(1): 3–16.

Hay, J. (1995). *Transformational Mentoring*. London: McGraw Hill.

International Coach Federation (2008). Code of ethics. www.coach/federation.org.

Kamvounias, P., McGrath-Champ, S., & Yip, J. (2008). '"Gifts" in mentoring: Mentees' reflections on an academic development program', *International Journal for Academic Development*, 13(1), 17–25.

Klasen, N. and Clutterbuck, D. (2002). *Implementing Mentoring Schemes*. Oxford: Butterworth.

Knight, P. and Trowler, P. (1999). 'Organisational socialisation and induction in universities: reconceptualising theory and practice', *Higher Education Journal*, 37: 177–195.

Knight, P., Tait, J. and Yorke, M. (2006). 'The professional learning of teachers in higher education', *Studies in Higher Education*, 31(3): 319–339.

Land, R. (2004). *Educational Development: Discourse, Identity and Practice*. Maidenhead, UK: Society for Research into Higher Education and Open University Press.

Lumsden, P. and Eagle, L. (2014). 'Dialogue as a developmental tool', *Educational Developments*, 15(3): 13–16.

Megginson, D. and Clutterbuck, D. (1995). *Mentoring in Action: A Practical Guide for Managers*. London: Kogan Page.

Piccinin, S., Cristi, C. and McCoy, M. (1999). 'The impact of individual consultation on student ratings of teaching', *International Journal for Academic Development*, 4(2): 75–88.

Rogers, J. (2004). *Coaching Skills: A Handbook*. Maidenhead, UK: Open University Press.

Schein, E. (2000). 'Coaching and consultation: are they the same?' In Goldsmith, M., Lyons l. and Freas, A. (eds), *Coaching for Leadership*. San Francisco: Jossey Bass.

SEDA-PDF. (n.d.). Retrieved 23 May 2015 from www.seda.ac.uk/pdf.

Senge, P. (1994). *The Fifth Discipline Field Book: Strategies and Tools for Building a Learning Organisation*. London: Nicholas Brearley Publishing.

Spiller, D. (2002). 'Conversations for change: mentoring conversations for induction into an academic career'. Presentation to a joint conference of the Staff and Educational Development Association and the All Ireland Society for Higher Education, Dublin.

UK Professional Standards Framework (UKPSF) | The Higher Education Academy. (n.d.). Retrieved 23 May 2015 from www.heacademy.ac.uk/professional-recognition/uk-professional-standards-framework-ukpsf.

Waugh, N. (2014). 'Carry on Campus', *Chartered Institute of Personnel and Development: People Management*. August 2014: 42–44.

Webb, G. (1996) 'Theories of staff development: development and understanding', *International Journal for Academic Development*, 1(1): 63–69.

Chapter 7

Supporting part-time teachers and contract faculty

Fran Beaton and Ellen Sims

Summary

Unprecedented increase in access to higher education over the past decade, particularly in the UK and Canada, has required Higher Education Institutions (HEIs) to employ more instructors, increasingly on contractually limited arrangements. What began as a short-term solution has now become the norm in many countries. In some disciplines, for example professional and practice-based subjects, there is a history of employing staff/faculty on a contractual basis, bringing valuable professional and industrial experience. Contextual pressures influence universities: changing expectations of their nature and purpose, the relationship between students and universities, changes in curriculum and teaching. At the same time, potential students and future employers scrutinise student satisfaction with the quality of their education. Public support for permanent/tenured positions has declined (Kezar, Maxey and Eaton 2014) and there is a demand for a more flexible workforce.

These conceptual and practical considerations are crucial to effective support for part-time and contractual staff. This chapter includes a series of case studies and examples from the literature, intended to illuminate good practice in the support and development of these instructors.

Links to web sources referenced in this chapter can be found at www.seda .ac.uk/apad.

Acknowledgements

The authors would like to acknowledge Tricia Thorpe and Pat Atkins for their contributions to the case studies in this chapter.

Introduction

This chapter begins with some definitions and attempts to identify, then explore, why these are significant in the broader educational context. The question of different understandings of what we mean by part-time staff, the work they are expected to undertake and their relationships with the institutions in which they work is central. We consider, too, national and institutional practices, chiefly in the UK and Canada, and:

- How these issues manifest in different national and policy contexts
- The possible roles of the academic/educational developer in influencing institutional decisions, policy and practice
- The implications for the recruitment, retention and support for part-time staff

These are illustrated by case studies drawn from different disciplinary fields and national contexts, illustrating key aspects of effective (or not!) support for part-time staff and identifying key messages for their support and development. We suggest, however, that while institutional support for these staff is essential, an effective institution will have structures and strategies to encourage all staff to develop their full potential. Thus, the robustness of support and enabling structures for part-time staff could be considered a litmus test for developmental support more generally.

Who are we talking about, and what do they do?

Definitions and terminology referring to this group can vary according both to country and institution. A selection of terms used in the literature and in practice include:

- Sessional
- Casual/non-career teacher
- Graduate assistant
- Graduate teaching assistant
- Contract or contract-limited faculty
- Tutor
- Visiting/associate lecturer
- Adjunct/contingent faculty
- Non-standard academics (a particularly broad and vague category)

For the purposes of this chapter we will use the term 'part-timers' unless we are referring to a specific sub-group.

Part-time teachers are a diverse group. Beaton and Gilbert (2013: 5) note that:

> ...it is becoming increasingly obvious that there are many different types of people who might be classified as having a non-standard academic post [so it is] important to consider the ways in which we might identify this elusive group.

Gappa and Leslie (1993) identify that some may be part-time from choice, for instance combining professional practice with teaching. These practitioner-teachers are employed elsewhere but come in to share special expertise, to 'connect students to the cutting edge ideas and practices of the professions' (Chan, 2010: 39). They model practice and embody professional knowledge (Chan, 2010; Trumble, 2010), maintaining expertise and status in both spheres. Others are part-time, aspiring academics hoping for a full-time or established roles, cobbling together enough work to survive (e.g. Bettinger, 2010; Bettinger and Long, 2004; Kezar et al., 2014; Jones, Gopaul, Weinrib, Metcalfe, Fisher, Gingras and Rubenson, 2014).

Part-timers within and between institutions have differing roles and responsibilities and different kinds of contracts. In Canada (Jones et al., 2014) and the US (Kezar et al., 2014), alternative arrangements vary widely by institution and discipline, and can be idiosyncratic. Typically they focus on teaching (although this may vary by discipline), demonstrating, leading seminars, providing occasional specialist input, supporting students and marking student work. As academic employment becomes more global, there are implications for the changing nature of graduate education, for example the differences in teaching portfolio/dossier between the US and the UK. Between and often within institutions and locales there may be a variance in terminal qualifications required for teaching in HE. Hudd et al. (2009) suggest they have an important role to play in creating a culture of integrity on campus, as so much of the assessment of student learning falls to this group. What a part-timer does may also depend on their career stage: a postgraduate combining teaching with doctoral study has different responsibilities from an academic teaching part-time as a prelude to retirement, or a professional practice educator bringing workplace expertise. We note, too, the differences in the amount and variety of teaching undertaken. The UK postgraduate, for example, tends to have a more limited portfolio than their North American counterparts, with possible implications for their eventual employability as an academic in a global marketplace. That same global marketplace (for both staff and students) means that teachers and students from culturally and ethnically diverse backgrounds bring different expectations to their work concerning the role of the teacher and the engagement and motivation of their students. These in turn can bring both opportunities and challenges, for which part-timers must be prepared.

The broader context

The role of the university

The contribution of part-time staff needs to be set in the context of a number of changes which have influenced universities. These include changing expectations of the nature and purpose of universities, changing curricula and changes in the way in which these curricula are designed and taught. Some reflect broader trends and affect numerous aspects and players: students, institutional perceptions of what the general public and politicians believe universities are for, how the quality of teaching and research is decided and the implications for institutional prestige. Other UK examples of change include the rise of nursing as a graduate profession, the expansion of the university sector (both as a consequence of the 1992 Further and Higher Education Act and in the development of specialist HEIs such as conservatoires, schools of art and private providers), the relationship of teaching and research and the balance between teaching, research, administration, and enterprise. In some professional disciplines, such as social work, the curriculum is influenced by the requirements of a professional body, so staff may be involved in designing curricula which integrate aspects such as arranging and monitoring work placements. It may be important to note that in some countries such as Canada, the HE system is highly unionised, including support staff and contract faculty. Collective bargaining has been the primary mechanism for determining academic work. (Jones et al., 2014).

Policy developments

These are relevant in that higher education policy translates into legislation and thence into university structures and practices. There is a highly decentralised approach to HE policy in Canada, with responsibility for HE assigned to the provinces, supported by grants from federal government during times of expansion, and which is now shrinking. Changes in UK student funding have contributed to a changing relationship between students and universities, generating a discourse of students as consumers, or co-constructors of knowledge. UK universities are now required to publish Key Information Sets (HEFCE, n.d.), giving information to prospective students about aspects which are likely to influence their choice of course and of institution. The KIS includes student satisfaction ratings under five headings, covering academic and pastoral experiences and gathered nationally through an online National Student Survey (NSS) of final year undergraduates.

The results are published nationally and, as education journalist John Gill points out:

> Institutions have a delicate line to tread in being open about their organisations versus the pressures of competition. (Times Higher Education, 4 April 2013)

In Canada and the US, the National Survey of Student Engagement (NSSE, 2015) is widely subscribed to by colleges and universities and reports student responses to questions about their experience and interactions with peers, academics and the academic environment. For universities, the stakes are high: an excellent or poor NSS or NSSE score is perceived to have an effect on student recruitment with consequent implications for institutional fee income and standing. The question of teaching quality and the proportion of time spent on teaching and learning activities is also revisited in the KIS information. Because the feedback students give is holistic (there is no scope to name individual teachers) this pressures universities to ensure that the quality of teaching is high across the board.

This is not a point we contest, but it underlines the importance of quality professional development. We will amplify the importance of this later in the chapter.

The impact of contract faculty on quality

Some studies (e.g. Bettinger and Long, 2004) link part-timers to a decline in teaching quality. This may be due to a number of reasons, including their being made to feel like second-class citizens (Gappa and Leslie, 1993). Kezar (2012) suggests that this may contribute to a 'caste'-based faculty system and notes that teachers who are divided into different cultures do not usually interact. This impacts on students and the curriculum, as well as creating implications for professional development (see Chapter 4) and sharing of good practice. Kezar et al. (2014) document the negative impact on both institutional and student outcomes in the areas of retention, achievement, transfer and graduation rates. They list several conditions potentially affecting student learning: last minute hiring, affecting preparation time; lack of access to mentoring, orientation and professional development; exclusion from curriculum design and decision making; and lack of access to space and resources.

In contrast, Landrum (2009:25) found no significant differences in course evaluations and grade distributions between tenured faculty and part-timers, also noting that 'it appears they do the same with less'. Kezar et al. (2014) conclude that it is not the tenure track status alone that affects quality, but the appropriate policies and practice in place to support faculty. Landrum (2009) also found that where there is a difference, it is small and differs by discipline – where vocational knowledge is more valued, adjuncts may provide better teaching outcomes. Jones et al. (2014:347) note that contingent faculty ' ... make important contributions... and complement the work of faculty with more traditional workloads'. Gunderman (2006:134) suggests that, as a result of educational compartmentalisation, specialists know more about less, and argues '[O]ne of our greatest opportunities as organizations is to increase the permeability of our internal boundaries.' It is worth noting that a large number of the authors cited in this chapter recommend an increase in opportunities for interactions between part-timers and full-time, permanent academic staff, to improve the student and staff experiences, as well as to benefit the institution (see Chapter 4). Meixner, Kruck and Madden (2010) reviewed the literature on the relationship of instructor type and student success, some of which is quoted elsewhere in this chapter, and found contradictions and the need for further study. However, it is often noted in the literature that institutional support for faculty can improve student success and experience.

Staff development needs and support

Recognition of the importance of teaching quality has been evidenced by the setting up of centres of teaching excellence, such as University Learning and Teaching Enhancement units. Lyons (2007) suggests that there is some argument that staff development is inconsequential as adjuncts have weak ties to the institution. However, he counters that they do so much of the teaching that their development should be taken seriously. Burk (2000, in Meixner et al. 2010:143) suggests that part-time faculty *are* at risk through 'institutional neglect', which can include exclusion from development opportunities. Kezar et al. (2014:7) find that ' ... prior studies and reports have been used to justify a positive working environment for tenured and tenure-track faculty' yet these rationales are not being applied to the 'new majority' (Gappa, 2008). Blackwell and Blakemore (2003:21) note, however, that 'for staff development, there is a major task in ensuring that part-time and casual staff receive...appropriate support'. Barriers to participation noted are: inconsistent and ineffective outreach (Meixner et al., 2010); poor communication and scheduling conflicts (Meixner et al., 2010; Anderson, 2007); and lack of payment for attendance (Anderson, 2007).

Anderson (2007) suggests that professional formation is both formal and informal, through academic development and less formal *ad hoc* encounters, and reflective practice. These *ad hoc* opportunities are not always available or practicable for part-time employees. Staff need help to identify their needs, but they are not usually part of the feedback process, except from students, and this is not always useful for this purpose.

Based on responses from faculty, Meixner et al. (2010) identified the need for developing skills to 'cultivate additional knowledge requisite for advancing university teaching', such as learning and teaching with technology; peer-review and exchange with other part-time faculty; course planning strategies and motivating students. Additional areas for development identified in the literature include: marking and assessment, teaching international students and avoiding plagiarism (Anderson, 2007); using discipline-based pedagogies such as dialogic approaches and problem based learning (Smith and Smith, 2012); and the need for training in interdisciplinary team teaching of medical students and curriculum development (Reuben, Fink, Vivell, Hirsch and Beck 1992).

The role of the academic developer

Schroeder (2010) suggests educational developers have an emerging role in organisational change at individual, departmental and institutional levels, through support and review and influence of institutional policy (see also Chapters 13 and 17). Debowski (2014) suggests this requires a more open, partnership model of working to change academic practice, and 'being present' to be able to recognise and accommodate needs. We accept that there are limits to what educational developers can achieve within an institution, although their cross-institutional role gives them a uniquely broad perspective. At the policy influencing level, educational developers can help identify issues to bring to senior management and make the case to be present at decision-making. Their responsibilities for various forms of provision (whether credit-bearing or not) give them an overview of the kinds of available and appropriate support, and the educational developer can play a strategic role in identifying gaps in support and making the case for these to be remedied (see Chapter 4). Developers are likely to have built relationships with individuals and programme teams on curriculum development or other aspects of academic practice, which can create a climate for critical friend questions about local arrangements, such as who has responsibility for supporting and developing part-time teachers. There may be limits to the educational developer's influence but this does not mean it is not worth a try. Case study 2 is an example of one such cross-institutional initiative designed to support postgraduates with teaching responsibilities – with a coda identifying the conditions which make such initiatives more likely to be effective.

The changing nature of academic work

So far this chapter has focused on who and what we teach. We turn now to the question of how we are expected to teach it. As noted, the focus of most part-time employment is teaching. There is an expectation of use of innovative approaches that are learner-centred and inclusive, whereas the nature of contract work does not often allow opportunities for support to achieve this. Globally, teaching and learning have been transformed by the explosion of ICT (information and communication technology) (see Chapter 8). At its simplest, this can mean teachers needing to know how to navigate an institutional Virtual Learning Environment. More complex uses of ICT may involve blended or distance learning. Teachers and academics are likely to be employed in several institutions in the course of their careers, so the widespread use of ICT means that capability will be expected. Those who do not have it may be put at a career disadvantage. Developing such capability is part of an individual's personal professional development (as discussed in Chapter 4). Since ICT has become integral to the learning experience of students, there are clear implications for the quality of that experience. Gunderman (2006:131) suggests that becoming good 'knowledge sharers' is essential to education, and acknowledges the value of technology for teaching and learning. However, he posits that information sharing is a collaborative process and 'no technology can replace a gifted teacher who thoroughly understands both the subject and the audience'.

There is, too, the question of research and scholarship in relation to the part-time teacher. The model of the full-time professoriate persists, but has been shown to be diminishing in many locales and becoming fragmented with the increasing use of contract teachers (Jones et al. 2014). Many of their full-time colleagues are expected to undertake and publish original research contributing to universities' research standing and funding, through (in the UK) the nationally applied Research Excellence Framework. The Canadian HE system is one where the professoriate are expected to 'maintain a balance of both research and teaching' (Jones et al. 2014:336), with both teaching and research being the mission of the university (ibid p. 339). However, not undertaking such research may inadvertently diminish individuals' chances of gaining more permanent positions, so it is important to develop a culture where part-timers have opportunities to develop a scholarly approach to their work. They should be expected to become familiar with different approaches to teaching e.g. uses of technology, student-centred learning and academic literacies for their immediate role, but also have opportunities to consider other aspects (such as research) which will affect their future careers. As HE recruitment and hiring become increasingly global, through casting a wider net as well as graduating a diverse population from which to draw future academics, part-timers need to have the opportunities to get to grips with these aspects.

In summary, institutions need to ensure that professional development addresses multiple facets of the academic role, enables all staff to develop their capability in their current role and some degree of future-proofing. In Australia, the RED report (Percy et al., 2008) identified the numerous challenges of an increasingly casualised workforce. The report calls for a systematic approach to the recruitment, induction and professional development of increasing numbers of part-time staff, estimated at that time as undertaking between 20 and 50 per cent of teaching, and linking this both to quality of teaching and broader integration into the academic community. In Canada, the HEQCO study (Field et al., 2014) similarly identifies employment trends which, although varying across institutions in Ontario, indicate an increase in the employment of part-time instructors in most HEIs to meet increasing enrolments due to increased access. The study calls for further research into the potential implications for quality and student success of these trends. We suggest that the integration and development of **all** staff need to be approached holistically, attended to by all areas of an institution which a member of staff, whether full-time or part-time, permanent/tenured or on time-limited contract, encounters. The practicalities of involving part-timers need attention too: involvement in discussion and the extent of agency which a part-timer feels they have, and more basic but important aspects such as payment for attending meetings and eligibility for recognition. Attending to these aspects increases the benefits to part-time and contract teachers (the group concerned in our first case study), their full-time colleagues, their students and the educational processes and outcomes of the institution.

Supporting graduate teaching assistants (GTAs): a Canterbury Tale

These GTAs are postgraduate students at the University of Kent, UK, registered for PhDs. They had been awarded university postgraduate scholarships to support their studies, of which one condition was that they should undertake some teaching. For those in the humanities and social sciences this typically involved leading seminars and/or workshops, with some degree of agency about how they set about the actual teaching. In the sciences, the role was more commonly working as a lab demonstrator under the direction of a permanent member of staff, or

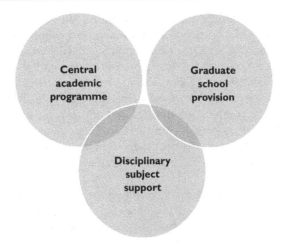

Figure 7.1 GTA support at the University of Kent

responding to individual students' questions as and when required in problems classes or practicals. Across all faculties there were variations in GTA involvement in other aspects, such as assessing student work.

A trigger for developing a range of support for these GTAs was that they had been told in their letter of appointment that central support for teaching development would be available, but the nature of the support was not made clear. Thus, many of these students were applying for places on a centrally run Postgraduate Certificate. This had originally been developed with full-time probationary staff in mind (and those responsible for the PgCert were initially unaware of the need to expand provision). The sudden spike in demand for places for part-timers considerably outstripped what the central team was able to offer. As part-time staff were having to wait up to six months to begin the course, this meant that they were often flying blind at the point at which they were embarking on their first taste of teaching. This had obvious implications from the point of view of the students they were about to start teaching and a wider equity issue in terms of the support available for this group of staff. In terms of the broader picture too, all UK universities' postgraduate students complete a nationally administered Postgraduate Research Experience Survey (HEA, n.d.), which includes a question about the extent and usefulness of support offered them to develop their teaching.

Once the situation became clearer, academic developers, in consultation with the graduate school, set up one-day workshop sessions, repeated several times on different campuses to cover the basics of university teaching and complemented by two further layers of provision. Firstly, sessions were run by each faculty, led by experienced staff (often university teaching prize winners) to provide a context for more discipline-specific considerations and to take account of the specific requirements for different GTAs. Secondly, individual schools (departments) set up regular workshop series to consider the detail of teaching in, for example, politics or languages, to address the specific context for science demonstrators and those simultaneously engaging in practice, and HE teaching in disciplines such as creative and performing arts, led by a named member of the permanent staff who takes responsibility for GTAs. The combination of these sessions acted as initial preparation, enabled the central team to identify demand and make a business case for expanding provision, and set up a progression route to the centrally taught programme as places became available. Overall provision was well received by participants.

These experiences highlighted three interrelated issues. First and foremost, communication is all. Institutional planning needs to be coherent and anticipatory as far as possible. Secondly, there needs to be a balance of discipline-transcendent and discipline-specific provision; as with any such group, participants from different disciplines have much to learn from each other, but there needs to be a forum where context-specific questions can be aired. Finally, some disciplinary specialists who take on the role of GTA (or indeed other kinds of) support have reported that this kind of work is not necessarily recognised in workload allocation models or reward structures.

Our second case study, contributed by Pat Atkins, Assistant Director (Associate Lecturer Support and Professional Development) at the Open University, UK illustrates a holistic approach to integrating and supporting part-time tutors.

Part-time staff at the heart of the student experience

Introduction: structures and processes

The UK Open University (OU) was created in 1969 as one of the earliest distance learning universities. Today it has roughly 200,000 students at any one time (Atkins, 2008). It has a full range of traditional academic, professional and vocational curricula.

When the OU was created it designed organisational structures to support its vision of becoming a university for all rather than for an elite. Like other mass-production systems of its time it divided up the work between roles. Full-time academics carry out research, design curricula and work with others to create distance teaching materials and assessment, but do not generally interact directly with students. On almost all modules, groups of around 20 students are supported by an associate lecturer (AL), part-timers normally working about six hours a week on teaching-only contracts, facilitating student learning on one module through feedback and marking of assignments, delivery of tuition (tutorials, face to face and/or using online synchronous technologies, asynchronous teaching in the VLE) and reactive remedial support when a student encounters problems.

The OU integrates ALs into the university through mechanisms designed to overcome the potential problems of delivering a consistent and coherent experience to large numbers of students spread across a wide geographic area. Key features include AL induction and access to professional development; marking guidelines, developed by full-time staff; and ensuring ALs make use of the multimedia module materials available to students.

AL professional development – a partnership

The wider university, the faculty, the module teams and the student support teams all have an interest in how ALs are integrated into the academic communities of the university and how they do their job. ALs themselves are often as expert as any in how to do it well. This case study includes two examples of very different approaches to AL staff development. What they share is central design and distributed delivery. In these two cases, the 'centre' is a central team acting for the whole university but in other cases the 'centre' may be a Faculty, a module team or a student support team.

AL support – career development and staff appraisal (CDSA)

Like most organisations the OU has a scheme to enable each member of staff to have an annual, recorded discussion with their line-manager about their current performance and career aspirations. The university extended this to ALs in 2011. Delivering such a process at a distance, with AL– to line-manager ratios of approximately 30:1, posed challenges. The university aimed to make the AL processes as similar to other staff Career Development and Staff Appraisal (CDSA) processes as possible. However, in setting up central support systems and sources of advice and guidance for AL line managers, the need for some adaptations emerged. For example, it was agreed that ALs would only have a CDSA discussion every two years and less frequent follow-up discussions of objectives. The implementation project decided to start rolling out the process to early adopters as soon as possible, to develop some case studies on which to base wider staff development for both ALs and their line managers. Resistance to the new processes from both groups of staff was mitigated by hearing the voice of colleagues who had found the CDSA discussions helpful and enjoyable, a significant factor in building acceptability.

Two years on almost all ALs who had passed probation have had a CDSA discussion with their line manager, agreed objectives and written up a small development plan, to go on their records. Lessons from the implementation are still being learnt and some of the innovations being sought for ALs may also feed back into improving CDSA for other staff. For example, it is clear that ALs need a fully online process; at the moment (2014) there is an agreement that CDSA reports should be filed on paper and no electronic copies retained. The staff responsible for AL CDSA are leading the drive to get that changed.

Teaching online using 'OULive'

The staff who use online synchronous technologies (e.g. Blackboard 'Collaborate') most regularly in the university are ALs. Many of them have been users for a number of years, while others are still novices. As the need for more, and more advanced, skills became clear, the university decided to extend its resources to support this for ALs.

There already existed a very well-received basic course for ALs, taken over a week and requiring about six hours' time, in a cohort of about 20. However this can at some times in the year not be sufficient for demand, with new ALs tending to all start together and existing ALs finding that the module they are on suddenly requires them to up-skill. The model has therefore been extended to include online resources which ALs can engage with more as reference materials in their own time, including opportunities to join a role-play group. In this, the AL spends some time as the moderator delivering some learning to others about to try their hand, to give them real experience before meeting their group of students.

ALs needed more advanced resources through a course for advanced pedagogic use of 'OULive', run over two weeks and needing about eight hours' study and a set of resources designed for independent study with 'play spaces' built in. Both approaches allow ALs to test more advanced pedagogic and technological approaches, gather tips from other advanced users and think about how the tools work within an ALs own discipline.

Whilst the requirements were specified and agreed centrally within the University's AL e-Learning Development group, and overseen by staff who are regular experienced OULive proponents, the vast majority of the development and facilitation work was undertaken by ALs.

Key messages

- Structurally coherent, context-dependent and professionally relevant initial and continuing professional development
- Emphasis on peer learning and expertise

Art and design

Background

Art and design education provides opportunities to learn through authentic activities, and there is a long history of learning and teaching with practitioners. Smith and Smith (2012) suggest that design professionals may deliver knowledge and bridge gaps between the academy and creative practice, therefore the value of 'Non-Career Teachers' (NCTs) may be pedagogic as well economic. Teaching and learning in art and design is iterative and negotiated, with uncertain outcomes. Therefore there may be numerous dilemmas for design education when employing

TAs and NCTs, as there are substantive methodological and pedagogical differences between design and other disciplines, and most mainstream professional support does not prepare individuals for these diverse methods.

Britt (2013) provides evidence from a range of studies, including her own (ibid:57), which indicate that the creative practice of the teacher practitioner has significant influence on pedagogy, curriculum, increased student engagement and employment skills. They use their connections and knowledge to create industry-based opportunities and collaborations. One study (Clews and Mallinder, 2010) identified that teacher-practitioners would welcome staff development opportunities to become more confident and proficient in these areas. A further issue is the role of writing in art and design, and Britt (ibid:59) identifies that support for writing and research projects is needed by creative practitioner teachers.

Additional reasons for creative practitioner-teachers to engage with professional development 'include giving teachers the language of pedagogy to participate more fully in research and academic discourse; engaging students as co-researchers and building learning communities; and acknowledging the "liquidity" of knowledge and developing new forms of social engagement with the world'. (Sims 2009:138). The activities of learning and teaching development include evaluation of individual and local practices and scholarly approaches and contributions to the debates in art and design pedagogy in HE.

The principles of students engaging with practitioners noted for art and design have potential advantages for any field of practice.

Medical education

Background

Medical education has been influenced by policy and funding developments as well as philosophical positions on the nature and purpose of medical education that go far beyond the scope of this chapter. However, the role of the medical educator is considered as an example of practice-based teaching and learning models that, although changed over time (see e.g. Gunderman, 2006; Steinert et al., 2006; and Trumble, 2010) has long persisted. Gunderman (2006:6) suggests that 'we need to see in today's medical students and residents not only the future of medical practice, but the future of medical education... Yet faced with the daunting challenge of teaching medical students and residents everything they will need to know to be good physicians, we frequently forget to see them as educators. We treat them as passive recipients of education rather than future educators in their own right'. In this context, Steinert et al. (2006:498) suggest that faculty development has become an increasingly important component of medical education. Whereas it was once assumed that a competent basic or clinical scientist would naturally be an effective teacher, it is now acknowledged that preparation for teaching is essential.

Rao et al. (2013) assert that development is essential to provide academic skills not taught in medical training, such as curriculum design, but may be too narrowly focused on teaching and requiring response to other needs, such as leadership skills, as faculty roles are more diverse and demanding than in the past. They also argue development is essential for institutional morale and vitality to attract and retain faculty. Al-Eraky and McLean (2012) note that the expectations of medical academics now include clinical, college and university service as well as leadership and scholarly activities. They suggest that needs assessments may be wish lists, but managers need to consider the agendas when planning, given the cost and significance. In their analysis of development programs for medical education, Steinert et al. (2006) found need for practice that makes more use of theory linked to practice, stimulates reflective practice, extends programmes over time and re-examines the question of voluntary participation.

Medical faculty

Medical faculty are part-time in the sense that they also generally maintain clinical responsibilities. 'Practitioner-Teacher' might more closely describe their roles than 'part-timers', even though they may not be in the university full-time. They tend to be dedicated individuals who have the personal resources to give a lot in the interests of the continuance of their own profession, supporting Gunderman's (2006:8) view that being an educator is

> built into the very essence of what it means to be a doctor. The word doctor is derived from the Latin... docere, which means to teach. Hence to be a doctor is to be a teacher.

This puts them in a different category from other part-timers.

In one example explored, the academic development practice course offered is not mandatory for any of the permanent faculty: it is entirely up to the health practitioner-teachers if they decide to participate. Moreover, there are financial implications, which are sometimes borne by the faculty member, although others are subsidised by work or their faculty. There is also, as is increasingly available in the UK, US and Canada (Australia too), a generic, university-wide programme for all new lecturers, which is free and compulsory for those new to teaching in HE. There is variation across institutions as to whether these are discipline-focused or more generic. In our example, the medical educators' course tends to be preferred for its discipline-specificity as well as its rigour as it is all at Master's level, giving a thorough theoretical as well as practical grounding in education.

The one area in which this UK example has become compulsory is for the clinical teaching fellows. These are junior doctors (often after their first two years of training in hospitals, though sometimes more than that) who are considered as temporarily out of their career path. Most of them are, for one year, full- or nearly full-time teachers, based in the hospitals that take this institution's students on their clinical placements. A few may be doing varying amounts of clinical work but teaching undergraduates in hospital settings on a very frequent basis. Undertaking the course supports them in their teaching work and the institution reports that a number of them continue to the next level – the diploma – (in their academic practice development) after finishing their teaching year. This supports them in developing careers in which education will be a key factor, and some return later to progress to the MSc.

Recommendations from the literature

As the situation of using adjuncts is unlikely to change, the question becomes how to make the most of the situation (Schmidt, 2008). Some if this is addressed by academic development that is flexible and relevant and offered in different formats including online, shorter and more sustained formats, self-directed learning, facilitated mentoring and mentoring networks, orientation courses, instructional effectiveness, social activities, recognition and information resources (Lyons, 2007). Anderson (2007) suggests that formal development may not be appropriate or do-able and suggests instead occasional conferences, opportunities for sharing reflective processes and innovations such as a virtual staff room. Kezar (2012) suggests that the benefits of development programs are to students as well as faculty, with improved teaching and less work than having to support sessional staff *ad hoc*. Rao et al. (2013) state that many needs can be met by steering faculty members to appropriate mentors (see Chapter 6), courses or other activities, making use of existing resources to meet individual needs. However, Kezar (2012) and others (e.g. Burk 2000, in Meixner, 2010; Blackwell and Blakemore, 2003) suggest there is benefit in offering specific programs as well as those that bring part-time and full-time academics together.

Some issues can be addressed in faculty development, but also require policy and structural change to offer better compensation, more security and permanence and changes to structures so that longer, more formal and valuable roles can be undertaken (Hudd et al., 2009); to engender feelings of purpose, belonging and feeling valued, and being more strategic about where and whom they teach (Schmidt, 2008). Finally, there should be opportunities for 'evaluation responsive to and aligned with the contingent role' Kezar (2012:7) and feedback to allow opportunities to evidence good practice and identify development needs and aspirations.

Conclusion

The case studies and literature combine to highlight the need for better relationships and outcomes for part-timers, who have been identified in the literature as a concern and priority. Clarity is essential in establishing expectations, responsibilities and support, both at institutional and departmental levels.

If, as Blackwell and Blakemore (2003) suggest, strategic staff development is an institutional function, then to be effective it has to engage with institutional concerns and priorities and ensure that provision is holistic, relevant and accessible to all staff, with a sensitivity to the particular practical challenges which part-timers have. Further, as Lewis (2002) asserts, if one of the primary goals of academic development programmes is to help faculty members become happier and more productive members of the HE community, this is the most effective method for instilling commitment and change. While the discipline may be at the heart of academic endeavour, robust institution-wide structures and practices are the backbone of effective provision for part-time staff and those who support them.

References

Al-Eraky, M. M. and McLean, M. (2012). 'The Compass Model to plan faculty development programs', *Medical Education Development*, 2(4).

Anderson, V. (2007). 'Contingent and marginalised? Academic development and part-time teachers'. *International Journal for Academic Development*, 12(2): 111–121.

Atkins, P. (2008). 'Transformation and integration through research and enquiry: a Centre for Excellence in Teaching and Learning perspective'. In Weaver, M. (ed.), *Transformative Support Models in Higher Education: Educating the Whole Student* (pp.181–196), London: Facet Publishing.

Beaton, F. and Gilbert, A. eds. (2013). *Developing Effective Part-Time Teachers in Higher Education: New Approaches to Professional Development*. London: Routledge.

Bettinger, E. and Long, B.T. (2010). 'Does cheaper mean better? The impact of using adjunct instructors on student outcomes', *Review of Economics and Statistics*, 92(3).

Bettinger, E., and Long, B.T. (2004). 'Do college instructors matter? The effects of adjuncts and graduate assistants on students' interests and success'. National Bureau of Economic Research Working Paper Series, number 10370. www.nber.org/papers/w10370. Accessed 9 January 2015.

Blackwell, R. and Blackmore, P. (2003) (eds.). *Towards Strategic Staff Development in Higher Education*. Maidenhead, UK: SRHE and Open University Press.

Britt, H. (2013). 'Practice what you teach? Examining the significance and complexities of textile designer educator creative practice'. *Art, Design and Communication in Higher Education*, 12(1): 49–64.

Burk, N. M. (2000). 'The invisible professor at-risk: how departmental disconfirmation disempower adjunct faculty'. Paper presented at the 86th annual meeting of the National Communication Association, Seattle, WA.

Chan, J. (2010). 'The use of practitioners as part-time faculty in postsecondary professional education', *International Education Studies*, 3(4): 36–45.

Clews, D. and Mallinder, S. (2010). 'Looking out: Effective engagement with creative and cultural enterprise key report', Art Design Media Subject Centre, www.heacademy.ac.uk/node/3910.

Debowski, S. (2014) 'From agents of change to partners in arms: the emerging academic developer role', *International Journal for Academic Development*, 19(1): 50–56, DOI: 10.1080/1360144X.2013.862621.

Field, C. C., Jones, G. A., Karram Stephenson, G. and Khoyetsyan, A. (2014). *The 'Other' University Teachers: Non-Full-Time Instructors at Ontario Universities*. Toronto: Higher Education Quality Council of Ontario.

Gappa, J.M. and Leslie, D.W. (1993). *The Invisible Faculty.* San Francisco: Jossey-Bass.

Gappa, J.M. (2008). 'Today's majority: faculty outside the tenure system', *Change,* 40(4): 50–54.

Gunderman, R.B. (2006). *Achieving Excellence in Medical Education.* London: Springer Verlag.

HEA (n.d.). Postgraduate Research Experience Survey, Higher Education Academy, accessed at www.heacademy.ac.uk/consultancy-services/surveys/pres, 13 May 2015.

HEFCE (n.d.). Accessed at www.hefce.ac.uk/lt/unikis/, 12 May 2015.

Hudd, S.S., Apgar, C., Bronson, E.F. and Lee, R.G. (2009). 'Creating a campus culture of integrity: comparing the perspectives of full- and part-time faculty', *The Journal of Higher Education,* 80(2): 146–177.

Jones, G.A., Gopaul, B., Weinrib, J., Metcalfe, A.S., Fisher, D., Gingras, Y. and Rubenson, K. I. (2014). 'Teaching, research, and the Canadian professoriate'. In J.C. Shin U. Teichler, W.K. Cummings and A. Arimoto (eds.), *Teaching and Research in Contemporary Higher Education.* pp. 335–355. Springer: Dordrecht.

Kezar, A. (2012). *Embracing Non-tenure Track Faculty: Changing Campuses for the New Faculty Majority.* New York: Routledge.

Kezar, A., Maxey, D., and Eaton, J. (2014). 'An examination of the changing faculty: ensuring institutional quality and achieving desired student learning outcomes'. CHEA Occasional Paper. Institute for Research and Study of Accreditation and Quality Assurance. January 2014.

Landrum, R.E. (2009). 'Are there instructional differences between full-time and part-time faculty'? *College Teaching,* 57(1): 23–26.

Lewis, K.G. (2002). 'The process of individual consultation'. In Gillespie, K.H., Hilsen, L.R and Wadsworth, E.C. (2002) (eds.), *A Guide to Faculty Development: Practical Advice, Examples, and Resources.* Bolton, MA: Anker. pp. 59–73.

Lyons, R.E. (2007) (ed.). *Best Practices for Supporting Adjunct Faculty.* Bolton, MA: Anker.

Meixner, C., Kruck, S.E. and Madden, L.T. (2010). 'Inclusion of part-time faculty for the benefit of faculty and students'. *College Teaching,* 58(4): 141–147. http://dx.doi.org/10.1080/87567555.2010.484032.

NSSE. (2015). Retrieved from http://nsse.indiana.edu. Accessed 22 October 2015

Percy A, Scoufis, Parry, S., Goody, A., Hicks, M., Macdonald, I., Martinez, K., Szorenyi-Reischl, N., Ryan, Y., Wills, S. and Sheridan L (2008). 'The RED Report, Recognition – Enhancement – Development: The contribution of sessional teachers to higher education'. Sydney: Australian Learning and Teaching Council.

Rao, G., Kanter, S.L., Weisz, O.A., Thompson, A., Ratti, T. and Woodward, J. (2013). 'Individualized strategic planning for faculty development in medical schools', *Medical Education Development,* 3(2): 5–8.

Reuben, D.B, Fink, A., Vivell, S., Hirsch, S.H. and Beck, J.C. (1992). 'Use of non-physician professionals in teaching geriatrics to internal medicine and family practice residents', *Gerontology and Geriatrics Education,* 12(1): 69–77.

Schmidt, P. (2008). 'Use of part-time instructors tied to lower student success', *The Chronicle of Higher Education,* 55(12).

Schroeder, C. (2010). *Coming In from the Margins: Faculty Development's Emerging Organizational Development Role in Institutional Change.* Virginia: Stylus Publishing.

Sims, E. (2009). 'Perfecting Practice: Engaging with learning and teaching in the creative subjects'. In *Dialogues in Art and Design: Promoting and Sharing Excellence,* D. Clews (ed.), pp. 136–141. ADM-HEA/GLAD. ISBN 978-0-9558978-1-8.

Smith, K., and Smith, C. (2012). 'Non-career teachers in the design studio: economics, pedagogy and teacher development', *iJADE*, 31(1): 90–104.

Steinert, Y., Mann, K., and Centeno, A. et al. (2006). A systematic review of faculty development initiatives designed to improve teaching effectiveness in medical education: *BEME Guide No. 8. Med Teach* 28(6): 497–526. (downloaded from informahealthcare.com 28 January 2015)

Trumble, S. (2010). 'Clinicians who teach'. Editorial. *The Clinical Teacher*, 7: 1–2.

Chapter 8

Technologies and academic development

Keith Smyth, Sheila MacNeill and Peter Hartley

Summary

This chapter proposes a critical approach to new technologies, identifying what academic developers need to know and do, emphasising strategic engagement.

We offer conceptual frameworks to help us select appropriate technologies, including the Digital University Matrix, 5C (Connecting, Communicating, Curating, Collaborating and Creating) and 3E (Enhance, Extend, Empower).

We explore practical strategies including attention to technologies in courses for new staff; new ways of working with students such as the Change Agents' Network; and informing and working with institutional strategy.

Finally, we suggest issues requiring our continuing attention, including the changing expectations of learners, changing teaching roles, and new forms of delivery such as Massive Open Online Courses (MOOCs).

Links to web sources referenced in this chapter can be found at www.seda .ac.uk/apad.

Introduction

This chapter proposes a strategic and critical approach to the selection and use of broad classes of technologies, in teaching and learning and, based on this, in academic development. It explores what academic developers need to know and be able to do about learning technologies, considering both breadth and depth of knowledge and expertise. We avoid the obvious risk of instant obsolescence which would be the result of focusing on particular and specific technologies of the moment. Instead we concentrate on the functional and educational potential of current and emerging classes of technologies. To some extent academic developers should follow and respond to the introduction and use of new technologies by teachers and institutions. However, following the guidance in Chapters 10 and 16, we should also be willing to take a strategic and leading role.

The chapter concentrates on technology and academic development. For thoughtful and thought-provoking accounts of implications of technologies for teaching and pedagogy, you will find value in Laurillard (2012) and Beetham and Sharpe (2013).

Our approach to technology and development responds to three key questions, and we illustrate our responses with examples and case studies:

- Which conceptual frameworks can we use to select appropriate technologies?
- Which practical strategies can help us make the most effective use of technologies?
- What are the key issues that we need to monitor?

We emphasise the necessity of productive collaboration between academics, educational developers, learning technologists and others concerned with development in higher education, as technology comes to permeate thinking and practice, becoming at the same time increasingly ubiquitous and less and less visible, less and less remarkable. Perhaps a post-digital age is already arriving ('Preparing for the postdigital era', 2009)?

Conceptual frameworks

The Digital University Matrix

The concept of the Digital University – in broad terms the higher education institution that is digitally enabled and digitally agile in practice and thinking – is being widely debated within the sector, and different perspectives on what 'being digital' means are becoming embedded in the policy, provision and futures planning of higher education institutions. However, provision and futures planning of higher education institutions, trying to understand what being a Digital University might look like, are hampered by the term often being used in narrow contexts, mainly relating to digital technology and infrastructure or to developing skills and digital literacies. There are different, often competing understandings about the nature and meaning of digital as it relates to the university and higher education. These diverse perspectives, often informed by the responsibilities that different individuals or departments have for specific aspects of digital practice within the institution, represent a form of value pluralism (Johnson and Smyth, 2011). These present a key challenge in taking a broader view – and perhaps an aspirational one – of what it means for a university to be digital, if indeed that is an appropriate goal beyond the short term.

The Digital University Matrix (MacNeill 2012) was developed as a strategic model which could provide a multidimensional, holistic view of the concept of the Digital University.

The Conceptual Matrix (Figure 8.1) suggests four key constructs to identify the key dimensions of the Digital University:

- Digital Participation includes public engagement by the university with government digital policy, and the growing potential of social and consumerist interactions offered by digital technology and the Internet.

Digital Participation	Information Literacy
Civic role and responsibilities Community engagement Networks (human and digital) Technological affordances	High level concepts and perceptions influencing practice Staff & student engagement and development Effective development and use of infrastructure
Curriculum & Course Design	**Learning Environment**
Constructive alignment Curriculum representations, course management, pedagogical innovation Recruitment and marketing Reporting, data, analytics	Physical and digital Pedagogical and social Research and enquiry

Figure 8.1 Conceptual matrix for the digital university (MacNeill and Johnston in, 2012)

- Information Literacy enables participation through developing skills, and identifies those both of academic relevance and relating to personal development.
- Both Digital Participation and Information Literacy are channelled through the university's Learning Environment, which is conceived in both technological and, critically, in academic and pedagogical terms.
- All three then influence and condition Curriculum and Course Design.

The Conceptual Matrix can be used to ask key questions relating to each of the four quadrants. For example:

- How is Digital Participation managed in the university – is this within widening access initiatives or lifelong learning provision?
- Where is Information Literacy visible in the university – in library programmes, or perhaps in staff and student development?
- How is the Learning Environment currently conceived in the university – as a unified concept or divided between infrastructure and estate, or teaching and learning?
- Who has the locus in Curriculum and Course Design, development and management?
- Where do decisions reside? (If anywhere – the analysis by Noble and Pym [1970, p. 431–445], suggesting that, wherever you look, decisions seem to be taken somewhere else – still resonates.)
- How influential are overall institutional objectives on outcomes common to all courses (e.g. employability, citizenship) in shaping practice at ground level?

These questions illustrate how the Conceptual Matrix can be applied. The important point is that the matrix and the dimensions within it can help channel key activities such as synthesising relevant pedagogical literature and evidence, analysing particular institutional contexts and settings, and identifying plausible lines of action for change. Ultimately the Conceptual Matrix is intended to support the exploration of the overarching term and concept of the Digital University, and offer the potential to act as a catalyst for fundamental change throughout an institution from administration to learning and teaching, and from policy formation to practice.

Since being developed, the Conceptual Matrix and associated tools have successfully been applied in aiding strategic discussions and scoping possible future developments at a number of universities in the UK (including the University of Dundee, University of Greenwich and Glasgow Caledonian University), and also at Macquarie University in Sydney. However, perhaps the most significant application of the Conceptual Matrix thus far has been in the Digital Futures consultation undertaken at Edinburgh Napier University between 2013 and 2014. The Conceptual Matrix provided the guiding framework for initial discussions at Edinburgh Napier, including a mapping of internal practice, and provided a key reference point for the themes and issues that were then explored throughout the consultation.

The consultation produced a number of outputs, the main one being a final report (Digital Futures Working Group Recommendations [DFWG], 2014) with both short and long term strategic recommendations. These included:

- Providing structured opportunities within every programme, and at various levels, for learners to engage digitally with the professional and discipline-related communities that they will ultimately become part of.
- Locating the digital in a programme-focused approach to curricula including cross-cohort learning and learners contributing to digital bodies of knowledge.
- Establishing a digital innovation fund for rapid piloting of digital innovations and positioning the university as one that embraces digital practice.
- Strategic funding in key areas of digital research and scholarship, knowledge transfer, and expanding online CPD (continuing professional development).
- Harnessing open educational practices in ways that make sense for a post-1992 institution with a strong agenda to widen access.
- Improving the use of digital approaches to scholarship, research and knowledge transfer through enhanced academic development provision.

The final recommendation of the Digital Futures Working Group was to explore the potential of the digitally distributed curriculum as an organising concept for future developments. The idea of a digitally distributed curriculum was defined in the final report of the Digital Futures group as:

> ... one that provides an innovative learning and teaching experience, extends learning and teaching across cohorts and communities, can meet diverse

needs around work-based learning and CPD, and that is digitally sustainable as well as pedagogically progressive. (Digital Futures Working Group Recommendations, op. cit.)

5 Cs Framework

The 5 Cs Framework was originally designed as a thematic framework for the five-day open online course, #BYOD4L (Bring Your Own Device for Learning – an initiative we discuss later in this chapter). The five areas provided an underpinning theme for each day. The framework has now evolved into a wider pedagogical framework to:

> … foster social learning underpinned by critical and creative thinking and action. (Nerantzi and Beckingham, 2014)

The five areas are:

1 Connecting,
2 Communicating,
3 Curating,
4 Collaborating and
5 Creating.

They provide interrelated hooks for individual and collaborative learning opportunities, particularly when situated within learning scenarios, such as #BYOD4L, which utilise social, collaborative media. Although apparently simple, the framework can provide a rich interface for both educational developers and learners, and indeed educational developers as learners, to explore and contextualise a range of formal and informal learning scenarios and spaces both on and offline.

The #BYOD4L course runs daily tweetmeets for synchronous discussion around one of the five Cs. These provide an ideal opportunity for participants to experience using a #hashtag, and to find and follow like-minded colleagues, within an open online network. As more and more institutions become partners with the event, they are also offering face-to-face discussion sessions to augment the online activities. In some cases, participation in #BYOD4L is now formally recognised within institutional CPD processes ('Manchester Metropolitan University | BYOD4L on WordPress.com', 2014).

3E Framework

The 3E (Enhance, Extend, Empower) Framework ('3E Framework', 2012) was originally developed as the 3E Approach as part of the cross-institutional TESEP (Transforming and Enhancing the Student Experience through

Pedagogy, n.d.) project. The 3E Approach was conceived as a design tool, based on socio-constructivist principles, to support FE and HE lecturers across a range of disciplines and levels to redesign one or more of their own courses to increase learner autonomy, choice and engagement through blending classroom and online approaches (Smyth et al., 2010).

The 3E Approach was then revised and expanded as the 3E Framework in 2011, as the basis for Edinburgh Napier's Benchmark for the Use of Technology in Modules (Smyth et al., 2011; Smyth, 2013). The 3E Framework is designed to help inform good practice in technology-enhanced learning, teaching and assessment, with an emphasis on considering what is appropriate to the context (i.e. subject, level, learners, and tutor experience) in question. As a continuum it essentially illustrates how technology can be harnessed to:

- Increase active learning (Enhance);
- Give students direct responsibility for key aspects of their learning (Extend); and
- Underpin more sophisticated activities that reflect the nature of learning and working in professional environments (Empower).

At Edinburgh Napier University, the framework is available both as a document and as an online interactive resource – see Figure 8.2 and 'University benchmark

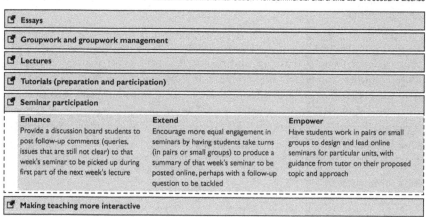

Enhance	Extend	Empower
Adopting technology in simple and effective ways to actively support students and increase their activity and self-responsibility	Further use of technology that facilitates key aspects of students' individual and collaborative learning and assessment through increasing their choice and control	Developed use of technology that requires higher order individual and collaborative learning that reflects how knowledge is created and used in the professional environment

This work is licensed under a
Creative Commons Attribution-NonCommercial-ShareAlike 2.5 UK: Scotland License

Essays

Groupwork and groupwork management

Lectures

Tutorials (preparation and participation)

Seminar participation

Enhance	Extend	Empower
Provide a discussion board students to post follow-up comments (queries, issues that are still not clear) to that week's seminar to be picked up during first part of the next week's lecture	Encourage more equal engagement in seminars by having students take turns (in pairs or small groups) to produce a summary of that week's seminar to be posted online, perhaps with a follow-up question to be tackled	Have students work in pairs or small groups to design and lead online seminars for particular units, with guidance from tutor on their proposed topic and approach

Making teaching more interactive

Figure 8.2 Online version of 3E Framework at Edinburgh Napier University (Smyth et al, n.d.)

for the use of technology in modules' (Smyth et al, n.d.). It includes illustrative examples of technology-enhanced learning for a range of learning, teaching and assessment activities, and also a series of examples of modules from across disciplines that are mapped to the framework.

The 3E Framework was made available via Creative Commons when it was first published by Edinburgh Napier in late 2011. Current contexts for the use of the 3E Framework include blended and online curriculum and course design, evaluation of technology-enhanced learning effectiveness, as the basis of institutional learning and teaching strategy, and to provide a common language within institutions for advancing practice in technology-enhanced learning, teaching and assessment. To date around 40 educational institutions that we know of, based within and beyond the UK, have implemented the 3E Framework or their own adaptation of it (see also Chapter 14.)

As we explore below, the 3E Framework has also been used extensively for academic development purposes including in taught programmes and continuing professional development provision for lecturers and teachers.

Practical strategies

Digital third spaces for learning

As our understanding and practice in the use of technology in higher education has evolved, we have seen a move away from the use of online technologies to deliver educational content and towards the use of online technologies as spaces to facilitate collaboration, cooperation, and content creation on the part of our learners.

The 5C and 3E Frameworks outlined in this chapter encourage this. However, another important and developing dimension to the application of online technologies in higher/further education lies in creating digital third spaces for collaborative learning that sit outside the institutional VLE. These can provide spaces for collaborative learning that cut across courses, disciplines, and formal and informal learning communities. This builds upon the ideas of Oldenburg (1991), who addressed the neutrality, mutual respect and opportunities to come together offered by physical third spaces in our communities. Educators have begun to explore how learning in digital third space might harness learners' digital literacies and networks in creative and empowering ways, and extend the opportunities for learning beyond the physical and virtual walls of the university (e.g. Gutierrez, 2008; Memarovic et al., 2014; Cronin, 2014). This encourages learning that is internationalised, multidisciplinary, and allows learners in higher education to engage and learn, within both the wider personal communities to which they already belong and the professional communities that they are aspiring to join.

Our view is that digital third spaces for learning will become increasingly important – as we develop academic practice using technology in higher/further education, and as universities try to become more authentic and more representative of the rest of the world in how they use digital tools and networks to learn, connect and participate.

Digital capability

Building digital capability ('Building digital capability', 2015) is also becoming an increasingly important overarching theme for institutional development. This is due in part to the increased adoption and acceptance of digital technologies and infrastructure across institutions. More importantly there is a growing recognition of the need to develop human capability in the form of developing and recognising the place of digital literacies both within the curriculum and in wider society.

Jisc has provided a useful definition of one element of digital capability, namely digital literacies, as:

> ... the capabilities which fit someone for living, learning and working in a digital society. ('Developing students' digital literacy', 2014)

As each of the models explored in this chapter highlights, the importance of developing staff and student confidence and capability with all aspects of digital participation is key to the success of any institution. Our existing practices and frameworks need to be revised in light of this. Jisc is now extending its work around supporting students' digital capabilities by developing a digital capability model to engage and support staff working in digital environments (as in Figure 8.3).

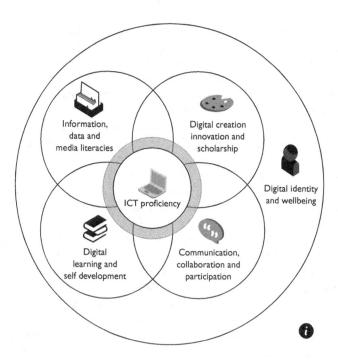

Figure 8.3 Digital capability model from Jisc (2015)

In response, educational developers need to be positioning themselves as digital scholars (Weller, 2011) exemplifying the use of digital technologies to extend their practice, research and dissemination in increasingly collaborative and open ways.

Very short courses

BYOD4L, described above in relation so the 5Cs Framework, is also important as a example of what we may call a very short course. Another is 'The 12 Apps of Christmas', (Rowell, forthcoming). This offers a quick introduction to tools for mobile learning through use of and conversation about, of course, 12 apps. It involves just a few minutes of work each day. The underlying model has wide applicability. Old models of IT training are much less relevant to apps, which usually take only a few minutes to obtain, explore/play with, and then decide whether and how to incorporate into one's repertoire/toolkit.

Trends and developments

We need to keep abreast, and where possible slightly ahead, of trends and developments in the application of current and emerging technologies. Among the most useful sources we have found are:

- Recent surveys from UCISA (the Universities and Colleges Information Systems Association). UCISA has been surveying the general use of IT in UK Higher Education since 1996/97. More important for this chapter is their recent work on technology-enhanced learning and on digital capabilities. Their first survey on digital capabilities was published in 2015. It makes many recommendations which echo our thoughts in this chapter, and identifies important barriers to progress including 'competing institutional strategies, institutional culture (and) departmental culture'. ('Digital Capabilities Survey Executive Summary', 2015)
- The NMC Horizon Report provides an American perspective. Their 2015 Higher Education Report identifies short, medium and longer-term trends and associated challenges and we have tried to cover these in this chapter. For example, their main short-term trends are BYOD and the Flipped Classroom. ('NMC Horizon Report: 2015 Higher Education Edition', 2015)
- Gartner claim to be 'the world's leading information technology research and advisory company'. ('Why Gartner Is Critical to Your Business', n.d.). They offer free information in addition to detailed reports for subscribing clients. Their Hype Cycles are widely quoted – charting the way that technologies can go through a cycle of possibly exaggerated claims and disillusion before (or if) they become embedded in routine practice. For an interesting discussion of the Hype Cycle and its application to MOOCs, see 'MOOCs and the Gartner Hype Cycle: A very slow tsunami', (2013)

- Numerous websites offer more speculative suggestions concerning the future. For example, the Future Tense blog recently included the argument by Dale Lately that 'The future of the Internet isn't Facebook. It's micronetworks'. (Lately, 2015)

Institutional strategy

A few years ago, a vice-principal at a large UK university proclaimed to one of us that his institution had 'got on top of e-learning'. Lowering his voice slightly (presumably, lest other people in the room latched on to his strategy), he revealed that his institution had invested in a major commercial VLE and that 'everyone is now on it'. Having sorted out his institutional strategy, he was moving on to other issues! (For a rather more sophisticated account of e-learning and strategy, see Sharpe et al. [2006] and Walker et al. [2011].)

Were we to repeat this conversation, we would point him to useful reports such as the one by Jones et al. (2013) on the potential of VLEs for advanced doctoral training. Noting the 'massive expansion' of VLEs and similar systems over the last two decades, they conclude that:

> ... online or 'virtual' provision provides enormous and valuable support for students in Higher Education at all levels from undergraduate teaching and learning to doctoral candidature. (ibid, page 34)

However, they also identify a number of critical challenges, including the 'danger of "McDonaldization of provision" which can arise from "one size fits all" models (which) tend towards the lowest common denominator'. (ibid, page 35) This example highlights the importance of a strategic approach to systems like the VLE. Academic developers need to be involved in this.

As an example of the tensions which might arise here, we can point to the contrast between initiatives like the work of Simon Thomson at Leeds Metropolitan University, providing both staff and students on a specific course with Google Nexus tablets and finding that this standardisation of technology delivered advantages to both groups, and initiatives which support the BYOD philosophy where the institution aims to support the student's own choice of technology.

The use of mobile devices in learning and teaching is another area where institutional strategy is important. For example, we await the outcomes of the initiative at an American college where all students are supplied with iPads which have their timetables preloaded and will flag up a message if the student is not in the right place at the right. The message goes to administrators and to parents (Welker, Urtnowski and Eng, 2015). Is this an example of helpful support, or a step too far in terms of intrusion and surveillance? This question also applies to some recent developments in learning analytics which we mention below.

Changes in our student populations

Increasingly affordable access to technology (and in turn to information), coupled with the increasing ubiquity of social networking, can be seen as disrupting the traditional nature of universities, as explored in Chapter 1. As technology and digital participation in its widest sense become more common-place, the technological and/or digital perceptions and abilities of our students and staff are also changing. At the turn of the twenty-first century the notion of digital natives and immigrants (Prensky, 2001) quickly gained traction, offering a logical or allegedly common-sense (Bennett et al., 2008) description of the technological skills and ability of the Internet generation. However, this model gained popularity, and almost universal acceptance, without significant evidence. As Bennett et al. (2008) said,

> The debate over digital natives is thus based on two key claims: (1) that a distinct generation of 'digital natives' exists; and (2) that education must fundamentally change to meet the needs of these 'digital natives'. These in turn are based on fundamental assumptions with weak empirical and theo-retical foundation.

The reality is far more nuanced. Whilst younger people may have a seemingly natural ability with technology, it is often at a functional level, often with particular kinds of functions and indeed particular kinds of devices. There are cognitive differences between individuals and tasks. In educational contexts there is still a need to ensure that students are constantly developing the digital capabilities needed for success in higher education and beyond.

The notion of digital visitors and residents (White and LeCornu, 2011) provides a more balanced approach and accompanying methodology to explore different modes of online engagement. Their distinction is based on the differ-ence between individuals who systematically integrate online activity into their daily routine – residents – and those who use online services on a more casual, irregular basis – visitors. This distinction focuses on online behaviour and makes no assumptions about age or social status. Someone who exhibits resident behav-iour tends to leave a digital social trace of their presence, whereas someone who is visiting leaves little or no easily discernable online trace or presence, although this distinction is probably fading year on year.

The visitor and resident mapping tool ('Visitors and Residents', 2014) is a simple matrix that can be used with learners and staff to help contextual-ise their professional and private online engagement. If undertaken regularly it provides an overview and insight into how and where online engagement is taking place. More importantly the workshop methodology surrounding the mapping exercise allows for meaningful discussion around a myriad of issues including confidence and privacy around online engagement for staff and students.

This is particularly useful in context of exploring and developing effective online collaborative spaces. For example, an HEA-funded study at Glasgow Caledonian University highlighted students' strategic use of online spaces for personal and professional use and common circumvention of professional network systems. There was an apparent correlation with more visitor-type behaviour to less interactive institutional spaces such as the VLE and the library. The study also concluded:

> With staff, we hope to use the trends and findings to help provide a focus on the design of learning activities. For example designing collaborative activities that allow collaboration to take place in a variety of places, but ensure that evidence of such activities is collated in a bounded, (at this point in time) institutionally provided space such as our VLE. We anecdotally know that some of our academic staff are at times uncomfortable using their personal (visitor and/or resident) places such as Facebook to interact in learning activities with students. We also know a key reason students feel comfortable and use these places is because staff are not there. (McElhinney and MacNeill, n.d.)

What do academic developers need to do?

They need to build their own and their team's expertise, use flexible conceptual frameworks, adopt an evidence-based approach to innovation, build collaborative networks across the organisation, and perhaps encourage innovative, even playful, approaches to using new technologies. This list of expectations may appear daunting. But the pressure can be alleviated by a team approach, where academic developers collaborate to cover the ground between them rather than expecting everyone to be expert in everything. Particular strategies which can be employed are as follows.

Role-modelling effective practice

Educational developers can harness current and emerging technologies in the academic staff development that they provide to the academic colleagues they support, encouraging both experimentation and critique. This book's final set of guidance to developers, in Chapter 18, incudes, 'Be exemplary'. A particularly important arena for this in the UK is the professional qualification in learning and teaching which is required of more and more university academics – in some universities, all. This is typically organised as a Postgraduate Certificate for new staff, or as an Accreditation of Prior (Experiential) Learning (AP(E)L) process for experienced staff, leading in either case to some grade of Fellowship of the Higher Education Academy. Applications of new technology within these courses and processes can function both as an exemplar (e.g. incorporating specific techniques such as a flipped classroom) and as a site for investigation and innovation (e.g. supporting academic staff to experiment with different techniques), perhaps evidenced through an eportfolio. Specific examples of which we have experience include the following.

Online options

As part of the revalidation of the Accelerate CPD framework at Glasgow Caledonian Univerity (Webteam@gcu, n.d.), a fully online option will be offered to staff members on distributed campuses. Many of the online activities will also be undertaken as part of the expansion of the current campus-based blended learning programme. It is hoped that this cascaded use of technology within a learning experience will impact on the use of technology within undergraduate/postgraduate teaching.

Incorporating the 3E Framework

One of the earliest implementations of the 3E Framework as a tool to support the effective embedding of technology in learning and teaching was as the curriculum design model for the MSc Blended and Online Education at Edinburgh Napier University. The MSc BOE is an online programme for academics and other education professionals. It aims to engage participants from the outset in developing their skill and expertise as online educators while modelling good practice along the way. This is partly achieved through the embedding of the 3E Framework within the design and delivery of the programme itself, particularly in relation to the first three modules that comprise the PgCert. These are designed to reflect each of the Enhance, Extend and Empower stages as illustrated in Figure 8.4.

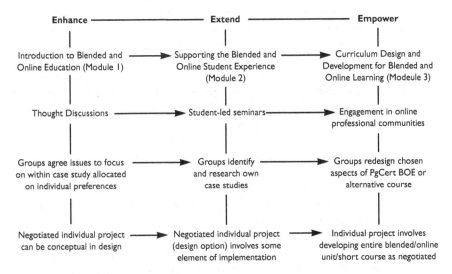

Figure 8.4 How the 3E Framework underpins the PgCert stage of the MSc BOE

In implementing the 3E Framework across the three core modules of the MSc BOE, the intention is build upon the well-established concept of scaffolding to move participants to a position of expertise in a structured but relatively rapid way, and to ensure that by the end of Module 3 PgCert completers and continuing participants will be equipped to sustain their own professional development. As Figure 8.4 indicates, this involves a move from tutor-led seminars in Module 1 to participant-led seminars in Module 2. These provide an opportunity to research a topic, and to develop skills in preparing and facilitating online discussions that can be taken back into the participants' own teaching practice. Similarly, in relation to individual work, in Module 1 participants undertake a project in designing for technology-enhanced learning that can be conceptual, but by Module 3 they move on to producing a blended or online course that is ready to go live. The 3E Framework-underpinned approach on the MSc BOE has proved successful to date, influencing the knowledge, skills and professional teaching practice of programme participants that is described more fully elsewhere (Smyth, 2009; 2013). What is important to the embedding of the 3E Framework across Edinburgh Napier, and in the institutions of other academics who take the programme, is that the participants on the MSc gain an in-depth experience and insight into the nature of the framework, and how activities informed by it can be implemented in their own practice. They also study the 3E Framework when exploring curriculum design models for blended and online courses in Module 3 of the programme.

Concept mapping to share and compare learner and tutor definitions of effective learning and teaching

David Hay and Ian Kinchin and colleagues at King's College, London, have used concept mapping extensively with staff and students as a way of eliciting and comparing understanding in a range of subject disciplines. (Hay and Kinchin, n.d.). This use has included work with university teachers on their conceptions of learning and teaching (Kinchin, 2012) and we have used a similar strategy with academic staff on a PGCert to compare perspectives and approaches. One advantage of this method is that maps are now very easy to prepare and share on computer, for example using CMap ('CmapTools', n.d.), The maps can be prepared either individually or collaboratively.

Another important area which lends itself to role-modelling is horizon scanning – reviewing developments in the use of technology in education which may have important implications for future practice. This can be achieved through collaboration. For example, as described earlier in this chapter, #BYOD4L exemplifies a crowd-sourced, bottom up collaborative, open, network-driven, learning experience. It is being sustained and developed through open, online collaboration. This allows it to be agile and adapt as community involvement ebbs and flows. It does not require funding for resources or platforms.

As increased use of digital technologies and social media impacts the core activities of teaching and research, the notion of digital scholarship (Weller, 2011) is gaining momentum to reflect how practice is increasingly networked, collaborative and open in nature. For example, self-publishing in particular via blogs is increasingly recognised as an effective way to promote research activities outwith traditional scholarly publishing routes. The LSE impact blog ('Maximising the impact of academic research', n.d.) has proved the impact of blogging and has evolved from being a research project to being an entity for sharing practice and ideas across a range of disciplines. Many educational developers and teams now share their practice via blogs.

This type of activity is increasingly being recognised as an important element of CPD. For example, one of the authors of this chapter, Sheila MacNeill, was awarded the ALT (Association for Learning Technology) Learning Technologist of the Year in 2013 for blogging activities (Smart, 2013). Reflecting on these developments, we also wonder if there is a new professional emerging – a hybrid of traditional academic developer/learning technologist. Are we seeing the emergence of the Digital Pedagogue? (e.g. Walker and MacNeill, 2015)

Building expertise

Repeated calls for progress have been made in enabling educators to use technology effectively by having them learn with technology in their own professions (Littlejohn, 2002; Oliver and Dempster, 2003; Mainka, 2007; Smyth, 2009). However, arguably it is only in very recent years that we have begun to see widespread developments in technology-supported, online forms of staff development for educators beyond technology-focused taught postgraduate programmes for academics. Some are described earlier in this chapter under 'Very Short Courses'. Academic developers need to expand on what they offer in this area, and also take further advantage of opportunities for professional development planning which encourages/enables engagement with new technology, e.g. use of eportfolios such as PebblePad or Mahara, whatever the university supports.

Evidence-based approaches

In an ideal world, all educational developers will be research-informed or research-active in the educational benefits and application of current and new technologies.

Educational developers should be instigating/supporting investigation and pilots of new technology, and we can identify useful recent examples such as the work on the flipped classroom by the University of Bath. (Martin, 2014).

Advising academic colleagues on how to evaluate and further develop the effectiveness of their own use of technology to support learning and teaching is an important development function. Some of the advice in Chapter 10 on evaluation may help.

Building collaboration

We need to build collaboration with other key groups in the organisation such as IT services, academic managers, and student support services. This includes engaging and working with learning technologists and building relationships with external agencies, e.g. in the UK, Jisc. Chapters 1 and 18 discuss this further.

Developing effective institutional strategies

As we have already indicated, an important role is shaping and implementing institutional learning and teaching strategy, including but not limited to e-learning strategy.

As an example of a recent development which we believe has the potential for significant impact and which has important strategic implications, we would cite the work on Students as Agents of Change, also highlighted in Chapter 14, such as the project of the same name at the University of Exeter, and the 'Student as Producer' initiative at the University of Lincoln. In the last couple of years, we have seen: the development of the Change Agents' Network for staff and students, and the associated SEDA qualification. Examples of involving students in investigation into the effective applications of technology for student learning include the Learning Futures development at the University of Westminster ('Learning Futures – University of Westminster', n.d.).

There is growing use of learning analytics ('NMC Horizon Report: 2013 Higher Education Edition', 2013, pp. 24–27; Sclater, 2014), using data generated through the use of VLEs and e-learning, to inform academic development for improved student learning. To use the Gartner Hype Cycle (op cit), learning analytics has been on the rise towards 'the peak of inflated expectations' over the past four years. A new research discipline is emerging, but it is still in its infancy. Data are only useful if you can do something with them. Data should provide 'actionable insights' (Cooper, 2012) that can be enacted, measured and shown to have impact on academic practice and student engagement and achievement. To do this takes time and skill. Educational developers should be at the heart of any work around learning data, to ensure that the data being collected do provide insights that can be translated into developing the curriculum to provide better meaningful engagement, feedback and learning.

Areas of challenge and opportunity for academic developers in relation to new technologies

Several issues remain unresolved and will influence educational practice at least over the next decade.

Social concerns about learning and the use of technology

As we were producing the final drafts of this chapter, a few studies received significant attention across print and broadcast media in the UK:

- 'Schools that ban mobile phones get better results' was the typical headline (Doward, 2015), reporting a study by Louis-Philippe Beland and Richard J. Murphy (Beland and Murphy, 2015), an earlier version of which you can find online (Beland and Murphy, 2013). Their data suggests that only a complete ban which is effectively enforced will have significant impact.

- 'Absent fathers and feminised schools are driving boys into a disconnected online world of porn and video games' was the subheading in *The Guardian's report* on 9 May 2015 (Jeffries, 2015), about Philip Zimbardo's new book (Zimbardo and Coulombe, 2015).
- 'Humans have shorter attention span than goldfish, thanks to smartphones' was the heading to the report by Leon Watson in *The Telegraph*, commenting on a study by Microsoft (Watson, 2015).

We do not have the space here to discuss these issues in detail. We include them to illustrate our argument that relationships between student learning and new technology are now areas of public concern. These concerns need to be recognised and dealt with by education at all levels. For example, the research on smartphones reported above does not offer much incentive to schools to consider the best ways of integrating mobile technology into the curriculum. If these and similar studies are widely publicised (and widely believed at face value), then we may have to work harder to deliver more balanced views of the advantages and limitations of new technologies.

Supporting new learners

What digital expectations and capabilities do new learners bring? What support do we offer to learners who are coming in to HE who need additional assistance in using, and learning to learn with, technology? As well as accounting for more fluent users of technology, we may also be making unwarranted assumptions about other students, in particular mature learners. Our impression is that many introductory IT courses for undergraduates have ceased, on the assumption that young people are now technologically fluent. But this may disguise some important problems. The variety of capability of students at entry may mean that individualised support is needed, matched to individual capabilities and needs.

Relationships between institutional and personal systems

Perhaps the most obvious example here is importance and impact of the virtual learning environment (VLE). On the one hand, the VLE is now regarded as an essential tool for student support. On the other hand, there are concerns that over-reliance on these institutional systems simply generates a more advanced form of student dependence. And what happens to them and their work when students leave and the VLE is no longer accessible? Have we prepared them sufficiently for independence in the digital and post-digital worlds?

Conclusion

Higher Education institutions must adopt a strategic and critical approach to the selection and use of broad classes of technologies to enhance learning, teaching and assessment, as well as other more general features of the student experience. Given the pace of development in new technology, the wrong kind of strategic approach could delay/discourage the very experimentation with new technologies which is a vital part of digital fluency. Strategy has to be agile and reflexive.

Educational developers can play an important role here by ensuring that they build their own and their team's expertise, use flexible conceptual frameworks, adopt an evidence-based approach to innovation, and build collaborative networks across the organisation. There are also some important and unresolved issues which educational developers need to monitor and engage with.

Acknowledgements

This chapter builds upon the work of many valued colleagues. We particularly wish to thank Chrissi Nerantzi and Sue Beckingham for their contributions to our development.

We also wish to thank the participants in the first workshop based on this chapter at the 2015 Solstice Conference at Edge Hill University for their comments and challenges.

References

3E Framework. (2012). Retrieved 18 May 2015 from http://3eeducation .org/?s=3e+framework.
Beetham, H. and Sharpe, R. (2013). *Rethinking Pedagogy for a Digital Age: Designing for 21st Century Learning* (2nd ed.). Routledge.
Beland, L. -P. and Murphy, R. (2015, May 12). 'How smart is it to allow students to use mobile phones at school?' Retrieved 26 June 2015 from http://theconversation .com/how-smart-is-it-to-allow-students-to-use-mobile-phones-at-school-40621.
Bennett, S. J., Maton, K. A. and Kervin, L. K. (2008). 'The "digital natives" debate: a critical review of the evidence', *British Journal of Educational Technology*, 39(5): 775–786.
'Building digital capability'. (26 June 2015). Retrieved 26 June 2015 from www.jisc .ac.uk/rd/projects/building-digital-capability.
Cooper, A. (2012, November 1). 'CETIS Analytics Series: What is Analytics? Definition and Essential Characteristics | cetis publications'. Retrieved 25 June 2015 from http://publications.cetis.org.uk/2012/521
CmapTools (n.d.). Retrieved 25 June 2015 from http://cmap.ihmc.us/.
Cronin, C. (24 July 2014). 'A conversation about third space, third place, and liminality'. Retrieved 25 June 2015, from https://catherinecronin.wordpress .com/2014/07/24/conversation/.
'Developing students' digital literacy'. (4 April 2014). Retrieved 25 June 2015 from www.jisc.ac.uk/guides/developing-students-digital-literacy.
DFWG (2014). *Digital Futures Working Group Recommendations*. Retrieved from http://staff.napier.ac.uk/services/vice-principal-academic/academic/ strategyactivity/DigitalFutures/Documents/Paper%20ENU-DFWG-25%20 Recommendations%20Final.pdf.
Digital Capabilities Survey Executive Summary (2015). Retrieved 25 June 2015 from https://www.jisc.ac.uk/blog/thriving-in-a-connected-age-digital-capability- and-digital-wellbeing-25-jun-2015.

Doward, J. (2015, May 16). 'Schools that ban mobile phones see better academic results'. *The Guardian*. The Guardian. Retrieved 25 June 2015 from http://www.theguardian.com/education/2015/may/16/schools-mobile-phones-academic-results.

Gutierrez, K.D. (2008). 'Developing a sociocritical literacy in the third space'. *Reading Research Quarterly*, 43(2): 148–164.

Hay, D., and Kinchin, I. (n.d.). King's College London – 'Visualising the student learning experience'. Retrieved 25 June 2015 from www.kcl.ac.uk/study/learningteaching/kli/research/projects/visual-learning-experience.aspx.

Jeffries, S. (9 May 2015). 'Psychologist Philip Zimbardo: "boys risk becoming addicted to porn, video games and Ritalin"'. *The Guardian*. Retrieved from www.theguardian.com/lifeandstyle/2015/may/09/philip-zimbardo-boys-are-a-mess.

Johnson, M. and Smyth, K. (2011). 'Diversity, value and technology: exposing value pluralism in institutional strategy'. *Campus-Wide Information Systems*, Special Issue on Learning Technology and Institutional Strategy, 28(4): 211–220.

Jones, C., Pryke, M. and Jones, R. (2013). The Potential of Virtual Learning and Virtual Learning Environments for Advanced Doctoral Training in the UK.

Kinchin, I.M. (2012). 'Visualising knowledge structures of university teaching to relate pedagogic theory and academic practice'. In J. Groccia, M. Alsudairi and W. Buskist (Eds.), *Handbook of College and University Teaching: A Global Perspective*. Thousand Oaks, CA: Sage. pp. 314–332.

Lately, D. (2015). 'The rise of the digital walled garden'. Retrieved 26 June 2015 from www.slate.com/authors.dale_lately.html.

Laurillard, D. (2012). *Teaching as a Design Science: Building Pedagogical Patterns for Learning and Technology*. Routledge.

Learning Futures – University of Westminster. (n.d.). Retrieved 25 June 2015 from www.westminster.ac.uk/study/current-students/student-news/student-news/2014/learning-futures.

Littlejohn, A. (2002). 'Improving continuing professional development in the use of ICT', *Journal of Computer Assisted Learning*, 18(2): 166–174.

MacNeill, S. (2012). 'A conversation around what it means to be a digital university', Sheila MacNeill. Retrieved 22 June 2015, from http://blogs.cetis.org.uk/sheilamacneill/2012/02/10/a-conversation-around-the-digital-university-part-2/.

Manchester Metropolitan University | BYOD4L on WordPress.com. (2014, May 9). Retrieved 12 June 2015 from https://byod4learning.wordpress.com/collaborators/manchester-metropolitan-university/.

Mainka, C. (2007). 'Putting staff first in staff development for the effective use of technology in teaching', *British Journal of Educational Technology*, 38(1): 158–160.

Martin, G. (2014). 'Flipping Technology'. In *Opportunities and challenges for academic development in a post-digital age*. Nottingham, UK: SEDA. Retrieved 24 June 2015 from www.seda.ac.uk/resources/files/18_Martin.pdf.

'Maximising the impact of academic research'. (n.d.). Retrieved 25 June 2015 from http://blogs.lse.ac.uk/impactofsocialsciences/.

McElhinney, E., and MacNeill, S. (n.d.). V&R case study. Retrieved 25 June 2015 from https://docs.google.com/document/d/1TzFR6GOSTKW5rUkP8Az45 8LsF00s6beWExzYwfCk0sg/edit?pli=1.

Memarovic, N. (2014, November 17). 'Rethinking Third Places: Contemporary Design With Technology'. Retrieved 26 June 2015 from http://ci-journal.net/index.php/ciej/article/view/1048/1116.

'MOOCs and the Gartner Hype Cycle: A very slow tsunami'. (13 September 2013). Retrieved 25 June 2015 from https://pando.com/2013/09/13/moocs-and-the-gartner-hype-cycle-a-very-slow-tsunami/.

Nerantzi, C. and Beckingham, S. (2014). 'BYOD4L – Our magical open box to enhance individuals' learning ecologies'. In Jackson, N. and Willis, J. (Eds.) *Lifewide Learning and Education in Universities and Colleges.* Lifewide Education. E-book available online: www.learninglives.co.uk/e-book.html.

NMC Horizon Report: 2015 Higher Education Edition. (2015). Retrieved 25 June 2015 from https://net.educause.edu/ir/library/pdf/HR2015.pdf.

Noble, T., and Pym, B. (1970). 'Collegial authority and the receding locus of power', *The British Journal of Sociology*, 21(4): 431–445.

Oldenburg, R. (1991). *The Great Good Place: Cafes, Coffee Shops, Community Centers, Beauty Parlors, General Stores, Bars, Hangouts and How They Get You Through the Day.* Marlowe & Co.

Oliver, M., and Dempster, A.D. (2003) 'Embedding e-learning practices'. In R. Blackwell & P. Blackmore (Eds.), *Towards Strategic Staff Development in Higher Education.* Maidenhead, UK: SRHE and Open University Press. pp. 142–153.

Prensky, M. (2001). 'Digital Natives, Digital Immigrants'. Retrieved from www .emeraldinsight.com/doi/abs/10.1108/10748120110424816.

'Preparing for the postdigital era'. (2009). Retrieved 27 May 2015 from https:// docs.google.com/document/d/1TkCUCisefPgrcG317_hZa4PwZoQ8m7- rL5AJF6PazHHQ/preview.

Rowell, C. (forthcoming). 'Reflections on the 12 Apps of Christmas at Regent's University London', *Educational Developments* 16.3, SEDA.

Sclater, N. (2014). 'Learning analytics: the current state of play in UK higher and further education'. Jisc. Retrieved from http://repository.jisc.ac.uk/5657/1/ Learning_analytics_report.pdf.

Sharpe, R., Benfield, G. and Francis, R. (2006). 'Implementing a university e-learning strategy: levers for change within academic schools', *Research in Learning Technology*, 14(2): 135–151.

Smart, C. (12 September 2013). 'Sheila MacNeill is awarded ALT Learning Technologist of the Year 2013 – Cetis – expert advice on educational technology and standards'. Retrieved 25 June 2015 from www.cetis.org.uk/sheila-macneill- is-awarded-alt-learning-technologist-of-the-year-2013/.

Smyth, K., Comrie, A., Gray, M. and Mayes, T. (2010). 'Embedding and sustaining change in technology-enhanced education: lessons learned from a cross-institutional transformation project'. Invited paper for *Education in the North*, Issue 18. Available online at www.abdn.ac.uk/eitn/display .php?article_id=65.

Smyth, K., Bruce, S., Fotheringham, J. and Mainka, C. (2011). 'Benchmark for the use of technology in modules'. Edinburgh Napier University. Available online at http://staff.napier.ac.uk/services/vice-principal-academic/academic/TEL/ TechBenchmark/Documents/3E%20Framework.pdf

Smyth, K., Bruce, S., Fotheringham, J. and Mainka, C. (n.d.). 'University benchmark for the use of technology in modules'. (n.d.). Retrieved 24 June 2015 from http://staff .napier.ac.uk/services/vice-principal-academic/academic/TEL/TechBenchmark/ Pages/home.aspx.

Smyth, K. (2013) 'Sharing and shaping effective institutional practice in TEL through the 3E Framework'. In S. Greener (Ed.), *Case Studies in e-learning*. Reading, UK: Academic Publishing International. pp. 141–159.

TESEP (n.d.) Accessed 28 October 2015 from http://www.webarchive.org.uk/ wayback/archive/20140614153959/http://www.jisc.ac.uk/media/ documents/programmes/elearningsfc/sfcbooklettesep.pdf.

'Visitors and Residents'. (2014). Retrieved 25 June 2015 from www.jiscinfonet .ac.uk/infokits/evaluating-services/visitors-residents/.

Walker, D., Sloan, D., Boyle, L. and Walsh, L. (2011). 'Informing TEL strategy through formal and informal channels: a case study', *Campus Wide Information Systems*, 28(4): 289–293.

Walker, D. and MacNeill, S. (2015). 'Learning technologist as digital pedagogue'. In D. Hopkins (Ed.), *The Really Useful #EdTech Book*. David Hopkins. pp. 91–105.

Watson, L. (15 May 2015). Humans have shorter attention span than goldfish, thanks to smartphones. *The Telegraph*. Telegraph.co.uk. Retrieved from www.telegraph.co.uk/news/science/science-news/11607315/Humans-have-shorter-attention-span-than-goldfish-thanks-to-smartphones.html.

Webteam@gcu. (n.d.). Accelerate/CPD | GCU LEAD | Glasgow Caledonian University | Scotland, UK. Retrieved 25 June 2015 from www.gcu.ac.uk/lead/leadthemes/acceleratecpd/.

Welker, K., Urtnowski, S., and Eng, J. (7 February 2015). 'Taking attendance: Class120 app alerts parents when students skip class'. Retrieved 26 June 2015 from www.nbcnews.com/nightly-news/taking-attendance-class120-app-alerts-parents-when-students-skip-class-n301951.

Weller, M., (2011). *The Digital Scholar How Technology is Transforming Scholarly Practice*. Bloomsbury Open Publishing.

White, D. S. and LeCornu, A. L. (23 August 2011). 'Visitors and residents: a new typology for online engagement'. Retrieved 25 June 2015 from http://firstmonday.org/ojs/index.php/fm/article/view/3171/3049.

Zimbardo, P. and Coulombe, N. D. (2015). *Man Disconnected: How Technology Has Sabotaged What It Means to be Male*. Rider. See also Jeffries (2015).

Chapter 9

Quality assurance and quality enhancement

Rowena Pelik

Summary

This chapter explores what characterises approaches to quality assurance and quality enhancement by external quality agencies, looking at definitions and at practices associated with each. It explores why Quality Assurance and Quality Enhancement are often seen in oppositional terms, both philosophically and in the associated practices.

It discusses how QE, with its stronger future and improvement focus, can provide a positive context for academic developers to encourage engagement with student learning and pedagogic practices. It explores the productive alignment of assurance with enhancement in mature quality systems in the creation of internal quality cultures centred on learning, development and enhancement.

Links to web sources referenced in this chapter can be found at www.seda .ac.uk/apad.

Introduction

This chapter explores approaches to quality and the external quality assurance of learning and teaching in university sector institutions (i.e. national approaches to whole-institution review). It examines how the premise behind the approach to quality assurance can impact on the development of internal quality cultures and help create, limit or deny space for academic developers. The enhancement-led approach in Scotland is used as a running case study throughout.

Characteristics and definitions explores what characterises quality assurance and quality enhancement, examines some definitions and associated practices, and outlines a general shift towards enhancement.

Quality enhancement in Scotland describes, and draws lessons for developers from, a well established and mature enhancement-led approach based on an integrated Quality Enhancement Framework.

A further look at definitions and approaches analyses in more detail the complex relationships between enhancement and assurance, and suggests the conditions necessary for an enhancement-led approach to thrive.

Roles and opportunities for academic development as part of quality emphasises the importance of a clear goal for enhancement – in the case of Scotland, this goal is improvement in the effectiveness of the learning experiences of students. It also, among other issues, describes the importance of student engagement in QA and QE and the key role of academic developers as agents of change.

Finally, *continuing challenges* acknowledges tensions around both institutions' and individuals' approaches to quality and confirms the essential role of developers in helping to develop a culture of quality.

Characteristics and definitions

Over the last decade, quality assurance across Europe has moved towards more enhancement-oriented approaches (Kastelliz et al., 2014). This reflects factors including the growing maturity of institutions in their internal quality assurance and, following one or more initial cycles of external review, greater trust in both institutions and external quality processes.

Quality enhancement was hardly part of the language of quality in the early 1990s (e.g. Green, 1994, Ellis, 1993). Quality was then, and has remained, a contested territory. The last two decades have seen the birth or growth of national quality assurance agencies and quality assessment regimes. Some are enshrined in legislation, others are a requirement of funding, some involve accreditation or formal recognition. Some national approaches focus on programme accreditation, and may or may not also include whole-institution review. Some draw heavily on data and survey information, others on notions of risk; and some are enhancement-led. Kastelliz et al. (2014) outlines the current range within Europe and Griffiths (2014) their evolution in England. Some approaches are self-referential, assessing universities again their own mission and objectives; others have external frameworks or criteria. Some national approaches have enabled ranking, while others have been deliberately designed to avoid comparisons.

Quality is not only about assurance or enhancement; it also involves systems, management and culture. The European University Association (EUA) define a quality culture as combining 'shared values, beliefs, expectations and commitments towards quality' and 'a structural/managerial element with defined processes that enhance quality and aim at coordinating efforts' (Sursock, 2011, p. 9, quoting EUA, 2006). *Quality assurance* is the generic term, but it has frequently come to be used pejoratively, gathering a burden of negative association, perhaps from associations with quality control, a concept seen as at odds with the values of a university. Quality Assurance has been associated with inspection, regulation, bureaucracy, tick-box exercise, performance measurement, managerialism; with a process done to rather than done with. The language of quality assurance is value-laden, although the values will vary according to context. Some quality assurance agencies and national systems, for example, use the term *quality audit*, and see this positively, whereas in the UK *audit* has gathered negative connotations and has been replaced by *review*. Quality enhancement, in contrast, is widely associated with a focus on improvement, on the future, on the effectiveness of practice, although there is not universal support or enthusiasm for quality enhancement, which some see as lacking the rigor of audit.

To explore what the contested minefield of quality means for academic developers, the characterisation of quality into the two broad areas, of quality assurance (QA) and quality enhancement (QE), is necessary.

When both internal and external quality systems are enhancement-led, both are working towards excellence and to ensuring the best student learning experience, perhaps even the best student learning – more on this in Chapter 10 on outcomes and evaluation. The goal is excellence within available resources. External quality enhancement works with an institution's mission, goals and values. Internal quality enhancement is marked by initiatives to improve educational quality at all levels, from the strategic to the individual, and will enable both the achievement of larger strategic goals and the setting and meeting of more local priorities, for example being responsive to discipline variations.

The powerful forces of league tables, ranking, national statistics and published survey outcomes have further complicated the territory of quality. Metrics are attractive to government, funding bodies and university management. The National Student Survey in the UK has had a powerful impact on what university managers have prioritised. Authors including Graham Gibbs argue persuasively for a more considered use of metrics and indicators – those that impact upon learning gain and encourage effective academic practices (Gibbs 2010 and 2012). Performance indicators can support improvement, but can also be a distraction when the target or the ranking becomes the focus, rather than the quality of the student learning experience and student learning.

Both internal and external quality systems necessarily involve an element of reporting and judgement; exposing and, for external review, putting on public record how well the programme/department/institution is doing. Thus quality is rarely greeted with unqualified enthusiasm, and is often resisted. Demands for accountability for public funding, or assurance for fee-paying students, and the confirmation for stakeholders of the validity of qualifications, make it unlikely that there will cease to be a requirement for external quality assurance process, even in the most mature and high-trust national systems. There will likely be continued resistance to the concept and/or the implementation of quality, even as the language keeps moving on, seeking to retain focus on the purpose, not the mechanisms, of quality.

Where approaches to quality shift from checking past performance towards a focus on the future and improvement, they provide greater opportunities for academic developers to engage with student learning and pedagogic practices.

Quality enhancement in Scotland

Quality enhancement in Scotland represents a well-established and mature enhancement-led approach. The approach to quality in Scotland was designed as an integrated Quality Enhancement Framework (QEF). The QEF was developed in partnership by the key players – funding body, quality assurance agency, the university sector and students' representative body. Introduced in 2003, it is in its third cycle. It has retained strong support, partly because the approach demonstrably works (Scottish Funding Council, 2010, and Dempster et al., 2014) and also because it lives by its own values:

- Self-evaluation,
- Evidence-based external evaluation and review,
- Collaborative practices and partnership,
- Reflection,
- Maturity,
- Transparency,
- Openness and
- Trust.

Scotland's integrated framework has five elements:

1 Enhancement-Led Institutional Review (ELIR),
2 Institution-led quality review,
3 Public information,
4 Student engagement in quality, and
5 The programme of national Enhancement Themes ('Enhancement Themes', n.d.).

Consensus around the QEF was achieved because there was already a climate of trust, and because the key agencies involved in its creation worked in partnership with a common aim toward common values. The QEF was jointly developed and agreed in 2003 by the Scottish Funding Council, the funding body; Universities Scotland, the representative body of the universities; QAA Scotland, the quality assurance agency; and National Union of Students Scotland, the students' representative body. Different areas of responsibility were clear and the interrelationship between them well understood, including the assumption that enhancement includes assurance. The QEF embraces internal responsibilities, external elements and collaborative aspects, with accountability and public reporting.

The QEF was designed, and ELIR developed, to move beyond confirming that threshold standards and expectations are being met, and to ask institutions *how* they are working strategically to enhance the quality of their students' learning experiences, *how* they are engaging and working with their students to improve learning. From its inception in 2003, ELIR included student reviewers as full and equal members of review teams. This helped, alongside other initiatives arising from the creation of the QEF such as Student Participation in Quality Scotland (sparqs), to produce a step change in student participation and engagement in internal and external approaches to quality assurance – and to make manifest that a primary focus of quality activity is students and their learning.

Self-evaluation exemplifies how the whole system reflects its basic tenets. Self-evaluation is expected, in the review of internal academic units and services by institutions and of institutions by QAA Scotland as part of ELIR. The QEF has been subject to independent evaluation. Before each new cycle, QAA Scotland and the partners to the QEF reflect critically on ELIR as it is revised and enhanced before the next cycle. Also QAA Scotland has commissioned research to explore institutions approaches to self-evaluation to support continuing development (Maher, 2013a and b). In an enhancement culture, the job is never done.

What has the Quality Enhancement Framework meant for academic practice and for those seeking to support academic development? The QEF, with its stress on students and their learning, has helped Scotland move quickly and fundamentally towards student-centred approaches to learning (Mayes, 2014).

Elements of the QEF play complementary roles:

- The Enhancement Themes have had an impact, through the work conducted as part of each theme and by foregrounding the importance of learning and teaching. The themes have supported change and provided space for collective development and interchange.
- ELIR is used variously within institutions to support and encourage change, and to describe an institution's strategic approach and its priorities for enhancement, for supporting and developing staff and for disseminating effective practice. Institutions reflect on the effectiveness of their approaches to identifying and sharing good practice, to engaging and supporting staff and the effectiveness of the approach to promoting good practice in learning and teaching (QAA Scotland, 2012).
- Institution-led quality review has created space for reflection and action at a subject or departmental level.

In broad terms, our enhancement-led approach encourages engagement with teaching and learning and provides a stage for conversations about learning. In doing so, it provides fertile opportunity for academic developers.

Informal conversations with vice principals and heads of academic development units in the autumn of 2014 revealed how the enhancement-led approach has helped to engender a positive engagement with teaching. One said that the focus on enhancement encourages colleagues to truly reflect on the effectiveness of the learning experience, and to innovate to improve things further, to encourage colleagues to be outward looking, to require external engagement, to identify and engage with best practice. Another described how the culture of enhancement had enabled his institution to develop reflective practitioners who are individually and collectively evaluating practice to enhance the learner experience.

A number emphasised the contrast with cultures of audit, which were seen as a restraint, as inward looking, as about compliance. They saw enhancement as forward looking, helping to make quality activities meaningful, more about practice than process. Broadly, this has created a culture favourable to academic developers. One leader of an academic practice unit emphasised how the enhancement-led approach was more likely to get buy-in from practitioners. She referred to the 'massive power of a sector working collectively to improve student learning' (personal correspondence, 2014). The QEF has given concern with learning and teaching a validity beyond educational developers.

Academic developers can work with academic staff to stress the academic relevance of quality-related activity. In Scotland, the QAA Enhancement Themes make this a more readily available option. The themes relate directly to student learning and academic challenges. The themes lend themselves to productive working between academic development units and academic staff – as members of institutional teams and as part of a collective endeavour that, as national themes, goes beyond individual institutions. In theme-related work there is the opportunity to explore questions with colleagues across the university sector in Scotland. The Enhancement Themes enable a deeper and fuller exploration of a territory than any one institution could have achieved alone. Sceptics may argue that much of this activity would have happened anyway. Nonetheless, the involvement of QAA Scotland, and hence the connection with external review and with national collaborative activity, adds an element of public accountability. This encourages engagement and the desire to evidence impact, and thus provides opportunities for academic developers.

The 2014–17 Enhancement Theme, *Student Transitions*, is particularly well suited to active and deep involvement by students. All students will face a series of transitions as part of their studies. All university teachers must support students through these transitions. The universality of the challenges inherent in this theme provides opportunities for academic developers within institutions and working collaboratively between institutions.

The approach to quality enhancement in Scotland has continued to evolve. This evolution has hopefully enabled academic developers to encourage and enable the journey from teacher-centred to learner-centred approaches. In Scotland, the purpose of effective quality assurance in universities is to help create a climate in which students can learn effectively and achieve their potential, to help make good teaching better, and to help ensure a focus on student learning and achievement. Good quality assurance should add value, and result in the enhancement of quality (the student learning experience). This notion of quality does not set QA against QE; they are part of the same intent.

A further look at definitions and approaches

However, this integrated account of quality does not lie at the centre of all approaches to quality assurance. The approach to quality in some national systems examines the functioning of the quality system itself, not whether the results of the system lead to beneficial change in teaching and learning. In offering recommendations, identifying strengths and areas of good practice, it encourages improvements to the quality system. This is sometimes described as enhancement-led. But this approach to quality is primarily about process, not about practice. It does not give a natural space to academic developers. It does serve to illustrate, however, that the debate is not so much about QA or QE, but about the purpose of the approach to quality. Systems approaches can be favoured because they are providing conclusions, not about academic quality and academic standards, but about quality systems. Similarly, some institutions' and agencies' approaches to quality are self-referential. They test an institution against its own aims and objectives and in light of its own mission. They ask how it is doing in its own terms. Such approaches can be primarily about improvement and enhancement. They can be favoured where there is either strong resistance to comparability or no common ground or framework for comparison.

A functioning system is essential if quality improvement is to be sustained. Any system will tend to break down and cease to be effective if the elements do not work together, or if some elements are demonised – for example performance indicators, assurance processes, or auditors. Again the issue is not QA v. QE, but rather the effectiveness and fit of the quality system, how it is perceived, how it works, how it is used, and for what purposes.

Fully functioning quality systems have effective follow-up for the action planning which results, and feedback systems to those who have contributed. In an enhancement system, quality is an inclusive process – many of the players will see the outcome of their contribution as part of the process. Enhancement-oriented approaches to quality include evaluation and feedback loops. This enables participants to see the benefits of their engagement. Feedback is not a bolt-on. Many institutions have good quality processes, but do not yet have fully functioning quality systems.

So, QA and QE are not wholly separate worlds; all QE must include assurance, and, once you get beyond the basics, QA processes should lead forward to QE actions. Why then are they often seen as poles apart? Often, it is not the approaches that are poles apart, but rather how they are characterised (or perhaps caricatured?), or simply how they are experienced, by some of the players. QA can be seen as an audit approach, about ticking the box; about compliance, checking and inspection; an imposed and burdensome bureaucracy; a distraction from the real business of research and teaching. QE can be seen as lacking rigour and hard quantifiable outcomes.

Any approach to quality assurance that is overly managerial, removed from disciplinary norms, primarily process-oriented, about paper more than practice, rigid and inflexible, is likely to be less effective in enhancing the quality of educational practice or of the student learning experience within higher education. In the UK at least, QA and audit have come to be associated largely with this negative set of meanings. QA and QE may be handy labels, but they do not say very much about the quality that is being assured or enhanced.

Quality enhancement is a demanding approach. It has operated best to date in mature, high-trust sectors. It does not lend itself to more market/consumer-oriented, competitive systems where its values of sharing, openness, self-evaluation and improvement can be threatened by competition and by compliance and complaint cultures. It pre-supposes a level of maturity that would be more challenging for those newly establishing quality cultures or new to the delivery of degree education.

Roles and opportunities for academic development as part of quality

Accepting that the university sector will be subject to external quality assurance and will operate internal quality process – what are the choices and what are the implications for academic developers? The overall purpose of QA is to check; the purpose of QE is to improve. A mature quality culture uses information and processes to evaluate, reflect and improve. Academic developers may train and explain, but the joy of academic development is to know that, through constructive challenge, you have helped to enable *beneficial* change, helped colleagues to create more effective learning opportunities and deepened their engagement with academic practice. Constructive challenge works best where it is possible to take risks, such as in a QE environment.

What implications does an enhancement-led approach to quality have for academic developers?

Enhancement in Scotland is based on the premise that you can always improve. This denies complacency. It is a demanding premise – you can, indeed should, always do more. Processes must not become routine, but must stimulate new approaches to evaluation and to practice. Such enhancement is flexible and responsive. It involves a commitment to a *way of working*, to questioning and to change. A culture that accepts this drive to improve, and the questioning challenge which goes with it, offers ideal opportunities for academic developers to work with academic staff to develop academic practice.

The approach to enhancement in Scotland is far more than simple continuous improvement (potentially indiscriminate and uncritical). Enhancement has to have purpose. The ELIR Handbook states:

> The Scottish sector has defined enhancement as **taking deliberate steps to bring about improvement in the effectiveness of the learning experiences of students.** (bold in original)

The handbook goes on to say that enhancement-led institutional review 'has a focus on the institution's strategic approach to enhancement, which will be implemented at multiple levels within the institution'. It explains that, 'in order to take deliberate steps, it is expected that the institution will have a clear strategic vision of the enhancement it is seeking to bring about' (QAA Scotland, 2012, p. 3). In summary: vision + purpose + process.

Critical and open self-evaluation is vital. Good internal quality systems should encourage and enable this at individual, programme, departmental and institutional levels, ensuring that each contributes and adds value and richness, building up and completing a picture. Good self-evaluation requires trust, openness and honesty. It is not easy.

Enhancement-based approaches will have self-evaluation at their core; critical, honest, and as the starting point for a dialogue. The importance and centrality of self-evaluation is indicated in the ELIR Handbook:

> The approach the institution takes to self-evaluation will form a significant focus in ELIR. This is because considerable confidence can be derived from an institution that has systematic arrangements in place for evaluating its strengths and identifying and addressing potential risks to quality and academic standards. In an enhancement-led approach institutions also identify ways in which the student learning experience could be improved, whether or not threshold quality is at risk. (QAA Scotland, 2012, p. 3)

Being outward-looking and actively seeking to learn from the practice of others is a third key characteristic of the approach in Scotland. This is in part about scholarship and evidence-based practice; in part about being willing to share your own practice and to learn from the practice of others – and be active in doing both – and in part about exploring comparative practice. A number of aspects are deliberately run together here (learning from the practice of others + dissemination and sharing + collegiate or collaborative practice), as it is the linkage between them all which most characterises enhancement-oriented practice in Scotland. This grouping needs to be evident at all levels – from the individual academic to the external quality assurance agency itself. Collaboration and connectivity across the sector in Scotland is a strong and distinctive element of national practice – a whole sector working together to improve student learning. Institutions make reference to the value of inter-institutional dialogue and to sharing practice and challenges.

The final characteristic to emphasise is student involvement and engagement. Students and their learning are at the heart of what we are all seeking to achieve. This brings the other strands together. It is the quality of the student learning experience that we are seeking to enhance – any enhancement-oriented culture will seek to achieve this by involving and engaging students. Institutions will seek to engage students as active participants in their learning, in the development of the curriculum and of learning and teaching approaches and as parties to decision-making at all levels. Students need to be partners in quality enhancement, in helping to identify the areas in which change is needed, if learning is to be better supported or more effective, and in helping identify and articulate what is important for learners. Students should be able to suggest change, help agree priorities, and suggest how change can best be achieved. In Scottish universities, students frequently work with staff on enhancement projects, or themselves lead projects and initiatives. Students' active involvement helps to emphasise their own prime responsibility for their own learning, and confirms how awareness of learning (their own and others) will help them within their immediate studies and throughout their careers. In Scotland we believe that you cannot design an outstanding educational experience without strong student engagement. Academic developers have played core roles in helping develop effective way to achieve the deep involvement of students and making empowering students less scary.

Academic developers will typically reflect the shared values of an institution and be part of the efforts to coordinate quality enhancement activity. Whether they operate in an assurance- or an enhancement-oriented way will, obviously, depend on factors including the value system of an institution, the nature of any external quality system, the leadership above or within an academic development unit, and the culture and belief systems of those they are seeking to influence.

Academic developers may be placed in, or chose to take, more assurance-oriented roles. These are often easier to operate and to manage. Assurance and compliance tasks may arise from an enhancement initiative by being taken forward in a directive way, for example, by making an activity or a requirement mandatory and ticking the box. This is not necessarily a flawed approach so long as means and ends are not confused. For example: if the problem is *consistency* in research supervision, then the answer may be mandatory supervisor training; but if the problem is the *effectiveness* of research supervision, then mandatory training will only be one element. The quality enhancement option is the bigger challenge: it involves hearts and minds, it implies resisting those who want to reduce things to the measurable, it means accepting that the essential goal is never fully achieved (you can always improve). With something as complex as learning as part of degree education in universities, improvement is always possible. Too much is changing all the time for academic quality to stand still. Quality Enhancement is about the effectiveness and impact of activity.

Academic developers can find themselves in an uncomfortable space between the mechanistic and the developmental approaches to quality. They can find their developmental role being used as a tool of managerial change. Academic developers may be judged, for instance, by numbers of staff attending professional development events or trained in a particular piece of educational technology; these can be measured. Effectiveness is harder to measure. (This is considered in Chapter 10 on outcomes and evaluation.) A developmental intervention is likely to have diffused as well as direct influence. The extent to which changes improve the learning experience of students may or may not be readily measurable. Learning by staff is as multidimensional as learning by students – we can occasionally correlate factors, but only rarely point to undeniable causal relationships. It can be tempting to make use of external drivers to get buy-in or to require mandatory involvement – including (mis)using enhancement-led approaches to review. But, despite these difficulties, academic developers can play a useful part in helping to identify evidence of the effectiveness of teaching innovations.

Staff development is important for achievement and success in both QA and QE regimes and approaches. A performance-driven QA culture will likely encourage continuous improvement and responsive change, and thus will likely provide opportunities for academic development, but may be built more on competition, even fear of failure, than on the reflective professionalism encouraged in QE. Marketisation and competition for students are more likely to produce a focus on quantifiable measures (contact hours, employment rates, etc.) than some of the less easily measured aspects of learning. An enhancement-led culture may make use of metrics and indicators, but it is not readily defined nor driven by mechanistic approaches. Change is observable and can be evidenced but not easily measured – the aim, above all, is to benefit students and their learning. The quality of the learning experienced by students may be reflected in numbers (those successfully progressing or completing, or in 'satisfaction' scores), but it is best motivated by a focus on good learning, for *these* students in *this* discipline, in *this* institution.

Where else do quality systems create the space for academic developers? Academic developers can help move a quality culture from assurance to enhancement. Self-evaluation provides opportunities for academic developers to work with colleagues to develop capacity for the self-evaluation of teaching, as well as on the areas identified for improvement resulting from self-evaluation. They can encourage colleagues to move from the individual: 'How can I evaluate my teaching?': to the programme: 'How can *we* evaluate how our teaching is working *together* to provide an effective overall learning experience for the students we have?' This will include asking: 'How does the information and feedback we have help us to improve learning? Do we need different information or to ask different questions of our learners? How can we involve students in critical reflection on learning in ways that is helpful, not only for future delivery but also for their present learning?' These are forward-looking, improvement-oriented questions. Academic staff can and will ask these kinds of questions of themselves. The involvement of academic developers brings both the challenge provided by a critical friend outwith the teaching team and the opportunity to bring alternative perspectives to the discussion. The involvement of academic developers thus supports and enables the sharing of effective practice and productive internal conversations between disciplines.

The relationship between development and departmental staff is more likely to be productive and fruitful if academic developers have become a part of routine monitoring and review processes, and part of a day-to-day culture of reflective practice, openness to new ideas and desire to improve. Whether they have been allowed into the space is not dependant on the dominant model of quality, even if it is more likely in a QE model. It is most likely in a quality culture which is strongly committed to enhancement/improvement, and believes that commitment can result from a performance-driven QA model, from good academic leadership or from being enhancement-led.

The principal challenge is not the quality system, it is finding how improving approaches to teaching, learning and assessment can be made welcome rather than threatening to individual academics/programme teams/departments. The suggestion of a need to improve or change can be seen to imply that what you currently do isn't good enough. This prompts resistance and challenge. Enhancement accepts that there will at times be issues and weaknesses, and that these must be addressed, but accepts that, for most, change and innovation are about becoming or remaining excellent. A recent small survey (Cannell and Gilmour, 2013) revealed that staff can find it easier to identify training needs (e.g. how to use a piece of educational technology) than to voice development needs around pedagogy (e.g. the pedagogical implications and possibilities of educational technologies to enhance student learning, or what notions of the 'flipped classroom' really mean for my practice). It is OK to be unsure how to use text wall technology, but not OK to be unsure how to use it pedagogically. The embedded and early involvement of academic development would surely mean that fewer staff would develop anxieties about pedagogic approaches.

Quality Enhancement can provide space for academic developers in a range of important ways. Academic developers can also play a valuable part in supporting risk-taking. Innovation and risk-taking are more prevalent in a QE rather than a QA culture. However, given that the risk is to students' learning, risk-taking is still challenging. QE accepts risk, and accepts that not every teaching innovation will be successful. QA is less likely to encourage experimentation, innovation and risk. Academic developers can help ensure that innovations are well planned and well supported, and can help ensure that students are brought on board. In a QE culture, change and innovation are *undertaken with* students, not *done to* them. This is important; some studies have shown that student satisfaction scores will tend to go down when innovations are first introduced.

As a breed, academic developers are change agents, working for improvement. They can be key advocates for enhancement-led approaches, and can use their skills to devise development opportunities that draw the doubters and the resistant into the change agenda. Quality enhancement in this sense has, as its basis, the professionalism of academic staff as reflective academic practitioners. The ELIR Handbook stresses the importance of change management within enhancement:

> Fundamental to enhancement is the management of change. Enhancement involves doing new things or doing established things in different ways. Both of these involve the need to manage a process of change from current to future activity. A key element for institutions will be the ability to identify and manage the risks associated with the change process. ELIR supports institutions adopting an ambitious approach to their enhancement activity and promotes managed risk taking. (QAA Scotland, 2012, p. 5)

Continuing challenges

This closing section seeks to bring the strands together and considers continuing tensions, challenges and opportunities.

Quality offers a fertile ground for academic developers, but developers are not yet always sufficiently included as part of quality processes and systems. They are still too frequently turned to, or wheeled in, to help address problems revealed by QA. Were academic developers there from the onset, embedded in processes and discussions at a local level, more development interventions would be undertaken early, as new challenges or issues emerge.

Quality enhancement seeks to work with the grain of academic professionalism. The processes used within a QE approach need to provide information that is *useful* and *important* to academic staff. In a local context, the information produced by quality processes will be derived from practice and needs in the discipline area, from discussions with students and amongst staff, from programme data, from the questions of external panel members and external examiners. The information may be challenging, even uncomfortable; but it will be relevant. Academic developers working with local discipline-oriented agendas can offer effective ways for staff and students to achieve the aims and actions they have themselves identified as important, as well as to make sense of wider strategic agendas.

The challenge for academic developers changes as quality processes move away from the local disciplinary context and towards institutional, strategic, and external considerations. Information produced by quality processes typically begins to be summarised or generalised, to lose the connection. If this is not carefully handled, academic developers can be seen as doing to and imposing on, not working with. Quality is cast as an unwelcome burden. Potentially, so are academic developers. They need to be skilled mediators and persuaders, sitting, as they often are, between various interests.

The purpose of QE is beneficial change. Thus in QE the goal is to use a review to help you understand where you are and how effectively you are meeting your goals, and to help you devise better grounded plans. QE is about working with all the players involved, in partnership.

The challenges and tensions are widely recognised. The EUA report *Examining Quality Culture Part II* notes that just fewer than half the universities it surveyed had units which supported academic development (Sursock, 2011, p. 45, referencing EUA, 2010). It gives examples illustrating a range, from the more implicit to more explicit links between staff development schemes and quality systems (Sursock, 2011, p. 45–47). In one example, a quality assurance scheme was introduced as staff development. This neatly avoided issues around the language of quality by not 'referring to it as a quality assurance initiative' (ibid, p. 47). Overall this EUA 2011 Report suggests that a positive quality culture can cope with explicit links between quality and staff development, whereas the two are more likely to be disassociated where there is 'QA fatigue' (ibid, p. 49).

The challenges of establishing an effective internal quality culture and successfully countering the forces of resistance and cynicism remain. There are new challenges ahead. The next shift in quality appears to be around notions of 'learning gain', and a greater stress on factors that evidence has shown affect educational quality, as discussed in Gibbs (2010 and 2012). Under a short section headed 'quality enhancement processes', the essential role of academic development is described. Gibbs states: 'collecting student feedback on teaching has little or no impact on improving teaching' (Weimer and Lenze, 1997) *unless it is accompanied by other processes such as the teacher consulting with an educational expert*, especially when preceded by the expert observing teaching and meeting students (Piccinin et al., 1999) (Gibbs, 2010, p. 37) – my italics. Running themes in Gibbs (2010) include the importance of the teaching team, debate about teaching, and communities of practice, which are explored in detail in Chapter 11. Academic developers are the ideal support system for department heads and teaching teams committed to quality. Developers have the right skill set to help teaching teams foreground in their academic practice those methods shown to promote effective learning and to truly place learners and learning at the centre of university education.

Gibbs (2010, pp. 21–22) suggests and quotes Chickering and Gamson's *Seven Principles of Good Practice in Undergraduate Education* (1987). Also worthy of attention are the conclusions of the Teaching and Learning Research Programme, which additionally give valuable attention to issues of policy as well as practice around learning and teaching (TLRP, 2008).

Quality enhancement is about continuing relationships, not occasional visits. Relationships take time to build and to maintain. The enhancement-led approach in Scotland features an annual discussion between each institution and officers from QAA Scotland, as well as support in preparation for review, for example, commenting on an institution's draft Reflective Analysis. The approach in Scotland has enabled the development of enhancement-based quality cultures. It has enabled academic developers to move into the space created by the emphasis on the quality of the student learning experience – on learning, development and dissemination – and to use this emphasis to advance academic practice. This will be successfully achieved when supported by strong internal working relationships and a sense of shared endeavour – a true quality culture.

References

Cannell, P., and Gilmour, A. (2013). *Staff: Enhancing Teaching Final Project Report*. Glasgow: QAA.

Chickering, A. W., and Gamson, Z. F. (1987). 'Seven principles for good practice in undergraduate education', AAHE Bulletin, 39(7): 3–7.

Dempster, S., Saunders, M., and Dalglish, D. (2014). *Evaluation of the Enhancement Themes 2014: Final Report*. Centre for Higher Education Research, Evaluation and Enhancement, Department of Educational Research, Lancaster University. Glasgow: QAA.

Ellis, R. (ed.) (1993). *Quality Assurance for University Teaching*. Buckingham: SRHE and Open University Press.

'Enhancement Themes' (n.d.). The Enhancement Themes website, retrieved 22 May 2015 from www.enhancementthemes.ac.uk.

EUA (2006). *Quality Culture in European Universities: A Bottom-up Approach. Report on the Three Rounds of the Quality Culture Project 2002–2006*. Brussels: EUA.

Gibbs, G. (2010). *Dimensions of Quality*. York: Higher Education Academy.

Gibbs, G. (2012). 'Implications of *Dimensions of Quality* in a market environment'. York: Higher Education Academy.

Green, D. (ed.) (1994). *What is Quality in Higher Education?* Buckingham: SRHE and Open University Press.

Griffiths, A. (2014). 'The birth of the quality agencies'. Gloucester: QAA. Paper published on the web at www.qaa.ac.uk/en/ImprovingHigherEducation/Documents/Executive-Summary-Risk-Based-Approach.pdf.

Kastelliz, D., Kohler, A., and Muller Strassnig, A. (2014). Part I: Synopsis. In D. Kastelliz, B. Mitterauer (Eds.), *Quality Audit in the European Higher Education Area: A Comparison of Approaches*. Vienna: AQ Austria.

Maher, P. (2013a). *Effective Approaches to Evaluation in the Scottish University Sector: What Makes Self-evaluation Work?* Glasgow: QAA.

Maher, P. (2013b). *Institutional Approaches to Self-evaluation (IASE): Project Report*. Glasgow: QAA.

Mayes, T. (2014). *Developing and Supporting the Curriculum: Summary Report*. Glasgow: QAA. Paper publishhed on the web at www.enhancementthemes .ac.uk/pages/docdetail/docs/publications/developing-and-supporting-the-curriculum-summary-report.

Piccinin, S., Cristi, C. and McCoy, M. (1999). 'The impact of individual consultation on student ratings of teaching', *International Journal of Academic Development*, 4(2): 76–88.

QAA Scotland. (2012). *Enhancement-led Institutional Review: Handbook 2012*. Glasgow: QAA.

Scottish Funding Council. (2010). *Second Annual Report of the Evaluation of the Quality Enhancement Framework*. Centre for the Study of Education and Training, Department of Educational Research, Lancaster University. Edinburgh: SFC.

Sursock, A. (2011). *Examining Quality Culture Part II: Processes and Tools – Participation, Ownership and Bureaucracy*. Brussels: European University Association, available at www.eua.be/pubs/Examining_Quality_Culture_Part_II.pdf, accessed 22 May 2015.

TLRP (2008). TLRP's evidence-informed pedagogic principles, ESRC – TLRP. 2012.

Weimer, M. and Lenze, L.F. (1997) 'Instructional interventions: a review of the literature on efforts to improve instruction', in R. P. Perry and J. C. Smart (eds) *Effective Teaching in Higher Education: Research and Practice*. New York: Agathon Press.

Chapter 10

'Is it working?'

Outcomes, monitoring and evaluation

Lorraine Stefani and David Baume

Summary

This chapter works with three principal ideas:

1 It is very important to establish, at a very early stage in planning, and as clearly as possible, what any academic development venture is intended to achieve, what its intended outcomes are. These may, by negotiation, be changed; but they should always be clear.

2 These intended outcomes provide a secure basis for monitoring (on the way through) and evaluating (at or after the end of) the venture, and thereby both for guiding the venture to success and for learning to inform future development ventures.

3 These intended outcomes should be increasingly ambitious, as academic development takes a leading role in changing higher education.

The chapter seeks to justify and extend these ideas, and to provide practical guidance on implementing them, in the complex and sometimes messy world of higher education.

On terminology – Evaluation is used here to mean making evidence-informed judgments about the value or effectiveness of an educational process. Where the authors speak of assessment, we mean making judgments on the work of individual students. These usages are common in UK and UK-influenced higher education. We are aware that assessment and evaluation can carry almost the reverse meanings in many US-influenced systems and institutions. *Thanks to Chris Knapper and Robert Cannon for guidance on this clarification.*

Links to web sources referenced in this chapter can be found at www.seda .ac.uk/apad.

Introduction

The primary intention of this chapter is to support academic developers to plan, monitor and evaluate their work in a range of ways, in order to provide accurate and usable evidence of effectiveness and added value.

To evidence our value, we developers need to ask difficult questions about what it is that we are evaluating (e.g. Stefani, 2010; Cousin, 2009) as a start to taking a more consistent and scholarly approach to investigating our own work and to creating an improved discourse of evaluation.

We suggest starting with a clear articulation; preferably derived from negotiation with stakeholder groups; of the intended **outcomes** of any academic development endeavour. The **activities** that developers undertake and the **outputs** that we produce are mainly important insofar as they contribute to the **outcomes** to be achieved. This process of identifying intended outcomes is illustrated later through two hypothetical case studies. Golding (2013) talks eloquently of the loss, the restrictions, which result from defining ourselves by what we do rather than by what we achieve.

A shifting narrative is developing around what exactly is to be evaluated or measured. Terms including *impact* (Gray and Radloff, 2008), *added value* and *return on investment* are increasingly used (Stefani, 2013). These may be experienced as unwelcome management-speak. But they may be the language of our managers. And they can be addressed in rigorous, scholarly and professional ways.

There are two sets of voices in this chapter, giving two perspectives on the response to this shifting narrative. Briefly, one voice is a voice in the literal sense and the other in the metaphorical sense. Geographically, a hemisphere separates us. Through our engagement and collaboration in this project we decided to give weight to each of our distinctive voices, and our knowledge, understanding and experience of the challenging topic of providing evaluative evidence of effectiveness of academic development.

In the first parts we explore further the relationships between activities, outputs and outcomes, and posit reasons for monitoring and evaluating any development venture. We provide practical examples of a scholarly and research-informed approach to evaluating and evidencing the organisational benefits of academic development.

In the latter parts, we explore a shifting approach to evidencing the value of our endeavours as we assert the leadership role of developers in promoting and contributing to enhanced organisational performance (Schroeder et al., 2011).

'What are we trying to achieve?' – Activities, outputs and outcomes

Ask an academic developer about their work, and they will typically talk about planning and running projects (Chapter 14), consulting (Chapter 5), running CPD (Chapter 4), responding to or initiating policies and strategies (Chapter 17), liaising, planning and running events and programmes, producing resources, and of course going to meetings. They will talk about what they do, maybe also about what they produce, and the attendant challenges and opportunities.

But, underpinning all this, we suggest, should be sustained, even relentless, attention to what each of these many activities and products is intending to achieve. In what particular ways is each of them, alone or together, helping to improve learning in the university? This, presumably, is the ultimate goal of most of the work of an academic developer. Not all of our work may be immediately described in these terms. We may work with other parts of the university towards more local and intermediate goals. But it is good to keep an eye on the overarching goal, a goal which can usually be achieved in many different ways (see Chapter 1 for further discussion).

To illustrate this account of outcomes and their importance, two hypothetical project case studies are offered. The case studies suggest the kinds of conversations that might be had between developer and clients in such projects.

Hypothetical Case Study 1: 'Learning experience' or 'learning'?

Kreber (2010) in Stefani (2010) speaks of enhancing the student learning experience as a primary goal of academic development. This formulation is widely used. Development projects are often planned with a primary goal of enhancing the student learning experience.

No one would wish students to have a poor learning experience. But a good learning experience is surely not sufficient. HE is not primarily a visitor attraction or a theme park. Our aim is surely to enhance student learning, not just the student learning experience. A good learning experience may be a long step on the road to good learning. But it is not the whole journey.

Note that the phrase 'good learning' can carry two meanings here. Both are valid. Good learning can indeed mean students having an enjoyable, stimulating, inspiring and etc. experience of learning. And good learning can mean students having developed a wider and deeper range of capabilities, qualities: whatever we wish as the effects of higher education. We suggest that the latter meaning is the more important. But if we want to make either or both of these into intended outcomes, we need to be explicit about them.

It may be felt that enhancing student learning is too ambitious a goal for a university, let alone for an academic development unit. We would disagree. As always in academic development work, and in many other kinds of work besides, it is good to keep our ultimate goal in our sights; to keep checking that we are on the way to the mountaintop, fog-shrouded and distant though it may well be, as we grub about, however purposefully, in the foothills. We should only back off from our ultimate goals when evidence persuades us that they are unattainable. And, even then, we should still work towards the most ambitious intermediate or proxy goals, plausible substitutes or stand-ins, that we may be able, with effort and ingenuity, to identify and attain. We have to remain ambitious, else what is the point?

A critical question for us to address is: How can we show that student learning has been enhanced?

- We could compare what graduates know with what they knew in previous years. However, we may feel that a degree should signify much more than knowledge. So we we shall move on to the next suggestion.
- We could compare what graduates can do, learning outcomes demonstrably achieved and consequently grades awarded, with student attainment in previous years. The assessment processes of the university should generate such data, although we may have to dig deep into course outcomes and assessment methods and marking schemes as well as assessment results to retrieve and to calibrate the data in such a way that it can be used to address our questions. If the data are hard to find, this suggests another challenge for the developers – helping the university to ensure that its (summative) assessment processes are achieving what they should achieve – evidencing student attainment.
- Taking a still more ambitious approach, we could compare data from previous years on what graduates actually do; in educational and professional language, we could explore the values and policies and beliefs, as well as capabilities and knowledge, that demonstrably inform their practice. This of course is only possible if these values and etc. are assessed. Many professions, disciplines and universities espouse such values. Rarely do they explicitly assess the enactment, and then the impact of the espousal and the enactment. A role for developers could and arguably should be to enable the university to assess these values, so that they are real rather than empty, substantial rather than rhetorical.

There are difficulties with these proposals. Students differ from year to year. Also, students are not just students – they are real people who also live in the real, sometimes challenging and messy, world. The widespread norm-referencing of our assessment procedures grading on the curve as it is sometimes called, the elastic ruler, in plain language the manipulation of groups of student marks to reflect the view that, overall, this cohort of students will do as well as last year's – camouflages improvements (and of course the opposite) in learning from year to year. However, such apparent difficulties and obstacles are there to be tackled and challenged, not immediately surrendered to.

The major pitfall with the language of *student experience* is that it may encourage us to be satisfied with enhancing student satisfaction. Student satisfaction is a weak evaluation measure, as explored in a later section of this chapter on levels of evaluation. Students should be informed and active partners in planning, undertaking and reviewing demanding and rewarding experiences that clearly lead to learning; learning that students, academics, disciplines and professions and employers all value. We may need, for example, to address external requirements, such as the UK National Student Survey ('The National Student Survey 2015', 2015), that focus on good student learning experiences. In such cases we also need to do some detailed work, involving staff and students, to identify what a good learning experience would be; what it would look and feel like; and how it leads to good learning. We need to analyse more robustly what constitutes good learning.

(At the start of this section we express reservations about Kreber's [2010] view that *enhancing the student learning experience* should be a primary goal of academic development. We add here that Kreber's chapter also contains much with which we strongly agree, including a powerful statement of the necessary emancipatory role of teaching. Evaluating the nature and extent of student emancipation is a wonderful challenge!)

As illustrated in Hypothetical Case Study 1, and taken further in the final section of this chapter: We believe that developers should start with ambitious goals. Chapter 2 on identifying needs explores this further. Enhancing student learning, and all the many interpretations of this – and the intermediate goals that flow from these interpretations; together with goals from the university, from disciplines, professions and employers, students and government – will keep us busy for decades to come.

Not all of these goals will initially be formulated as clear outcomes. But we need to clarify and negotiate them into operational form; into acceptable, inspiring, usable, and of course evaluable, outcomes. We must negotiate with people, and we must negotiate our way with, around and through policies and strategies and systems. This clarification and these negotiations are not simply technical activities. Discoveries and decisions will be made during these processes of clarification and negotiation, sometimes important ones. This clarification of outcomes, facilitated well, is a profoundly developmental process for all who take part – another strong argument for involving as many stakeholders as is feasible.

Any aim or aspiration can be operationalised, and thus its attainment evaluated, to some extent at least. There are many possible approaches to this. Some are suggested in a second hypothetical case study, based around a real example:

Hypothetical Case Study 2: 'Enhancing the status of teaching'

A university policy aim might be to enhance the status of teaching. This is a laudable aim; but vague.

A non-rhetorical question to begin with: How would you identify the status of teaching in your university, and track its changes over time?

Let's try to sharpen the aim.

We might try to achieve a more rigorous definition. We could negotiate university meanings – university meanings, not the meanings; we are developers, not writers of dictionaries – for terms including *enhance*, *status*, even *teaching*. Defining is often useful. For example we might debate whether teaching should be taken to include every function that directly affects student learning. We could produce lists of teaching and learning-support functions. We might try to assess the scale and nature of the contribution of each function, from published research, or from local surveys and studies. The analysis, the investigation, the conversations we generate can be useful, if kept within reason. It will be clear when the conversations have stopped being useful – people will cease to participate. Stop well short of this point!

Alternatively, we could take a more direct approach and ask the question – 'What would indicate an enhanced status of teaching'? We could decide, again using ideas from the literature, and/or we could ask within the university. We could devise and implement a survey to identify the current status of teaching. This would rapidly reveal some of the many meanings of the status of teaching. Analysing these, seeking a core, seeking context-specific (for example, discipline-specific) local variants, and feeding in any research-based accounts, all start to give an account of the status of teaching with which we can work.

Remember that the overall aim is to enhance the status of teaching. This means that one criterion for a useful account of the status of teaching is that it should offer a sense of direction or quantity or quality. Our account should enable us to identify enhancement over a baseline. In enhancement work, it's good to know which way is up.

There is a further, again complementary, approach. Instead of seeking definitions of words or of phrases, we could seek indicators, possible current and future indicators of the status of teaching, and also of efforts to enhance it. Indicators, not proof. Determinable, not measurable. Better than nothing – sometimes much better.

Examples of possible indicators of a university acting to enhance the status of teaching include:

- A formal teaching awards scheme – a plausible indicator that an institution is seeking to enhance the status of teaching. Beyond this, the number of scheme applications and awards each year, the rewards given to and more broadly the fuss made of award winners; these are all further indicators of an institution taking seriously the enhancement of the status of teaching.
- Promotions criteria that include teaching – indicating that teaching is being given high status. We should want to know that these criteria are being used, and also that they are widely believed to be being used. Publishing criterion-referenced citations for promotions would be one way to evidence this.

• Teaching ability being emphasised in recruitment advertisements, and taken seriously in selection processes, would be a further positive sign.
• Encouragement, support and/or a requirement for staff to gain and maintain teaching qualifications.
• Systematic peer observation and feedback on teaching, and evidence of the results being used to inform changes to practice and the planning of individuals' further development.
• Mentoring of new teachers by teachers of proven excellence.

Many other approaches to increasing the status of teaching are of course possible, and no doubt are being enacted around the world. What these and other possible approaches have in common is that they show explicit rewards, recognition and/or requirement, at institutional and/or local level, for staff to teach well, to improve their teaching, and to enhance the status of teaching.

Of course most of these processes could be implemented well or badly, strongly or feebly. All could be respected or not by academic staff, managers and students. All could be subverted or diminished by other policies and strategies which value, or are perceived as valuing, other kinds of activity – most obviously research or administration – more highly than teaching. Nonetheless, a university implementing such measures, and putting some effort into evaluating their effectiveness, could make a decent claim to be committed to enhancing the status, and also the quality, of teaching.

In this consideration of enhancing the status of teaching, academic developers have many possible roles. They can help universities, schools and departments to identify possible good academic practices that are broadly compatible with the norms and values of the institution, accepting also that one of the more challenging roles of the developers is sometimes to help the institution to shift its norms and values. Developers can make productive connections across the institution. They can help to identify, clarify and refine goals that are both appropriate and evaluable. And they can help institutions to identify, understand and learn from what is working.

At some point a developer will also want to ask – 'Why do we seek to enhance the status of teaching?'

Why and for whom? Purposes and audiences for monitoring and evaluation

Audiences for evaluation typically include those who commissioned whatever is being evaluated – the main stakeholders in it, those principally involved in and affected by it, and any wider communities who may be interested.

When times were easier, different reports could be written for different audiences. No more. An evaluator should probably write a summary report, just a few pages, which addresses the main questions that have been asked, and provides conclusions and recommendations, key points of learning, and perhaps an overview of how resources were used. Detailed data, methodology and longer discussions are best confined to an appendix, accessible to those with a particular interest.

There are perhaps four main reasons to monitor and evaluate. A good evaluation will address all four purposes:

1 Accountability

The report should show that the resources allocated to the project were properly expended.

The report should also describe and illustrate, up front, the extent to which the project achieved its original intended outcomes, or of course negotiated variations thereof.

2 Explanation

As well as showing whether and to what extent a project achieved its intended outcomes, a good evaluation also offers some explanation of why. Evaluation thus has affinities with research, although evaluation also has purposes beyond research, beyond seeking evidence-based understanding and explanation. Some relations between evaluation and research are considered in a later section of this chapter. When those undertaking and evaluating a project can, at least in part, explain why it has had the effects that it has had, it becomes easier to increase the effectiveness both of the current project and of future projects.

Development activities also have unexpected outcomes. These, too, should be noted, and attempts made to explain them.

3 Contributing to improvement

This follows directly from the previous point. Monitoring should be a frequent, indeed as close as possible to a continuing, feature of the operation of any academic development venture. This means that, from the earliest possible moment, learning can be fed back into the operation and the improvement of the venture.

4 Enhancing capacity for evaluation

If we believe that evaluation is a useful process, then we may wish to help our colleagues – whether other developers, academics, administrators, managers or other supporters of learning – to develop some further enthusiasm for and capability in evaluation, beyond what they bring from their original discipline or profession. A good way to do this is to involve them in the evaluation process.

The long road from awareness to return on investment – levels of evaluation

The model of evaluation shown below is adapted from Kirkpatrick (1994). It suggests a ladder of levels of evaluation. The Kirkpatrick model of evaluation has four levels:

1   **Reaction**: To what degree do participants react favourably to a development event/opportunity? The happy-sheet typically measures immediate reactions.
2   **Learning**: To what degree have participants acquired the intended knowledge, skills, attitudes, confidence and commitment as a result of their participation in a development event? 'What have you learned'? is a useful question for a feedback sheet, although it only captures an immediate account of what has been learned.
3   **Behaviour**: To what extent did participants apply what they learned during the development event when they returned to their working environment? This requires a follow-up survey, possibly some months later.
4   **Results**: To what extent has the performance of the organisation changed as a result of the development opportunity and subsequent actions by participants? Commonly tracked in business, this is rarely studied in academic settings.

In our extended model, there are ten steps. An evaluation strategy can go as far along the ladder as our resources; and, if we may briefly be mischievous, our courage (do you really want to know?); allow. But, we suggest, to stop at level 3 of the extended model is to stop much too soon, before we have collected data that we can use to determine the effectiveness of our work.

The ladder is presented here as a tool for evaluation. It can, however, also be used as a tool for planning development events or processes.

The questions can be modified to reflect the nature of the particular activity being evaluated. Further questions can be added as required or appropriate to what is being evaluated and the questions of concern to the developer and evaluator.

Table 10.1 Ten levels of evaluation, adapted from Kirkpatrick (1994)

Level	Label	Typical question(s)
1	Awareness & knowledge	What proportion of the intended stakeholders knew about the activity?
2	Expectations	What did stakeholders want, need, expect from it?
3	Reactions	Did it meet their needs? Did they like it?
4	Suggestions	How did they feel could it be improved?
5	Engagement	In what particular ways did stakeholders engage with it?
6	Learning	What did people learn from it?
7	Planning	What use do people plan to make of what they have learned?
8	Applying	What use have people made of what they learned?
9	Student learning	What effect has their changed practice had on student learning?
10	Return on investment	Were the costs of the activity, process or project at least recouped through increased efficiency, effectiveness, quality – on whatever the institution places financial value – of teaching and learning?

It will be clear that some questions are to be asked before, others during and still others at various intervals afterwards.

The quest to explain – research and evaluation

Part-way through a fascinating evaluation, the thought has occurred to many an evaluator – *this would make a great paper!* Ashwin and Trigwell's (2004) work, after Rowland (2000), in Baume and Kahn (2004), advise caution on this. Ashwin and Trigwell value what they call *scholarly investigation* as an important part of academic development. They offer three, sometimes slightly overlapping, levels of investigation:

1 **Personal investigation**, leading to personal knowledge that informs only one's own practice; reported perhaps in a notebook (or a blog); verified only by the investigator.
2 **Local investigation**, leading to local knowledge that can inform the practice of a defined group – for example a development unit, a programme team, even an institution; disseminated through conversation or report or seminar or website; verified by members of the same group.
3 **National or international investigation**, leading to journal-published or conference-presented research; verified through peer review.

Work at each of these three levels should be scholarly, both conceptually and methodologically, certainly informed by, and at least prepared to contribute (at level 1 and 2, after further work) to the literature. But, at level 2, issues of confidentiality, of audience, of the purpose of the evaluation, all mean that converting an evaluation report into a paper for publication can be very problematic. Ashwin and Trigwell (2004, p. 122) conclude: '...this decision about which level of investigation is appropriate is one that generally needs to be made prior to the investigation taking place'. Researching academic development is considered in Chapter 12.

Approaches to evaluation under conditions of complexity

We have suggested that developers often work with the ultimate goal to improve student learning. But many factors affect student learning. And our work is mediated through the work of academics and institutions, among others (Gordon in Stefani, 2010). How can we identify our contribution and our effects?

We can decide that this problem is so difficult that it is impossible to address it, and then struggle to defend the effectiveness of our work when the next budget pressures come. Or we can undertake a little rational analysis, and be pleased to have achieved at least a partial account of the effects of our work.

Two main approaches can be taken to meeting the challenge:

Identify the connections

We can seek to identify the main links and networks of influence, and evaluate each separately.

Developers typically seek to influence both policy and practice.

Identifying contribution to policy is difficult, but usually possible, at least in part. Especially if the developer drafts the policy paper. But even when the developer simply contributes to discussions and makes suggestions, then it is usually possible to at least outline their contribution to the final policy, even in the complex mix of debate and redrafting.

For example: The ADU supports the writing and introduction of a new learning and teaching strategy, and runs development events for staff on the new approaches to teaching and learning that the policy espouses or suggests or implies. Informed by the new strategy and the development events – and of course by other factors – staff make some identifiable changes to their teaching practice. As a result of these changes – and, of course, again, of other factors – student learning changes, again in identifiable ways.

Evaluation can follow this relatively short and simple chain/network. Not perfectly – but well enough to give valuable data and understanding. Doing so may contravene two usually unspoken developers' commandments – 'Be humble' and 'Do not claim credit for what you helped to achieve', both commandments underpinned by the old saw, 'It's amazing what you can achieve if you don't care who gets the credit'. Deciding how humble to be, and for what audiences, is yet another difficult decision that developers have to make.

Use existing results

Another approach is to use existing research data that may suggest appropriate proxy measures, intermediate measures, rather than investigating everything from scratch.

We do not have to evaluate every link in the chain. For example, Rust (1998) established that some 90 per cent of participants in well-run staff development workshops reported implementing ideas that they heard or developed during the workshop. This research-based knowledge allows us, with some although of course not total confidence, to assume that well-run workshops – in particular, workshops that allow participants sufficient time and support, not just to hear new ideas but to plan how they might implement them – are a good and defensible proxy measure for changes to teaching methods. Of course, if we have time, we could replicate Rust's work in any particular setting, and no doubt learn more about how workshops affect the teaching behaviour of academics. (More on workshops in Chapter 18, on futures.)

If we want to know what factors affected an academic's decisions to make changes to their practice, we can ask them. We will get a partial, but probably still somewhat useful, account.

All that remains is to identify changes in student behaviour and changes in student learning. The teacher is likely to want to know whether the changed teaching methods are having any effect on the behaviour and then the learning of their students. Neither of these is particularly difficult to identify. Information on changes in what students do, and in particular in the work that they produce, is readily available to the teacher, particularly in the age of the VLE. And information on changes in performance on a particular task, or particular kinds of tasks, is also available through the conventional processes of assessment.

If we want to know what factors affected a student's decision to make changes to their practice, and perhaps changes in their learning, we can ask them. Again, we will get a partial, but probably still somewhat useful, account.

We know that we are presenting here an optimistic, even idealistic, account. We know that there can be logistical and political and cultural difficulties at every step. Sometimes it is useful to look up from the everyday difficulties and consider how things might be – in this case, what a university committed to learning about and improving its processes might be like. And then, as developers, work to help the university become a little more like this.

Outcomes and evaluation as political acts

Defining intended outcomes is in part a political act, in several senses. Defining intended outcomes seeks to influence others, sometimes many others. Negotiating intended outcomes is more participative, but still political, offering a particular view of participatory good practice. Such defining also presents and reinforces a particular view, of education and academic development, as, at least in part, rational and goal-directed activities. Defining affects, and is affected by, how the organisation functions, and to what and whose ends. Sometimes – for example, though helping to define, and then seeking to support implementation of, policy – it seeks to exert influence. Recognition of such factors may help us understand any resistance we encounter as we suggest and negotiate the intended outcomes for a piece of work. The eventual outcomes may be less pure than we would wish, informed by factors beyond what we know about the conditions for good student learning. But we can find and then achieve better outcomes when we make the compromises that we have to make in an explicit and clear-eyed way.

Evaluation is or can be similarly a political act. Clients sometimes tell evaluators, whether internal or external to the university, in more or less direct terms, what they want the evaluation to show. They may seek to influence evaluation reports. More generally, when money has been spent and reputations and egos are in play – which is to say, usually – it will be clear to the evaluator what kinds of evaluation results will and will not be welcome. The best situation is for the evaluator to be appointed and funded independently from the funding of what is being evaluated. But often the evaluator is funded from within the project budget, which means that the evaluator may face biting the hand that feeds. What is an evaluator to do?

- The evaluator should be involved from the start of the project. They can help to clarify outcomes, to help ensure that outcomes are both attainable and evaluable. They can also advise on intermediate outcomes, way-points along the journey. This all reduces the chance of the project failing.

- They can act as formative as well as summative evaluator, providing continuing monitoring, feedback and guidance, again increasing the chance of the project staying on track.
- They can involve the whole project team in formative evaluation, collecting and making sense of outcomes–related data. This again increases the likelihood that the project will stay on track. It also enhances evaluation capability, which as suggested above is a valid goal for an evaluator and a developer.
- Alone or with the project team, the evaluator may be able, by keeping a focus on ultimate and then intermediate outcomes, to see early indications that some intended outcomes are no longer attainable, or indeed appropriate, and help the project team revise or renegotiate goals.

The model suggested here of the embedded evaluator, the evaluator as member of the project team, as evaluation consultant as well as evaluator, has dangers. The term *embedded* was chosen to bring echoes of the reporters embedded with fighting forces in wars, and to remind us of fears of loss of objectivity; hopefully in the case of developers without the physical danger. The evaluation contract must be clear. It must describe the evaluator's roles and responsibilities, rights and duties.

Clear project outcomes make it easier for an evaluator to judge how far these outcomes have been achieved. The evaluation contract can very usefully say that the evaluator will submit their report to the project team to check for matters of accuracy, but that the evaluator retains full responsibility for the judgements they make. The project team may of course choose to provide a written response to the evaluation. A rewarding part of the evaluator role is the continuing conversation with the project team, perhaps acting as a kind of critical friend, to develop together a clearer understanding of how and why, as well as what, the project is achieving.

If the project wants an honest evaluation, it should not hire an evaluator who is hungry for the work. If the evaluator wants to stay honest, they have to be willing to be critical. Evaluators have to hope that their reputation comes from doing good work, not from saying what the clients want to hear. Like so much academic development work, evaluation requires values, indeed courage, as well as skills.

The relationship between the narrative of academic development and evaluation

In this final section we pull back from detailed consideration of principles and practice and raise the issue of the twenty-first century narrative of academic development. This narrative presents us with more ambitious goals, and hence more challenges to evaluation. We suggest that courageous leadership is required of academic developers in promoting, supporting and evidencing ambitious change goals, and then establishing a robust link between academic development interventions and enhanced organisational performance, perhaps moving towards identifying the Return on Investment referred to earlier in this chapter.

Schroeder and associates (2011) provide a road map for academic developers for the future. They affirm the mission-critical role for faculty developers in this time of immense flux and uncertainty for universities. Along with other commentators (e.g. Gordon, 2010), they emphasise that the broad-based institution-level changes that are underway involve many players, not only academic and educational developers. This might well be a positive indication that academic developers have been highly successful over the past decades in contributing to enhanced organisational performance – many staff across our faculties are now also contributing more to organisational success through their enhanced performance and academic practice.

So what of our future if we can show that we have been successful in our endeavours to date? Do we do more of the same, or should we reshape our narrative and mission for the twenty-first century? Schroeder and her colleagues suggest strongly that faculty developers should merge the traditional responsibilities and services of the past several decades with a **leadership** role as **organisational developers**. It is the leadership issue that is significant, recognising that as academic developers we are, or can be, leaders within the organisation, and as such we need to recognise ourselves as role models of leaderly behaviour. Relations between academic development and university leadership are considered further in Chapter 16.

Similarly, national organisations associated with sector-wide enhancement in learning, teaching and the student experience are promoting the leadership role of academic development. This, together with national and institutional links between Quality Assurance and Quality Enhancement, is explored in the Scottish context in Chapter 9. In Australia the government-funded Office of Learning and Teaching (OLT) promotes and supports *change* in higher education institutions for the enhancement of learning and teaching. The Leadership Foundation in the UK has a similar role.

The responsibilities of OLT include:

- Providing grants to academics and professional staff to explore, develop and implement innovations in learning and teaching and to develop leadership capabilities
- Commissioning work on issues of strategic significance to the higher education sector to inform policy development and practice in relation to learning and teaching
- Managing a suite of awards to celebrate, recognise and value teaching excellence and programs that enhance student learning
- Funding fellowships and secondments for leading educators to address significant national educational issues

The mandate of the Office of Learning and Teaching (OLT) Australia invites academic developers to influence policy at institutional and national level on the basis of research-informed practice and evidence. The emphasis on *leadership* and *leading change* invites us to:

- Establish a robust link between academic development activities and interventions and sustainable organisational change and development
- Build leadership capacity and capability
- Adapt to changing institutional and student expectations
- Enhance organisational performance

Framing our contribution as developers in this way in turn invites a highly strategic approach to evaluating and evidencing our added value.

We can also point to work carried out by the Council of Australian Directors of Academic Development. CADAD (2011) is an extensive document with templates that could be modified to form the basis for developing Key Performance Indicators (KPIs) within any institutional academic development unit. The authors of the CADAD report, leaders in the broad field of academic development, have presented the work of academic development units as falling within eight key domains of influence which should resonate well with most developers:

- Strategy, policy, governance
- Learning and teaching
- Scholarship of teaching and learning
- Professional development
- Credit bearing programmes in HE
- Curriculum development
- Engagement (internal and external)
- Academic Development Unit Effectiveness

Within these key domains are sub-domains. For example the sub-domains for 'strategy, policy and governance' include strategic advice, strategic planning, governance, policy development and implementation. Scoping statements are provided along with guidance on levels of practice and levels of performance. This Benchmarking Guide encompasses and complements many of the previous strategies for presenting evidence outlined in this chapter.

That the benchmarks start with our role in strategy, policy and governance is indicative of the expectation of leadership by academic developers.

The Benchmarking domain of Academic Development Unit Effectiveness encompasses the sub-domains of Mission and Strategic Alignment, Leadership and Management, Impact and Quality Assurance and Enhancement.

The Benchmark Guide should support AD directors, their units and their institutions in better understanding the strategic potential of academic development. The guide is designed to enable effective evaluation and to enhance academic development unit performance regardless of their combinations of functions and models of delivery.

As ever, though, it is relatively easy to show what has been done and what has been produced. The challenge is to show what has been achieved. The more strategic and leadership-focussed academic development becomes, the longer and more complex the chains and networks of influence typically become. The ladder of levels of evaluation is still applicable. When evaluating our work for the purposes of providing effective indicators of achievement, the basic principles – clear outcomes, rigorous evaluation – will always be applicable.

Conclusion

A valuable contribution developers can make to their institution is to help the institution to clarify intended outcomes, at scales and levels from local to institutional, and then evaluate their attainment. Self-evaluation, with some degree of external moderation, is a powerful learning tool, just as is self-assessment for students. These are not routine administrative activities, not chores. They are an integral part of practice, to be undertaken in a scholarly and professional way, and demonstrably contributing to the continuing improvement of the institution. The developer as evaluator perhaps becomes at least in part an evaluation consultant, embedding their work and their ethos and then moving on to fresh challenges.

References

Ashwin, P., and Trigwell, K. (2004). 'Investigating staff and educational development'. In D. Baume and P. Kahn (Eds.), *Enhancing Staff and Educational Development* (pp. 117–131). London: RoutledgeFalmer.

Baume, D., and Kahn, P. (2004). *Enhancing Staff and Educational Development*. London: RoutledgeFalmer.

CADAD (2010). *Benchmarking Performance of Academic Development Units in Australian Universities.* Retrieved 10 June 2015 from www.cadad.edu.au/pluginfile.php/401/course/section/78/Benchmarking_Re.

Cousin, G. (2009). *Researching Higher Education: An Introduction to Contemporary Methods and Approaches.* Taylor & Francis.

Cousin, G. (2013). 'Evidencing the Value of Educational Development by Asking Awkward Questions', in *Evidencing the Value of Educational Development* (Bamber, V., Ed.) SEDA Special 34, pp. 19–21.

Golding, C. (2013). 'Blinkered conceptions of academic development', *International Journal for Academic Development,* 19(2): 150–152.

Gordon, G. (2010). 'The quality agenda: where does academic development sit?' In L. Stefani (Ed.), *Evaluating the Effectiveness of Academic Development Practice: Principles and Practice* (pp. 31–44). New York: Taylor & Francis.

Gray, K., and Radloff, A. (2008). 'The idea of impact and its implications for academic development work'. *International Journal for Academic Development,* 13(2): 97–106.

Kirkpatrick, D. (1994). *Evaluating Training Programs.* San Francisco, CA: Berrett-Koehler Publishers, Inc.

Kreber, C. (2010). 'Demonstrating fitness for purpose: phronesis and authenticity as overarching purposes'. In L. Stefani (Ed.), *Evaluating the Effectiveness of*

Academic Development Practice: Principles and Practice (pp. 45–58). New York: Taylor & Francis.

Rowland, S. (Ed.). (2000). *The Enquiring University Teacher (Society for Research into Higher Education)* (1st ed.). Philadelphia, PA: Society for Research into Higher Education & Open University Press.

Rust, C. (1998). 'The impact of educational development workshops on teachers' practice', *International Journal for Academic Development*, 3(1): 72–80.

Schroeder, C. (Ed.). (2011). *Coming in from the Margins: Faculty Development's Emerging Organizational Development Role in Institutional Change*. United States: Stylus Publishing.

Stefani, L. (2010). *Evaluating the Effectiveness of Academic Development: Principles and Practice*. New York: Routledge.

Stefani, L. (2013). 'Learning to dance in the rain: shifting the narrative of academic development', in *Evidencing the Value of Educational Development* (Bamber, V., Ed.) SEDA Special 34.

The National Student Survey 2015. (n.d.). Retrieved 29 April 2015 from www.thestudentsurvey.com.

Chapter 11

Working with networks, microcultures and communities

Katarina Mårtensson and Torgny Roxå

'I have really become inspired to do new things in my teaching through this pedagogical course, but I cannot do it. My colleagues are like a wet blanket over everything'. (Participant in a pedagogical course, 2003)

Summary

This chapter draws on a sociocultural perspective on academic development. It briefly introduces some current theoretical frameworks, including social network theory, organisational culture and communities of practice. It shows how these models can be used to design a variety of academic development activities. The purpose of using this perspective is to help academic developers support not only individual teachers but also the collegial context in which the teachers are professionally active. Case studies and quotations from academics are included.

Links to web sources referenced in this chapter can be found at www.seda .ac.uk/apad.

Introduction – some factors acting for and against change

Academic teachers do not act in isolation. On the contrary, they form their understanding of teaching and learning, and conduct their teaching practice, in relation to a context that includes their disciplinary community, students, academic colleagues, leaders, the organisation and society. For decades, academic developers have organised formal learning opportunities for academic teachers through workshops, courses and programmes. Academic developers have engaged in various development projects, and lately also worked strategically with leaders and managers (Gibbs, 2013). Evaluations of such activities, in search for evidence of meaningful and substantial impact on academic teaching and student learning, repeatedly indicate that the impact is not straightforward (Chalmers et al., 2012; Gibbs and Coffey, 2004; Prosser et al., 2006). This is explored further in Chapter 10 of this book, on monitoring and evaluation. The evaluation results are generally positive in terms of satisfied participants, who adopt a more student-/learning-centred approach (Prosser and Trigwell, 1999) to their teaching after they have completed a staff development programme. However, less is known about the effects on an organisational level (Trigwell, 2012). In fact, evaluation studies hitherto indicate that the effects differ depending on how the academics' collegial contexts value teaching and academic development programmes, as illustrated by the quote at the head of this chapter. Informal structures in the various contexts where academic teachers are active thus appear to mediate the impact of formal academic development activities.

Learning through formal academic development activities is therefore not straightforward, since it is blended with informal learning during day-to-day interaction with colleagues. Knight (2006) critiques pedagogical courses as a means of professional development: 'learning to teach is not, mainly, a formal process: non-formal, practice-based learning is more significant' (Knight, 2006:29). Knight argues that enhancement of teaching and educational professional development should have as its main focus the non-formal, daily practice of the academic teachers and their working environments rather than focusing on formal educational training programmes. In other words, there are many indicators that teachers' social and collegial contexts strongly influence their ways of talking about, valuing and practising teaching. This obviously has implications for academic developers. In this chapter we argue that the more academic developers can grow our awareness of and design activities in order to target these local academic contexts, the more efficient will our work be.

This chapter aims to help academic developers to understand how institutionalised norms and traditions in local academic workplaces influence the construction of knowledge about teaching and student learning, and consequently teaching practices. The text applies a sociocultural perspective to academic teachers in their collegial contexts, and highlights the implications for academic development. Firstly, a theoretical framework is sketched, drawing upon literature on social networks, organisational culture and communities of practice. Secondly the implications for academic development are outlined, with practical examples. Finally, academic developers themselves are considered as a collegial community.

Theoretical framework – considering organisational culture

Since academic developers are mostly employed by, and work in, higher education organisations, we need ways to understand organisations and development in and of the organisation. Van Maanen (2007; further developed in Ancona et al., 2009); helpfully defines three different lenses with which we can analyse and understand an organisation:

1 The *strategic design* lens, which reveals how an organisation is intended to work, often illustrated with charts of boxes and arrows on an organisation's website;

2 The *political* lens, through which we can see different interests, stakeholders, alliances and power struggles within an organisation; and

3 The *cultural* lens, through which we can see the norms, habits, traditions and acts of meaning-making constructed through day-to-day interactions and activities in the organisation.

Van Maanen emphasises that the three are partly overlapping, and all are needed in order to fully understand an organisation. In this chapter we will highlight what we can see and understand by using mainly the third, the cultural lens. Organisational culture, as described by Alvesson (2002), is what constitutes a group and makes it visible in relation to its background. Organisational culture is usually considered to comprise group-specific norms, behaviours, and ways of talking and acting. More colloquially, culture is widely described as 'the way we do things around here'. It is useful to explore how elements of organisational culture are developed over long periods of time. We argue here that this is where our efforts as academic developers first and foremost should be directed in order to have effect.

Recent research shows that academic teachers have a few trusted colleagues with whom they discuss teaching seriously (Pataraia, Falconer, Margaryan, Littlejohn and Fincher, 2014; Roxå and Mårtensson, 2009; Thomson, 2013). Pataraia and colleagues (2014) use social network analysis to show how academics actively seek support from expert colleagues in order to develop their teaching capacity. Roxå and Mårtensson (2009) mapped the number of significant others (Berger and Luckmann, 1966) that academic teachers have in relation to teaching, and the character of the conversations. The study showed that teachers have five to ten trusted people with whom they discuss teaching in order to try new ideas or discuss challenges in relation to teaching and student learning. Arguably it is during these interactions that teachers construct and maintain beliefs and conceptions about teaching. These trusted few are labelled the teacher's *significant network* (Roxå and Mårtensson, 2009). Thomson (2013) interviewed academics about their conversations on teaching with departmental colleagues, and describes the functions of such conversations as overall supporting the learning about teaching. So, it seems fair to conclude that academic teachers rely on informal networks when they learn about teaching. These networks, however, may not necessarily follow the strategically designed organisation, such as departmental boundaries. Thus, any higher education organisation can be considered as containing a large number of interwoven networks, making up a complex web of meaning-making interactions.

With direct relevance for academic developers, Trowler (2008, 2009) takes a sociocultural point of view. He argues that any attempt to change or develop teaching should focus on the individual teacher within his or her various professional, disciplinary contexts – be that departments, teaching-teams, or work-groups. Trowler has usefully described the traditions constructed in such collegial academic contexts as *teaching and learning regimes (TLR)*. These regimes are socially constructed cultural structures consisting of tacit assumptions, implicit theories about teaching, learning and students; as well as recurrent practices, conventions of appropriateness, and power issues. Trowler convincingly shows how such teaching and learning regimes affect individual teachers' thinking and practice in relation to teaching and student learning, both for good and for bad.

> In one TLR reported to the authors, students were generally considered as 'enemies', constantly demanding higher grades than they deserve. A strategy in practice would then be to give quite substantial, critical feedback on student assignments, so that students in the end were relieved that they actually passed the course.

> In another TLR, students were rather considered as future colleagues, with implications in terms of how feedback to their assignments would be verbalised more constructively and supportive.

As research on student learning indicates the importance of feedback and formative assessment (see for instance Hattie, 2008; O'Donovan, Rust, Price and Carroll, 2006) these two different teaching and learning regimes and their resulting feedback strategies would clearly have completely different outcomes on student learning.

Jawitz (2009) studied how new academics learn how to assess and grade student work in different disciplinary contexts within the same university. He clearly demonstrates how different assessing and grading traditions have developed over time in different collegial contexts. For example, in one context the new academic does the marking completely isolated from colleagues' opinions, whilst in another context the new academic is gradually introduced in assessment practices through a shared collegial seminar with discussions and negotiations about relevant issues on assessing and marking.

Related to Jawitz' (2009) findings, Roxå and Mårtensson (2011/2013) studied five so called *microcultures* in a research-intensive university. Microcultures were defined as local work-contexts where the members over time develop traditions and habits in a similar way to that described above. Over time, the members collaboratively form versions of the overall academic culture in their respective institution. A microculture can be a department, a workgroup, a disciplinary community or something similar. It doesn't necessarily follow the formally designed organisational boundaries. In Roxå and Mårtensson's study, the microcultures, strong in both research and teaching, were characterised by high internal trust; intense interaction, communication and collegial support; high demands on students paired with active support for learning; and rich collaborations external to the microculture. Some of the teachers involved would for instance teach in pairs, share all teaching material with each other, act as critical friends to each other, or initiate a readers' club across disciplines in relation to their challenge of forming a joint international master's programme. Each microculture was significantly influenced by their own story about themselves and who they were, but they also had a clear idea of where they were going, and what the purpose of their existence was. These future-oriented visions could be about changing the society, improving the industry or developing the profession.

Jawitz' findings, together with Trowler's description of teaching and learning regimes, as well as Roxå and Mårtensson's exploration of academic microcultures, convincingly illustrate how teaching traditions over time become internalised and institutionalised, and how they influence teachers towards certain teaching and assessment methods, perspectives on students, learning, etc.

A widespread and lately much used model for designing professional development builds on the idea of *communities of practice* (Wenger, 1999). Wenger and Snyder (2000) define communities of practice (CoP) as 'groups of people informally bound together by shared expertise and passion for a joint enterprise' (p. 139). So, in relation to the above, a community of practice would always also constitute a microculture. But an academic microculture is not necessarily a community of practice – at least not in relation to teaching, and as defined by Wenger. For a detailed account of this, see also Roxå and Mårtensson (2015). A key task for any CoP is to *define its domain*. Unless members feel personally connected to the group's area of expertise and interest once it has been defined, they will not fully commit themselves to the work of the community (ibid., p. 144). In relation to academic development, the domain could be teaching and student learning, and any aspect of this, including assessment and programme design. Although CoPs are fundamentally informal and self-organising, they can still benefit from *cultivation* (ibid., p. 143). This means they can be nurtured and supported in different ways, although this needs to be done in a way which respects the current CoP. In the US, for instance, Cox (2004) reports on the benefits of learning communities as a means for academic teachers to jointly learn about and improve their teaching.

One key aspect of cultivating a CoP – for instance the task of academic developers responsible for an academic professional development programme – is the use of *events;* i.e. bringing members of the community together, for different *types* of activities and with a certain *rhythm* in order to gain momentum for the group and secure the ongoing interaction. In practice, this means that academic developers can make sure that a group of people regularly come together for a learning/development purpose. Another aspect of cultivation concerns *connectivity*, meaning that it is important to enable a rich fabric of connections among those involved – getting people together, and securing interaction between members through multiple media. So, again in reference to a programme this means that academic developers need to make sure there are rich opportunities face-to-face and online for participants to interact with each other, discussing aspects and sharing experiences of teaching and learning. Even grouping people and making sure that the setting of the room and opportunities for informal conversations at breaks support connectivity. Members of a CoP deepen their mutual commitment when they take the responsibility for a learning agenda, so a third key aspect is a *learning project*, which pushes their practice further. Activities might include exploring a knowledge domain or finding gaps in the community's practice and defining projects to close the gaps. So in a programme it is important that participants get the opportunity to explore a phenomenon in relation to their own teaching and their students' learning, and that participants share and discuss these phenomena with each other. Fourthly, a community has to consider what *artefacts* or tangible traces of learning are meaningful, and who should produce and maintain them, so they will remain useful as the community evolves. This can be made possible in several ways, such as papers, posters, presentations and the like that display the result of the learning projects that participants have engaged in.

Finally, in terms of *leadership*, a CoP depends on internal leadership; it is not 'managed' in a corporate way (Wenger and Snyder, 2000). However, the role of a *community coordinator* is crucial. Academic developers could be considered as community coordinators, when designing formal academic development programmes, building on the idea of CoP. But a community also needs additional and multiple forms of leadership. The balance between these forms of leadership will change over time.

Some implications for academic development

> While I came up with the initial plan for my course, it has been designed and carried out as a close collaboration between virtually all teachers at my department, as well as a few external teachers. My colleagues, with their experience, enthusiasm and constructive suggestions and ideas, have been invaluable to the creation and carrying out of the course. I can only hope that other new employees receive the same backing when they present their ideas to colleagues at other departments. (Participant in a pedagogical course, 2010)

Below we will highlight some implications for academic development practice based on the ideas outlined above. We argue that academic developers can both directly and indirectly address the local collegial contexts. Consequently, appropriate activities can be built into formally designed academic development programmes, but at the same time academic developers can also work more directly with the academics' local contexts. In the next section we will therefore showcase some examples of how we have used these perspectives in the academic development work at our university. These activities are further developed in Mårtensson (2014); Mårtensson, Roxå and Olsson (2011); and Roxå, Olsson and Mårtensson (2008).

Academic development programmes

The quote above originates from a follow-up study of some of the pedagogical courses at our university (Larsson and Mårtensson, 2014). The pedagogical courses in our university are designed with the intention to support *both* the individual academic teachers *and* their collegial contexts in improving teaching and student learning. The courses are modularised and usually comprise between 80–200 hours of participants' time, of which roughly 30 per cent are contact hours. All courses are related to nationally established goals and outcomes for such programmes (Lindberg-Sand and Sonesson, 2008). Some courses have participants exclusively from one faculty, whereas other courses have participants from across the university. The courses are all based on the model of communities of practice, as described above, and also aim to support teachers to engage in *scholarship of teaching and learning* (Boyer, 1990; Kreber, 2002) by relating their own teaching practices to educational literature in their assignments. The written course assignment, which here constitutes one *artefact* in Wenger's model, is peer-reviewed and discussed by fellow participants within the pedagogical course and also discussed with one or more 'critical friends' (Handal, 1999) at the participants' own department. Comments from these critical friends are to be included in the final version of the assignment. Participants have a large degree of freedom to choose the content of the assignment, so that it matches their perceived learning needs, in relation to their disciplinary prerequisites, and where they are in their teaching careers.

The participants also choose their own critical friends. These may be one or two trusted colleagues within the teacher's significant network, or colleagues who teach on the same course, or others. Some participants choose their programme leader or director of studies as critical friends, thereby being able to connect their project to a formal local leader. In the study by Larsson and Mårtensson (2014) it was evident that the critical friend component of the courses contributed to the fact that nearly 80 per cent of the 130 respondents claimed that they had partly or fully been able to implement improvements in their teaching after taking the pedagogical course.

Case study – choosing an appropriate critical friend

Karen is a PhD student who attends a pedagogical course. Her supervisor who is a professor of her discipline has advised her not to engage too much in 'such nonsense'. In her assignment she chooses to analyse and suggest improvements, based on educational literature and research, for a course in her discipline. Previously, she has given a few lectures in this particular course, for which the professor is responsible. When deciding on whom to use as a critical friend to read and comment on her draft assignment, she hesitates to ask the professor, knowing his negative attitude to pedagogical courses. However, she decides to ask him anyway. After all he is responsible for the course that her assignment concerns. She returns from the conversation, her face shining, saying that first of all, after reading her text, the professor wanted to give her more influence over the course design, and teaching in the course, based on her analysis and informed suggestions for improvements. Secondly, the professor had said: 'If this is what you do in the pedagogical courses, I will have to re-evaluate my judgment of them'.

The example above shows the value of designing academic development programmes with the participants' social collegial context in mind. Furthermore, it shows how specific activities built into the design of such programmes can help to bridge between the programme, educational theory and the participants' teaching context. The written assignments constitute scholarly *artefacts* that can be used, as exemplified above, to influence and strengthen conversations within collegial networks, so called *strong ties* (Granovetter, 1973) signified by high density in interactions and emotional relatedness. The main principle is to design assignments that are considered meaningful and worthwhile for *both* the individual participant *and* for his/her teaching context. Another way we do this at our university is to encourage participants to discuss, and perhaps even define, their course assignment together with their director of studies – in the Swedish system the director of studies is their closest leader in relation to teaching. By doing so they can negotiate the assignment and its meaning for the local practice already at the outset of the course. This, in turn, implies that the instructions and design of the assignment need to be somewhat open for interpretation and local adjustments.

Working with the academics' collegial contexts

As a further complement to how academic developers can design academic development programmes, we can also work directly with the social and collegial context of the teachers, in several ways:

- *Consultation*: at the end of pedagogical courses we offer to consult with the participants' teaching teams, departments or microcultures in relation to any chosen topic of their concern in relation to teaching and learning. Individual teachers, who may find it difficult to inspire or persuade colleagues to rethink their teaching practice, can invite academic developers to come to a departmental seminar, or run a workshop, or just participate in a collegial conversation about the chosen topic. These consultations can be a stand-alone event, or become a longer commitment where academic developers follow a group of teachers and their efforts to develop their curriculum, or certain aspects of it. Consultation is also offered outside the courses, and to any sector of the university: individual teachers, groups of teachers, departments, program coordinators and boards, senior faculty management, student union, and administrative support units. The topics covered are basically everything related to teaching and learning. In one of our faculties, consultation time is advertised, and different groups of teachers can, quite informally, apply for such time. The main criterion for receiving this kind of consultation is that it involves more than one individual teacher and therefore encourages collegial interactions rather than just individual support.

- *Collegial course*: As an extension of the above, a department, a working group, a teaching team or a similar group of colleagues can apply for a *collegial course* ('Collegial Project Course', n.d.). This is a pedagogical course organised especially for a group of academic teachers who share a local working context. They read about, discuss, and document a particular aspect of teaching of their own choice. The course is led collaboratively by a teacher in the discipline and an academic developer. The aim is to offer consultancy inside the immediate and informal processes of a microculture in relation to the development of teaching and student learning.
- *Development projects*: academic developers can work together with academic teachers on specific projects.

Case study – curriculum redesign, team-working

The journalism curriculum was criticised by the external national quality agency. A group of teachers decided to take the criticism seriously as an opportunity to redesign their curriculum as well as to support the idea of working as a team rather that a set of individuals. They engaged an academic developer to support the process. The one-year long process consisted of a number of seminars and workshops where different aspects of the curriculum were critically investigated. The teachers, and the director of studies, who was leading the process, wrote drafts of course syllabi, instructions for assignments, etc. These were all discussed in the group and set in relation to other journalism curricula in the country, to external experts' comments, and to educational literature. At the end of the year a new curriculum was launched, which was also approved by the quality agency.

The examples above illustrate how academic developers can take the perspectives of social networks, microcultures and communities of practise into account and work with them directly, in one sense from the inside. Academic developers need to find strategies to develop such relations suitable for the context they are active in. In our university that has come about through offering the collegial consultancy to faculty deans, to heads of departments and to programme coordinators who have wanted to initiate development. On one occasion an academic developer invited herself to a faculty meeting with all the heads of departments. She presented the numbers of teachers from that faculty who had participated in pedagogical courses over the past two years, and also how many hours of engagement for developing teaching that corresponded to. The question to the heads of departments was in what way they made use of all those hours. The resulting discussion made visible that the courses are deliberately designed to be sensitive to the teachers' and departments' working conditions. Following this discussion, new routines were established for how a better alignment between pedagogical courses and the local microculture could be supported.

It is also important to consider the networks and microcultures that academics are part of in a system (Roxå, Mårtensson and Alveteg, 2010). The pattern of microcultures together, analytically, form a complex web that comprises programmes, departments, schools and faculties in a university, thereby making up the *meso-level* of the organisation (Hannah and Lester, 2009; Roxå, 2014). The university-level or even the national level would consequently be considered the macro-level. Following from this, and as pointed out by Hannah and Lester (2009) and Mårtensson (2014), it can be fruitful and effective for academic and organisational development to build bridges between different microcultures. These can be what Granovetter (1973) calls *weak ties*, signified by less dense and less frequent interaction than the strong ties.

From an academic development point of view, one potential approach is to make the assignments that are written within pedagogical courses – the artefacts – into resources available to forthcoming cohorts of participants, for instance through a database or a website. From an organisational point of view, such as a faculty or a university, supporting weak ties can include having a campus newsletter and campus conferences on teaching and learning, as well as blogs and other arenas with the opportunity for various microcultures across the university to influence and be influenced by each other (Mårtensson, 2014).

Academic developers as a community

So, if these perspectives are useful in our ways of working with academic teachers, are they also useful when considering ourselves, our roles as academic developers and our own professional development?

Academic developers around the world have a lot in common, perhaps a shared passion to develop and enhance teaching and learning in higher education. We also share some practices, even if we work in different national and institutional contexts. And we participate in the exploration, meaning-making, and development of academic development as a field. This passion becomes visible, not the least through the worldwide organisation ICED and its biennial conferences (described elsewhere in this book, including in Chapter 1), as well as in publications in *IJAD*, the *International Journal for Academic Development*. Many countries have national networks for academic developers, including SEDA in the UK, POD in the US, DUN in Denmark, HERDSA in Australasia, UniPed in Norway, Red-U in Spain and Swednet in Sweden. Professional development of academic developers might come about naturally through respective network or participation in conferences etc. The development of academic developers is considered further in Chapters 1 and 3. However, such development can also be fuelled by more systematic approaches using the Communities of Practice-model as a design tool. From 2001 to 2012, in the UK, the SEDA Summer School, open also for participants from other countries, was a three-day intensive course for new academic developers. For those participating it was an opportunity to learn for instance how to run a workshop, how to initiate and support change, how to evaluate effects of academic development activities. In the following, another initiative, in Sweden, will be described briefly. For further details, see Roxå and Mårtensson (2008), and Mårtensson and Roxå (2014).

Strategic Educational Development – a national course

In 2004, the Swedish government assigned Swednet to provide professional development for academic developers. Swednet came up with several suggestions, one of which was a national course for academic developers on the topic 'Strategic Educational Development'. The course was given twice, each time with roughly 20 participants. The authors of this chapter were the course leaders, together with a senior academic developer from another Swedish university. The course spanned one year, corresponded to five weeks of participant time, with two start-off days where the whole group met, a five-day retreat in the middle, and two end-of-course days. In between, course participants worked on a project anchored in their own institutional context and with a character of being strategic in relation to academic development. 'Strategic' here meant doing something that targeted not only individual academics, but had a larger scope, including for example: the implementation of an institutional policy related to teaching and learning, evaluating a programme on teaching and learning for academics, developing a scheme for rewarding excellent teaching, changing institutional course evaluation practices, creating support for educational leaders, etc. Some of the projects resulting from this initiative are reported in a special issue of *Higher Education Research and Development* (Vol. 27, issue 2, 2008).

Key features of this initiative, based on the significant traits of cultivating a CoP, were:

- The learning *projects* that each course participant (i.e. academic developer) worked on during the course. These were written up as draft reports at several points of time during the course. They had to be scholarly, i.e. underpinned by relevant literature, and they were continuously peer-reviewed and discussed within the group. This way, *participation in meaning-making*, was secured over time. The resulting *artefacts*, the reports, could be used for dissemination within participants' institutions, and to other academic developers.
- *Connectivity* was secured, as enough time was provided for people to get to know each other and develop trust. Discussions on for the participants, relevant and important topics were organised in a fairly small group during several face-to-face meetings, not least the retreat mid-ways. A web-platform facilitated interactions between meetings.
- Over the year the course lasted, the participants processed their projects, followed up on previous discussions, and by doing so developed a sense of belonging. In the end each participant's *identity* was affected (Mårtensson and Roxå, 2014).
- *Coordination*: Although the course leaders had a formal role mainly consisting of organising times and places to meet, suggesting readings, and inviting guests, the group itself took the lead using shared experiences.

After the two occasions the course was offered, participants who had taken the course represented almost 50 per cent of the Swedish higher education institutions. Later, a national follow-up conference was organised, with both cohorts invited to share updates on their strategic projects (Mårtensson, 2009). The Swedish network for educational development, Swednet (www.swednetwork.se), is currently planning on organising a similar course.

Conclusion

In this chapter we have argued that it is the academic teachers' daily practices, and meaning-making interactions with their colleagues, that will have the strongest influence on how individual teachers think and act in relation to teaching and student learning. We have used a theoretical framework that captures social networks, academic microcultures in the 'meso' or middle level of the organisation and used communities of practice as a specific framing of such collegial contexts. While doing this we have drawn on van Maanen's (2007) model of three lenses – strategic design, political and cultural – to understand an organisation, we acknowledge that all three are important. This chapter has particularly picked up on the third of these, aspects of the organisational cultural environment, since we consider this to be the most important for academic development to address. We claim that it is mainly through day-to-day interactions and meaning-making processes in collegial contexts that academics develop their understanding and practices of teaching. We have argued that academic developers may benefit from taking these collegial contexts into account when designing activities and support for the development of teaching and learning within an institution. We also have provided examples from our own university of what academic developers can do. The chapter thus outlines how academic developers can work in several different ways to support, not only individual academics, but also their collegial contexts in which their teaching is practiced. By designing academic development with the specific purpose of supporting *both* individuals *and* their local context, their *microculture*, we think academic development initiatives can reach a greater potential in their endeavour to improve student learning.

It is our hope that this text can inspire other academic developers to engage with passion in a networked web of meaning-making and enhancement processes within their own institutional contexts.

References

Alvesson, M. (2002). *Understanding Organizational Culture*. London: Sage.

Ancona, D. G., Kochan, T. A., Scully, M., Van Maanen, J. and Westney, D. E. (2009). *Managing for the Future. Organizational Behaviour and Processes*. Mason, OH: South Western Cengage Learning.

Berger, P. and Luckmann, T. (1966). *The Social Construction of Reality. A Treatise in the Sociology of Knowledge*. Penguin Books.

Boyer, E. (1990). *Scholarship Reconsidered: Priorities of the Professoriate*. Princeton, NJ: The Carnegie Foundation.

Chalmers, D., Stoney, S., Goody, A., Goerke, V. and Gardiner, D. (2012). 'Measuring the effectiveness of academic professional development. Identification and implementation of indicators and measures of effectiveness of teaching preparation programmes for academics in higher education' (Ref: SP10-1840). The University of Western Australia Curtin.

Collegial Project Course (n.d.). retrieved 25 May 2015 from www.lth.se/fileadmin/lth/genombrottet/KursplanGB_S21_KK2v__eng.pdf.

Cox, M. (2004). 'Introduction to faculty learning communities'. *New Directions for Teaching and Learning*. 2004(97): 5–23.

Gibbs, G. (2013). 'Reflections on the changing nature of educational development', *International Journal for Academic Development*, DOI:10.1080/13601 44X.2013.751691.

Gibbs, G. and Coffey, M. (2004). 'The impact of training of university teachers on their teaching skills, their approach to teaching and the approach to learning of their students', *Active Learning in Higher Education*, 5: 87–100.

Granovetter, M. (1973). 'The strength of weak ties', *American Journal of Sociology*, 78(6): 1360–1380.

Handal, G. (1999). 'Consultation using critical friends', *New Directions for Teaching and Learning*, 79: 59–70.

Hannah, S., and Lester, P. (2009). 'A multilevel approach to building and leading learning organisations', *The Leadership Quarterly*, 20: 34–48.

Hattie, J. (2008). *Visible Learning: A Synthesis of Over 800 Meta-Analyses Relating to Achievement*. Routledge.

Jawitz, J. (2009). 'Learning in the academic workplace: The harmonization of the collective and the individual habitus', *Studies in Higher Education*, 34(6): 601–614.

Knight, P. (2006). 'Quality enhancement and educational professional development', *Quality in Higher Education*, 12(1): 29–40.

Kreber, C. (2002). 'Teaching excellence, teaching expertise and the scholarship of teaching', *Innovative Higher Education*, 27(1): 5–23.

Larsson, M., and Mårtensson, K. (2014). 'From individual to collegial – the impact of project-based teacher training programmes.' Presentation at the ISSOTL-conference *Nurturing Creativity and Passion in Teaching*, Quebec, Canada, October 22–25, 2014.

Lindberg-Sand, Å., and Sonesson, A., (2008). 'Compulsory higher education teacher training in Sweden: development of a national standards framework based on the scholarship of teaching and learning', *Tertiary Education and Management*, 14(2): 123–139.

Mårtensson, K. (2014). *Influencing teaching and learning microcultures. Academic development in a research-intensive university*. PhD thesis, Department of Design Sciences, Faculty of Engineering, Lund University. Media-Tryck, Lund.

Mårtensson, K. (Ed., 2009). Strategisk pedagogisk utveckling – proceedings [Strategic educational development – proceedings]. Lund University, Centre for Educational Development.

Mårtensson, K., and Roxå, T. (2014). 'Promoting learning and professional development through communities of practice', *Perspectives on Pedagogy and Practice*, 5: 1–21.

Mårtensson, K., Roxå, T. and Olsson, T. (2011). 'Developing a quality culture through the scholarship of teaching and learning', *Higher Education Research and Development*, 30(1): 51–62.

O'Donovan, B., Rust, C., Price, M. and Carroll, J. (2006). '"Staying the distance": The unfolding story of discovery and development through long-term collaborative research into assessment', *Brookes e-Journal of Learning and Teaching*, 1(4): 1–4.

Pataraia, N., Falconer, I., Margaryan, A., Littlejohn, A. and Fincher, S. (2014). '"Who do you talk to about your teaching?": networking activities among university teachers'. *Frontline Learning Research*, 2(2). http://dx.doi.org/10.14786/flr.v2i2.89.

Prosser, M. and Trigwell, K. (1999). *Understanding Learning and Teaching: The Experience in Higher Education*. Buckingham: SRHE and Open University Press.

Prosser, M., Rickinson, M., Bence, V., Hanbury, A. and Kulej, M. (2006). *Formative Evaluation of Accredited Programmes*. York: The Higher Education Academy.

Roxå, T. (2014). *Microcultures in the meso level of higher education organisations – the Commons, the Club, the Market and the Square*. PhD thesis. Department of Design Sciences, Faculty of Engineering, Lund University. Media-Tryck, Lund.

Roxå, T. and Mårtensson, K. (2015). 'Microcultures and informal learning: a heuristic guiding analysis of conditions for informal learning in local higher education workplaces', *International Journal for Academic Development*, 20(2), 193–205.

Roxå, T. and Mårtensson, K. (2011/printed 2013) *Understanding strong academic microcultures. An exploratory study*. Report. Lund University. Available at www.ced.lu.se/marrtensson--roxa-2011.aspx

Roxå, T. and Mårtensson, K. (2009). 'Significant conversations and significant networks – exploring the backstage of the teaching arena'. *Studies in Higher Education*, 34(5), 547–559.

Roxå, T. and K. Mårtensson (2008) 'Strategic educational development: a national Swedish initiative to support change in higher education'. *Higher Education Research and Development*, 27(2), 155–168.

Roxå, T., Mårtensson, K., and Alveteg, M. (2010) 'Understanding and influencing teaching and learning cultures at university – a network approach'. *Higher Education* 62, 99–111; Online First, 25 September 2010.

Roxå, T., Ohlsson, T. and Mårtensson, K. (2008). 'Appropriate use of theory in the scholarship of teaching and learning as a strategy for institutional development'. *Arts and Humanities in Higher Education* 7, 276–294.

Thomson, K.E. (2013). *The nature of academics' informal conversation about teaching*. PhD thesis, University of Sydney, Sydney, Australia.

Trigwell, K. (2012). 'Evaluating the impact of university teaching development programmes. Methodologies that ask why there is an impact'. In E. Simon and G. Pleschová (Eds.) *Teacher Development in Higher Education. Existing Programmes, Programme Impact, and Future Trends* (pp. 257–273). New York and London: Routledge.

Trowler, P. (2009). 'Beyond epistemological essentialism: academic tribes in the twenty-first century'. In C. Kreber (Ed.) *The University and Its Disciplines – Within and Beyond Disciplinary Boundaries* (pp. 181–195). London, Routledge.

Trowler, P. (2008). *Cultures and Change in Higher Education. Theories and Practice*. Gordonsville, Palgrave Macmillan.

Van Maanen, J. (2007). *Three Perspectives on Organizational Change*. Powerpoint presentation at a Dean for Undergraduate Leadership Retreat, June 15, MIT, Cambridge, MA.

Wenger, E. (1999). *Communities of Practice. Learning, Meaning and Identity*. Cambridge, Cambridge University Press.

Wenger, E. and Snyder, W.M. (2000). 'Communities of practice: The organizational frontier'. *Harvard Business Review*, reprint R00110; January–February.

Chapter 12

Researching academic development

Kathryn Sutherland and Barbara Grant

Summary

This chapter explores the nature and purposes of academic development, and relates this exploration to an analysis of what, how and for whom research in academic development has been and is undertaken. The history and the growth of research in academic development are reviewed. Current trends in academic development research are identified, through analysis of recent issues of three journals and through categorisation of papers by research paradigm and methodology. Topics and futures for research into and the scholarship of educational development are suggested. The chapter concludes with advice to new academic developers on how to become researchers of academic development.

Links to web sources referenced in this chapter can be found at www.seda.ac .uk/apad.

Introduction

In placing ourselves in the academy as practitioners and scholars, several big questions have perplexed academic development researchers. One has concerned our identity as a discipline. Are we a disciplinary community with all the rules and supposed privileges associated with such a claim (Bath and Smith, 2004)? Or are we, as others have suggested, a distinctive field of practice (Clegg, 2009; Shay, 2012), influenced by many disciplinary communities, backgrounds, leanings, histories? Or should we, as still others have proposed, be resisting any such classification, identification or categorisation (Grant, 2007; Lee and McWilliam, 2008; Webb, 1996)?

A second cluster of questions concerns the communities and purposes we serve (academics, students, institutions, governments, ourselves?) – and, thus, for whom we do our research. As Stefani and Baume suggest in Chapter 10, on evaluation, many academic developers are expected to produce evidence-based evaluation of their work in order to ensure their unit's (if not their own) survival through the securing of ongoing funding. Much of our day-to-day research may be directed towards producing evidence of the effectiveness, or impact, of our own and others' practices. Yet this accountability regime does not always resonate with the kind of research and writing that brings us joy and intellectual stimulation (Peseta, 2007). Slightly more academic developers come from narrative literary fields than come from scientific backgrounds (Green and Little, 2015), and take a scholarly approach that favours questioning, storytelling, and opening up ideas for scrutiny and debate, rather than pinning down the claimed best evidence or identifying conclusive claims of certainty. Thus, academic development research serves many masters – from the vice-chancellor who wants to know that it is worth continuing to fund the operation of a Learning and Teaching Centre or where to direct a discretionary fund for digital learning innovations, to the academics whom we try to convince a practice is worth attempting, to national centres for higher education and government funding bodies who solicit or desire research on the impact of large-scale empirical teaching and learning projects, to ourselves as a community of practitioners and as individual researchers/scholars. Is there space for different kinds of research and are we reaching all these stakeholders?

A third set of questions relates to *what* and *how* we are researching. What and who are the subjects of our research? For example, Chapter 11 reports and applies extensive research into development with communities of academics. What methodologies and methods do we employ to investigate the answers to our research questions? What theories inform our approaches? By focusing on these questions in the light of past and current practice in academic development research, this chapter aims to open space for further conversation, especially about what kinds of research questions and designs, and modes of writing, we might pursue in the future. We look at the research that academic developers have been and are doing in, on, for and about academic development, as well as consider the likelihood that much of our research is about learning and teaching, and about helping others to do research into *their* teaching and learning. We also point new academic developers in the direction of good readings on research in academic development and, to a lesser extent, higher education more broadly.

History of research in academic development

As a field of practice, academic (or educational) development dates back up to six decades across diverse national sites including Australia (Lee, Manathunga and Kandlbinder, 2008), Aotearoa New Zealand (Barrow, Grant and Brailsford, 2010), the UK (Gibbs, 2013), South Africa (Boughey and Niven, 2012) and the US (Felten et al., 2007; Sorcinelli, Austin, Eddy and Beach, 2006). During this time, it has been variously referred to as a discipline (Bath and Smith, 2004), a community (Boughey and Niven, 2012), and a project (Clegg, 2009; Peseta, 2007). In what follows, we use the concept of a field to refer to the group of people engaging in academic development practice, research and scholarship, rather than using other terms such as *discipline* or *profession*. Both of us are resistant to staking a claim for identity as an academic profession or discipline for reasons explained elsewhere (Grant, 2007). And, while there is not space in this chapter to summarise all earlier accounts of research in and on academic development, we hope that the work we cite might offer an enticement to further reading for those who may wish to delve more into academic development histories.

At various points in the history of our field, different academic generations of developers have been identified (Lee et al., 2008), from the pathfinders of the 1960s and 70s, to the pathbreakers of the 1980s and 90s, to the precarious workers of the 2000s. First-generation developers have differing recollections of the place of research during the emerging years of the field, and scholarly accounts from different countries/regions imply varying approaches. In some places, such as the Universities of Melbourne (Lee et al., 2008) and Auckland (Barrow et al., 2010), academic development emerged out of an institutional research unit; in others, research did not feature prominently until the 1980s (Lee et al., 2008, p. 98; Scott, 2009) or even later (Felten, Kalish, Pingree and Plank, 2007; Gibbs, 2013).

In the US, Felten and colleagues (2007) claim that, while '[e]ducational development has been a growing field for the last 50 years or so... for most of that time it has been a practice-based discipline with little in the way of systematic study of its range, its activities, or especially its outcomes' (p. 94). Similarly, in Australia, Lonsdale claimed that, in the early days, '[r]esearch, or a good understanding of the processes we were dealing with, did not guide our early work. In fact research in the field was discouraged in a number of universities; the expectation was that educational development units would concentrate on providing services, and not engage in research or other academic activities carried out by colleagues in other parts of the university' (Lee et al., 2008, p. 98). By contrast, Falk, described as having 'played a foundational role in making a place for teaching and learning in Australia' (p. 16) and influencing the first and second generation of academic developers in that country, remembers that, from the beginning, her work and that of the Centre for the Study of Higher Education was 'fundamentally supported by research' (p. 30).

In South Africa, similar uneven patterns were evident, though often for more political reasons: Boughey and Niven (2012) claim that certain:

> Communities of practice in Academic Development were more research productive than others at particular times and ... that the mechanisms underlying this productivity related strongly to the epistemological resources that were available in these communities. (p. 651)

In a similar vein, Scott (2009) suggests historical and political contexts prevented the little research that was happening in academic development in South Africa from being published beyond national conference proceedings or in local institutional documents.

In the UK, research in higher education has been prevalent for many years, but more latterly there has been a recognition that research on and for academic development, as a particular field within higher education, was increasingly necessary.

Eggins and Macdonald's (2003) book, *The Scholarship of Academic Development*, arose from the joint SEDA and SRHE conference in 1999 that came at 'a key moment when the academic community was beginning to recognise that there was a need for rigorous research studies on academic development itself' (p. xi). Around the same time, Brew (2002) also called for more research *in* academic development, but acknowledged 'there rarely seems time to indulge in what often feels like the *luxury* of research' (p. 112, our italics).

Thirteen years on, many more academic developers are researching and publishing as a matter of necessity, not luxury. Research and publication are now an expected part of our jobs and in many countries, like New Zealand, government-imposed research exercises require those of us on academic contracts to be active researchers. In South Africa:

> [c]hanges in the state-funding formula in the early 2000s have meant that research production also became more lucrative, with articles in accredited journals attracting substantial income. This has put pressure on those working in the movement to research and publish, if only because of the institutional income produced. (Boughey and Niven, 2012, p. 651)

Even as Fraser and Ling (2014) point to a downturn in the number of academic developers being appointed on academic contracts, this does not necessarily appear to be preventing academic developers from engaging in research activity, although it might shape the kind of work they are doing: in a survey of UK educational developers, Gosling noted that:

> 72.5% of EDUs [Educational Development Units] now saw undertaking or contributing to pedagogic research as part of their function and 67.5% saw their role as sponsoring research into teaching and learning. (cited in Fraser and Ling, 2014, p. 228)

In the past couple of decades, published research for and on academic development has increased greatly. The *International Journal for Academic Development* (*IJAD*), the flagship journal of the International Consortium for Educational Development, published its first volume in 1996, consisting of two issues and around 200 pages of articles, reviews and notes. By 2013, the journal had expanded its output to four issues and 400+ pages per year. Similar growth is seen in higher education research in general (Tight, 2012), with more articles published on academic development practices, approaches and problems – written by and for academic developers, sometimes in partnership with other academics and practitioners. This period has also seen an increase in the publication of research questioning the focus, breadth, approaches, theories and methodologies of academic development.

Origins of academic development more broadly are explored in Chapter 18, on futures.

What were we researching?

Practice in the field has shifted from a focus on teaching and the individual academic to a focus on learning and students (Fraser and Ling, 2014), and more recently to communities of academics (Chapter 11) and institution- and sector-wide education concerns and agendas (Jones, 2010; Fraser and Ling 2014). So too has published research in academic development. Brew (2003) provides a succinct summary of the kinds of topics that academic developer researchers have focussed on over the years:

> Basic research into students' learning, teaching methods and their effectiveness, conceptions of teaching, conceptions of the subject matter held by students and their teachers, effects of particular aspects of the learning environment on students' learning experiences has been the mainstay of academic development work.... [T]he adult education literature has also been important, as has literature on personal and organizational transformation, the research on higher education policy, as well as more specific theoretical and practical literatures, for example situated cognition, cognitive changes, critical theory, postmodernism and on specific aspects of teaching and learning: assessment, group work, information technology in teaching and learning, and so on. (Brew, 2003, p. 170)

More recently, Kandlbinder and Peseta (2009) have summarised the key concepts taught in postgraduate certificates of higher education in Australasia and the UK. They identified the following five concepts and their associated authors:

1 Reflective practice (Schön, Brookfield);
2 Constructive alignment (Biggs);
3 Student approaches to learning (Marton and Säljö; Ramsden);
4 Scholarship of teaching (Boyer);
5 Assessment-driven learning (Gibbs and Simpson).

The work and influence of the proponents (original and subsequent) of these concepts can be recognised in the pages of many academic development and higher education journals. Many of these men (for they are all men – see Kandlbinder [2014] on the gendered state of citations in higher education research) feature among the most cited researchers in the English-speaking higher education literature (Tight, 2008). Some commentators see the *consumption* of teaching and learning research as a professional responsibility: academic developers are 'repositories of knowledge' about research on learning and teaching (Macdonald, 2002) and 'translators' of pedagogical research for those with whom we work (Peseta, 2007). In this view, we should be attentive readers and consumers, keeping up-to-date with the broad literature on teaching and learning, in order to be knowledgeable practitioners (Jones, 2010). Others argue that academic developers must also be *scholars and researchers* of teaching and learning, producing new knowledge that challenges, changes, critiques, and informs the field (Brew 2002; Grant 2013).

For whom were we researching?

In *IJAD's* first-ever editorial, Baume identified some audiences for academic development research: *IJAD* would be a journal, he declared, with a distinctive focus on:

> ... the processes of helping institutions, departments, course teams and individual staff to research into, reflect on and develop policy and practice about teaching, learning and assessment and other activities in support of learning. (Baume, 1996, p. 4)

The articles published would represent research on and for teaching and learning, for institutions, and for their staff, as well as on and for the academic developers; they would also be 'much concerned with the nature and philosophy of, as well as the practice of, academic developers' (Baume, 1996, p. 5). As Macdonald acknowledged less than a decade later, however:

> ... the obvious tensions between supporting managerial top-down initiatives and the needs or wishes of 'ordinary' staff mean that academic developers can sometimes feel like either the filling in a sandwich or a cushion between conflicting interests. (2003, p. 9)

Academic developers need to balance the expectations of these different audiences – academics and managers – and find the right language to meet the needs of both without buying into 'managerialist language' (Jones, 2010) that might alienate some of their audience. They also need to balance an expectation that they will produce the practically useful research findings academics seek (Blackmore and Blackwell, 2006; Little, 2014), with the need to talk to each other through their research (Clegg, 2009) by producing critical and theoretical work that can inform their professional practice. And they need to think of their own academic careers and decide:

> ... how much time to spend carrying out strategic research to provide information for institutional managers and how much time to spend on research which will bring the credibility and the rewards needed for promotion and career advancement. (Brew, 2003, p. 173)

A desire for academic credibility (Brew, 2002; Orrell, 2008; Jones, 2010) has seen calls for academic development to stake a claim as an academic discipline in its own right (Bath and Smith, 2004). Many in the field appear keen to work towards such an identity: a survey of POD members in the US and Canada identified a desire among faculty developers for working towards gaining:

> ... more respect and credibility as a field or discipline of study ... [which are] linked to the field's ability to articulate a body of scholarly knowledge, standards, and core competencies that defines it, and to build on the research base already laid for the scholarship of teaching. (Sorcinelli et al., 2006, p. 142)

Other researchers argue, however, that academic development is still in its infancy and has not yet built a strong or distinctive enough, shared, scholarly base to make this claim (Clegg, 2012; Felten et al., 2007; Grant, 2007; Harland and Staniforth, 2008; Lee and McWilliam, 2008; Shay, 2012).

Whether we are a discipline, a field, or a profession, academic developers must write for others – academics, students, university leaders and managers, and government policy-makers – as well as for each other. Not all our work needs to be concerned with what we or others *do* (Grant, 2013); it can also be about *who* we are (Lee and McWilliam, 2008), *why* we do what we do (Clegg, 2009), and how we *feel* when we do what we do (Peseta, 2007). In a poignant article, Peseta calls for more attention to what we conceive of as useful, publishable, readable research in academic development. She argues that the institutional agendas prescribing many of our research projects – and the turn to a privileging of evidence-based research – have seen academic development research narrow its focus. Foreshadowing Graham Gibbs' (2013) complaint about the 'affect-free' nature of much academic development work in recent years, Peseta calls for more narrative, more feeling, more accounts of difficulty and failure, so that we might read and feel the full range of our practices and experiences in our writing.

How were we researching?

The breadth of academic developers' prior disciplinary experiences and expertise means that both our practice and research will manifest in divergent ways. Such divergence can be illuminating, in that it opens up many different ways of viewing the world and the people with whom we work, *and* limiting, in that we do not share a core theoretical or methodological language (Little, 2014).

Tight (2004) has claimed that, in the last decade of the twentieth century, the overlapping communities of practice conducting research into higher education had produced research that was, in the main, a-theoretical. However, academic development was identified by Tight as a more highly theorised field than many others, as evidenced by the number of articles in his sample that employed explicit theoretical perspectives and methodologies:

> Where theory is explicit, the authors appear more likely to be based in a social science department or academic development unit, rather than an education department or higher education research centre. (Tight, 2004, p. 395)

Since then, Tight (2012) has analysed a slightly different, but overlapping, sample of higher education journals, and identified an overall increase in engagement with theory in the intervening decade. His more recent sample did not, however, include *IJAD*, and only 10 per cent of the contributing authors to the 567 articles were academic developers.

So, what are some of the theoretical perspectives and methodologies that academic developers have been using in their research? In that first issue of *IJAD*, Graham Webb (1996) named 'reflective practice', 'deep and surface' approaches to learning (phenomenography) and 'emancipatory action research' as key theoretical frames influencing the interpretation and enactment of academic development. Macdonald (2003) also identified action research and phenomenography as particularly prominent research approaches in the history of academic development, along with evaluation (discussed in Chapter 10). In more recent years, the research approaches appearing in the field have broadened, featuring methods as diverse as questionnaires, interviews, textual and documentary analysis, conversational dialogues, structural equation modelling, (auto)biographical narratives, focus groups, and participant or video observations. As in education research more generally, there are 'no standard, off-the-peg approaches' (Wisdom, 2002, p. 224).

What and how are we researching now? Current trends in academic development research

To explore current trends in academic development research, we looked at the research methodologies, methods, and theoretical frameworks for all the academic development-related articles in three peer-reviewed publications across 2013. Each publication – *Higher Education Research and Development* (*HERD*), the *International Journal for Academic Development* (*IJAD*) and *To Improve the Academy: Resources for Faculty, Instructional, and Organizational Development* (*TIA*) – is associated with a professional organisation with strong ties to academic development and is briefly introduced here.

Higher Education Research and Development (HERD) (Vol. 32)

HERD is the learned journal of the Higher Education Research and Development Society of Australasia (HERDSA). Published since 1982, it has grown from a largely regional peer-reviewed journal to an international one with six issues each year. In terms of content, the journal has a broad higher education focus, as seen in its Aims and Scope:

> HERD... publishes scholarly articles that make a significant and original contribution to the theory, practice or research of higher education. We welcome empirical, theoretical, philosophical and historical articles and essays that address higher education in any of its dimensions. (HERD 32(6) [2013] inside back cover)

With academic development as only one area of higher education among many, and with a publication criterion that accepted articles must make a new contribution to the field, the journal does not publish case studies of practice nor does it usually publish evaluation studies of an author's own practice unless the work is researched or theorised in a novel way. In 2013, *HERD* published 71 articles altogether across six issues: nine of these articles focused on academic development.

International Journal for Academic Development (IJAD) (Vol. 18)

IJAD is the journal of the International Consortium for Educational Development ('ICED', n.d.), which currently (2015) has 24 member organisations across the world, and whose aims include: helping partner organisations develop their capacity for educational development in higher education through the sharing of good practice, problems and solutions. Published since 1996, and with a panel of four co-editors and four associate editors from four different continents, the stated purpose of *IJAD* is to:

> ... enable academic/educational/faculty developers in higher education across the world to exchange ideas about practice and extend the theory of educational development, with the goal of improving the quality of higher education internationally. (*IJAD*'s Aims and Scope)

IJAD publishes scholarly articles on any aspect of academic development, as well as reflections on research and on practice. In 2013, four issues were published with a total of 25 articles, all of which focused on academic development.

To Improve the Academy (TIA): Resources for faculty, instructional, and organisational development (Vol. 32)

TIA is the flagship journal for the Professional and Organizational Development Network in the US. (In 2014, it changed its subtitle to *A Journal of Educational Development*.) As the POD President at the time described:

> Part of the strategic dimension is the emphasis on research-based principles. This new articulation is grounded in POD's current strategic plan, particularly goal #4: Advancing evidence-based practice among our members. Establishing a strong research orientation, and a practice grounded in empirically gathered evidence, is part of the ongoing professionalization of the field and it is also needed to maintain relevance. (DiPietro, 2014)

In 2013, *TIA* published 21 chapters in one volume, all of which focused on academic development.

Categorisation of papers for inclusion in analysis

Based on a careful reading of the article title, abstract, keywords and reference list, followed by a faster read of the article content, we grouped the 55 academic development articles found across the three publications for 2013 into the following three categories:

1 Original research, as defined in New Zealand's Performance-Based Research Fund Guidelines:

> [R]esearch is original investigation undertaken in order to contribute to knowledge and understanding ... It typically involves enquiry of an experimental or critical nature driven by hypotheses or intellectual positions capable of rigorous assessment by experts in a given discipline. It is an independent, creative, cumulative and often long-term activity conducted by people with specialist knowledge about the theories, methods and information concerning their field of enquiry. Its findings must be open to scrutiny and formal evaluation by others in the field, and this may be achieved through publication or public presentation.... Research includes contribution to the intellectual infrastructure of subjects and disciplines (e.g. dictionaries and scholarly editions). It also includes the experimental development of design or construction solutions, as well as investigation that leads to new or substantially improved materials, devices, products or processes. (TEC, 2013, p. 25)

   Original research can be theoretically and/or empirically based, and can be in various forms, such as research articles or scholarly essays. In assigning papers to this category, we noted the methodology used (if it was mentioned explicitly or could be deduced from other details in the paper) and the methods.

2 Evaluation studies of the author's/s' own practice, which do not meet the PBRF definition's requirement for independence.

3 Scholarly case-studies of the author's/s' own practice, which do not meet the PBRF definition's requirements for original investigation, nor for independence.

Looking across this body of work, it is interesting to note several features: overall, 47 per cent comprises original research while evaluations of practice constitute 22 per cent, and scholarly case studies of practice 31 per cent. Most of the articles written in categories 2 and 3 are found in *IJAD* (category 2) and *TIA* (category 3), suggesting there may be different cultures of enquiry in different countries, or related to different professional organisations (as well as diverse criteria for acceptability by each publication). It is common across all three journals for articles to be co-authored: of the 55 articles analysed, just 16 (or 29 per cent) were sole-authored. Most of the 79 authors are academic developers (47), followed by discipline-based academics (19), then higher education researchers or consultants (11), and one each from learning support and organisational/strategic development.

Table 12.1 Articles categorised by type

Journal	Original research	Evaluations of practice	Scholarly case-studies	Total
HERD	6	2	1	9
IJAD	13	7	5	25
TIA	7	3	11	21
Total	**26**	**12**	**17**	**55**

For the ensuing analysis and discussion, we focus on the 26 articles categorised as fully meeting the standards of original academic research. The set comprises 18 empirically based research articles, six that are theory and/or scholarship-based (in the mode of a scholarly essay), and two 'structured reviews' of the literature.

Categorisation of papers by research paradigm

In order to make sense of the range of research approaches used in this set of articles, we first grouped these papers following a research paradigm typology developed by one of the authors with Lynne Giddings (Grant and Giddings, 2002). This typology draws on the work of other scholars, notably Patti Lather (1991), to propose the presence of four broad paradigms in social science research: positivist/post-positivist, interpretivist, radical/critical, and post-structuralist (each is explained in more detail below). Table 12.2 shows the paradigms with the research papers mapped onto them. In most cases, authors did not describe their work in terms of its paradigm, so we have made judgments based on the available evidence.

Well over half (15 of 26) the research articles in our sample were situated in the positivist/post-positivist paradigm. In fact, all 15 are *post*-positivist in that they are based on qualitative data (although alongside quantitative, in some cases). Post-positivism marks the expansion of logical positivism's boundaries to include the collection and analysis of qualitative data in social (including education) research. By and large, work within the post-positivist paradigm takes the existing 'reality' of the institution as a given, eschews theory, and reports data in descriptive categories and themes understood to be representations of an underlying truth.

What of the remaining 11 articles? Eight are interpretivist, that is, more concerned to understand subjective experiences of phenomena than to pursue the cause and effect or prediction and control relationships that preoccupy post-positivist researchers, and more explicit about the theoretical framing of their data analysis. Three fall within the broad critical and post-critical traditions: two are located in the post-structuralist paradigm and one in the radical/critical. The relative absence of research from these paradigms may be because they are heavily theorised modes of enquiry and unattractive in what is essentially a practice-focused field. Moreover, they entail a researcher stance of suspicion towards data's

Table 12.2 Articles categorised by paradigm

Journal	Positivist/ post-positivist	Interpretivist	Radical/ critical	Post-structuralist	Total
HERD	5			1	6
IJAD	7	5		1	13
TIA	3	3	1		7
Total	15	8	1	2	26

meanings, which is at odds with ideas about the importance of representing participants – or their 'voice' – faithfully. Another obstacle to the value of radical/critical and post-structuralist research may arise from the attenuated relationship between findings produced and prescriptions for practice. In our experience, many academic developers prefer not to think in these latter registers and, as most are not trained as education researchers – two-thirds hold their highest qualification in a discipline other than education (Green and Little, 2015) – they find much educational and social theory (beyond the restricted group of concepts mentioned by Kandlbinder and Peseta [2009]) difficult to come to grips with.

Categorisation of papers by method/ology[1] used

As a second step, we categorised the papers according to method/ology used, following the classification used by Tight (2012) for his higher education research sample. He identifies three predominant and three subsidiary method/ologies. In order, they are:

- Surveys and multivariate analyses
- Documentary analyses (focusing on policy, practice or the literature, whether a simple discussion or more sophisticated analysis), and
- Interview-based studies, including focus groups, life history, oral history, participatory interviews

and

- Auto/biographical and observational studies ('biographical')
- Conceptual analysis (usually literature discussion on a particular concept), and
- Phenomenography.

In Table 12.3, we summarise the method/ologies found in our sample. Phenomenography is not included, as we found no examples, which was somewhat surprising given how prominent phenomenography appears to have been in earlier academic development research (Macdonald, 2003; Webb, 1996).

Our sample of articles mirrors the pattern of predominance found by Tight (2012). At just under a third ($n=8$), the largest single group of the articles was categorised under 'surveys and multivariate analyses', which is not surprising given the findings shown in Table 12.2: these are the classic methods of post-positivist social research. Just three (of the eight) articles included detailed statistical analyses of data, while the remaining five reported only descriptive statistics. The most common method employed in this category was the survey questionnaire, which could be online or paper-based.

Just under a quarter ($n=7$) of the research articles in our sample were based on documentary analyses, which (as we have categorised them) included a wide variety of documents. Researchers analysed institutional policy documents, archival documents, webpages, written first-person accounts or narratives (including, on occasion, those of the author her/himself, perhaps in the form of field-notes based on observations), the published research literature, citation analysis and videos.

A slightly smaller number of studies reported using interviews ($n=5$), which could be either face-to-face or by telephone, individual or group-based (focus groups or roundtables), or have a particular form such as the 'professional dialogue'. There was the same number of articles categorised as conceptual analyses ($n=5$), which were typically essay-style articles exploring some concept or model.

This brief analysis shows there are some strongly shared objects of researcher attention: not only the traditional topics of teaching and learning, but also a variety of inquiries into the broader work of, and socialisation into, academic work, including (occasionally) research. At the same time, however, our sample suggests an absence of a shared scholarly base in the sense of a commonly drawn-on body of theory. The most commonly used paradigm (positivism/post-positivism) is usually accompanied by an absence of explicit theory, resting implicitly on the assumptions of positivist science. In the other articles, a range of theories is touched upon (mostly fairly lightly) including transformative learning, appreciative inquiry, reflective practice, constructive alignment, connectivism, and activity theory. Lastly, there is no common or expected method/ology for engaging in academic development research: although half the articles

Table 12.3 Articles categorised by method/ologies

Journal	Surveys & multivariate analyses	Documentary analyses	Interview-based	Biographical	Conceptual analysis	Total
HERD	3	2		1		6
IJAD	2	3	4		4	13
TIA	3	2	1		1	7
Total	8	7	5	1	5	26

use surveys of some kind or interviews, there is also a notable degree of variety beyond these core practices.

This finding signals an absence of what some commentators have long been calling for as a sign of academic development's maturity as an academic field or discipline: a core knowledge base (Margaret Buckridge cited in Lee et al., 2008); a clearly defined supporting theory (Sorcinelli et al., 2006) or theories (Shay 2012); a shared language, texts and standards of quality for our research (Little, 2014); and a common set of research methods (Felten et al., 2007). On the other hand, this is not so different from the wider field of educational studies, in which there are research interest groups that ignore each other's existence.

What of the future for researching academic development?

> Given the complexity of the games, players need a more critical scholarship. (Lee and McWilliam, 2008, p. 76)
>
> [F]ar from producing triumphalist accounts of practice, academic development remains profoundly self-questioning, torn between its new-found influence, the felt fragility of some of its claims to effectiveness and the instability of its power bases. (Clegg, 2009, p. 409)

In order to avoid the many pitfalls of amnesia, academic development researchers need to heed the call to know our history/ies (Lee and McWilliam, 2008; Boughey and Niven 2012; Moses in Lee et al., 2008; Clegg 2009). As we have found by looking at one year's worth of publication across three journals, there is a trove of published research in the field. Commentators have already surveyed the field and identified areas in need of further work. For example, in 2002, Brew (2002) listed five research zones she thinks academic developers should pursue:

1 Research into policies, practices, strategies of higher education in general
2 Basic research into student learning
3 Institutional research and evaluation
4 Action research as an integral part of professional practice (particularly working with academic staff on action research investigating their own practice but also action research on academic developers' own practice)
5 Research into methodologies for educational research. (pp. 117–118)

Thirteen years after Brew compiled her list, we can see that three of these areas are in focus but the first and the fifth are largely not. Research into policies, practices, strategies of higher education in general is under-represented in our sample, while that into the methodologies for educational research was absent. In addition, there was little by way of critically reflective commentaries on the method/ ologies used – and sometimes little explicit description of them as well. As we go into the future, we might consider paying more attention to both: the context in which we work – those increasingly globalised policies, practices and strategies of higher education – and to how we do our research differently and better. Both areas offer us possibilities for asking new questions, having new conversations and producing new knowledge.

In addition, we might think about how to build better, shared definitions of what Scholarship of Educational Development, SoED (Felten et al., 2007) research means. We need to find and articulate its common language and guiding principles, while still paying attention to the diversity of our field and its audiences. In building on and extending our knowledge bases together, we want to continue to ask: what approaches are we privileging and why? What methods would best help us answer *this* question? (Little, 2014, p. 7). How can we work together to draw on our wide variety of disciplinary methods, experiences, and expertise to discover a common ground, but also reach beyond the familiar and 'enrich our scholarship and expand our vision of what is possible' (Little, 2014, p. 7)?

Lastly, academic developers can undertake research that contributes not only to the knowledge economy but also to social justice and to the 'public good' (Leibowitz, 2012). From his South African context, Scott (2009) calls for more *radical* pedagogies, educational agendas and scholarship, as well as more engagement with practitioners and scholars in countries beyond the 'English-speaking first world' (Scott, 2009, p. 45). We could be contemplating action research (and other types of research) partnerships with those marginalised in our own contexts or those in countries where academic development is a nascent field. Jointly we can research issues of importance to our institutions and societies in order to shed light on knotty problems and maybe even propose practical, sustainable solutions. For example, Wisker (2012) describes a project with women academics in Iraq that aims to uncover the barriers to their development.

Advice to new academic developers

As we close this chapter, we pass on our best advice to those of you who might be about to start researching in the field and those keen to (re)invigorate their understanding of the field:

1   Review the first three years of *IJAD* – there are many good articles by leading researchers/practitioners in the field and you will start to get a feel for the kind of research that has been done in the past.
2   Get hold of a good book on researching higher education. For an accessible and practical overview of common research method/ologies used in higher education research (many of which we have seen reflected in the pages of academic development journals), see Glynis Cousin's book, *Researching Learning in Higher Education* (2009). She provides an overview of 11 different methods, explains their provenance and their key proponents, unpacks the ways in which the methods are applied, and provides examples from higher education research of such application. It is a useful book for new

academic developers seeking an overview of different research approaches and for more experienced academic developers interested in reading about a new way of conducting their research.

3 If you come from a discipline outside of education, don't assume you have to throw your old method/ologies (your research expertise) away. Think how to use them and look around for others who are doing this kind of academic development research. They are out there!

4 Once you've found your feet, don't keep them stuck in one place. Read beyond the common research method/ologies into newer ones (at least new for education/higher education/academic development). Look at books on ethnography and autoethnography (for example Chang, 2008; Pelias, 2004); books that problematise the idea of 'voice' (for example Jackson and Mazzei, 2009), or some other core concept/assumption; books that explore different theories and what they have to offer research (for example Jackson and Mazzei, 2012), or that explore indigenous ways of researching (for example, Smith, 1999).

5 Having read in, of, about, and around the field of academic development, read some more.

6 Then, write. Add your voice to those we've cited here and help us all to grow, define, shape, and influence our field, our thinking, our scholarship and our practice.

Note

1 Tight (2102) deliberately conflates methodology and method under the 'compound-term method/ology' on the grounds that it 'reflects what is commonly found in the research literature on higher education (and other topics)' (p. 9). We have followed his practice in this chapter, despite understanding methodology and methods as distinctive aspects of research design and practice (Grant and Giddings, 2002, pp. 12–13).

References

Barrow, M., Grant, B. M. and Brailsford, I. (2010). 'Heroic aspirations: the emergence of academic development in a New Zealand university', *New Zealand Journal of Educational Studies*, 45(1): 33–47.

Bath, D. and Smith, C. (2004). 'Academic developers: an academic tribe claiming their territory in higher education', *International Journal for Academic Development*, 9(1): 9–27.

Baume, D. (1996). 'Editorial', *International Journal for Academic Development*, 1(1): 3–5.

Blackmore, P. and Blackwell, R. (2006). 'Strategic leadership in academic development', *Studies in Higher Education*, 31(3): 373–387.

Boughey, C. and Niven, P. (2012). 'The emergence of research in the South African academic development movement', *Higher Education Research & Development*, 31(5): 641–653.

Brew, A. (2002). 'Research and the academic developer: a new agenda', *International Journal for Academic Development*, 7(2): 112–122.

Brew, A. (2003). 'The future of research and scholarship in academic development'. pp. 165–181 in H. Eggins and R. Macdonald, eds., *The Scholarship of Academic Development*. Buckingham: SRHE and Open University Press.

Chang, H. (2008). *Autoethnography as Method*. Walnut Creek, CA: Left Coast Press.

Clegg, S. (2009). 'Forms of knowing and academic development practice', *Studies in Higher Education*, 34(4): 403–416.

Clegg, S. (2012). 'Conceptualising higher education research and/or academic development as "fields": a critical analysis', *Higher Education Research and Development*, 31(5): 667–678.

Cousin, G. (2009). *Researching Learning in Higher Education: An Introduction to Contemporary Methods and Approaches*. New York: Routledge.

DiPietro, M. (2014). 'Tracing the evolution of educational development through the POD Network's institute for new faculty developers', *To Improve the Academy*, 33: 113–130. doi:10.1002/tia2.20009.

Eggins, H. and Macdonald, R. (2003). (Eds.) *The Scholarship of Academic Development*. Buckingham: SRHE and Open University Press.

Felten, P., Kalish, A., Pingree, A. and Plank, K. (2007). 'Toward a scholarship of teaching and learning in educational development', *To Improve the Academy: Resources of Faculty, Instructional, and Organizational Development*, 25: 93–108.

Fraser, K. and Ling, P. (2014). 'How academic is academic development?' *International Journal for Academic Development*, 19(3): 226–241.

Gibbs, G. (2003). 'Researching the training of university teachers: Conceptual frameworks and research tools'. pp. 129–140 in H. Eggins and R. Macdonald, eds, *The Scholarship of Academic Development*. Buckingham: SRHE and Open University Press.

Gibbs, G. (2013). 'Reflections on the changing nature of educational development', *International Journal for Academic Development*, 18(1): 4–14.

Grant, B. (2007). 'The mourning after: academic development in a time of doubt', *International Journal for Academic Development*, 12(1): 35–43.

Grant, B. (2013). 'The rush to scholasticism', *International Journal for Academic Development*, 18(1): 15–17.

Grant, B. and Giddings, L. S. (2002). 'Making sense of methodologies: a paradigm framework for the novice researcher', *Contemporary Nurse*, 13(1): 10–28.

Green, D. and Little, D. (2013). 'Academic development on the margins', *Studies in Higher Education*, 38(4): 523–537.

Green, D. and Little, D. (2015, forthcoming). 'Family portrait: a profile of educational developers around the world', *International Journal for Academic Development*.

Harland, T. and Staniforth, D. (2008). 'A family of strangers: the fragmented nature of academic development', *Teaching in Higher Education*, 13(6): 669–678.

ICED. (n.d.). Retrieved 25 May 2015 from http://icedonline.net/about-us/aims/.

Jackson, A. Y. and Mazzei, L. A. (Eds.) (2009). *Voice in Qualitative Inquiry: Challenging Conventional, Interpretive, and Critical Conceptions in Qualitative Research*. London & New York: Routledge.

Jackson, A. Y. and Mazzei, L. A. (2012). *Thinking with Theory in Qualitative Research: Viewing Data Across Multiple Perspectives*. Abingdon, Oxon; New York, NY: Routledge.

Jones, A. (2010). 'Examining the public face of academic development', *International Journal for Academic Development*, 15(3): 241–251.

Kandlbinder, P. (2014). 'Signature concepts of women researchers in higher education learning and teaching', *Studies in Higher Education*, 39(9): 1562–1572.

Kandlbinder, P. and Peseta, T. (2009). 'Key concepts in postgraduate certificates in higher education teaching and learning in Australasia and the United Kingdom', *International Journal for Academic Development*, 14(1): 19–31.

Lather, P. (1991). *Getting Smart: Feminist Research and Pedagogy With/in the Postmodern*. New York: Routledge.

Lee, A., Manathunga, C. and Kandlbinder, P. (2008). *Making a Place: An Oral History of Academic Development in Australia*. Milperra, NSW: HERDSA.

Lee, A. and McWilliam, E. (2008). 'What game are we in? Living with academic development', *International Journal for Academic Development*, 13(1): 67–77.

Leibowitz, B. (2012). 'Introduction: reflections on higher education and the public good', pp. xvii–xxvii in *Higher Education for the Public Good: Views from the South*. Stoke on Trent: Trentham Books.

Little, D. (2014). 'Reflections on the state of the scholarship of educational development', *To Improve the Academy*, 33(1): 1–13.

Macdonald, R. (2002). 'Educational development: research, evaluation and changing practice in higher education'. pp. 3–13 in Macdonald, R. and Wisdom, J. (eds.), *Academic and Educational Development: Research, Evaluation and Changing Practice in Higher Education*. London: Kogan Page.

Macdonald, R. (2003). 'Developing a scholarship of academic development: Setting the context,' pp. 1–10 in H. Eggins and R. Macdonald, eds., *The Scholarship of Academic Development*. Buckingham: SRHE and Open University Press.

Macdonald, R. and Wisdom, J. (Eds.) (2002). *Academic and Educational Development: Research, Evaluation and Changing Practice in Higher Education*. London: Kogan Page.

Orrell, J. (2008). 'Review, reactions and reminiscences', pp. 168–176 in A. Lee, C. Manathunga and P. Kandlbinder (Eds.), *Making a Place: An Oral History of Academic Development in Australia*. Milperra, NSW: HERDSA.

Pelias, R. (2004). *A Methodology of the Heart: Evoking Academic and Daily Life*. Walnut Creek, CA: Altamira Press.

Peseta, T. (2007). 'Troubling our desires for research and writing within the academic development project', *International Journal for Academic Development*, 12(1): 15–23.

Scott, I. (2009). 'Academic development in South African higher education', pp. 21–49 in E. Bitzer (Ed.), *Higher Education in South Africa: A Scholarly Look Behind the Scenes*. Stellenbosch, South Africa: SUN MeDIA.

Shay, S. (2012). 'Educational development as a field: are we there yet?', *Higher Education Research and Development*, 31(3): 311–323.

Smith, L. T. (1999). *Decolonizing Methodologies: Research and Indigenous Peoples*. London & Dunedin: Zed Books Ltd. and Otago University Press.

Sorcinelli, M., Austin, A., Eddy, P. and Beach, A. (2006). *Creating the Future of Faculty Development: Learning from the Past, Understanding the Present*. Bolton, MA: Anker.

TEC (2013). *Performance-Based Research Fund Quality Evaluation Guidelines 2012*. Wellington: Tertiary Education Commission.

Tight, M. (2004). 'Research into higher education: an a-theoretical community of practice?', *Higher Education Research and Development*, 23(4): 395–411.

Tight, M. (2008). 'Higher education research as tribe, territory and/or community: a co-citation analysis', *Higher Education*, 55: 593–605.

Tight, M. (2012). 'Higher education research 2000–2010: changing journal publication patterns', *Higher Education Research and Development*, 31(5): 723–740.

Tight, M. (2014). 'Discipline and theory in higher education research', *Research Papers in Education*, 29(1): 93–110.

Webb, G. (1996). 'Theories of staff development: development and understanding', *International Journal for Academic Development*, 1(1): 63–69.

Webber, T., Bourner, T. and O'Hara, S. (2003). 'Practitioner-centred research on academic development in higher education', pp. 117–128 in H. Eggins and R. Macdonald (eds.), *The Scholarship of Academic Development*. Buckingham: SRHE and Open University Press.

Wisdom, J. (2002). 'Towards a culture of evaluation', pp. 217–234 in R. Macdonald and J. Wisdom (eds.), *Academic and Educational Development: Research, Evaluation and Changing Practice in Higher Education*. London: Kogan Page.

Wisker, G. (2012). 'Educational development for the public good', pp. 203–215 in B. Leibowitz (ed.), *Higher Education for the Public Good: Views from the South*. Stellenbosch, South Africa: Trentham Books and SUN MeDIA.

Chapter 13

Managing and leading change

Models and practices

Celia Popovic and Kathryn M. Plank

Summary

We explore five models – grass roots, Faculty-led, strategic, community building and research-based – that may help developers to manage and lead change, rather than merely responding to it. In each case, we analyse when the model works best, and why, and include a case study illustrating the approach. Actual practice may not fit neatly into a single model, or into the three-stage process – creating a climate for change, engaging and enabling the organisation and implementing and sustaining the change – that we describe and use. In practice, of course, we often use combinations of models. But models help us to conceptualise our work and make it more intentional.

Links to web sources referenced in this chapter can be found at www.seda. ac.uk/apad.

What is the challenge?

As we see in other chapters of this book, academic development is all about change – whether that change involves helping an individual academic change teaching methods, navigating the constant changes in instructional technology, or responding to larger changes in the world of higher education. Change in higher education can be disruptive and revolutionary, or it can be incremental and part of a bigger, long-range plan. Sometimes it is led by senior management, perhaps as they interpret national or sectoral policy; and sometimes it emerges from individuals. Sometimes it is a naturally occurring, predictable development, and sometimes it seemingly comes out of nowhere. Change is not always easy, or welcome, or good. The challenge for developers is to be open to change but not to be constantly swayed, to know when (and how) to force change, to facilitate it, to leverage it, and, if necessary, to resist it.

What do we know from the literature?

Much of the literature on change concerns commercial organisations. This may be our first challenge – to identify the ways in which universities variously are and are not like commercial organisations, and thus bring particular challenges.

Universities are complex, messy organisations, with particular cultures, unclear lines of authority and an inbuilt resistance to change, certainly around pedagogy (Boyce 2003, Christensen and Eyring 2011). It is not uncommon for teachers to work in isolation, not to feel a personal connection to institutional goals, and to have a strong belief in their own personal and professional autonomy. To be effective, an academic developer must manage and lead change within the context of this difficult environment; otherwise, 'using concepts foreign to the values of the academy will most likely fail to engage the very people who must bring about the change' (Kezar 2001, p. vi).

We have drawn on literature on *change management* and *community engagement*, as well as that of *academic development* to identify key issues and develop a strategy for academic developers to lead change in higher education.

Change management is more likely to occur and be sustainable when the end point is clearly identified, there is a clear path for change and there is genuine engagement with the community. The literature suggests three stages in a successful change management process: creating a climate for change, engaging and enabling the organisation, and implementing and sustaining the change (Kotter 1996). Change involves working with individuals as well as with structures and policies. In a university environment we may not have some of the rewards and sanctions available in a commercial organisation. For example we may not be able to require all teachers to attend a workshop, or penalise those who flagrantly ignore a directive to create learning outcomes (see Chapter 4). In creating the climate for change we need to engage with rational arguments, as well as appeal to the emotions of those we wish to influence (Heath and Heath 2010). It may not be sufficient to argue for the benefits of student-centred learning, for example, purely on a rational level (e.g., student-centred learning leads to improved student experience). We may also need to appeal on an emotional level to effect actual engagement, as opposed to lip service (e.g., students in a student-centred learning environment are more pleasant and rewarding to teach than those in a traditional teacher-centred environment).

Universities are a community comprising distinct groups, including faculty, contract faculty, teaching assistants, support staff, administrators, librarians, IT, student services, and of course, students. At times there are, or may be perceived to be, competing demands within the community. Furthermore, those wishing to bring about change are themselves part of the community. Often the change that is desired is multiple and ongoing. It is not one self-contained project.

Community engagement literature emphasises the need for a catalyst to bring about change, but at the same time the necessity to build the capacity of the community as a whole to take ownership of the enterprise (Frank and Smith, 1999). Without this, an endeavour will fail, as it will lack the basis to be sustained. An Academic Development Unit (ADU) and a few allies such as associate deans and senior administration may be able to instigate change, but without the genuine commitment of teachers, students and the rest of the community, any change will be short lived and superficial.

Academic development is informed in part by adult education social theories of learning and constructivism (Vygotsky, 1987; Lave and Wenger, 1991). While changes in attitudes to teaching and learning are often focused initially on changing individual instructors' behaviour; through written resources, consultations, and workshops, for example; meaningful change is more effective and sustainable when the change includes engagement at a strategic level, including policy formation (Gibbs, 2013; Knapper, 2012) and changes in institutional culture.

As we think about effecting change, it's also useful to consider recent literature that explores the organisational positioning of academic developers. As Little and Green (2012) describe, academic developers reside in a liminal space, between other units, between disciplines, between levels of organisation (e.g., between higher administration and university teachers). This positioning, which can sometimes make the developer feel caught in the middle, can also be an ideal position from which to facilitate change. Kezar and Lester (2009) describe faculty development centres as an example of integrating structures because they can 'connect their mission to broader goals (such as improving institutional student outcomes) that require collaboration among faculty across units to determine institution-wide outcomes.' (p. 129).

Developing a strategic approach to leading change

If we combine the findings from these three bodies of literature, we can start with a foundation of Kotter's (1996) three stages for change management, incorporate a focus on community engagement, and develop a strategic approach that works within the context of academic development.

Stage 1. First we need to *create a climate for change*. As academic developers, sometimes we are the catalysts for change, but other times we are enacting change for others. As we enter into the process, it is important for us to ask questions such as whose change are we advancing and for what purpose? Where is the change coming from? What is the motivation behind the call for change?

Once we understand the origin of the change, we can adopt a model or models for change that will best fit the context. For example, in the case study below illustrating the emergent model, although academic developers were key to the change process, the desire for change emerged from one of the academic disciplines and the subject leader in that field took the most visible role.

Also part of creating a climate for change is creating 'a culture of risk' (Kezar 2001), and providing the support necessary to help people take risks, such as the resources described in the University of Arts example of creating a standardised feedback form.

Stage 2. Secondly we need to *engage and enable the organisation*. To do this we need to communicate the vision, enable action, and 'connect the change process to individual and institutional identity' (Kezar 2001). To keep motivation high, it helps to create short-term wins. In this middle stage we get the change underway and we motivate by showing progress.

At this stage, it is also important to build community around the change, to engage stakeholders and allies. A key role for a developer often lies in observing, listening, and understanding the culture of the institution, and understanding with whom to align (and sometimes whom not to be seen as aligned with). Sometimes, as described in The Greenhouse case study below, the developer leads change by letting the community take the lead.

Stage 3. In the third stage we need to *implement and sustain the change*, and we need to avoid declaring victory too early. Too many change initiatives fail because the change leaders mistake progress for the finishing post. We need to consolidate improvements while producing still more change, and we need to institutionalise the change. By this stage it is imperative to have embedded the vision in the community, to ensure a continuous cycle of improvement.

The three steps are not a once-only cycle. As we respond to the continuous need for improvement, we will engage with this cycle repeatedly. As we work through the cycle, and answer the questions presented to us at each stage, we can make decisions about the models to use in leading that change. The remainder of this chapter focuses on five models to help guide developers in leading change.

Introduction to five models of practice

The five models of or approaches to change described here – grass roots, Faculty-led, strategic, community building and research-based – do not comprise an exhaustive list, but are ones that seem highly applicable to the work of academic developers. They are also not discrete models but rather in practice often occur in combination. Each is described with examples as illustrations of those most frequently adopted. The point isn't to pick a model and follow it, but to have a toolkit of various approaches which you can draw from in different situations and combine as necessary.

For each model, we use a SWOT analysis to explore the positives and negatives of each model for immediate effectiveness as well as for long-term impact. We also discuss contexts in which they are suitable and provide case studies to illustrate each model or combination of models.

Grass roots

The grass roots model is an individual-focused approach. The Academic Development Unit (ADU) alone or in partnership with Faculties, offers one-off workshops, provides *ad hoc* resources, and holds one-on-one consultations. This approach has been shown to be highly regarded by those who engage with it. However, it can also be relatively inefficient (although Piccinin et al. [1999]

show considerable impact on individual academics from even a single coaching session). Individual-focussed work generally has a low impact across an institution; however, when combined with other approaches it can work as a way to funnel and promote interest in the ADU. The activities themselves may have low institutional impact, but they can lead someone who attends a workshop on one topic to give greater thought to their teaching and lead to them being more willing to engage in other activities in the future (see Chapter 18 for further discussion). Satisfied participants may spread the word to their colleagues, and help to gradually build the centre's reputation. Some of the individual-focused activities can be developed to contribute to the community-building model described below.

Examples of grass roots activities

- One-on-one or peer consultations
- Teaching observations
- Lunchtime workshop series
- Website resources and links

Table 13.1 SWOT analysis of the grass roots model

Immediate effectiveness	Strength	Weakness
	Popular with individuals Is familiar, people think they know what to expect	Low impact and often inefficient use of resources Hit and miss – individual need may not coincide with the timing of a workshop Rarely results in meaningful change at the institutional level
Long-term impact on organisational culture	Opportunity	Threat
	Allows the ADU to gradually build provision May lead to development of a culture of teaching from the bottom up May be seen as less threatening to individuals than a top down approach	The centre may remain individually focused, never moving on to a strategic approach, especially if this is the only model used

Case study of a grass roots approach – brown-bag lunches at York University

When the Teaching Commons (ADU) was launched at York in 2012 they started from nothing. There was a mission to raise the profile of teaching across the institution and there were three developers, one of whom was the director. There was a need to provide offerings so that prospective users would have an idea of what was available. Even though the developers were fairly sure that such workshops in isolation would have limited long-term effect, they felt it was imperative to offer a series. They were called Brown Bag, indicating they would take place at lunchtime but the participants would be expected to bring their own lunches.

The series, rather as expected, had mixed results. The topics were chosen following a survey of new faculty. During the orientation event faculty were taken through a planning exercise designed to encourage them to identify any support they might need. They were given a choice of topics and space for their own comments and asked to rank the topics they would most like see included in the series. Despite this admittedly superficial needs analysis, attendance at the workshops was extremely low with at most five or six people attending from a pool of 1400 tenure track and 1500 contract faculty. Professors were not asked when they would like to attend or when they would like the work-shops. This may have been partly to blame for the low attendance.

This was not regarded as a failure, as although the team would have wel-comed a healthier level of attendance, the workshops served another service. They signalled the areas of expertise or source of support available from the centre – including course design, managing large classes, experiential education and writing learning outcomes.

This case study does illustrate one of the weaknesses of the grass roots model – it is subject to the whims of individuals and the challenges presented by multiple diary responsibilities.

Faculty-led

Faculties (schools, departments), rather than the ADU, take the lead in suggest-ing the focus for activity. The Faculty has a sense of ownership, as an event is tailored to their context using discipline specific examples, addressing Faculty-specific policies and issues, and engaging with Faculty members as presenters and exemplars as well as participants.

The engagement and motivation of the individual contact person in a Faculty, as well as their seniority and perceived credibility, can make a huge difference to the level of engagement. An event initially designed for one Faculty may then be offered, suitably re-versioned, to others, or pan-university. Key to the success of this model is the nurturing of relationships with gatekeepers and influencers in the faculty. However, any member of a Faculty who engages with the ADU in any capacity should be regarded as a potential ally. Also, it is important to ensure that the key influencers are aware of the centre's successes, have a clear picture of what is possible, and are encouraged to see themselves as partners in the process. The centre may have more success if it is willing to allow others to take the credit for some projects and events.

Examples of Faculty-led activities

- Faculty-hosted workshops
- ADU contributing to a Faculty committee on a teaching related issue
- Responding to requests for alternative delivery models or redesigning a workshop for a specific discipline or Faculty

Table 13.2 SWOT analysis of the Faculty-led model

Immediate effectiveness	Strength	Weakness
	Get buy-in because responses are directly relevant to the Faculty's needs	More vocal and larger Faculties may dominate, and get more than their fair share of resource
	Tailor provision to the specific context of participants, Faculty wide or at department level	Lack of over-arching strategy as the provision is responsive not proactive.
	Faculty has a sense of ownership as they suggest the activities	Dependent on the commitment of the Faculty contact person/group and their relationship with the ADU
Long-term impact on organisational culture	Opportunity	Threat
	Faculties inspire or even compete with each other	If the support is provided in-house (i.e. Faculty specific development rather than from a central unit) the institution could lose the advantage of economies of scale of a central unit
	Can be responsive to emergencies	
	Can repurpose resources created for one Faculty with another using their examples and context	
	Chance for inter-Faculty projects as the teaching ADU has oversight of needs in different areas and can bring them together	

Case study of a Faculty-led approach – improving assessment

The contributor of this case study requested that this example be anonymised.

A persistent challenge in many subject areas is the achievement of an assessment strategy that is reliable, valid, fair and well understood by students. Recognising this, a school approached the academic development team with a request for staff development activities that would help the school achieve these assessment characteristics. Two development events were organised and facilitated by a senior academic developer. However, the champion for the events was the school's own Architecture programmes subject leader; he very visibly took the role of defining the need and recruiting the participants. The events were seen as internal events, rather than something contracted out to an academic development unit.

Subsequently a similar assessment event was organised for the staff of a separate department in another school. The framework for this event was very similar to the original event (similar issues, similar responses), but once again, the event was championed by the head of the department. Presented as an internal event, it was designed to the department's own specifications, with the academic developer bringing a bespoke expertise to a local problem.

During the subsequent academic session the department head reported positively on increased consistency in staff assessment behaviour and favourable responses from students.

Strategic

This approach is so named because it is linked to the university strategy, and is tied to overarching priorities which may be led by the institution or the government. This model sees the ADU as a key player in the development as well as the implementation of teaching-related policy. (The developer's roles in contributing to policy is explored in more detail in Chapter 17).

As well as influencing strategy, the centre can act as a central hub in a hub and spoke model of provision where the spokes are Faculties or departments. At its most organised, the institution has a teaching and learning strategy, which identifies in detail the aims and priorities for the institution. Each Faculty is expected to show, on an annual basis, how they are furthering the institutional strategy. Generally this involves each Faculty developing its own local Teaching and Learning Strategy.

In some examples, each Faculty has a teaching and learning committee. The ADU also has a committee – each Faculty sends a representative from their own committee to the centre's committee. This enables priorities and concerns to be shared across the institution, and communication about teaching issues is encouraged both between Faculty and administration, and among Faculties.

Examples of strategic activities

- ADU has a presence on teaching-related university policy committees and working groups
- Provision of events and courses tied to the achievement of policy aims
- Formation of a strategy to assist in the evaluation of all programs at the university
- Creation of teaching awards

Table 13.3 SWOT analysis of the strategic model

Immediate effectiveness	Strength	Weakness
	Consistency of approach across the University	Local issues may be side-lined
	Reduction of localised activity and therefore better use of resources	May lose buy-in if instructors sense a top-down approach ignoring local needs
	Clarity of aims for the University as a whole	
	Increased sense of the institution as a community	
Long-term impact on organisational culture	*Opportunity*	*Threat*
	The institution can roll out university wide initiatives in a relatively consistent manner. This approach may become embedded in the culture facilitating future initiatives.	Some Faculties may resist if they feel their autonomy is threatened.

Case study of a strategic approach – reviewing the ADU at MMU

By Penny Sweasey

In order to review the organisational and operational aspects of the ADU (CELT) at Manchester Metropolitan University (MMU), the Director Penny Sweasey consulted widely with faculty and central stakeholders to develop an approach to academic development across the university.

This led to the formulation of MMU's new Strategy for Learning and Teaching which informs the work of CELT. This included the re-validation of CELT's accredited programmes, and a framework for flexible and responsive CPD was introduced to significantly increase levels of engagement from staff.

Three strands of activity emerged:

- Policy and Strategic Framework Development and Implementation including linking several institutional strategies directly or indirectly related to teaching and learning. Examples include peer observation, an academic probation period, linkage of teaching and learning with research and knowledge exchange, and promotion criteria linked to teaching.

- Staff Development Programme and CPD Portfolio of flexible modes and routes – the strategy puts the student experience in terms of learning and teaching policy at the forefront; but more can be done to articulate what this looks like in the university's classroom and seminars. CELT's CPD offer is enhanced through a professional recognition scheme and a portfolio of staff learning opportunities focused on career stage and role.

- Supporting strategies to promote Student Engagement, Inclusion, Retention and Success. Our focus on the 'academic environment in which student learning can thrive' extends beyond the quality of teaching to the quality of academic relationships forged between students and their tutors – it is this which will have the greatest impact on retention and success.

With its new and high-profile approach to learning, teaching and assessment, CELT is well placed as the champion of the strategy around the university.

Case study of a strategic approach – improving assessment at UAL

By Shân Wareing

As Dean of Learning and Teaching Development at the University of the Arts, London (UAL), I was concerned about fairness and standards in assessment. Assessment standards were implicit, and students complained in surveys about bias and subjectivity. There was also a gap in attainment between white and Black and Minority Ethnic (BME) students greater than the national average. A pedagogically ideal process would have involved extensive staff development to maximise academic buy-in to the project, and innovative, discipline-specific, locally owned solutions. However, I estimated that using that approach it would take six years before we would see significant institutional level change, given the context of an institution of 20,000 students, distributed across 12 campuses, where half the teaching was undertaken by staff on hourly paid contracts (because of the high number of practitioners teaching); and allowing for the time required to deliver the staff development on the scale required, the numbers of people who would be unable to attend the first or second time development sessions were offered, the staff who wouldn't engage, and the length of time it would take for staff to design in the changes required, have them validated, and implement them effectively. I therefore went against the grain in both educational development and art and design pedagogy, and in nine months developed and implemented institutional marking criteria and a standardised feedback form. The design and development process included: a working group with institution wide membership; a pilot in each distinct area; regular reporting to university committees; close liaison between educational development and the quality and standards office; commissioning a designer to produce the forms; a DVD and website with the background information, videos and downloadable documents; and a series of roadshow seminars in the different campuses to brief academics on the changes. The change was very controversial, but was followed over the next three years by a 12 per cent rise in scores on National Student Survey questions relating to assessment and feedback. The ethnicity attainment gap did not close, but all degree results rose by 3–4 per cent. And within a year of introducing the undergraduate marking criteria, staff and students requested that the university implement a variation of the same system for taught Masters courses.

Case study of a strategic approach – boosting the use of social media at SHU

By Sue Beckingham

Within two Faculties at Sheffield Hallam University (SHU) Sue Beckingham (Educational Developer) and Dr Alison Purvis (Head of Learning and Teaching) identified a need to take a more strategic approach to educate and guide staff and students in their use of social media. The faculties worked with Helen Rodger from the central Quality Enhancement and Student Success team to develop a social media strategy through open dialogue and collaborative guidance.

The development and implementation of the strategy features a strong emphasis on collaborative relationships across different areas of the institution and was informed by the needs and priorities of the staff and students in order to be fit for purpose. The elements that have enabled a strategic approach to this emergent work are that we:

- Recognised the boundaries of our responsibility
- Prioritised needs based on resources and potential impact
- Championed collaboration
- Placed value on listening to staff and students
- Understood the constant evolution of social media
- Challenged and questioned
- Ensured guidance was inclusive
- Promoted authenticity

The outcomes include a rich collection of resources using different media, the development of a Social Media CoLab and communities of practice collaboratively exploring, using and evaluating the use of social media; and the support of the university to embed the use of these and other technologies to enhance the learning experience.

Community-building

This model may emerge from a grass roots model, but has the potential for greater impact and culture change than a purely individual targeted approach. Activities and resources are focused on breaking down the individualism common in teaching, and encourage the sharing of ideas, peer support and networking. The ADU has a key role to play in facilitating the development of these communities, but if successful the communities become self-sustaining. The support that the centre can provide may include identifying common points of interest that would lend themselves to special interest groups, encouraging potential members to join in and providing space to meet – this space may be physical or could be virtual, or a combination of both.

Examples of community-building activities

- Teacher Talk sessions where instructors are invited to attend regular meetings on themed topics
- Journal club, face to face or online, where instructors read and discuss a predetermined article on a topical teaching related issue
- Creation of learning communities – groups of self-identified instructors work together on a given topic with a specific aim in mind
- Teaching and learning conference – sharing of good practice, colleagues learn from each other

Table 13.4 SWOT analysis of the community-building model

Immediate effectiveness	Strength	Weakness
	Speeds up the development of a teaching focused culture	May lack an overarching strategy if left to evolve without guidance
	Provides avenues for teaching related discussions to take place	Interest groups may not reflect the institutional priorities
	Enables teachers at any level of experience, discipline or position in the hierarchy to learn from each other	Powerful or influential individuals may subvert the focus to pet projects or hobby interests

(continued)

Table 13.4 SWOT analysis of the community-building model (continue)

Long-term impact on organisational culture	Opportunity	Threat
	Interest groups within the university may be able to link with others regionally and beyond.	Without an overarching strategy this could result in a collection of disparate groups that lack focus or clearly defined goals.
	Highly motivated small groups can achieve a great deal, for example publish guides on teaching topics.	
	Once they get going self interest groups can be self-sustaining and help to build a culture that values teaching.	

Case study of a community-building approach – The Greenhouse at MMU

By Chrissi Nerantzi

The Greenhouse is an academic development intervention that has the characteristics of the Community Building model. It was brought to life by an academic developer (Chrissi Nerantzi) from the Centre for Excellence in Learning and Teaching at Manchester Metropolitan University (MMU) in the UK in January 2014. The idea was to create a space for creative practitioners from around the institution to come together, to share ideas linked to innovative learning and teaching practices, to experiment together with new pedagogical ideas but also to support each other and identify opportunities for cross-disciplinary collaboration. Gatherings are organised in different locations around the campus once per month, by a different creative gardener each time who is also leading the related Greenhouse activity. The Greenhouse uses social media to extend opportunities for sharing and support in between the monthly gatherings and has become much more than a mere physical space. It is a supportive community and a developmental ecosystem. There is a sense of belonging and commitment to the idea, to creative thinking, actions and practices. The community itself is the heart and soul of the Greenhouse while the developer, who set up this initiative, sees herself as a fellow member. She seeded the idea and nurtured its development. However, the Greenhouse would neither survive nor thrive without its members and what they bring to the community.

Research-based

This model draws strength from avoiding the binary opposition of teaching and research that is often presented and indeed experienced as a tension both for the individual faculty member and in the way university policy is perceived. There is an extensive movement arguing for a scholarly approach to university teaching (often referred to as SoTL – Scholarship of Teaching and Learning). Proponents (Healey 2005) support linking the two areas of academic work in several ways. These include using examples from one's research in one's teaching; developing research skills in students as a learning technique; and applying research approaches to answer questions about one's own teaching (identifying good questions, framing them as research queries and then investigating them, perhaps even publishing, at least locally). This latter approach has been used to great effect both to engage researchers in teaching and to produce innovative solutions to teaching challenges. The research-based model may be linked to the community-building model to identify shared concerns and the resulting research findings. The research may be led by developers, or they may facilitate this process while other colleagues take the lead.

Examples of research-based activities

- Action Learning Sets linked to action research projects
- Funding for small-scale research projects
- Workshops on social science and education research methods for faculty from other disciplines
- Writing retreats
- Information about teaching related conferences

Table 13.5 SWOT analysis of the research-based model

Immediate effectiveness	Strength	Weakness
	Combines faculty members' joint concern with teaching and research Scholarly approaches to teaching have been shown to produce better learning environments If teachers take a research approach to their teaching they may be more willing to learn about other teaching innovations and research findings.	Research can become the tail wagging the teaching dog – can be difficult to keep the focus on the teaching Pedagogic research and publications are not universally valued as equal to similar work in a discipline

(continued)

Table 13.5 SWOT analysis of the research-based model (continued)

Long-term impact on organisational culture	Opportunity	Threat
	If promotion decisions acknowledge publications in pedagogy, professors are more likely to engage such that teaching quality improves. The research / teaching gap is narrowed. Teaching becomes a demonstrably more scholarly activity, and thus has higher status.	Need to consider ethics in involving students as subjects for research Limited funds are available for pedagogic research, it may be necessary to avoid diverting funds away from teaching to support teaching related research.

Case study of a research-based approach – developing scholarly habits at Victoria University of Wellington

Developing Scholarly Habits (DSH) is a year-long programme for early career academics in the Faculty of Humanities and Social Sciences at Victoria University of Wellington in New Zealand (Sutherland and Willis, 2013). It begins with a three-day off-site retreat, with another retreat held mid-term in the final semester. Participants also meet monthly with the whole group at which they discuss highlights and challenges from the previous month, and ask questions of a panel of experts or participate in a workshop on a topic they have chosen to learn more about. Topics have included preparing a book proposal, developing a social media presence, speed reading, time management and contributing to academic journals. At the monthly meetings, participants also receive the task they must complete over the next month. In between monthly meetings, they meet with their assigned trio of peers to complete the task (if it is a group activity) or discuss the findings from their individual task completion. Tasks have included: preparation of (and peer feedback on) a promotion application, peer observation of teaching, interviewing academic role models about their success and career paths in academia, identifying service opportunities, completing a time-use log and writing a letter to a future DSH participant.

Case study of a research-based approach – enhancing digital capabilities through communities of practice at UAL

This second case study from Shân Wareing combines community building and research-based approaches.

Like many academic developers, I was strongly influenced by Etienne Wenger's work on Communities of Practice. As a result, I designed and implemented a university project which was based on communities of practice identifying their technology-enhanced learning goals and being supported to become self-sustaining in developing their digital literacies. At the time I was working in an arts university, and the project was called DIAL, for Digital Integration into Arts Learning. The project was made possible with funding from Jisc, a national organisation which supports IT and learning technologies in UK higher and further education. I appointed a project manager and we use the project funding to support small community-based projects to trial the model. We wanted to see whether the communities could effectively increase the digital literacies of all members, and become self-sustaining, and to develop materials and resources to support other students and staff in their digital literacies. The project manager was a technician at the university, who really loved his new work, and ended up presenting it at international conferences. The project had a positive impact on digital literacies of students and staff at UAL.

DIAL was built on the premise that an academic community is an effective site to develop the digital literacies of their members, for several reasons. Communities (a course, a discipline area) include students and staff with varying level of skills from novice to expert. Communities are good structures for developing skills because people already have relationships, helping communication and trust. In a community, support can be timely, relevant and proportionate – you can ask someone a question and receive an answer that helps you inside a few seconds. Also, communities to some extent share goals, and undertake collaborative projects, which allow digital literacies to be developed in context, and for specific purposes. They can be self-sustaining in terms of digital literacies: once communities know how to support each other in developing the skills they collectively need; they can help each other and learn new skills with less or no intervention from outside.

Integrating the approaches

This hopefully useful but also somewhat artificial distinction between various models may mask the day-to-day reality, where developers adopt a combination of approaches. What works in one institution won't work in another, and even within an institution and over time we may find some approaches work better than others.

The five models described above are unlikely to be successful if any one approach is used in isolation. In the past the grass roots model has been used by some teaching support centres to limited effect. It is unlikely that any of the others would be used alone. And any approach should be both informed by strategy and policy and rooted in and owned by one or more communities if it to have any reasonable chance of success. Hence this final case study:

Case study – bringing it all together

By Rowena Pelik

The Quality Enhancement Framework in Scotland, established in 2003, includes nationally set and agreed Enhancement Themes, managed and led by QAA Scotland. This is discussed in greater detail in Chapter 9. The themes frame a wide array of activity at sector, institutional and local levels, be it Faculty, school/department or subject, and is characterised by a strategic and collective approach to change. Enhancement is defined as *taking deliberate steps to bring about improvement in the effectiveness of the learning experiences of students (QAA 2012)*. The themes are chosen by the sector to reflect a dominant concern in teaching and learning. They are typically addressed variously through commissioned work, institutional activity, sector events, an annual conference and the creation of resources housed on the Enhancement Themes website. The latter form an open educational resource that is widely used by academic developers and teaching staff both in Scotland and internationally.

This approach is interesting as it embodies and encourages each of the identified models. It is **strategic**, reflecting institutional and sector-wide priorities for change. Each institution takes forward the current theme in ways that are relevant to its own ways of working and is responsible for delivering a number of agreed outputs. Many institutions make use of **grass roots** and **emergent** approaches in encouraging activity under the theme. Thus many have established enhancement funds that individuals or teams can bid into to pursue initiatives. Increasingly, these funds are used to encourage student-led enhancement projects. Outcomes presented at internal teaching conferences act as **community building** within institutions and, through presentations and posters at theme events, across the sector. Work at sector level further supports collaborative and collegiate sharing which also builds community and drives academic practice forward. Work commissioned by the theme is **research-based** and leads on to the publication of reports and conference presentations.

References

Boyce, M (2003). 'Organizational Learning is Essential to Achieving and Sustaining Change in Higher Education', *Innovative Higher Education*, 28(2).

Christensen, C. M. and Eyring, H. J. (2011). *The Innovation University: Changing the DNA of Higher Education from the Inside Out*, Jossey-Bass.

Frank, F. and Smith, A. (1999). *The Community Development Handbook: A tool to build community capacity*, Labour Market Learning and Development Unit, Human Resources Development Canada.

Gibbs, G. (2013). 'Reflections on the changing nature of educational development', *International Journal for Academic Development*, 18(1): pp. 4–14.

Healey, M. (2005). 'Linking research and teaching: exploring disciplinary spaces and the role of inquiry based learning', in Barnett, R. (ed.) (2005), *Reshaping the University: New Relationships between Research, Scholarship and Teaching*. McGraw Hill and Open University Press.

Heath, C. and Heath, D. (2010). *Switch: How to Change Things When Change is Hard*. New York: Random House.

Kezar, A. J. (2001). *Understanding and Facilitating Organizational Change in the 21st Century: Recent Research and Conceptualizations*. ASHE-ERIC Higher Education Report, 28.4. Jossey-Bass Higher and Adult Education Series.

Kezar, A. J., and Lester, J. (2009). *Organizing Higher Education for Collaboration: A Guide for Campus Leaders*, San Francisco: Jossey-Bass.

Knapper, C. (2012). 'The impact of training on teacher effectiveness: Canadian practices and policies'. Video Keynote.

Kotter, J. P. (1996). *Leading Change*. Harvard Business School Press.

QAA (2012). Enhancement-led institutional review: Handbook. Enhancement themes website. www.enhancementthemes.ac.uk/.

Lave, J. and Wenger, E. (1991). *Situated Learning: Legitimate peripheral participation*, New York: Cambridge University Press.

Little, D. and D. A. Green (2012). 'Betwixt and between? Academic developers in the margins', *International Journal for Academic Development, Special Issue: Political Geographies in Academic Development*, 17(3): 203–215.

Piccinin, S., Cristi, C. and McCoy, M. (1999). 'The impact of individual consultation on student ratings of teaching', *International Journal of Academic Development*, 4(2): 76–88.

Sutherland, K. and Willis, D. (2013). 'A relational and holistic approach to the changing academic environment: a faculty-based academic development programme for early career academics', pp. 39–42, in R. Macdonald (ed.), *Supporting Educational Change: SEDA Special 33*. London: SEDA.

Vygotsky, L. (1987). *Collected Works*, Vol. 1. New York: Plenum.

Chapter 14

Managing and leading projects and project teams

Nancy Turner and Peter Hartley

Summary

The project – a piece of work with defined goals, process, start and end points – has long been an essential item in the academic developer's toolkit. Irrespective of changes to external funding for them, projects should remain a mainstay. However, we cannot rely on traditional project methodologies. In particular, we must ensure that the project is conceived and undertaken as a change process rather than as an isolated event, and that outcomes and outputs are integrated into learning environments. This means changing the ways we conceptualise, plan and then run projects. We use examples of recent and current projects from two national contexts, Canada and the UK.

Links to web sources referenced in this chapter can be found at www.seda .ac.uk/apad.

Acknowledgements

The authors would like to thank all the individuals involved in the work the case studies included in this chapter highlight, many of whom we have been privileged to work with and learn from. We would also like to thank members of the Bay View Alliance – Lorne Whitehead, Mary Huber and Pat Hutchings – for their input into the BVA case study.

Introduction

Opportunities for externally funded projects tend to be cyclical in higher education. For example, funding opportunities are currently very limited in the UK, after more than two and a half decades of good support. By contrast, funded projects are on the rise in some parts of Canada. We argue that the project approach, whether from large-scale externally funded projects, major institutionally led change initiatives or smaller funded projects or pilots in specific areas of the developer's own institution, remains an essential element of our practice. However, we argue here that we need to change how we conceive and employ project management techniques and tools.

We need to modify the project mindset, adopting techniques and strategies which ensure that the project is conceived of and enacted as a change process, that valuable processes and tools used effectively in project management are aligned to the objectives of our work, and that outcomes and outputs are more effectively embedded and integrated into the longer term life and work of the institution. Reframing the project in this way, as an essential component of our development activities and as an element in the change process, can help us support the many different needs and opportunities for academic development identified in Chapter 2. (Timmermans [2014] reports that developers' most often identified threshold concept in academic development is facilitating a change process.)

Learning from history

The role and status of educational development projects has changed over the years in different ways in different countries to reflect the broader social and economic context of higher and further education. A brief comparison of developments in the UK and Canada will illustrate this point and highlight the need for change in our approach.

In the UK, a string of national programmes over the last 25 or so years enabled educational developers and development units to lead or support major funded projects and expand their staffing and expertise. Some of the early initiatives are reviewed in Martin, Yorke and Baume (2002). Programmes included:

- £311m from November 2004 to March 2011 to 'reward teaching excellence' though the establishment of 72 Centres for Excellence in Teaching and Learning (CETLs) in universities across the UK, supported by the national funding body (HEFCE).
- Major programmes to support and evaluate innovation in learning and teaching including the Fund for the Development of Teaching and Learning (FDTL – £36m from October 1996 to July 2008), the Teaching Quality Enhancement Fund (TQEF – £158m from August 2006 to August 2009), the Teaching and Learning Technology Programme (TLTP – £33m from May 1993 to June 2004), and the Curriculum Development and Curriculum Delivery Programmes supported by the Joint Information Systems Committee (Jisc).
- Collaborative research and development programmes such as the National Teaching Fellow (NTF) Group Projects, supported by the Higher Education Academy (HEA).

This funding has reduced or disappeared. Funding for CETLs was discontinued after the initial awards were completed in 2010; there are currently no major funding calls from Jisc; and the NTF Group Projects were also discontinued, although the individual Fellowship scheme is still operating. In the same time period, the organising agencies have scaled back and been redefined, including changing roles for the HEA and Jisc. While these changes have been largely driven by economic pressures, they have also been influenced by the criticism of initiatives that are judged not to have had the anticipated or expected impact on the sector as a whole (e.g. Trowler, Ashwin and Saunders, 2014). Following such evaluations, a topic of concern in the UK is that traditional project approaches have not been able to extend or embed outcomes into mainstream educational provision.

In Canada, higher education (HE) is funded and governed at the level of the province. Historical involvement with projects in HE has therefore varied considerably across the country. For the most part, however, there has been a dearth of project-based funding available to HE. This trend has shifted recently in Ontario, where the Higher Education Quality Council of Ontario (HEQCO) has been opening up competitive calls for research projects into varying aspects of HE policy and practice. Many of these have been awarded to academic developers, and some are being undertaken through cross-institutional collaborations between Institutional Educational Development Units. Furthermore there has been a push for increased use of eLearning from the Provincial Government, with the aim of increasing flexibility for students, enabling them in theory at least to take courses (modules) from any Ontario University. The response to calls for a share of $42 million has been led by academic developers in most institutions. It is unclear whether these approaches will continue in Ontario, and whether they will begin in other provinces.

While project work is often conceived as arising from receipt of external funding, projects can and do occur without external funding. As we will argue here, projects can be a very powerful mechanism for organising many aspects of academic development work to bring about change in higher education. The need to achieve and demonstrate long-term and wide-scale impact from all academic development work, including that organised and presented as project work, has become more pressing. Approaches to monitoring and evaluation are described in Chapter 10.

Here, we identify and discuss three key issues for academic developers seeking to utilise projects to enable change and to increase the impact of these projects, both within their own institutions and more broadly across the sector:

- Reviewing and revising our definitions of project work.
- Redefining roles and team structures.
- Ensuring appropriate methodologies.

As we work through these issues, we will highlight key practical steps, summarised in Table 14.2, which academic developers can take to enhance the impact of their projects.

Redefining 'the project'

Before we reflect on different definitions of the project, it is worth explaining why we are so concerned about the conceptualisations of the project approach.

In the introduction to this chapter, we suggested that there was a project mindset. We have borrowed this term from the now considerable body of research in the social sciences which demonstrates the power of our expectations and assumptions in determining our behaviour (Dweck, 2006). The work of Dweck and a host of other studies demonstrate that adopting a particular definition of, or perspective on, a situation can influence our behaviour in ways that we may not be fully aware of (Chabris and Simons, 2010). Our own practical experience of project approaches and methodologies suggests that problems often arise because participants have misleading or conflicting expectations and assumptions about the situation, which are not recognised or surfaced. We also have to contend with the complexities of the language which we use to explain and justify our intentions. There is considerable research on the ways that language can be used to frame our understanding and to favour particular approaches to action. So our definitions (both explicit and implicit) are important in the ways that they can either liberate or limit our approach.

From this perspective, we think it is essential to interrogate the way that projects are typically conceptualised. Regardless of scale or funding arrangements, projects have typically been identified with the following principal characteristics:

- A finite and defined piece of work;
- Particular pre-defined intended outcomes;
- Start and finish dates; and
- Employing defined resources.

A typical and oft-quoted definition comes from the UK Office of Government Commerce, which defines a project as:

> [A] unique set of co-ordinated activities, with definite starting and finishing points, undertaken by an individual or team to meet specific objectives within defined time, cost and performance parameters. (Quoted in Project management, 2014)

One practical difficulty with this definition is that the project can be seen as a largely self-contained piece of work which is completed by the end date. But adopting this approach can minimise impact, as little attention is paid to the subsequent embedding and support which may be necessary for longer-term effect. Often we think about projects producing the artefact (policy, new learning environment, etc.). We may forget about the practices that need to change across the institution in response to and in working with the artefact. In the extreme, the agents that will be enacting or interacting with the artefact are left out of the scope of what a project considers. The work to support change across the institution needs to be considered as a key aspect of, or accompaniment to, the project if it is to succeed. Only by paying sufficient attention to these issues will we realise the full advantages of the project approach, as summarised in Table 14.1 below.

Table 14.1 Advantages and limitations of the conventional project approach

Features of the project approach	Advantages	Limitations
Definite timescale	Can help planning and scheduling	May not pay sufficient attention to embedding and long-term impact
Clear objectives	Help to focus attention and provide a clear mechanism for evaluation of process and outcome	May be interpreted too rigidly and/or be inflexible when circumstances change
Defined and distributed responsibilities	Everyone knows what they should be doing and all team members have responsibility for progressing objectives	May be interpreted too rigidly and/or be inflexible when circumstances change Can be a challenge to ensure work is completed across a diverse team
Teams created that do not necessarily align neatly with organisational structures	Means that inter and cross-team collaboration can be facilitated as well as meaningful stakeholder involvement. The ideal outcomes are those co-created and co-owned by a group that cuts across institutional structures and hierarchies.	Can create issues in forming a shared vision of what the process and outcome of the project might be Conflicting interests can, at times, be difficult to manage.
Structured and focused consultation with stakeholders	Can enhance the alignment of the project to the needs of the community the project aims to serve	Can be time-consuming and costly
Collaborative work within the project team to achieve objectives	If the process is well constructed and participants are open, the project is an opportunity for participants to learn from and with each other leading to personal and professional growth, exposure of team members to broader perspectives and increased understanding of the practices and values of others within and outside the organisation.	All participants need to be ready and willing and possibly supported in collaboration if the process is to function effectively and particularly if full benefits are to be achieved.

To capitalise on these advantages and to minimise the limitations, we argue that project definition and planning must always be undertaken from a change management perspective. A successful project must pay explicit attention to developing collaborative processes within the project team, to involving stakeholders at all points in the project, to how this involvement can in and of itself be part of the change process, and to how the outputs and thereby the outcomes can be disseminated and extended beyond the project team and the planned schedule. Table 14.2 suggests practical steps which we can take to achieve this expanded definition of the project, to enhancing impact whilst maintaining the advantages of the project approach.

The case studies which, sometimes interspersed with sections considering issues in the use of projects, form the rest of this chapter are our selection of recent and continuing projects which illustrate these practical steps through using different strategies.

Table 14.2 Practical steps to enhance project impact and sustainability in higher education

Practical step	Illustrated by specific case studies in this chapter
Integrating and embedding projects in broader institutional change	1, 2, 3, 7
Publishing and promoting outcomes and processes as widely as possible, both inside and outside the home institution	1, 7
Engaging a broad range of stakeholders in conceiving, planning and implementing the project	2, 3, 5
Using the project to enhance understanding of our own processes	3, 6
Adopting agile and less time intensive approaches to project management	6
Adopting project processes and structures which can foster improved long-term relationships and future collaborations	4, 5, 7
Improving communication and coordination within and between projects and sub-projects	4, 5, 7
Enabling more meaningful student engagement to ensure they, as the primary stakeholder group, are both creators and beneficiaries of the project	5

Case study 1: The 3E Framework – enhance, extend, empower – from Edinburgh Napier University: Moving from specific project objectives to flexible institutional change

The 3E Framework (Smyth, 2013) offers an inclusive and flexible approach to the use of new technology in learning and teaching. It has now been adopted and adapted by a number of other universities.

The framework started with the specific aim of helping further and higher education lecturers to extend and embed their use of learning technology as part of course redesign. This approach was then revised and expanded for use at Edinburgh Napier University and published under Creative Commons in 2011.

The framework supports lecturers who wish to integrate learning technologies into their modules by offering examples and inspiration at three levels – enhance, extend, and empower. These three levels reflect the different experience and aspirations of different lecturers. The framework also provides models for lecturers to move through the levels – from enhancement to empowerment. The framework has now been used in different ways by a range of other universities in the UK and abroad, including at York (as an evaluation tool), Sussex (adapted for assessment and feedback), Leeds Metropolitan (now Leeds Beckett) (as the starting point for their 4E Framework), and in Greece as part of a government-funded schools curriculum project. Links to all these projects and others can be found in Keith Smyth's 3E Education blog ('3E Approach', 2012). The use of this framework with learning technologies is described in Chapter 8.

In many ways, the development of this framework exemplifies the approach to projects which we are advocating in this chapter – starting from a project with specific objectives, and then adopting a change management approach to exploit its potential. Among the key components of the change management were:

- Ensuring that the framework was integrated and embedded in broader institutional change at Edinburgh Napier.
- Publishing the framework widely to facilitate its use across the institution and to enable other institutions to adopt and adapt it.
- Using an inclusive approach which catered for staff at different stages of development with new technology.

Case study 2: University of the Arts London (UAL) VLE review and implementation project: Use of a project to collaboratively establish a new vision for the use of learning technology

This was a major institutional change project. It entailed reviewing options, selecting a new Virtual Learning Environment (VLE), shifting from a proprietary to an open source platform, along with the transition and implementation of the new platform. This was undertaken at a large collegiate art, design and communication specialist institution that historically had made little use of the VLE. The project was therefore intended to examine some of the reasons for the low uptake as part of the review process, and to align selection of the new tool with the culture to better meet the needs of the colleges. Another key goal of the project was to establish new working relationships across central service units to better support the VLE. The review identified five key characteristics that the new VLE needed to provide:

a   *Openness.* Course sites that can be easily opened to staff and students as well as to external collaborators and guests
b   *Contextual fit.* A structure that matches the way in which UAL courses are delivered (e.g. virtual spaces for programmes, courses, years and units)
c   *User Experience and Interface.* An improved user experience and user interface designed for an arts university
d   *Flexibility and Mobility.* A more flexible and agile VLE model that allows for greater responsiveness to institutional strategy and changes in technology
e   *Pedagogic fit.* The learning environment should be student-centred, with the capacity for student-led activity

It also provided a road map for learning technology at the institution, based on extensive consultation with senior and middle managers, academics and students across the institution. This fed into the selection process, which involved key stakeholders from across the institution.

Once the new platform was selected, the implementation project was managed centrally by a project board chaired by a pro vice chancellor from one of the six colleges that make up UAL and having staff and student representatives. The project had several additional components. These included:

• A design advisory board drawn from experts in academic departments,
• Several student focus groups, and
• In-depth involvement by student representatives in all levels of the project.

In addition, implementation boards were established at each college to manage the local planning, customisation and implementation of the environment. The entire process was intended to engage the academic community to consider what learning technologies could be used for at present, what their aspirations were in using it to support student learning, and collectively to shape an environment and support services that enabled those aspirations.

The whole project ran over four years with review and selection taking 1.5 years and the implementation taking 2.5. The project is now complete. However, the longer-term impacts of establishing a collective understanding of where the institution is going in use of learning technology, and the alignment of the infrastructure and support to enable achievement of that, are still in progress. The progress of change in attitudes to and practices in learning technology across programmes began at the initiation of the review process and developed throughout the formal project. The dialogue, debate and decisions made shaped both the project and the understanding of the individuals participating in them. The project board, in a slightly modified form, has been retained to provide continuing input and oversight into development of learning technologies across the university.

Case study 3: The Gwenna Moss Centre for Teaching Effectiveness (GMCTE) at the University of Saskatchewan: Use of project teams to develop a shared understanding of academic development work

The GMCTE had traditionally operated with small teams or individuals within the unit undertaking specific duties. Coordination across all areas was led by the Director of the Centre. Several changes at the University of Saskatchewan over six months meant that the GMCTE was called to shift its work and function within a new management structure. The changes meant there was less capacity for one person to direct the work of many, and so a distributed leadership model was implemented, with each staff member at the centre leading one or more areas of work.

These leads headed up cross-unit teams, often including individuals from outside the unit. The teams were connected to the area of service concerned, to progress work that would have previously been owned by small groups or an individual. The newly formed teams developed objectives for the year that aligned with a set of guiding principles which acted as an initial set of espoused values (Schein, 2004), and served as the starting point for a vision of how the work could be undertaken. These teams were loosely managed projects with a lead, individual contributors, and a set of clear objectives to be achieved within a timeframe. The teams continued to work together as the year progressed, focused on achieving these objectives through participation in regular discussions and joint work in enacting them. As the year progressed, some of the objectives evolved due to changing circumstances or new unexpected opportunities. The teams were able to make these decisions collectively and respond to emerging needs in an agile way.

A process was also implemented for each area of service to share progress and challenges in their work with the wider team. This allowed for the individual areas to benefit from the input of the whole team, and allowed for each team member to conceive the areas of service as contributing to the mandate of the centre and achievement of the common goals. The process also allowed the team to reflect explicitly on each area of service in the context of the emerging understanding of how the centre effects change across the institution.

This approach was implemented to engender leadership and collaboration across the team, to break down internal unit structures and to cross external institutional boundaries. The intent, in line with social learning theory, was also to develop a clearer shared understanding of our practice as a unit through the collaborative process of setting, implementing and evaluating a set of objectives (Wenger, 2000). Projects included the revision and implementation of a graduate professional skills certificate, creating a framework for supporting the development of intercultural competence across the institution, and developing online resources for the centre's website in line with institutional strategic priorities amongst many others.

Establishing effective roles and team structures

Academic developers can be positioned in varying roles within projects, often determined by where in the project life cycle they become involved. As initiators of projects, academic developers are well positioned to lead or strategically invite leadership from another part of the institution. As project managers, academic developers can navigate the course of a project, influence its strategic positioning, build relationships across an institution and generate conversations that will begin the change process in advance of implementation. As project team members, academic developers can be active in contributing and drawing out the ideas of others, facilitating collaboration, and having input into the direction the project takes. In all of these positions within a project, the academic developer will need to be welcoming of and open to the opinions of others, keep the improvement of student learning at the fore of any programme outcomes, and keep project outcomes flexible and responsive to changing environments and local contexts. In addition, academic developers need to ensure that the role and team structures employed within a project are the most appropriate to achieve the objectives and enable change management. To meet this enlarged range of needs, we need to consider moving beyond conventional or traditional project team structures.

The conventional role and team structure adopted by many educational projects has used a combination of steering group, formal evaluation, and project director(s) leading a team who are responsible for delivering the outcomes and outputs. The formality and complexity of this structure typically varies with the size of the project.

Again there are both conceptual and practical issues with this conventional approach:

- Will all the relevant stakeholders be engaged?
- Do the structures allow for input from all parts of an institution and implementation to vary appropriately based on local cultures?
- Can evaluation be designed in a way that allows for it to impact the project at varying points?
- Will the final evaluation deliver useful insights for the future?
- Is this structure sufficiently sensitive to accommodate changes in the context in which the project is being undertaken?
- How do we create an effective working team to ensure the quality of the deliverables?

We can learn from recent literature into the nature of effective working groups (e.g. West, 2012) and from innovation in methods of group discussion and problem-solving (such as Ketso and Open Space – see Weblinks). We can explore a range of alternative techniques to answer these issues and potentially deliver more flexible outcomes. For example, the role of project sponsor is often used to ensure senior management engagement. We can also consider projects as change processes that require varying types of engagement from stakeholder groups, ranging from voices to consultants to partners, with the latter having the possible outcomes of shared ownership and buy-in to the intended change.

Case study 4: The CAMEL project and the use of Critical Friends: Developing communities of practice within and between projects

A number of useful approaches and techniques have emerged from the major programmes of academic innovation funded in the UK by Jisc and HEA. We point to some of their innovations at programme level in case study 8 below. Here, we want to focus on innovations in project team structures and processes which emerged from the CAMEL project.

CAMEL (n.d.) stands for Collaborative Approaches to the Management of E-Learning. The project brought together representatives from different institutions to share experience and expertise and build a Community of Practice. The approach was based on a model originally developed and used by Uruguayan farmers as a self-help strategy. Based on this model, key features of the CAMEL approach included:

- Collaborative planning
- Open discussion with nothing hidden
- Making tacit knowledge explicit
- Expert facilitation
- Formal evaluation

From this project, and from subsequent use of the CAMEL approach in programmes funded by Jisc and by HEA, a model of expert facilitation has emerged – the 'Critical Friend' (Critical friends, 2014).

The essence of this role was captured by John Macbeath (Critical friends, op. cit.):

> Perhaps the critical friend comes closest to what might be regarded as 'true friendship' – a successful marrying of unconditional support and unconditional critique.

Both conceptually and practically, this role is very different from the traditional role of external evaluator, where the focus is on ensuring that project outcomes and outputs are delivered and where there is often a sense of personal distance or detachment between the evaluator role and the project team. This is explored further in Chapter 10. This does not mean that the critical friend is less concerned with outcomes and outputs, rather that the continuing process of project support and critique has a much more developmental and proactive role.

Case study 5: Ensuring meaningful student engagement: The development of students as change agents and co-workers

The impact of any educational intervention obviously depends on how it is received by students and its effects on student learning. It is therefore no surprise that developers have been looking for ways of enhancing the engagement of students with projects and initiatives as they develop, rather than simply presenting students with a fait accompli when the project is implemented. As a result, an increasing number of academic development projects have included students in more meaningful and varied ways than the conventional student representative on the steering group. Problems with a limited representative role include the weight of responsibility this places on the one or two student reps, and the way that their influence can be diluted through the heavy hand of committee bureaucracy.

Successful initiatives have included work on specific study roles such as the work on students as producers at the University of Lincoln (Neary, 2010). These initiatives have enabled students to partner with staff on specific studies and investigations, and have often been linked to opportunities for publication and other forms of professional development. But perhaps the most significant initiatives for the themes of this chapter are those which aim to engage students with continuing change on a broader scale.

Perhaps the best-known single initiative of this type in the UK is the 'Students as Change Agents' project at Exeter. We could also have used this project as an example of the successful move from project to institutional process:

> Students from across the university have contributed to this initiative, carrying out a series of research projects on their learning and teaching environment, selecting concerns raised through student-staff liaison committees (SSLCs), and providing recommendations and solutions to improve their experience. (Dunne and Zandstra, 2011, p. 2)

There is a formal application process and support system with Change Agent Representatives. Other universities now offer similar schemes, often with opportunities to earn some form of academic credit (e.g. at the University of Nottingham – see Weblinks).

There have also been experiments with the student role in specific educational change projects. A good example here is the work led by the University of Greenwich on their 'Digital Literacy in Transition' project (funded by Jisc as part of their Digital Literacy Programme). This project used studentships as part of a cross-university interdisciplinary research group. (The success of this initiative led to further funding to set up the Change Agents' Network, which in turn has piloted a course and qualification for participants, in partnership with SEDA ['CANLearn', n.d.].)

McMaster University in Canada has also initiated a programme of student engagement in change projects that are relevant to both the Educational Development Centre and the students themselves ('MIIETL: McMaster Institute for Innovation & Excellence in Teaching & Learning Student Engagement', n.d.).

Developers can use this sort of professional support and accreditation as an incentive for student engagement, as more universities extend the role of students in their programmes of change. As a final example of this latter development, we can point to the use of students as student engagement leads in the Learning Futures Programme at the University of Westminster (see Weblinks).

Appropriate management and methodology

Project management in education often uses specific strategies and techniques which are used in other areas of organisational planning. A leading example in the UK is Prince2 (for PRojects IN Controlled Environments), which was extended well beyond its original focus on IT projects to become the 'required methodology for all UK Government commissioned projects' (Court, 2006, p. 2).

The Prince2 method includes a sequence of recommended stages, particular role descriptions, and strict document control. It has been used by a number of universities, and in some national projects. The equivalent of Prince2 in North America is the PMP designation (see Weblinks). It, like Prince2, has well developed foundational and practice standards.

There is a strong emphasis on control in the Prince methodology. This is allied to a very tight definition of outputs and outcomes. This is not surprising, given its origins in IT – when you are designing an IT system you need to be very clear about the required functions. There are many well-publicised examples of major systems which have failed because of inadequate specification. However, we may not be able to (or feel is appropriate to) define outcomes so rigidly in higher education. If you are aiming to improve aspects of the student experience such as engagement, inclusivity or employability, then the very definition of those terms may need to change in the course of the project. A much more iterative project process may therefore be required.

There are alternative frameworks which may offer more flexibility in an educational context. For example, Jisc offers a scaled down version of Prince2 ('Project Management', 2014). This aims to offer a 'user-friendly framework' which provides more of a focus on people, in order 'to give due emphasis on the skills required to manage the people aspects and the organisational change that any project will inevitably bring about'. This approach suggests a start-up phase which happens only once, and then elements which can recur in an iterative cycle: 'Planning, Managing Phases and Controlling, form an iterative cycle that may repeat many times before the project is complete'.

As well as adapting the Prince2 approach to make it more education-friendly, Jisc has used a variety of approaches on their large-scale programmes which were designed to enhance collaboration and dissemination and which can be adapted to other contexts. For example, the Curriculum Design and Curriculum Development programme ('Curriculum design', 2012) used meetings which every project in the programme was obliged to attend and where progress and issues could be shared. Sharing was encouraged with a variety of methods including marketplace sessions to identify the potential for mutual assistance and critical review sessions (using the 'Dragon's Den' format borrowed from the UK TV programme where inventors make a pitch to a panel of prospective investors). In these sessions, projects could receive quick and incisive feedback from their peers on progress and issues.

The earlier Emerge project (Sharpe and Clarke, 2009) used a community-building approach. The programme established a community of interested experts in the field of e-learning before issuing the conventional call for project proposals. The community was used to help shape the priorities and criteria for funding through open events and structured workshops.

Another approach gaining in popularity is Agile project management (see Weblinks). This approach counters the Prince2 linear approach, in which outcomes are rigidly defined at the outset and worked towards in incremental steps. The Agile technique involves iterative cycles of work that are highly collaborative and result in outcomes (or prototypes of the outcomes) along the way. This in turn allows continuous refinement or completion of a larger more complex task in smaller chunks.

Our examples represent different ways of overcoming the inherent inflexibilities of highly structured approaches to project management, whilst keeping the accountability and clarity benefits of formal project management.

Case study 6: Minimising project paperwork and bureaucracy: The 'two-sides-of-the page' approach from the Bradford project on Inclusivity

This project was one of ten in the HEA's inclusion change programme 'Developing and Embedding Inclusive Policy and Practice in Higher Education', launched in April 2007 (May and Bridger, 2010). The University of Bradford project aimed to develop an inclusive campus.

For the purposes of this chapter, we focus on the simplified approach to project administration which was highlighted by the programme consultants as a particular strength. Rather than use the initially suggested approach to project management, which seemed to the Bradford team to be heavily based on Prince2 methodology, the team decided that a simpler approach was necessary to focus attention on the overall aims of the project and assist collaborative communication. The team settled on a two-sides-of-the-page approach. Two documents provided the main agenda for each team meeting – a one-page concept map which summarised the main objectives and required activities of the project, and an action tracker which recorded progress on each of the agreed actions. The action tracker obviously expanded to significantly more than one page as the project developed, but the team felt that this very simple set of documents maintained a constant focus on the very ambitious overall objectives.

A concept map has advantages over a traditional project description. It can provide an overview of the key components and the relationships between them, which can be difficult to demonstrate in a written text. This reflects the considerable literature on concept mapping as an important tool for the 'improvement of education and the creation and use of knowledge' (Novak, 2010, p. xiv). The development of accessible software across a range of platforms (PC, Mac and now iPad) means that users can create maps of the sort used in this chapter after only a few minutes of learning.

Case study 7: The Bayview Alliance (BVA): Capitalising on shared goals across institutions

The BVA (see Weblinks) is another type of collaboration across HE institutions, loosely based on a networked improvement community model designed to facilitate connections across projects in ways that advance shared goals. A group of nine North American research-intensive universities sharing the common goal of increasing the adaptation, implementation and integration of evidence-based teaching approaches, the BVA studies the development of departmental cultures that support effective teaching and learning. A core principle of the work is that institutions can achieve more by collaborating and sharing practice than working in isolation.

A steering committee of representatives from each member institution governs the BVA, which organises its work through several research action clusters (RACs) with each RAC led by one member institution. The RACs enable institutions to connect locally-based research projects under a common theme (e.g. the impact of faculty development on use of active learning spaces). Institutions outside the BVA may also be invited to join RACs if their work aligns, allowing for expanded input and new perspectives to be added where appropriate. Member institutions choose to join RACs if they are engaged in or wish to initiate projects that fit the theme. A key aspect of the work of RACs is the sharing of processes, methods and tools as they are developed and sharing data about outcomes. In this way, the RAC groups can discuss and contribute to elements of the members' projects as they evolve, and maintain an agile project management approach.

Each RAC involves a set of connected projects where process and outcomes are shared and refined through an iterative process that is informed by and informs work being completed across the network. Institutions implement interventions designed to promote positive culture change and study their effects. They create prototypes, tools and methods that can be refined through input from other BVA participants and adapted by other institutions for their own use. The participants share, practice, collaborate, and learn from each other, building understanding of effective teaching enhancement practices in HE. Findings can be shared and implemented more quickly than would be the case if institutions undertook this work on their own and shared outcomes only through formal dissemination and publication routes.

In addition to the benefits that the BVA brings to its member institutions, its second key purpose is to benefit the broader higher education community. Beyond dissemination of the results of the research projects, the BVA also works to share knowledge about networked improvement and inquiry within higher education. Increasingly the BVA is doing this in ways that, at scale, model networked improvement and inquiry.

Conclusions

Academic developers are being called on increasingly to initiate, lead and undertake institution-wide initiatives. Setting up activities as projects can be very helpful, as it concentrates the mind on intended outcomes, methods, timescale and resources. But we must also take account of change management issues, and ensure that outcomes are embedded and sustainable. The variety of examples in this chapter from across the HE sector suggests ways we can incorporate the advantages of project methodologies into successful change management. Taken together, these examples highlight some key issues for academic developers:

- The importance of conceiving and implementing projects in line with social learning theory, recognising that change occurs in dialogue, collaboration and shared practice.
- The need for the work of change to begin from the first discussion of what the focus and objectives of the project should be, and to continue on through evaluation of outcomes after the project.
- The opportunity that projects provide to generate evidence of impact against clearly defined objectives. This is becoming increasingly important for academic developers as we need to justify institutional investment in enhancement endeavours.
- The importance of monitoring and evaluation as a continuous process which is established as early as possible in the project. This and the previous bullet point are explored in more detail in Chapter 10 on monitoring and evaluation.

As a final example, we include Figure 14.1 – a concept map outlining key questions which can be applied to most if not all academic development projects and which has now been used to organise the evaluation activities on several national

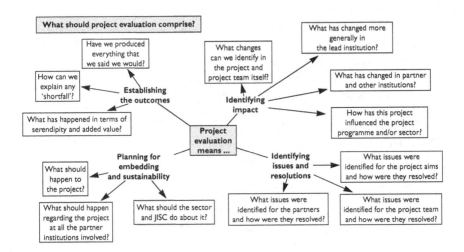

Figure 14.1 Key issues for project evaluation

development projects. This map includes a number of critical points, including the distinction between outcomes and impact, and the importance of embedding the project outcomes and sustainability.

We need to adopt techniques and strategies which ensure that project outcomes and outputs are more effectively embedded and integrated into learning environments. A focussing on embedding will capitalise on projects as structured and purposeful collaborative work, work that benefits from bringing together individuals with different perspectives from within or outside an organisation. This focus will also situate projects as an opportunity to develop stronger connections and shared understandings across institutional structures. This chapter has included a range of strategies and techniques which academic developers can use to enhance their deployment of project methods as a valuable part of the change process.

Weblinks

'3E Approach': Keith Smyth's 3E Education blog:
http://3eeducation.org/?s=3e+framework
Agile project management:
www.allaboutagile.com/what-is-agile-10-key-principles/
Bay View Alliance:
http://bayviewalliance.org
Bradford inclusive campus project:
www-new1.heacademy.ac.uk/assets/documents/inclusion/Developing
    EmbeddingInclusivePP_Report.pdf
CAMEL project:
www.jisc.ac.uk/guides/change-management/camel-approach
Change Agents' Network:
www.jisc.ac.uk/rd/projects/change-agents-network
Cmap software:
www.ihmc.us/cmaptools.php
Curriculum Design Programme: typical meeting agenda:
www.webarchive.org.uk/wayback/archive/20140614155506/
www.jisc.ac.uk/whatwedo/programmes/elearning/curriculumdesign/
    progmtgoct11.aspx
Digital Literacy in Transition:
www2.gre.ac.uk/research/centres/ecentre/projects/dl-in-transition
JISC Infokit re Critical Friends:
www.jisc.ac.uk/guides/change-management/critical-friends
Jisc on project management:
www.jisc.ac.uk/guides/project-management

Ketso:

www.ketso.com

Learning Futures Programme at the University of Westminster:

www.westminster.ac.uk/study/current-students/student-news/student-news/2014/
learning-futures-programme-student-engagement-taskforce

OpenSpace:

http://openspaceworld.org/wp2/

PMP:

www.pmi.org/PMBOK-Guide-and-Standards.aspx

Students as change agents:

http://jiscdesignstudio.pbworks.com/w/page/31087422/Students%20as%20
Change%20Agents

At University of Nottingham:

www.nottingham.ac.uk/currentstudents/studentopportunities/students-as-change-
agents.aspx

At McMaster University:

http://miietl.mcmaster.ca/site/student-engagement/

References

3E Framework (2012). Retrieved 11 June 2015 from http://3eeducation.org/?s=
3e+framework.

CANLearn. (n.d.). Retrieved 19 April 2015 from www.canlearn.co.uk/.

Chabris, C. and Simons. D. (2011). *The Invisible Gorilla: And Other Ways Our
Intuition Deceives Us*. London: HarperCollins.

Court, R. (2006). 'An introduction to PRINCE2 project methodology'. Chartered
Institute of Management Accountants. Retrieved 19 April 2015 from www
.cimaglobal.com/Documents/ImportedDocuments/PRINCE2_P5_article.pdf.

Critical friends. (2011). Retrieved 19 April 2015 from http://www.jiscinfonet.ac.uk/
infokits/critical-friends/.

Curriculum design. (2012). Retrieved 21 October 2015 from www.jisc.ac.uk/
guides/change-management/critical-friends.

Dweck, C. S. (2008). *Mindset. The New Psychology of Success*. New York: Ballantine.

Dunne, E. and Zandstra, R. (2011). *Students as Change Agents. New Ways of Engaging
with Learning and Teaching in Higher Education*. Bristol: HE Subject Centre for
Education. Retrieved from http://escalate.ac.uk/downloads/8244.pdf.

Martin, P., Yorke, M. and Baume, C. (eds.) (2002). *Managing Development Projects:
Effective Management for Maximum Impact*. London: RoutledgeFalmer.

May, H. and Bridger, K. (2010). 'Developing and embedding inclusive policy and
practice in higher education'. York: Higher Education Academy. Accessed at
www.heacademy.ac.uk/sites/default/files/DevelopingEmbeddingInclusivePP_
Report.pdf.

MIIETL: McMaster Institute for Innovation & Excellence in Teaching & Learning.
(n.d.). Retrieved 11 June 2015 from http://miietl.mcmaster.ca/site/
student-engagement/.

Neary, M. (2010). 'Student as producer: a pedagogy for the avant-garde?', *Learning
Exchange*, 1(1).

Novak, J. D. (2010). *Learning, Creating, and Using Knowledge: Concept Maps as Facilitative Tools in Schools and Corporations.* London: Routledge.

Project management. (2014). Retrieved 28 October 2015 from www.jisc.ac.uk/guides/project-management

Schein, E. H. (2004). *Organizational Culture and Leadership.* 3rd edition. San Francisco: Jossey-Bass.

Sharpe, R. and Clarke, P. (2006). 'A community-based programme of support'. In Roberts, G. (Ed.), *JISC Emerge: A User-Centred Social Learning Media Hub,* pp. 20–25.

Smyth, K. (2013). 'Sharing and shaping effective institutional practice in TEL through the 3E Framework'. In S. Greener (Ed.), *Case studies in e-learning.* Reading: Academic Publishing International, pp. 141–159.

Timmermans, J. A. (2014). 'Identifying threshold concepts in the careers of educational developers', *International Journal for Academic Development,* 19(4): 305–317.

Trowler, P., Ashwin, P. and Saunders, M. (2014). 'The role of HEFCE in teaching and learning enhancement: a review of evaluative evidence'. York: The Higher Education Academy. Retrieved 11 June April 2015 from www.heacademy.ac.uk/sites/default/files/downloads/The_role_of_HEFCE_in_TL_Enhancement_final_report.pdf.

Wenger, E. (2000). 'Communities of practice and social learning systems', *Organization,* 7(2): 225–246.

West, M.A. (2012). *Effective Teamwork: Practical Lessons from Organisational Research.* 3rd edition. Oxford: BPS Blackwell.

Chapter 15

Leading an academic development unit

Julie Hall and David A. Green

Summary

In this chapter, the authors use theoretical frameworks to explore key issues faced by leaders (sometimes also called heads, managers or directors) of Academic Development Units (ADUs). They focus on the importance of values for an ADU's success, the difficulties of balancing individual and institutional priorities, the unusual HE context (in which most colleagues are themselves experts), the pros and cons of collaboration across the institution, and the role of ADUs in institutional change. Using real case studies from the USA and the UK, the authors illustrate these issues with topics as diverse as changing assessment practices, technological change, curriculum review and mentoring schemes.

Links to web sources referenced in this chapter can be found at www.seda.ac.uk/apad.

Context reigns supreme

Academic Development Units (ADUs) are configured in many ways, with contrasting remits, varied institutional locations, and different reporting structures. Each of these factors means that there are 'no fixed recipes' (Leibowitz, 2014, p. 73) when it comes to leading an ADU, just as there are no fixed recipes for how to teach well or how to help students learn. In other words, context reigns supreme as you think through how best to lead your unit.

Fortunately, we are not operating in a knowledge vacuum. Even if we lack rich studies on directing and managing ADUs, there is much research that we can bring to bear in our decision-making, and so the aim of this chapter is to provide examples of how the literature has helped us lead our own units. Where appropriate, we provide short case studies to vivify the research and illustrate how these theories and frameworks might play out in reality. The purpose behind this approach is twofold.

Firstly, it is easy to fall into the trap of surveying other ADUs and then shoe-horning their approaches into our own institutions, regardless of our different contexts. So in this chapter, our aim is to encourage you to work out your underlying framework and values so that your approach to leading your unit is well-grounded in the literature. This will help you make good decisions about what to say 'yes' to and what to decline. Here, we are following Kurt Lewin's (1951, p. 169) adage that, 'There is nothing so practical as a good theory,' and will provide different examples for specific situations and questions.

Secondly, as developers, we work with academics and we *are* academics – or at least we believe we should be. And as the 'academics' academic', the 'meta-academic,' so to speak, we need as best we can to model exemplary approaches to our work (Baume and Kahn, 2004). To that end, using theoretical models to underpin what we do is a way for us to signal that being an academic leader can be informed by research, be carefully considered, and applied in a nuanced way to acknowledge the peculiarities of working in the 'knowledge business'. We are in the unusual situation where most of our colleagues have been educated to the highest level in their fields and are therefore forever – and rightly – asking, 'Why'? If we can demonstrate that we have thought through the whys and have strong guiding principles, then this can only enhance the reputation of our ADUs and therefore improve our chances of affecting change in our institutions. In other words, it's a question of credibility.

The models and theories we provide in this chapter are not necessarily ground-breaking and many are not new, but we have seen them work successfully. Where a model doesn't sit comfortably with you, we trust that you will seek out alternative frameworks that allow you to be true to yourself as an academic leader and effective in your own institutional context.

Defining and establishing an ADU based on values

While few people have the luxury of designing an ADU from scratch, it is common to have to review and adapt a unit to new demands, often linked to changes in learning and teaching practices. In this section we focus on three factors that we see as critical for the leader in creating or realigning an ADU. First, vision-building as a way of underpinning the ADU with values, purpose and integrity; second, managing upwards; and, finally, building the ADU team. This might be summarised as how the ADU works, its role and its people.

The ADU's role is often to coordinate and drive educational change, a multi-level social process which Michael Fullan (1992, p. 109) reminds us is 'technically simple and socially complex'. We have found the values of our professional networks (SEDA and POD) helpful across the two dimensions of vision. The first is developing a shared vision for the ADU to provide clear direction and a mechanism for deciding what tasks to take on; the second is a shared vision for how to work – the strategies to ensure changes happen in particular ways. The values of POD and SEDA emphasise an inclusive and critical approach and a shared sense of purpose in both the content of our work and the process. SEDA's values ensure that in the end, the ADU recognises change as a learning experience for everyone involved. A common pitfall is to focus on *what* the unit should do – how a course for new lecturers might be designed or redesigned, for example – and *who* should lead it. Yet we have found that in the long run, it is more helpful when establishing and adapting an ADU to focus on *how* the unit should work.

As an ADU leader, you can find yourself Janus-faced: developing trust with academic colleagues while requiring the ADU to be championed by a senior university manager – usually someone who has responsibility for teaching quality or the student experience. This is a key relationship because this senior leader can create the conditions for or against engagement with the ADU (see Chapter 16). Some senior managers will not fully appreciate the complexities of academic development and many are often under pressure to develop a strategy at speed. The senior manager may also, at least at an early stage, be unaware of academic development as change management, seeing the ADU for example as merely the place to train people to teach more effectively. ADU leaders must therefore be alert to managing upwards, as well as managing their own team and its change processes. This process can be further complicated when a new senior manager takes over – someone who may well decide to change the focus of the ADU, requiring the leader to defend the unit, argue for its existence or redevelop it with a different remit (often driven by a new Learning and Teaching Strategy). Resilience is therefore an important quality for the leader alongside the ability to be flexible, and to pause, reflect and plan for new agendas. Managing upwards can involve providing articles (or summaries) for the senior manager to read, pointing them to research evidence, being honest and authentic when taking principled positions, and collecting institutional data to analyse what is happening.

There seems to be little consistency in staffing models across ADU teams because of the variation in university traditions, structures and missions. Many ADUs focus on early-career academics, so one common gap for unit leaders to address early is facilitating ongoing, cumulative learning to develop conceptions, skills and behaviour among more experienced academics. Further complicating matters, government funding in Australia (Parrish and Lafoe, 2008) and the UK (HEFCE, 2011) in recent years has enabled distributed leadership models that recognise disciplinary expertise and aim to build a community of academic development. Your team therefore may be large or small, may be based in the ADU or embedded in academic teams, may cover a range of roles or may have a single aim. Given these dissimilar configurations, compounded by the diverse career pathways into academic development (MacDonald and Stockley, 2010) and the frequent reorganisation of ADUs (Gosling, 2009; Holt, Palmer and Challis, 2011), unit leaders often have to help colleagues cope with a sense of displacement or reorientation. Developers can feel the strains of operating on the 'fault lines' (Rowland, 2002, p. 53) of higher education, being 'caught in the middle' (Hicks, 2005, p. 175) between senior managers and academics. We suggest that time to discuss feelings of discomfort, identity and marginality within the ADU team is valuable.

As the team grows in size or complexity the leader also needs to ensure a focus on the processes of change and on modelling collaborative working (Chapter 13 explores some models of change). In this way good ideas and stories can be shared, practices can be scrutinised and consistency of vision can be maintained, as well as celebrating jobs done well. Throughout, the leader should emphasise that the ADU must model good practice to academic colleagues and senior managers and thus there is pressure to ensure that any event, intervention or piece of research is of the highest quality, with evidence where possible to indicate its worth. This then refocuses the ADU on embodying and enacting its underlying values in all its work – the highest level of the Taxonomy of the Affective Domain (Krathwohl, Bloom and Masia, 1964).

Case study: Using POD's ethical guidelines to shape the mission of an ADU and how it is led

The website of the POD Network in the US includes ethical guidelines for educational developers that can be used to shape the values and work of an ADU (POD, n.d.). These guidelines have led many US units to demarcate their work with academics as 'confidential, formative and voluntary'. The confidential component means that academics feel comfortable raising difficulties they are experiencing without fear of reprisal. The formative aspect protects developers from having to pass judgment on (re-)appointments or promotions and so ensures that the developer–academic relationship is not simultaneously developmental and judgmental. The voluntary piece flows naturally from the other two: if someone is 'required' by their supervisor to see a developer, then the ADU's confidentiality policy means the supervisor cannot find out about it, so if the conversation *does* take place, it is inherently voluntary. These three policies can help ADUs decide what to say yes or no to and provide helpful buffers that keep the ADU out of the power dynamics that can dilute a unit's effectiveness.

For example, one ADU in the US runs a programme for new academics, but the provost's office decides who must attend; the ADU helps teams develop their programme assessments, but a quality assurance office evaluates it. The ADU's underlying values help it navigate changing institutional politics and priorities with integrity, while ensuring all along that academics can continue to trust a unit that is specifically designed to help them develop in their roles.

Managing the balance between supporting individuals and meeting strategic priorities

In many countries, ADU work is changing, creating new challenges for ADU leaders:

> Leading new initiatives may seem like a great idea, even if we don't have much experience of doing it, but this may well involve stopping doing what some of us are used to doing – such as being responsive to requests. It may involve rationing help and effort in line with institutional priorities rather

than following one's nose or the noses of our most frequent and valued clients. (Gibbs, 2000, p. 1)

Over the last ten years in the UK, for example, government funds have been provided for large-scale institutional initiatives such as the Centres for Excellence in Teaching and Learning. Yet changes directed from on high, even with funding attached, do not in themselves automatically lead to improvements in the student learning experience. Elton (1992) argued that enhancement, empowerment and enthusiasm to make changes come to nothing without academic development expertise. ADU leaders have to develop and nurture this expertise and navigate a route from supporting individuals to large strategic change projects.

A number of ADUs have their historical roots in voluntary preparation programmes for new academics or individual pedagogic support. This personalised work has often resulted in rich communities of academics attuned to pedagogic practices and can form a firm foundation for effective ADU involvement in important strategic projects.

Writing about educational change in the school system, Fullan (2008) points to a challenge for leaders to remain alert to the real issues for academics and students while being able to take a strategic view and prioritise the focus of effort. Heifetz and Linsky (2002, p. 50) describe this skill as 'getting off the dance floor and going to the balcony' – the mental activity of stepping back in the midst of action and asking, 'What's really going on here?' The ADU leader has to get things done while maintaining a powerful value-based compass and a peripheral vision to what might be either problematic or a convenient academic development opportunity. Leaders can be effective when they have the ability to move back and forth, making interventions, observing their impact in real time, and then returning to the action. They and their ADU colleagues are in effect learning continuously and then working out how to share this learning across the university. The unit leader has a responsibility to be clear with ADU colleagues about the strategic priorities for the unit, ensuring the unit is seen as valuable in meeting strategic needs while maintaining a reputation so that the ADU is trusted by academics on the ground.

Case study: Embedding learning technologies with a focus on pedagogy

When one UK university decided to use a virtual learning environment to supplement all undergraduate teaching, the Learning Technology team, not the ADU, was asked to lead the project. Many academics were nervous about new technologies and reluctant to spend valuable time creating virtual classrooms. The strategy of the Learning Technology team was based on a training model with the aim of showing academics how to use the technology and some examples of good practice. During the process, several individual academics and course teams requested meetings with the academic developers. Some wanted to discuss how they might adapt their practice for the online environment while others wanted a safe space to raise concerns about a reduction in face-to-face teaching and support. The developers had a unique insight into reactions in academic departments, so the ADU leader spoke with the head of Learning Technology and the senior manager with responsibility for Learning and Teaching to suggest a new approach involving the ADU. He argued that this would ensure that the technology would enhance student learning, rather than simply being a repository for lecture notes and articles. He also made the case for a strategic approach to adapting pedagogic practices that recognised micro-cultures in the disciplines. Together the two leaders and their teams redeveloped the implementation plan to include examples of scholarship in disciplinary e-pedagogies and e-assessment, a one-day conference to raise concerns and share good practice and a mentor scheme for academic teams to review their courses and redesign them as required.

Establishing a unit that values academics' expertise

If one of our aims as academic developers is to transform higher education – to help students and academics reach their potential – then a positive and constructive relationship with academics themselves is clearly essential. Ultimately, they decide how a course will proceed, how to use their time, how to conduct themselves in the classroom. They understand their disciplines in ways that we are unlikely ever to (unless we previously studied the same field) and are specifically employed for their expertise. Decisions made at the level of the individual or academic department therefore make an enormous difference to student success – and in turn the success of our institutions.

A risk for us as developers when working with individuals and departments – particularly early in our careers, when enthusiasm for student learning can overshadow all else – is that we may disregard academics' expertise and insider knowledge, and instead try to impose an oversimplified one-size-fits-all approach to higher education that treats academics as novices with little of value to offer. Even when our ideas may be well-founded, we may end up presenting them using a particular epistemological framework that conflicts with the values or methods of a discipline or department, leading our contributions to appear counterproductive or intellectually flimsy. In turn, we may overlook the potential cognitive dissonance academics can experience when their identity as a subject expert rubs up against being a pedagogical novice. This tension is explored further in Chapter 3 on professionalism.

Catherine Manathunga's work (2006, 2007) on post-colonial approaches to academic development provides a helpful framework to capture this tension and proposes an alternative route that may be more productive. She identifies the trap of colonial condescension toward academics – viewing them as 'pedagogically "unwashed" disciplinary-based colleagues' – whereby we as developers believe 'we understand the "principles" of teaching and learning and can "help" our poor, underdeveloped content-driven colleagues to finally become pedagogically sound' (2006, p. 24). It can be easy to forget that we are working with subject experts who, whether through dialogue with us or through trial and error on their own, can often find appropriately tailored disciplinary responses to the pedagogical issues they face.

Manathunga advises that we should 'sacrifice our claims to being an *authority* on teaching and learning' (2006, p. 26) and to acknowledge and explore the power dynamics that are present in our work with academics – and in their work with students. By taking this stance, we can 'openly air the tensions, ambivalences, and anxieties experienced by academic developers', creating space to discuss 'some of the unresolved tensions and dilemmas embedded in all aspects of teaching and learning' (Manathunga, 2007, p. 31).

So as an ADU leader, a key role – especially when working with new developers – is to establish a culture that strongly values disciplinary expertise and aims to build on it, rather than inadvertently undermining it through well-intentioned attempts at imposing ready-made solutions from the outside. Entering conversations with academic colleagues with a sceptical lens toward some of the HE research and its underlying assumptions – just as academics do in other disciplines – opens us up to frank conversation and the potential for more creative, locally appropriate solutions. It can also help release some of the tension that we and our academic colleagues may feel when policies or practices conflict with our own values in education.

Case study: Candid conversations

As a way of allowing academics to let off steam while engaging with tricky or controversial topics, the ADU at one US university introduced the format of 'candid conversations' – late afternoon gatherings on current issues on campus, often with a more pointed or sceptical title and a short description that invites debate and (cordial) disagreement. For example, past sessions have included 'Infantilizing our students? Attendance, surveillance, and the degradation of learning', based on the work of Bruce Macfarlane (2013), and 'Outcomes schmoutcomes' (n.d.). The latter of these addresses a perennially problematic area for many developers: how to implement the learning outcomes agenda so as to comply with requirements from the university, accreditors or the government, while still providing a useful framework for programme teams and for students. Through a candid conversation – where there is no agenda other than to provide the context at the start (for instance, 'Here is what is required of us all and here are some of the key objections; where would you like to begin?') – academics have the opportunity to share their thoughts and to process the issue as a group before we can move on to look at how we might implement the outcomes agenda in a way that is beneficial.

Providing a venue to tease out the inherent flaws in both the policies and how they might be implemented locally matters. Academics feel heard and can jointly devise new and more imaginative solutions that tick the right boxes institutionally while more importantly being meaningful for the programme and student learning. The 'candid conversations' format at this institution has become a regular feature, and incidentally requires far less preparation and planning by the ADU than a more traditional academic development workshop, since all that is required is the framework.

Managing the ADU's collaborations with other centres

As good academic citizens, ADUs also often collaborate with other centres to put on events or run projects that cross over areas of expertise or territory. Common collaborations are with learning technologies (when they are separate units) or learner development programmes, but also areas such as human resources, libraries or external funding offices. (Chapter 1 provides a longer list of examples.) Being able to tap into this expertise and combine it with our own in academic development helps us reach new audiences on our campuses, hopefully creating new allies and stronger cross-campus connections. With our knowledge of how to run successful events for academics – something many other offices on campus may find tricky – we can find ourselves in the luxurious position of having more requests for collaborations than we are able to fulfil.

Yet collaborations are often also problematic. If your ADU has a clear set of values and organises its programming in particular ways (for instance, by not being directive, but being more open, as discussed earlier in this chapter), you may discover tensions when your collaborators' models conflict, requiring you to spend longer discussing and coaching in advance of the session so as to ensure that you are comfortable being associated with it. (This extra workload can counteract the potential advantage of being able to do more, too.) If the remits of the collaborating centres are also close (such as between ADUs and learning technology centres; see Little and Green, 2012), then there can be additional territorial tensions: Who will academics follow up with? When does one unit refer a person on to the next? A further conundrum can be the varying reputations of the collaborating centres. If the ADU has a good reputation among academics and your collaborating centre does not, how can you be sure that your profile is maintained and the partner's enhanced? Often a reputation deficit comes back to underlying principles and values, so major philosophical differences – and disagreements – are easily possible. Agreeing a common approach to your collaboration and checking in and reviewing regularly with the other centre's leader will be key. Chapter 18 says more about collaboration.

To make the most of collaborations, we suggest using Ray Land's 'Orientations to educational development' (2000, 2004), which offers a smorgasbord of potential ways to act, from the 'entrepreneurial' developer who may look for external drivers and funding to achieve a unit's aims, to the 'researcher', who expresses education research in a range of formats to be accessible to different disciplinary ways of thinking.

Depending on our partners in collaborations, we may wish or need to take different orientations to be most effective. If, for instance, we notice academics struggling due to increased research expectations or fears of job losses, then adopting the 'romantic' orientation – which emphasises both the intellectual and emotional – may lead us to partner with counselling services or human resources on stress and resilience; alternatively, taking an 'opportunist' orientation – looking for institutional 'cracks' or levers – may lead us to seek connections with an institutionally highly funded, but academically not well-regarded, unit to run a joint event on an area of common interest that lends itself to the ADU's critical, academically driven philosophy. Land's orientations model thereby helps us be more creative about developing connections on our campuses and enables ADUs to be adaptable in evolving institutional contexts.

Case study: Collaborative working to ensure quality assurance levers lead to academic development

Academic teams were rarely using the ADU to help them enhance their degree programmes at one UK university, so the ADU leader looked for pre-existing institutional 'levers' that might nudge people to engage with the ADU. Every five years the university quality assurance office organised a review of each programme at the university. In preparation, programme teams needed to analyse trends in attainment, retention and recruitment and explain the rationale behind curriculum content and assessment methods. The final report would be sent to a mixed group of external specialists, student representatives and peers from across the university, followed by a quality assurance review event with the academic team and head of department. These meetings commonly resulted in an action plan before the course was confirmed for the following five years. The ADU leader collaborated with the quality assurance office to adapt the process of drawing up the report so that the ADU could work with the academic team and contribute to the analysis and explanation – and, even more importantly, be involved in the action planning after the review meeting.

In addition, the ADU offered training in curriculum design and assessment practices to student representatives and peer reviewers. The result was a more informed discussion at review meetings, action plans based on good practice and scholarship, and an increased number of academic teams using the ADU.

Leading an ADU as a vehicle for institutional change

ADUs are driving strategic change more regularly in universities. This contribution to strategic change is important and valuable in raising the status of our units, bringing them into the centre of the university and indicating their worth. It also brings challenges. As we have mentioned, there is a threat that ADUs can be seen as coercive – undermining the work that has been undertaken to build trust with academic colleagues. In addition, individual members of an ADU may be uncomfortable working in this way, especially if the changes the ADU is being asked to support are not wholly welcomed by academics. Yet change is central to our working lives.

Identifying a set of stages to operationalise the strategic change can be helpful, yet change in universities is complex and many activities may not in the end turn out to be sequential or within the grasp of the ADU. For this reason a more helpful approach may be to consider the process of engagement with the various people involved – your own team, academics in the departments, and the senior managers you will be working with. It is also important that ADU leaders pay some attention to models and theories of change (see Chapter 13).

A wide-ranging change to assessment patterns, for example, can make individuals so angry and animated that ADU teams often need to adopt approaches to acknowledge this while enabling people to move forward. Understanding that anger and resistance have their place in change management is important: Kurt Lewin's (1948) work on unfreezing behaviour, the root of many modern change models, can be helpful in such situations. Lewin argues that people need to arrive at an understanding that change is necessary in order to move away from current comfort zones. For the ADU Leader, this first stage of strategic change is about preparing the ADU and academic colleagues before the change, and ideally creating a situation in which people come to want the change or at least realise that it is necessary. The ADU can build on the trust and personal relationships it has developed in the past, and again can consciously choose the appropriate approach using scholarship such as Land's (2000) orientations and the shared experience of the ADU team. The leader can take steps within the ADU team to facilitate change by providing:

- An evidence base for a richer picture of the current situation (such as attainment patterns, non-continuation data or a national perspective);
- Opportunities for academics to air their anxieties and interrogate the need for change with senior managers;

- Opportunities for academic teams to explore and plan future ways of working, with ADU colleagues offering examples of good practice and research evidence from elsewhere;
- Opportunities for senior managers to hear alternative approaches to the same problem;
- Plans for new ways of working and reinforcing the changed practices.

Case study: Using a whole-university conference to address issues around changing assessment patterns to improve student continuation

Proposals to change assessment were causing some concerns in one UK university. The ADU leader worked with a range of university colleagues to design a programme for a day-long conference. It was essential that senior managers and academics contributed ideas and felt some responsibility for the event. With the ADU leader's knowledge of the sector, change management and scholarship in this area, she was able to provide a steer in terms of outside speakers, the statistical evidence that underpinned the issue and the conference activities. Experienced workshop facilitators were hired, academics from other universities and her own were invited to share experiences of assessment change and the vice-chancellor set the context. The unit leader knew that there had to be time to address people's concerns – and provide that 'unfreezing' opportunity – and so also suggested a Q & A session with a panel of senior directors and students. In one-to-one pre-conference meetings, ADU colleagues rehearsed with them the kind of questions that might arise.

The conference was a success in that it allowed academics to share concerns, learn from others and understand the wider context for the university. The ADU was critical to the design of the conference and the pro-vice-chancellor recognised that this had made a difference to the change process. The ADU continued to work with academic teams and students after the conference to ensure changes were pedagogically sound and embedded into courses. A number of academic staff began to be seen as 'assessment experts' and a community of practice developed (Wenger, 1998). The ADU also conducted a full evaluation the following year.

Conclusion: Some lessons learnt from our own experiences

Throughout this chapter we have sought to share the scholarship and values that have helped us as leaders of ADUs. We have demonstrated some of the critical skills required and the attention we believe that should be placed on dialogue that recognises the particular location of academic development work in the academy.

In offering a chapter on leading ADUs, we further suggest that this kind of leadership merits more research. New understandings of the ADU leader role specifically and the ADU role more generally are required if we are to meet the challenges ahead.

To sum up we offer some of key lessons we have learnt as ADU leaders:

- There are no fixed recipes to leading an ADU.
- Time spent on establishing the unit's underpinning values and principles aids decision-making and brings benefits in the longer term.
- Directing an ADU is as much about managing upward as it is managing the team.
- Leading an ADU requires resilience so that we are prepared for our units to be disbanded, reshaped or reconstituted and can work through those changes.
- In some situations, we will need to adopt uncomfortable or atypical orientations in order to succeed.
- We can and should use appropriate research to underpin our work, our processes and our rationales.

Acknowledgements

Thank you to the colleagues who shared their stories for this chapter and to those who have helped us to develop our own styles as leaders.

References

Baume, D. and Kahn, P. (2004). 'How shall we enhance staff and educational development?' In D. Baume and P. Kahn (Eds.), *Enhancing Staff and Educational Development* (pp. 185–194). London: RoutledgeFalmer.

Elton, L. (1992). 'Quality enhancement and academic professionalism', *The New Academic*, 3(5): 1.

Fullan, M. (1992). 'Causes/processes of implementation and continuation'. In N. Bennett, M. Crawford and C. Riches (Eds.), *Managing Sustained Change* (pp. 109–129). Milton Keynes: Open University Press.

Fullan, M. (2008). *The Six Secrets of Change: What the Best Leaders Do to Help Their Organizations Survive and Thrive*. San Francisco: Jossey-Bass.

Gibbs, G. (2000). 'Learning and teaching strategies: the implications for educational development', *Educational Developments*, 1(1): 1.

Gosling, D. (2009). 'Educational development in the UK: a complex and contradictory reality', *International Journal for Academic Development*, 14: 5–18.

HEFCE. (2011). Summative evaluation of the CETL programme - Higher Education Funding Council for England. Retrieved 5 November 2015 from http://www.hefce.ac.uk/pubs/rereports/Year/2011/cetlsummevaln/Title,92265,en.html.

Heifetz, R. and Linsky, M. (2002). *Leadership on the Line: Staying Alive Through the Dangers of Leading*. Boston: Harvard Business School Press.

Hicks, M. (2005). 'Academic developers as change agents: caught in the middle'. Refereed paper presented at the 28th HERDSA conference, Sydney. Retrieved from www.herdsa.org.au/wp-content/uploads/conference/2005/pdf/refereed/paper_315.pdf.

Holt, D., Palmer, S. and Challis, D. (2011). 'Changing perspectives: teaching and learning centres' strategic contributions to academic development in Australian higher education', *International Journal for Academic Development*, 16: 5–17.

Krathwohl, D. R., Bloom, B. S. and Masia, B. B. (1964). *Taxonomy of Educational Objectives: The Classification of Educational Goals: Handbook 2, Affective Domain.* London: Longmans, Green.

Land, R. (2000). 'Orientations to educational development', *Educational Developments*, 1: 19–23.

Land, R. (2004). *Educational Development: Discourse, Identity and Practice.* Maidenhead, UK: Open University Press/McGraw-Hill.

Leibowitz, B. (2014). 'Academic development: no fixed recipes', *International Journal for Academic Development*, 19(2): 73–75.

Lewin, K. (1948). 'Action research and minority problems.' In G. W. Lewin (Ed.). *Resolving Social Conflicts.* New York: Harper & Row.

Lewin, K. (1951). *Field Theory in Social Science: Selected Theoretical Papers.* Ed. D. Cartwright. New York: Harper & Row.

Little, D. and Green, D. A. (2012). 'Betwixt and between: academic developers in the margins', *International Journal for Academic Development*, 17(3): 203–215.

MacDonald, J. and Stockley, D. (Eds.). (2010). 'Pathways to the profession of educational development [special issue]', *New Directions for Teaching and Learning*, 122.

Macfarlane, B. (2013). 'The surveillance of learning: a critical analysis of university attendance policies', *Higher Education Quarterly*, 67(4): 358–373.

Manathunga, C. (2006). 'Doing educational development ambivalently: post-colonial approaches to educational development?', *International Journal for Academic Development*, 11: 19–29.

Manathunga, C. (2007). '"Unhomely" academic developer identities: more post-colonial explorations', *International Journal for Academic Development*, 12(1): 25–34.

'Outcomes schmoutcomes'. Accessed 28 October 2015 from https://www.seattleu.edu/faculty-development/events/past/candid.

Parrish, D. and Lafoe, G. (2008). *The Green Report: The Development of Leadership Capacity in Higher Education.* Australian Government Office for Learning and Teaching. Retrieved from www.olt.gov.au/resource-green-report-uow-2008.

POD (n.d.). Ethical Guidelines, available at http://podnetwork.org/about-us/what-is-faculty-development/ethical-guidelines. Accessed 18 May 2015.

Rowland, S. (2002). 'Overcoming fragmentation in professional life: the challenge for academic development', *Higher Education Quarterly*, 56(1): 52–64.

Wenger, E. (1998). *Communities of Practice: Learning, Meaning, and Identity.* Cambridge: Cambridge University Press.

Chapter 16

Academic development and senior management

Sally Brown and Shân Wareing

Summary

This chapter reviews the management issues associated with overseeing academic development units and ensuring they help to deliver the institution's strategic priorities; considers why academic developers in particular can make effective and useful senior managers; explores what kinds of activities academic developers can undertake that support their senior managers in making educational changes; and offers advice to academic developers about moving to more senior roles and to new PVCs on how to manage their first months in post.

Links to web sources referenced in this chapter can be found at www.seda .ac.uk/apad.

Introduction

Implementing real change in assessment, learning and teaching in higher education is best effected when academic developers work in close partnership with their senior managers, particularly PVCs, Vice Rectors and Deputy Principals of Higher Education providers (collectively referred to as PVCs hereafter). In this chapter, drawing on our own experiences as both academic developers and PVCs, we offer some perspectives on how to make such partnerships work. Case studies are based on our own experiences and those of others who have similarly joined senior management teams, quotations from whom are derived from personal correspondence with the authors.

Our backgrounds

Both of the authors have held posts as Pro Vice-Chancellors in post-92 UK universities, and previously worked as academic developers. We were attracted to a PVC role as a way to increase our impact and extend our ability to deliver what we saw as important improvements to the student and the staff experience at our universities. The community which nurtured us personally and professionally was the Staff and Educational Development Association (SEDA), which has been a source of our professional development through conference and workshops, and also more importantly, a network of like-minded colleagues providing advice, mentoring and intellectual challenge. Being academic developers, and working in and chairing SEDA committees including the executive committee as co-chairs of SEDA, gave us a grounding in enabling action and change with colleagues with whom we had no direct line management relationship. This was tremendously helpful when we came to senior leadership roles in universities.

Academic developers and institutional strategic change

The relationship between academic developers and institutional strategy and change is dynamic, and a lot of ground has been travelled over the last 20 years. One career generation ago, learning and teaching were often not a university-level priority, at least not in practice even if they were in the rhetoric. It was not uncommon to find academic developers working at odds with the culture or strategic direction of their institution, acting in accordance with their values but feeling marginalised and insecure. In the UK, the days are now largely passed when senior staff observed aloud that the University PgCert in Learning and Teaching formed a barrier to institutional progress, or (usually) when new lecturers fail their PgCert but pass their probation. Most academic developers are appointed now into UK higher education providers with an institutional emphasis on learning and teaching and on students' experience and success. This change, from counter-culture to mainstream, enables academic developers to align their work directly and visibly with the institutional mission and strategy.

It probably goes without saying that working in alignment with the institutional mission and strategy is important for academic developers. This principle became more apparent as our institutional responsibilities increased. Reasons include:

1   The PVC can champion and resource the unit better if the purpose and success of the PVC and the EDU are closely aligned.
2   It is easier to communicate clearly the message and purpose of the unit if they are aligned to institutional strategy. Being unable to align academic development activity with an institutional goal makes communication difficult for the academic development unit, which can lead to its institutional obscurity, compromising its effectiveness.
3   The strategically aligned academic development unit can more easily collaborate with other academic departments and professional services, working towards the same organisational goals, creating critical mass and supportive networks.

So the work of the academic development unit and the institution must be strategically aligned. (Chapter 15 says much more about leading an academic development unit, and Chapter 17 about academic development and institutional policy and strategy.) To achieve this strategic alignment between the ADU and the institution, the obvious starting place is published institutional strategy documents. But these can be dated, at too high a level or too all-inclusive to be very helpful. Being in touch with current thinking, achieved through talking to senior managers and paying close attention to relevant committee papers and minutes, can be a more effective way to make sure the academic development unit is perceived as institutionally relevant.

Looking externally, academic developers' access to national and international trends and research can contribute valuable professional expertise to institutional planning. 'Horizon scanning' and 'seeing round the bend' help institutions to plan for the future, so it is important to maintain external networks, to read reports and research outputs, to monitor policy changes, and to share what is learned.

Never underestimate the importance of explaining what your strategic goals are: to your team colleagues, to your boss, to the wider university, and to the outside world, and how they align to the university goals. These acts of communication allow people to share assumptions, analyse misconceptions, question perceived gaps, spot potential collaborative activity and areas for mutual support. Herding cats or moving a graveyard are common metaphors for managing a university. If you can courteously and constructively make it really clear to people what they are being asked to do and why, a surprising number of people may be willing to cooperate with you. Achieving really effective communication is a complex task: apparently clear messages can be confusing if underlying assumptions are at variance with other university initiatives. An active communication strategy, sharing values, processes and plans in creative, relevant, interesting ways is vital to strategic change.

Even with perfectly clear communication, interests may genuinely collide or philosophies diverge. Institutional politics, and indeed sector and national politics, can be a significant challenge for academic developers. Successful institutional influence requires pragmatism and resilience. Surviving and thriving in an environment where there is a gap between the rhetoric (espoused values) and the values revealed by actions can be disconcerting, difficult, and stressful. Ways of dealing with situations which seem to challenge deeply held values include keeping calm in the moment and not jumping to conclusions about other people's intentions, maintaining a sense of proportion, keeping sight of your ultimate goals, and seeking out and maintaining networks for peer support. In challenging times, it remains important to keep the faith and to stay true to the values which brought you into education in the first place.

> When I became a Pro Vice-Chancellor, I remember an educational development colleague saying 'don't forget us, grappling with the day to day business of teaching and learning at the coal face.' I try not to. However strategic my thinking needs to be, I try to always validate it against my core personal, professional and pedagogic principles and a dose of common sense. I try to talk to practitioners and, crucially, actively listen to those around me. Most importantly, I try to be authentic and open in my approach. But the key test

for any big idea or decision is 'will this improve things for our students?' and that test is as true and valid now as when I was a school teacher, lecturer, programme leader and educational developer. (Dr Claire Taylor, Pro Vice-Chancellor, St Mary's University, Twickenham, London)

The interface between academic developers and senior managers

Senior managers enter PVC Learning and Teaching roles from all kinds of backgrounds. Peter Wolf, Associate Vice-Provost (Teaching and Learning) Queen's University Canada told us:

My background is not a traditional academic one, in that I have worked as a professional staff [member], starting almost 20 years ago in academia as a counsellor and [working as a] distance education designer and academic developer before taking on formal educational leadership positions.

Lesley-Jane Eales-Reynolds of Kingston University came to her PVC position via a more traditional academic background, which served her in good stead for her senior roles:

My route into being a PVC at Kingston University was from being a Director of Learning and Teaching and pedagogic research, rather than being an academic developer as such. My background as a five-star researcher in Immunology who was a passionate teacher and a National Teaching Fellow, (retaining my research-profile in Immunology until relatively recently) led to me being a Deputy Director of a Health Sciences Institution and subsequently writing a successful bid for a HEFCE Centre for Excellence in Teaching and Learning. My work as the CETL Director and also my role as chair of the Association of National Teaching Fellows gave me a national profile and a set of skills that underpinned my application to be a PVC.

PVCs with a background in discipline leadership in Faculties may find engaging with academic developers a challenge. They may perceive academic development units as sources of unnecessary complications regarding what may superficially seem like straightforward issues. Both authors, in earlier roles, encountered senior managers who held relatively naïve views of staff development and institutional change.

Sharon Huttly, PVC at Lancaster University, argues that a transition to PVC from an academic role with recognised expertise in learning and teaching can be very helpful:

The pathway I took (i.e. academic to manager and leader) helped give me credibility in the eyes of the staff and an understanding of the competing pressures that academics are under in a research-intensive environment.

I believe that in turn this facilitated me in moving from a disciplinary base to a Faculty and then an institution-wide role. That empathy also assisted in dialogues with staff when planning and implementing change.

She continues that it is very important for senior managers to keep in touch with the changes academic staff are being asked to implement:

Throughout the different roles I've had, I have maintained an active teaching portfolio. Again this helps with credibility and gives me a better understanding of 'the issues on the ground' ... I also feel that I developed a role as a 'translator' – in order to undertake my learning and teaching leadership role I needed to network externally and build up a good understanding of the context, nationally and internationally, in which the institution operated. I then needed to sift through the many issues to foster debates around those most critical for the institution with respect to learning and teaching and to translate them into development of policy and practice where appropriate. I feel this sifting and translating for L&T are particularly important for research-strong HEIs where there are multiple agendas to address.

A pro vice-chancellor portfolio usually means managing multiple areas, and the post holder is unlikely to have the same level of expertise in all of them. Such leaders will frequently be managing specialists who know more than they do about that area of responsibility, and this can make building a trusting working relationship a challenge. Specialists and generalists can see the world differently; specialist academic developers may sometimes find their generalist manager lacking in understanding and nuanced judgement in their field. Mutual respect for what each other and a bit of patience enables people committed to an effective working relationship to manoeuvre around this inevitable gap. Being longer in the PVC role also means that, even in areas where you did have expertise, your knowledge of the detail can lose currency. For many managers this loss of expertise can feel like a wrench and a threat to their identity.

Pauline Kneale (PVC Teaching and Learning at Plymouth University) outlines some of these tensions:

For me one of the challenges has been my personal wish to maintain a research record as an academic alongside the workload as PVC. Coming from a Russell Group background, I am acutely aware that research, writing and PhD supervision is what justifies my continuing to hold the title of Professor. In some universities, especially where these roles are appointed rotationally, for example for a three or five year period before reverting back to one's discipline role, there is an expectation of preserving a day a week for one's own research. If one is to re-join a School in this way retaining academic credibility in one's discipline is vital. Finding time for research is challenging in any context, but perhaps more so in universities where the

PVC/DVC role is a full time administrative one. Ceasing to be research active may be an appointment deal-breaker at a later time.

A good working relationship between academic developers and their senior managers is valuable for both. Ideally the relationship between an academic developer and a PVC Learning and Teaching will be built on mutual trust and respect, underpinned by understanding each other's backgrounds and motivations. Academic developers working closely with a PVC necessarily need to familiarise themselves with the particular role their PVC holds and their level of currency and awareness concerning staff development and teaching and assessment approaches.

What can academic developers do to support institutional change?

Based on our experience, below are ten suggestions of ways in which academic developers can support institutional change.

1. Use academic development principles in institutional change

Academic development engenders a nuanced, sophisticated understanding of how people (students, individual staff members) grow and change. We know that students are not empty vessels to be filled with subject content, and that the responsibility for learning and attainment is shared in complex ways between the learner, the course team, and the institution. These principles also hold true for institutional learning and large-scale change processes.

> Having been a teacher and an academic developer I bring a deeply embedded sense of the practical realities of teaching and learning to my role. I see teaching as a relational activity; a two-way process of interaction, dialogue and challenge. I see all teachers as learners; understanding their contexts, environments and a multitude of factors that may enable or inhibit learning. These ways of seeing and being are foundational to my current role, where I continue to operate within a framework predicated upon relational and reflective dialogue. (Dr Claire Taylor, Pro Vice Chancellor, St Mary's University, Twickenham, London)

Appreciating that people are individuals and not empty spaces, that they need to understand the relevance of a policy before implementing it, and that they may have valid but hidden reasons for non-compliance, is fundamental to effective institutional change. Developing a new policy and informing staff about it in an email is not an effective approach to change management. Academic developers fully understand this in the context of student learning and staff development.

Joy Mighty, Associate Vice-President (Teaching and Learning) Carleton University Canada, suggests that the style a senior manager adopts can have high impact on the extent of success as a senior manager:

> I chose to be consultative, responsive, and collaborative rather than prescriptive. I spent the entire first semester in my new role meeting with deans, department heads, vice-presidents, committees, and student groups, asking them about their hopes, expectations, and needs with regard to teaching and the Teaching Centre. I also began compiling a list of volunteers, which grew throughout my tenure. By the second semester, I had a sense of key allies and supporters upon whom I could call and I established committees that became my internal community.

2. Develop shared priorities and goals

You need to know what your PVC is trying to achieve, what they regard as success, what for them counts as failure. Ask, and at the same time communicate your own goals. It is OK to have a journey of months or even years to come to a shared vision, as long as the direction of travel is on the whole drawing closer together. Peter Wolf from Queen's University Canada, further emphasises the importance of flexibility and collegiality:

> In the past decade, I have focused on program development and assessment processes that encourage further development of the transferable. This focus on disciplinary learning grounding transferable knowledge, skills and values is directly related to my experiences as my own life has evolved. The capacity-building, empathy and systems thinking that have served me well in my past work with individuals and programs continues to serve me well as I adapt to engaging with the different stakeholders, scale and scope of my new landscape.

3. Make sure the relationship works for both of you

As discussed above, good working relationships need trust. Trust allows us to overlook the inevitable flaws and miscommunications which all working and personal relationships contain, and keep the relationship on track through times of tension and even conflict. Trust allows us to take risks, and success absolutely depends on responsible risk taking. Investment of time and effort in the relationship with your manager is always worthwhile. Equally important is not to jeopardise it unnecessarily. Where you do have differences of opinion, these should be approached with sensitivity and with planning. You can be a critical friend to your PVC, but they need to trust you too, and not fear you will make it harder for them to undertake their role or compromise their effectiveness by embarrassing them in public. They may seem to hold a lot of power to you, but in reality they are also negotiating for resource and priority. They need you to cover their back, just as much as you need them to support you publicly.

4. Make your metrics work for you

We all know that life is more complicated than the top line figure, but a good metric which sums up the impact of an innovation or policy change can nail a debate. Work out what metrics matter to other people, and keep records of them as you go – numbers of staff attending events, applying for bids, seeing improvements in student achievement or feedback. Look for positive trends, and find a way to tell your story through convincing statistics and figures. This creates a space for you to operate in and makes it easier to take risks or ask for support next time. Metrics can demonstrate the power of your actions to change the experiences of students (Brown, 2011), resulting in measurable impact – for example in the take up of peer observation of teaching or improving National Student Survey results. Chapter 10 provides further suggestions on evidencing achievement.

5. Brief people in multiple ways and at multiple levels

It's easy to assume that what you do and why you do it is obvious to everyone because it is so clearly the right thing to be doing. In fact, no one knows anything about what you do unless you tell them, many times and in many ways. Write strategy documents, position papers, updates, reports. Give presentations and prepare 'elevator pitches' (short clear impressive statements you can produce when you find yourself trapped for a one minute ride to the top floor with the CEO, to cement the impression you are a person of vision, purpose and action). Tell people about things you do that they will be interested in, when you meet them in the corridor. Perhaps even more importantly, ask people what they think, and listen when they talk to you: they hear you better when they know you heard them. Linking your work to their goals is a good way to increase their buy-in and your influence.

6. Be a good team player

If you are fortunate in your colleagues, they will collaborate with you, cover for you, lend you funds or a member of their team for a project, and cheer you up when you are down; and you need to do the same for them. Someone sticking up for you, or being able to share resources with you when you are in a tight spot, can often be the difference between an initiative failing or succeeding. Senior management teams can be cut-throat environments. The best way to earn loyalty and support is to provide it to others.

7. Stay calm

When bad news is announced, or tempers fray, stay calm and listen. Ask dispassion-ate, analytical questions to understand the situation better. Don't react strongly, in the heat of the moment, because doing so can close down options. Buy time to assess what it is best to do. Women in senior management roles particularly are likely to be harshly judged if they react visibly to bad news or aggression, so it is worth cultivating techniques to cope with unpleasantness. Keep asking clarifying questions, rather than responding immediately. If you are not prepared to see your own words reproduced in the press or in court, it's probably best not to send an angry email, and if you are tempted to do so, wait at least until the next morning, when you've had time to think through repercussions.

8. Be the agent of your own destiny

Keep a strong sense of your own professionalism and agency. Focus on what you can accomplish, not what you can't. However, if you are thinking of moving into a senior management role yourself, Alan Wright Vice-Provost, Teaching and Learning, University of Windsor, Canada warns that it is hard for academic devel-opers to be seen as senior management material in their own institutions. He says:

> In Canada, the ten or so universities to have created equivalent positions to mine in the last few years have not filled them with the directors of their centres. They have either hired a centre director from another university or, exceptionally, hired a professor from their own university who did not work in academic development. If you seek a move up from centre leader you will have to move to a new university.

9. Use your networks

Academic developers benefit from exceptionally strong, useful, warm networks. There is more on this in Chapter 3 on professionalism. Developers are by and large pleased to share information and help each other. Joy Mighty argues for the power of the academic development community as a source of sustenance for senior managers:

> [From the educational development (ED) world] I discovered a whole new body of literature and a whole new world of ED associations and confer-ences, of which I had never heard. I learnt a great deal about the practice of ED from this external community and they became my family members, colleagues, and ultimately my trusted friends. As the years passed, what had at first been somewhat serendipitous became intentional, as I chose to participate actively in these communities. For example, I engaged in the scholarship of teaching and learning, presenting my research at national

and international conferences. I was elected as the inaugural chair of the Educational Developers Caucus (EDC) and later, the President of the Society for Teaching and Learning in Higher Education (STLHE). The latter role gave me the opportunity to represent Canada on the international stage, including membership on the Council of the International Consortium for Educational Development (ICED).

What she learned gave greater credibility in her role:

> Participating in these internal and external communities increased my knowledge and understanding of the higher educational landscape locally, nationally and internationally. More importantly, they garnered me respect not only among my ED peers, but also among the community of higher education administrators. When I later joined that community in the capacity of Associate Vice-President (Teaching and Learning) I was accepted as a peer with expertise that was sorely needed for all sorts of quality assurance, accountability, and reputational reasons.

10. Take an institutional perspective

In proposing actions that impact on the student experience, think through the implications for how changes you advocate may affect the wider organisational agenda, such as timetabling, estate management and construction, staff workloads, staff-management relations and employment policies. For example, if in the UK you are suggesting all staff will be required to achieve Fellowship of the Higher Education Academy, aligned with the UK Professional Standards Framework (see Chapter 3), which is increasingly being adopted internationally, you need to think through not only how this will impact on traditionally hard-to-reach groups like part-time and fractional staff, but also on your colleagues in the Senior Management Team who might or might not welcome the proposal to set a good example by applying for Principal Fellowship themselves.

Supporting the management of change

Academic developers can usefully ensure that the academic voice is heard in change management in relation to learning and teaching, by seeking out and reflecting the perspectives of classroom teachers, as Lueddeke argues:

> Too often new approaches are introduced by executive fiat or though a centralist management strategy, or, at worst through ad hoc and hurried planning interventions in response to years of benign neglect. It seems a rarity indeed for academics to genuinely feel that they are part of a meaningful, participatory decision-making process that values their experience or even their instinct for seeing potential pitfalls. (Lueddeke, 1999, p. 236)

Furthermore, academic developers can show academics and other staff an evidence-based rationale for changes that are being initiated in assessment, learning and teaching, and for sustaining those changes once they have been implemented. As Scott (2004) argues:

> Staff will not engage in a change effort and the learning that goes with it unless they can personally see that doing so is relevant, desirable, clear, distinctive and importantly feasible. Being appropriately involved in shaping an agreed change project and being clear on what is envisaged are also powerful motivators. Right from the outset, staff affected by each change will be weighing up the benefits of engaging and persevering with it against the costs. This is a process that carries on over the whole life cycle of every change effort. (Scott, 2004, p. 4)

There is a further key task for academic developers in embedding cultural changes in ways that empower academics and enable them to commit to change:

> It is a very wrong-headed notion, too, one that is, ironically in an 'age of empowerment' and 'flatter organisations', not only deeply disempowering, (in that it implies the way to empowerment can only be achieved by recourse to hierarchical authority), but also, even more importantly, that overlooks the crucial fact that values are only values if they are chosen voluntarily and as such cannot be imposed from the top. Thus initiatives that are solely top down are at best likely to evoke compliance with change rather than a genuine commitment to it. (McCaffery, 2004, p. 237)

Cuthbert, in a keynote on the 'Imaginative Curriculum in 2002', described managing in higher education as taking place in 'organised anarchy' (Cuthbert, 2002, p. 2). The task can seem overwhelming unless one is selective. The secret of success, he suggests, is unobtrusive management. He argued for a pragmatic approach, which recognises the limitations of what senior managers in isolation can achieve. Managers should:

> ... be concerned with identifying and maintaining the conditions necessary for organisational survival and responsiveness. Managers do best when they avoid making choices, but focus instead on influencing and selecting items for attention from the streams of problems, solutions and choice opportunities, and shaping the 'organisational garbage can' in which choices are sometimes made. By subtly deflecting, constraining or augmenting the streams of problems, solutions and choice opportunities, managers can influence events more tellingly than if they sought to make a decision. (Cuthbert, 2002, p. 2)

Chapter 13 says more about managing and leading change.

Advice for academic developers working with PVCs for learning and teaching

Working with an established PVC for learning and teaching

1. Find out everything you can about your PVC's role and responsibilities

Do this as soon as possible. Read the role description or the job advertisement to which they were appointed. Check out how closely they work with the head of the organisation (not always as much as you might imagine, since not all PVCs are automatically members of executive groups), the amount of autonomy they have as well as the level of budget controlled (often the latter is an indicator of the former). How many people directly report to your PVC? Do these include any heads of professional services units (e.g. library, IT services, student services, etc.)? Do they belong to any national or international bodies in relation to learning and teaching? What links do they have with professional, Regulatory and Subject bodies? And most importantly, what is the nature of the relationship between your PVC and Deans of Faculty (indeed some hold both titles)? Frequently there is an interesting balance of power and authority between Deans and PVCs, which can limit or expand the scope for managing change.

2. Explore their professional background

This will let you know how best you can work with them. For example, if your PVC speaks nationally and internationally on educational technologies, then you are unlikely to need to do much upward briefing on this topic, but if they have little obvious expertise in this area, this might be something you can help them with.

3. Brief upwards

Once you know more about your PVC's background and interests, you can start working on subtly briefing upwards. What areas is your PVC is likely to need to know about, and therefore may need some support on? Whether it is an element of the institutional strategy they will be leading on, or an innovative teaching method that might be unfamiliar, you can make lives easier by offering or providing unsolicited short, well-researched topical papers. These will enable them to talk confidently in meetings and enter into related activities well-prepared. Find out in what respects your predecessor in post (if you had one) was particularly valued by your PVC, and look at how best you can fill the gaps left behind.

4. Identify no-go areas

It can be time consuming to push for innovations which your PVC may be determined to avoid. For example, if you believe (rightly in our view) that providing multiple formative assessment opportunities for students is likely to enhance student learning significantly, improve retention and foster engagement (Nichol and Macfarlane-Dick, 2006) and your PVC has publicly stated that they require academics to reduce the number of assessment occasions in any module to just one, then don't advise colleagues to increase the number of assessed elements across their programmes. This might be an important area for you to work to with your PVC to view things differently. Such battles should not be fought in public if you are to maintain a good working relationship.

5. Identify what internal committees and working groups your PVC belongs to or chairs

This will help you to work out and suggest which ones you could usefully join, support, or persuade your PVC to delegate to you to chair. Many senior managers acknowledge the importance of using the committee system in a university to bring about meaningful change, rather than just compliance to directives. For example, your efforts in going round all the faculty boards discussing a peer observation policy (Brown, 2011) before taking it to academic board can pay off, if the contentious discussion can be had before the more formal occasion.

Working with a newly-appointed established PVC for learning and teaching

Much of the above advice will still apply, and also the following.

6. Find out about your new PVC's background

Have they come from a very different background (for example in the UK, from a research-focussed university to a more teaching-orientated university?) Knowing this will help you to offer helpful, targeted information.

7. Identify useful national/international conferences and events

Which of these are likely to be particularly helpful to your PVC? Suggest them, and (ideally) offer to go along with them. Or offer to go and report back on key areas of interest to the university (and do a very diligent job of this). You can also point them towards texts you find particularly useful (for example, new SEDA papers and the magazine *Educational Developments*, which offer up-to-date critiques of current developments).

8. Use your knowledge of existing networks and groupings within the university

You can help your new PVC become familiar with the ways of your university. For example, if your HEI has a network of Teaching Fellows or National Teaching

Fellows, you can invite your PVC to meet them in an occasion you have brokered to help your PVC find out who can be informative and helpful. By offering to lead such groups in providing useful critiques of draft policies, you can help your new PVC to gain consensus about new directions being taken, and potentially avoid the kind of crass, naïve or thoughtless interventions that sometimes new PVCs make in seeking impact in a new post.

And finally, for new senior managers ...

Some thoughts for those taking senior management roles for the first time, gleaned from our own experiences and those of our respondents:

- Don't commit to anything in first six weeks in office. People with an axe to grind are likely to beat a path to your door. It may be best to use the early period in office to acclimatise and learn as much as possible about the institutional environment before making any promises.
- Continue to use all available networks, including the professional organisations like SEDA, ANTF and ICED that may have sustained you in your previous roles. Also explore networks like the Higher Education Academy network in the UK for PVCs/DVCs as a means of broadening your understandings of similar and very different parallel roles. Such colleagues are likely to share many of the challenges and issues you face, and may be able to provide useful perspectives on addressing and resolving them.
- Maintain an external profile and build your internal visibility. It's often hard to manage time for all the committees and meetings you are likely to be required to attend or chair as well as making time for being visible on campus, listening to and meeting staff and students. It can be really helpful regularly to use all the campus cafes and refectories to make yourself available for informal but invaluable chats.
- Build good work habits, and recognise your own limits in terms of workload. It is a useful rule of thumb to assume that about 20 per cent of all the activities you undertake will deliver 80 per cent of the results, so it's a good idea to regularly review how you are spending your time, to ensure that you are directing your energies in the most productive directions. It is easy to be distracted by the urgent at the expense of the important, and most senior managers in these kinds of roles indicate that it simply isn't possible to do every potential task that presents itself (see Rob Cuthbert's [2002] encouraging account of keeping the chaos that accompanies the DVC's daily grind at bay by selecting the tasks for action that would result in disaster if not achieved in any given day).
- Seek out personal assistance to help you do your job properly. An effective PA/Executive Assistant can filter emails, screen visitors, and help you organise your day-to-day workload.

- Know your own strengths and weaknesses. Recruit specialist support for the areas you know are not your best. Keep on seeking extending and developing yourself by seeking training to enhance your capabilities in crucial areas (Sally Brown says, 'My most useful training for my PVC role was a three-day course on reading university accounts as a preparation for working with Senior Finance Officers from a perspective of some knowledge'. Shân Wareing says: 'For relevant projects, I always work closely with a project manager to pick up the details I overlook').

- Just like any university position, a PVC or DVC role can be exhausting, frustrating and demoralising, carrying with it much less power to make things happen than those who report to you always recognise. Nevertheless, being a senior manager with influence over learning and teaching can be immensely exciting, a great privilege and a genuine opportunity to make change that can impact directly on students' learning experiences. Celebrate the positives, enjoy the ride, and make the most of the chance to be an influence for the good.

References and further reading

Brown, S. (2012). 'Managing change in universities: a Sisyphean task?', *Quality in Higher Education*, 18(1): 139–46.

Brown, S. (2011). 'Bringing about positive change in higher education; a case study', *Quality Assurance in Education*, 19(3): 195–207, Emerald Bingley.

Cuthbert, R. (2002). 'Constructive alignment in the world of institutional management', presentation at the Imaginative Curriculum symposium, York Higher Education Academy. Available at www.heacademy.ac.uk/resources/detail/resource_database/id170_constructive_alignment_in_the_world.

Lueddeke, G. (1999). 'Toward a constructivist framework for guiding change and innovation in higher education', *Journal of Higher Education*, 70(3): 235–60.

McCaffery, P. (2004). *The Higher Education Manager's Handbook: Effective Leadership and Management in Universities and Colleges*. Abingdon: RoutledgeFalmer.

Nicol, D. J. and Macfarlane-Dick, D. (2006). 'Formative assessment and self-regulated learning: a model and seven principles of good feedback practice', *Studies in Higher Education*, 31(2): 199–218.

Race, P. with Chapman, F., Cooke, B., Leggott, D., Moore, D., Morris, S., Mothersdale, J., Penson, W., Rawnsley, S., Sanderson, C., Smith, L., Smith, S., Soosay, M., Stapleford, J., Timmis, I., Tum, J. and UK National Teaching Fellows. (2009). 'Using peer observation to enhance teaching'. LeedsMet Press. Retrieved 20 April 2015 from http://repository-intralibrary.leedsmet.ac.uk/open_virtual_file_path/i01n324964t/Using%20peer%20observation%20to%20enhance%20teaching.pdf.

Robertson, C. Robins, A. and Cox, R. (2009). 'Co-constructing an academic community ethos – challenging culture and managing change in higher education: a case study undertaken over two years', *Management in Education*, 23(1): 32–40.

Scott, P. (2004) *Change matters: making a difference in higher education*, keynote given at the European Universities Association Leadership Forum in Dublin, available at www.uws.edu.au/data/assets/pdf_file/0007/6892/AUQF_04_Paper_Scott.pdf (accessed 6 April 2013).

Chapter 17

Writing, contributing to and using institutional policies and strategies

Ian Solomonides

Summary

The chapter illustrates the predominately service-leadership orientation of central academic development unit in a large metropolitan university in Sydney, Australia. It describes some of the ways in which the unit and others in Australia have contributed to or engaged with strategy and policy to provide professional development and to effect change in their institutions and elsewhere in the sector. Based on examples of work completed, the author who is also the director of the unit reflects on what the implications might be for academic developers generally.

Links to web sources referenced in this chapter can be found at www.seda .ac.uk/apad.

Introduction

The political and economic environment in which academic development operates is contested and tricky to navigate. The work and indeed the existence of an Academic Development Unit (ADU) can be subject to acute change depending on national policy, prevailing executive sponsorship and budgetary constraint, with significant consequences for the sustainability of initiatives (Brew and Cahir, 2013). However, one constant that seems to run through the work of many ADUs and the work of their academic developers is the contribution they make to professional development, change management, and capacity building in the institutions they serve. This chapter is written primarily with reference to the professional learning and the organisational change that academic development supports and operates in, but see Chapter 13 for further discussion of change models. It is written from my perspective as a director of an ADU, in this case, the Learning and Teaching Centre at Macquarie University in Sydney, Australia, as well as from my responsibilities as part of the wider academic development community in Australia and perhaps beyond. I have provided a number of comments throughout the chapter on what the implications may be for academic developers in writing, contributing to or using institutional policy.

ADUs and their directors often provide leadership, advocacy and resources for policy implementation, if not the actual development and writing of policy itself.

Any involvement in policy can be contentious, as ADUs are often caught between the demands and needs of the institution and its management, and those of the individual members of staff to which professional development, training or service might be provided.

Background

At the time of writing, the Learning and Teaching Centre (LTC) at Macquarie University is one of the larger of its type in the Australian sector, having employed up to 80 staff at any one time of various levels and expertise to serve a university of around 45,000 students and 1,350 full-time equivalent academic staff. Of course the size of the LTC is a reflection of the work it undertakes, ranging from systems and operations associated with the University's Learning Management System and the broader learning technologies platform; support and materials conversion for students with accessibility needs; student evaluation of teaching; design and capability development work in technology enhanced learning and teaching; credentialed and non-credentialed professional learning, including a Masters in Higher Education; curriculum development and review; research supervision training; and, the promotion of scholarship for learning and teaching. Few of these activities come with a direct responsibility for policy and procedure, with the exception of enterprise level activities for which the LTC has oversight, including the learning technologies policies and procedures, under the auspices of the University's Academic Senate. Nevertheless, as I shall discuss later, ADUs like the LTC have a significant part to play in a more indirect but arguably significant role relative to strategic thinking and policy formation.

Academic development work and the ADUs in which it is managed vary in shape, size and constitution to an extent that it is difficult to provide a common description. The differences and similarities are well reported as are the ways in which '... institutions view developers as service or academic, or a mixture of both' (Di Napoli, 2014, p. 5). Around 10 per cent of the staff in my own unit are classed as academic, the majority as professional. The internal and external tensions – as well as opportunities – that this creates should be at least tacitly acknowledged, especially in an era of what Locke (2014, p. 12) calls the 'disaggregation of academic work' and Macfarlane calls the 'morphing' and 'unbundling' of academic practice and the 'rise of the para-academic' (2011). We are also witnessing the evolution of neo-liberal forces acting on higher education and the marketisation of learning and teaching across the globe, leading to what Zepke describes as variable affinities (Zepke, 2014, p. 4) between prevailing contextual forces and the work of universities.

The roles ADUs have played in the establishment of strategy, practice and institutional thinking are perhaps mostly located in the concept of service-leadership, enacted through various channels. In the case of the LTC this includes providing intelligence on national and international trends that feed into institutional awareness, thinking and planning; provision of systems for learning management, student evaluations of teaching, and administration workflows; data sets for institutional planning and risk management purposes; professional development;

responses to perceived quality issues such as casualisation (see Chapter 7); the general evidence-based support for curriculum innovation in the face of contemporary challenges; and, the hidden work common to many ADUs in establishing the climate, registers and impetus for change through communities of practice, scholarship, advocacy and consultancy. Many ADU staff are also involved in national projects or bodies designed to advance quality enhancement and assurance such as a peer review, moderation, etc. However, this work can come with some well-known risks such as mission creep, distraction from core business, and accusations that the ADU is not *directly serving* the needs of the institution (see Chapter 14 for further discussion of issues raised by projects). This last point in particular emphasises an imperative for ADUs to be as transparent as possible in maintaining working relationships with stakeholders and owners, faculties and offices, as well as individual academics in documenting their work for 'evidence of value' (Gunn, Creanor, Lent and Smyth, 2014, p. 29, and Chapter 10).

Implications

Writing and owning policy can be a risky business for the academic development unit, especially where the focus of the unit is primarily on service and support, as most ADUs tend see themselves as helping implement policy compared to owning and applying policy as a managerial tool. However, where it is appropriate to own policy, the policy should be developed in wide consultation with stakeholders to maximise a sense of ownership and awareness across the institution. The policy itself should set the context, outline key underlying principles, be definitive, and be succinct; these are the 'why' and 'what' aspects. Procedures describe the steps to achieve a policy outcome and those responsible for action. The procedures are the 'who', 'how' and 'when'.

Perhaps even more than writing policy, one of the critical roles members of ADUs play is to contribute to institutional thinking and the evidence that goes into policy and strategy development. Here the academic developer acts as a radar-scanner, monitoring the horizon for developments that need to be responded to or that can be used to enhance practice. Combined with their own expertise and experience, the academic developer contributes to institutional research by providing ideas, reports and recommendations as appropriate. A practice in the LTC is to prepare short papers under three headings that succinctly set out the issue(s) being considered, a discussion of the implications, and then a limited number of recommendations. This layout deliberately mimics the format of papers in University Executive Group meetings and so affords an easy transition up the chain if appropriate.

As a developer, and especially as a director of an ADU, one also has to advocate for best practice; to be prepared to bring evidence and advice to individuals and fora; and, to communicate messages in formats and style that maximise their effectiveness. This may not always be formal reports and recommendations, and could also come through new media outlets such a blogs or Twitter and the back channels of internal publication.

Impact of the UKPSF on strategy and policy in Australia

There is no doubt that the establishment of the UKPSF and associated accreditation and recognition pathways through the Higher Education Academy (HEA) have been a success in the UK sector and beyond. Affording higher educational staff recognition through a scheme based on their development has been shown to have significant impacts on institutional policy and strategy and individual academic practice (Turner, Oliver, McKenna, Hughes, Smith, Deepwell and Shrives, 2013). I have looked at the UKPSF ascendency with a certain amount of envy, disappointed at the lack of similar will in Australia to establish a climate of expectation for higher education teachers to be qualified and externally accredited.

Reading reports and commentary on the adoption of the UKPSF in the UK sector (e.g. Shrives, 2012; Bostock, 2013; Turner et al., 2013) one could conclude that there are variable affinities between external political and economic contexts, and the development of institutional policies and strategies for professional development frameworks, their resourcing, and reporting of outcomes. This is clearly in evidence in the Quality Assurance Agency (2013, p. 3) guidance on teaching qualifications where, '... the Higher Education Statistics Agency (HESA) will collect data on the teaching qualifications of academic staff as part of its staff record ...'. This includes a range of data that might be put forward at the institutional and course level, including staff gaining recognition through the HEA's Fellowship scheme and completion of credentialed qualifications such as postgraduate certificates in higher education. Viewed from afar, there also appears to be an economic imperative for the international expansion of the UKPSF, professional accreditation, and thereby the HEA Fellowships. There is a circle – virtuous or otherwise – driving the development of institutional policy and practice to meet external standards that satisfy the QAA, but that in part also provide fuel for the global business model of the HEA.

In stark contrast to the national and institutional drivers to accredit professional development courses and fellowship pathways exemplified in Tim Thornton's case study of the University of Huddersfield in the UK (Thornton, 2013), there are currently no national policies or indicators to promote similar professional recognition in Australia. There have been previous attempts by commonwealth governments of various political ideology to reward teaching innovation through performance schemes, grants, awards and the like, but no widespread demand for the professionalisation of teachers. In this vacuum, ADUs in a limited number of institutions in Australia have appropriated the UKPSF and the HEA fellowship scheme in the development of policy and strategy. An early adopter of the UKPSF and HEA fellowship scheme is the Australian National University (ANU), one of Australia's most prestigious institutions, but not one necessarily well known for promoting the scholarship of teaching as compared to research.

ANU, like several other Australian universities, has reconsidered its support for an internal Graduate Certificate in Higher Education prompted by concerns for workload, uptake of staff and government policy that effectively removed subsidised enrolment for these courses. The ADU at ANU integrated existing policy and strategy from the university's strategic plan into its plans for a new 'Educational Fellowship Scheme' (EFS). ANU's strategic plan, *ANU by 2020*, (Australian National University, 2011) sets targets for all new staff to complete a foundational course in learning and teaching and heralds a, '... greater push towards implementing campus-wide professional standards and professional recognition for teaching' (Beckman, personal communication, 2015).

ADU colleagues at ANU developed the supporting and thematically based Academic Professional Development program (APD); each theme comprising ten short, micro-credentialed modules called decamods, or alternatively a more customised, individually negotiated set of learning outcomes and activities (see Australian National University [n.d.] for further information and examples of decamods, the EFS and the APD). ANU also became the first institution in Australia to subscribe to the HEA, to have the HEA's first international accreditor (Elizabeth Beckman), and to begin awarding locally accredited HEA Fellowships. This is clearly stated in the compact (a negotiated agreement all Australian universities have with the Commonwealth):

> All applicants for all categories of fellowship will be required to submit an application under the EFS, with no other pathways. ... internal recognition processes will be fully integrated with the ANU Academic Professional Development (APD) program and the ANU Promotion Indicators in Education initiatives, and through these links as an integral part of ANU's staff development and promotions processes. (Department of Education and Training, 2013, p. 25)

The ANU initiative and its alignment of strategy and policy appears to be working, with:

> ... more than 300 academics a year taking up the diversity of modules, and gaining certificates for completion; ... more than 100 academics gaining HEA recognition in the first year of the EFS; educational leaders stepping up as role models and champions of the EFS; and peer engagement and mentoring approaches as the basis for fellowship application development and assessment. (Beckman, personal communication, 2015)

Implications

Know what works for your institution. Motivation, encouragement and incentive to engage with professional development will vary between individuals and relative to the context and the characteristics of the organisation. As a research intensive, highly selective university with minimal and dwindling uptake for its Graduate Certificate in Higher Education, the ANU needed to find a way in which staff would be encouraged and supported to engage in scholarship of teaching and learning activities. In this case, policy and strategy tacitly accepted the primacy of research over teaching whilst creating a clear expectation for professional recognition supported by a suite of development activities that were easy and efficient for staff to engage with. In promoting both the policy and the professional development, a deliberate tactic was adopted to recruit prominent members of staff to become early adopters, achieve fellowship status, and to lead some of the professional development activities.

Academic development as an agent for professionalism

Whilst the HEA Fellowship scheme gains ground in Australia, there have been several reports and a general desire for a more home grown process and mechanism to promote professionalisation; Australia has the opportunity, but currently lacks the structure. This missed opportunity was paralleled in the UK, as noted by William Locke, citing Lord Dearing:

> I am disappointed that academics themselves did not seize on the idea of a professional institute, run and owned by them, awarding associate and full fellowship memberships in recognition of their own profession and their achievement within it. I used to say that academe was the only profession I knew that does not collectively recognise, cherish and promote its own professional standards. (Dearing, 2007, p. 178, quoted in Locke, 2014)

Locke builds on this to make a useful suggestion, with implications well beyond the UK:

> As it tackles its own funding crisis due to the withdrawal of the majority of state sponsorship, the Higher Education Academy may like to reflect on this notion of a professional body for those with responsibilities for teaching and learning in higher education and the research and scholarship that underpins this. (Locke, 2014, p. 27)

Locke (2014, p. 26) goes on question the current primacy of individual rather than community development, an issue taken up in Chapter 11 on communities. Locke makes the distinction between professionalisation with connotations of external imposition and professionalism that emerges from within. These issues are considered further in Chapter 3. Locke's observations speak to something I believe is among the strategic responsibilities of ADUs and their directors, that is, the obligation to reflect on and where necessary challenge the zeitgeist, to advocate and lobby for action, and to responsibly promote best practice as fitting for the community of academic development and higher education. This view is commensurate with my role as President of the Council of Australian Directors of Academic Development (CADAD), membership of which includes my fellow directors and whose mission is to, 'To promote and advance research, policy and practice as it relates to the leadership, management and development of higher education learning and teaching' (CADAD, 2015). As such, CADAD will regularly contribute to the national higher education debate by responding to government discussion papers and calls for submission, providing occasional reports on contemporary issues, and funding small projects to support quality enhancement and assurance initiatives. CADAD Executive's most recent deliberations and proposals have been around the opportunities afforded by the UKPSF and HEA Fellowship scheme and indeed the potential for the creation of an Australian national body, along the lines of that called for by Locke.

Professional development, as discussed in Chapter 4, especially in the market-driven, neo-liberal higher education economy may have the positive appearance of progression, or more worryingly be seen as managerial control. This may be particularly evident where formal courses are viewed as a form of instrumental development, as has become the case in some institutions where targets are set for staff recognition and accreditation (Laycock and Shrives, 2009; Thornton, 2014), potentially leaving ADUs exposed to criticism by both executive management and by the constituents they serve, let alone posing existential challenges for the individual ADU staff who may find their own agency and values challenged if not compromised (Di Napoli, 2014). This leads some to argue that the professional development might better be promoted through action research type activity (Locke, 2014; Laycock and Shrives, 2009).

Academic development through professional learning

Most attempts to embed '… teaching criteria into policy, processes and practices require leadership, persistence and extensive engagement across institutional communities' (Chalmers, personal communication, 2015). This evokes notions of the personal and institutional capacity for dogged determination required in academic development and the sometimes very long game played to influence change, and provides more examples of how strategy and policy can be developed and enacted over time.

At the time of writing, Macquarie University is not sponsoring recognition of its staff through the HEA pathway. There has however been a long history of articulated professional learning opportunities, variously located and facilitated, with the LTC being the majority provider of these opportunities as exemplified in the Table 17.1. These offerings range from stand-alone workshops through to certification of higher degree research.

Nevertheless, the uptake of professional learning is sporadic and the LTC and others in the institution have long been advocates for a more systematic approach to continuing professional development. An example is the Tutor Induction

Implications

Academic development is a profession with its own norms and values, methods of enquiry and communities of practice. Academic developers need to know how to engage with that community as well as the local institutional community. As a director of an ADU and as President of CADAD I have a network I can solicit for advice and support, and together we can lobby for or respond to actions, policies and strategies that affect higher education. Similar networks, formal and informal, face-to-face or online, are often found at local, state, national and international levels, and engagement with these networks should be encouraged. For example, the Staff and Educational Development Association's (UK) Listserv mailing list, open to anyone, frequently has exchanges between academic developers seeking ideas, advice and discussion on a range of strategies and tactics related to many aspects of academic development.

Academic development is often a form of service leadership. Being a servant first and a leader second require humility and emotional intelligence. It often requires suspension of one's own assertions in favour of an organisational or policy directive. It is not for everyone...

Program (TIP) is one such offering, and an example of how ADUs like the LTC have a role to play in the evolution of practice as it moves from local to enterprise provision. TIP originated in the Faculty of Business and Economics as a process of enculturation and training for its high proportion of sessional tutors and shows how an ADU can work in partnership with a Faculty to contribute to and to use institutional strategy:

> The program is coordinated and administered by the TIP team, which comprises the Faculty Director of Learning and Teaching along with an Educational Developer or Designer (ED). ... Co-opting an ED from the LTC further ensures alignment and coherence with University Learning and Teaching Policies, strategic plans and visioning documents. (Huber, Hoadley and Wood, 2011, p. 14)

Following its inception, other faculties came to realise the benefits and affordances of TIP. What evolved, however, was a well-intentioned but somewhat chaotic mixture of expectations for and approaches to TIP across the university, triggering a review and evaluation before making recommendations to and receiving approval from the Pro-Vice Chancellor Learning and Teaching for a more consistent and coordinated policy for TIP (Harvey, 2015). The establishment of TIP as a coherent enterprise level course with clear expectations for tutor engagement illustrates the brokering role ADUs have in establishing but not necessarily owning policy and in the collaborative development of strategy.

Table 17.1 Examples of professional learning facilitated through the LTC

		Features	Examples	Assessment & Certification
1	**Knowledge, skills and information**	Development and updating of knowledge and skills One-off events Captures strategic need, current issues	Workshops, webinars, seminars Self-paced online modules LMS training Curriculum design and development workshops	None
2	**Theories, principles & practice**	A compulsory regime of activities introducing theoretical perspectives, or a short course providing an in-depth treatment of practice	Foundations in Learning and Teaching (FILT) Higher Degree Supervision Enhancement Flexible learning at Macquarie (FLaME) Tutor Induction Program	Certification of Completion
3	**Deepening the scholarship of learning and teaching**	Award courses – fully articulated Masters course in collaboration with the School of Education Research Degrees	Postgraduate courses in Higher Education Articulation from Foundations with credit for one unit in PG Certificate	PgCert PG Diploma Masters PhD

TIP is but one instance of compulsory and certificated professional development. The challenges for any ADU and the institutions within which they reside are how to encourage individual and collective engagement with various forms of development, and thereafter to reward and recognise that engagement. In what Holt, Palmer and Challis (2008, p. 50) call the mobilisation of teaching leaders within communities of practice, it is important that ADUs and their directors are able to recognise and influence the, '... important relationships between those: formal and informal roles; in different areas; and, operating at different levels of the organisation'. Strategic leadership and leverage of ADUs can be very important in driving innovation in policy and strategy, in institutional research and thinking and in delivering on the operational plans and projects that are forthcoming.

Capitalising on the positional leadership opportunities that I have as a director, as well as the distributed leadership network we have as an ADU, we have been able to build momentum around institutional awareness and interest in issues such: critically reflective practice; transitioning from norm based to criteria and standards based assessment; course development, review and accreditation; technology enhanced learning; and, exemplified below, the value propositions inherent in a positive student experience. Here the LTC has been instrumental in developing the evidence base foundational to any further articulation through policy, strategy and action. This evolving framework is shown in Table 17.2.

Table 17.2 Characteristics of the student experience at Macquarie University

OUTCOMES		BEFORE	DURING					AFTER
Organizational Goals and Values*	Individual Learner Goals		Academic	Para Academic	Student Support & Welfare	Amenity, Extracurricular & Social	Administration	
Transformative learning	Learning.	Awareness	Feeling of curriculum having coherence.	Integrated student induction.	Access to student support, information & advice.	Involvement in social integration activities that promote belonging.	Student-university congruence (through gatekeeping).	Employability
Student engagement	Employment.	Attraction	Consistent & common values.	Effective orientation.	Feeling that students have representation in decision-making.	Access to appropriate or 'fit for purpose' facilities.	Communications with families.	Leadership
Student representation	Research and enquiry.	Conversion	Involvement in authentic & experiential tasks.	Appropriate room allocation & timetabling.	Access to effective formal mentoring activities.	Availability of social, recreational & competition sport, dance, cultural clubs societies & venues.	Efficient enrolment.	Attachment
Student employability	Life experiences.		Involvement in work integrated learning.	Flexible scheduling relevant to need & preference.	Involvement of minority students, professional & academic staff as mentors.	Perceived quality or value for money of consumables.	Converged services.	Allegiance
Effective teaching	Optimism & confidence.		Good interaction with teachers.	Access to just-in-time help.	Access to financial aid.	Perceived quality or value for money of services & facilities.	Timely & consistent advising.	
Discovery and innovation	Engagement with curricular & co-curricular activities.		Cooperation between students.	Effective learning infrastructure.	Access to counseling & medical services.		Timely notification of results.	
Research training	Attendance at key activities.		Small group teaching.	Transparent student evaluation cycle.			Good service quality.	
Good Reputation	Positive relationships with others.		Timely & effective feedback.	Well-organized University activities.			Helpful staff.	
Effective services	Effort & vitality.		Learning with & about diversity.	Access to supplementary instruction.			Coherent communication.	
Scholarship	Resilience.		High expectations & defined standards of achievement for courses.				Effective communication & dissemination.	
Integrity	Emotional stability.							
Empowerment	Positive emotion.							
Inclusiveness								

Sustainability *As summarized from the University's Strategic Framework *Our University: A Framing of Futures*	Competence. Positive self-esteem. Organization of self & tasks. Appropriate time on task. Academic integrity. Reflection. Aptitude. Sense of belonging to institution, cohort, discipline etc.	High quality of teaching. Research & industry materials & activities as part of learning. Social integration for learning. Clear pathways & sequencing. Easily accessed materials. Community & service learning. Culminating projects & expositions. Choice & negotiation in assessment. Good advice available. Clear assessment criteria. Up-to-date learning materials. Relevant & in-context learning materials.	Access to resources when needed. Easy-to-navigate University systems & procedures. Helpful staff. Positive campus climate & culture. Access to regular & structured academic advising.	Affordable housing. Sense that MQ cares.	Acceptable transport options.

Implications

You've got to be in it to win it. There is no writing, contributing to and using institutional policies and strategies unless you create the conditions by which you can engage with them, as discussed in Chapter 16. This can be as simple as having a seat at a committee or working party; it may be systematised through responding to strategy with relevant professional development; and, most importantly, it is enabled through a, 'context of trust and a culture of respect coupled with effecting change through collaborative relationships' (Lefoe, 2013). I often say to academic developers that the work is out there, meaning in the faculties, schools and departments, as opposed to at a desk in the ADU. This is the winning of hearts and minds part of the job and the networking and brokering that ensures one is meeting local demand but also identifying the opportunities to maximise best practice wherever possible.

TIP is but one small example of many where the LTC has partnered with a department or faculty to move an initiative from innovation to wider adoption. One of the privileges of a centralised ADU is in the ability to look beyond local practice so as to ensure the success of a particular initiative or strategy at the enterprise level. However, this demands that the ADU and its staff are sufficiently knowledgeable of variations in local contexts and discipline practices, as well as relevant governing policies that might impact on innovation. This can be achieved by, for example, having ADU staff sit on faculty learning and teaching committees, and by ensuring ADU staff are critically engaged with policy and strategy development and review.

It is also important that the professional development offerings of the ADU respond to and support strategy. Academic developers should know how and where they support the learning and teaching or academic strategy and operational plans of the institution. In my own unit we review institutional plans on an annual basis, anticipating what might be needed and when, and incorporating actions into our own operation plans and projects. Some of these projects are intentionally labelled 'strategic' as discussed below.

This also enabled an opportunity to align the framework with the broader strategic framework of the university. Development of awareness, artefacts and resources like that in Table 17.2 and others exemplify the role ADUs and their staff can have in channelling the scholarship of theory and practice in contributing to policy and strategy.

Academic development through strategic change

It is important that directors and staff of ADUs have the skills and abilities to work with others as part of the critical stakeholder management required to develop or indeed respond to strategy and policy. Aside from the interpersonal skills required, more formal mechanisms such as the establishment of a steering committee or reference group can be valuable in obtaining stakeholder input, and in managing and extending the sphere of influence of a particular initiative. Aside from the attributes and skills of staff or the organisation of effort, it makes obvious sense to align resources and actions of the ADU with goals and objectives in strategic plans and initiatives; better still to be involved in the development of the plans themselves, to have actions and responsibilities therein, or to provide evidence that support the initiatives of one's executive sponsor.

The tripartite of development, strategy and implementation is suggested in Figure 17.1 and, 'This sandwich effect, before and after the planning process, reinforces the cyclical nature of planning and organisational development' (Rowley and Sherman, 2001, p. 243).

ADUs and their staff could find themselves involved in any aspect of these three stages, for example, providing leadership or knowledge development at one end of the sandwich whilst at the same time creating the methodologies for implementation at the other. Such has been the case with the development of the most recent Learning and Teaching Strategy in my institution. As the director of the ADU I have been fortunate enough to work with the Pro-Vice Chancellor Learning and Teaching in the conceptualisation and writing of the strategy, offering advice on content and style, as well as evidence to support its intentions. Indeed, it has been possible aligning LTC's work with support for the Learning and Teaching Strategy. In doing so, we found it useful to develop project briefs in consultation with the PVC, deliberately describing them as strategic projects. Strategic projects are conceptualised as enterprise or whole of office level projects commissioned to support the goals and strategic direction of the University or of the Learning and Teaching Centre. An example of a LTC strategic project brief is shown in Table 17.3.

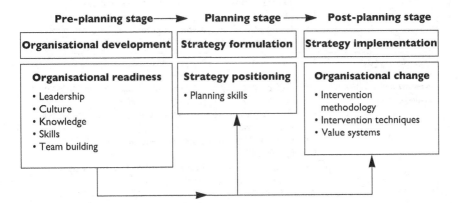

Figure 17.1 The integration of organisational development and strategic planning (from Rowley and Sherman, 2001, p. 244)

Table 17.3 Strategic project brief aligned to the learning and teaching strategy

Project Name	Learning and Teaching Framework Development (Design for Digital)	
Management	Helen (Project Lead) and Victoria (Project Coordinator)	
Project team	Iain, Deirdre, Rebecca, Ronell	
Purpose	The Learning and Teaching Strategy is built around 3 principles with an overarching structural approach. This project supports the PVC/DVC-A and the University community in the creation and adoption of the Learning and Teaching Framework and Strategy principle #2 "Design for Digital"	
Objectives	To develop resources and activities that support an approach to teaching that understands that, properly designed and utilised, digital technologies provide tremendous opportunities for better learning. It can also free up teaching time, and allow more effective student interaction in face-to-face engagements. Acknowledging that our student cohorts (like the broader world) are increasingly engaged with digital technologies, we need to fully develop emerging digital learning possibilities.	
Key stakeholders and / or needs	PVC/DVCA, AD's L&T, Staff, Students An evidence base and resources for professional learning in support of the emerging learning in and teaching framework and strategy	
Specifications	Resources fit for purpose and for various audiences (e.g. the PVC/DVC; Academic Staff; Heads of Department / Office etc.). Develop and refine a suite of resources to support an environment where: • All of our learning will be blended, with every unit offering a mix of face-to-face and online activities; • Our core curriculum content and assessment (including examinations) will be on open, accessible digital platforms; • Our suite of fully online programs will be strategically expanded and strengthened	
Target dates	**Start**	**End**
Key deliverables / milestones	• Design, prototype, evaluate and integrate in consultation with the Director LTC and PCV L&T • Regular inter and intra project team sharing of practice and findings • Consultation with other stakeholders (e.g. Associate Deans L&T) • Frequent, written outputs of materials for inclusion in the Learning and Teaching Strategy	

(continued)

Table 17.3 Strategic project brief aligned to the learning and teaching strategy
(continued)

Project Name	Learning and Teaching Framework Development (Design for Digital)
Inclusions	• The evidence base (Phase 1) • Alignment with other university strategies and frameworks (Phase 1) • Case studies of implementation (Phase 2) • Embedding and communication strategies (Phase 2/3) • Professional development resources (Phase 3) • Evaluation will be an ongoing consideration
Exclusions	L&T Strategy Principles #1 and #3
Key risks	Resources are not appropriate for the intended audiences
Assumptions	That there is an evidence base for the principles within the Learning Teaching Framework
Constraints	Alignment with other relevant institutional strategies
Cross-dependencies	Other designated Learning and Teaching Framework Resource Development projects
Notes	This project will require staged outputs over its lifetime (suggested above by three phases) to be discussed with Project Leads and Coordinator

Implications

Know who's who in the zoo. Regardless of the size or complexity of the ADU, the chances are that resources will need to be marshalled and managed and stakeholders included when implementing institutional strategy. Typically working parties and sub-committees are constituted to progress ideas and developments. Knowing who should be on the committees, for what reason and with what reach, or ensuring that you have a seat at them becomes desirable. Executive sponsorship can be effective as this affords greater positional leadership but just as important can be the distributed leadership of key influencers.

Poor planning leads to poor performance. There are finite resources in any institution. Despite this, many academic development projects and activities are open ended, poorly scoped, and suffer from mission creep and inefficiency. In my experience, very few academic developers are skilled project managers, which has implications for either internal professional development or the employment of people with appropriate skills. Chapter 14 of this book offers advice on planning and running projects to avoid these dangers.

Consider also the alignment of projects to strategic needs. Uniting policy or strategy with approach provides alignment with institutional imperatives. In the example of the strategic projects, the LTC has scoped projects that directly addresses aspects of the university's learning and teaching strategy, supporting the needs of the office of the PVC Learning and Teaching; acknowledging the need for support from elsewhere; and supporting the members of the academic community through the development of professional development resources and support needed for the enactment of the strategy. The impact of the project could be shown to support each end of the development to implementation sandwich.

Concluding remarks

Establishing the kind of thinking described above and maintaining the debate and momentum of change is crucial and should be central to the work of ADUs and their directors. However, strategy and policy best affect widespread change in pedagogic practice when supported by an institutional culture of learning and teaching that rewards excellence in teaching and views quality teaching as an important endeavour. Institutional policies also need to be embraced at a departmental level and, where appropriate, tailored to suit specific disciplines. One of the most effective ways in which ADUs can support this process is through the facilitation of communities of enquiry and practice; the bringing together of colleagues to partner in responding to, developing and enacting policy and strategy. Always located in the evidence, the work aims at once to build a ground swell of interest and enthusiasm across the academe and to ensure the executive leadership required for integrating strategy, policy and practice; the, 'unity in policy and approach' described by McInnis, Ramsden and Maconachie (2012). At Macquarie this means that we believe there exist many different strategies for teachers to develop, maintain and assess teaching skills ranging from the credentialed versus non-credentialed and to formal versus informal. This range of activity and opportunities therein are neatly summarised and discussed by Kennedy (2005), whose taxonomy described in Figure 17.2 suggests that members of the university community have available to them professional development of various types and orientation, within which they might develop skills, knowledge and values. Professional development must at its highest level of conception lead to transformative practice as described by Kennedy.

The notion of the transformative in the context of the work of the LTC is important as it responds directly to Macquarie University's overarching strategic framework and its first goal to, '… imbue our academic and professional staff with a culture of transformative learning …' (Macquarie University, 2013). It might

Model of CPD	Purpose of Model	
The transformative model The action research model	Transformative	↑
The community of practice model The coaching/mentoring model The standards-based model	Transitional	Increasing capacity for professional autonomy
The training model The deficit model The award-bearing model The cascade model	Transmission	

Figure 17.2 Models of continuing professional development modified from Kennedy (2005)

even be argued that the service-leadership orientation of the LTC presumes that in some, perhaps all, aspects of endeavour, the primary role of the LTC and other ADUs is not in writing, contributing to and using institutional policies and strategies per se, rather than in helping to create, '... the range of different conditions required for transformative practice' (Kennedy 2005, p. 246). Viewed through this lens, professional development involves helping individuals, collectives and the broad university community to contribute to, critique and ultimately implement strategy and policy.

Occupying as they also do a pivotal role between their own institutions and the broader sectors in which they reside, ADUs and their directors may also support the transformative agendas of the type described in CADAD's work earlier in this chapter. Here the contribution to strategy has the potential to fundamentally transform policy and practice across a sector, and should be perhaps be considered as one of the principle community engagement activities and vocational responsibilities of academic development and developers.

This chapter has provided an illustration of the service-leadership orientation of the LTC at Macquarie and some of the ways in which it approaches working with policy and practice, especially as it relates to professional development. I hope it serves as a useful example of how ADUs and their directors can at least influence the writing of policy and strategy, if not directly crafting them. Of course some policies and procedures sit comfortably within the purview of ADUs, especially if like the LTC, the office is responsible for significant aspects of university endeavour and operations, such as the educational technology platform in the case of the LTC. Indeed the LTC is the owner of the learning technologies policy and procedures precisely because it provides and has responsibility for access to, the management of, professional development within, and the quality assurance of the system. This affords the ADU and its director other opportunities for influencing strategy and policy through governance chain within which the policy resides and is reviewed.

ADUs often make indirect contributions to policy and strategy through their role in informing the community of issues, innovative developments, or providing responses to policy and legislative changes and so on. Of course this work can take place within one's office and organisation as well as outside it, as shown in the example of the evolution of TIP from a local to an enterprise level offering, or in the response to national agendas where the LTC prepared the ground by informing institutional thinking and advising on strategic responses, if not developing the strategy and policy directly. Here also was an example of my broader role within the higher education sector in working with CADAD. Working through CADAD or as an institutional representative has enabled involvement in several national debates related to higher education and specifically as it applies to academic development. This shows how the staff of ADUs can be important influencers in sector practice, inter-institutional cooperation, and political expectations.

Against the backdrop of the central role many ADUs have in providing opportunities for professional development and organisational capacity building, the service-leadership orientation highlights one of the key ambivalences of our work:

> ... while the ADs may hold the knowledge, they may not hold the power to translate that knowledge into widespread practice unless they have a strong sponsor who seeks similar outcomes. Instead, they must operate through influence, alliances, stealth, lobbying, and whatever other technique they can employ to be considered an important source of insight and ideas. (Debowski, 2014, p. 54)

My experience and that of the ADU I am privileged to be the director of lead me to conclude that ambivalence is less about contradiction and more about taking multidimensional approaches when writing, contributing to and using institutional policies and strategies. These various approaches, in part exemplified in this chapter, are somewhat messy, often long in gestation, and not always easy to record or justify; but they are crucially important if ADUs are to continue to provide foundational work for transformative continuing professional development effected in policy and strategy.

References

Australian National University (2011). *ANU by 2020*. Canberra: Australian National University, www.anu.edu.au/files/review/anu-2020-strategy.pdf.

ANU (n.d.). Australian National University Staff Education Teaching and Learning, available at http://chelt.anu.edu.au/staff-education/, accessed 18 May 2015.

Bostock, S. (2013). 'Developing SEDA's Professional Development Framework', *Educational Developments*, 14(1): 5–8. London: Staff and Educational Development Association.

Brew, A. and Cahir, J. (2013). 'Achieving sustainability in learning and teaching initiatives', *International Journal for Academic Development*, 19(4): 341–352, DOI: http://dx.doi.org/10.1080/1360144X.2013.848360.

CADAD (2015). *Constitution of the Council of Australian Directors of Academic Development*, www.cadad.edu.au.

Dearing, R. (2007). 'Higher education in the learning society'. The report of the National Committee of Inquiry into Higher Education (NCIHE), 1997.

Debowski, S. (2014). 'From agents of change to partners in arms: the emerging academic developer role', *International Journal for Academic Development*, 19(1): 50–56. http://dx.doi.org/10.1080/1360144X.2013.862621.

Department of Education and Training (2013). *2014–16 Mission-based Compact Between the Commonwealth of Australia and The Australian National University*, Canberra: Department of Education, https://docs.education.gov.au/system/files/doc/other/anu_2014-16_compact_final.pdf.

Di Napoli, R. (2014). 'Value gaming and political ontology: between resistance and compliance in academic development', *International Journal for Academic Development*, 19(1): 4–11, DOI: http://dx.doi.org/10.1080/1360144X.2013.848358.

Gunn, C., Creanor, L., Lent, N. and Smyth, K. (2014). 'Representing academic development', *Journal of Perspectives in Applied Academic Development*, 2(2): 24–30. http://jpaap.napier.ac.uk/index.php/JPAAP/article/view/92/pdf.

Harvey, M. (2015). Benchmarking leadership and advancement of standards for sessional teaching. Accessed 22 October 2015 from http://blasst.edu.au.

Holt, D., Palmer, S. and Challis, D. (2008). *Strategic Leadership and its Contribution to Improvements in Teaching and Learning in Higher Education*. Geelong: Deakin University. http://dro.deakin.edu.au/eserv/DU:30061199/holt-strategicleadership-2008.pdf.

Huber, E., Hoadley, S., and Wood, L. (2011). 'Teaching Induction Program: framework, design and delivery', *Asian Social Science*, 7(11): 13–19. www.ccsenet.org/journal/index.php/ass/article/view/12837/8968.

Kennedy, A. (2005). 'Models of CPD: a framework for analysis', *Journal of In-service Education*, 31(2).

Laycock, M. and Shrives, L. (eds.) (2009). *Embedding CPD in Higher Education*, London: Staff and Educational Development Association.

Lefoe, G. (2013). *Evaluating Distributed Leadership in Learning and Teaching*, presentation to the Council of Australian Directors of Academic Development. Victoria University, Melbourne, April 2013.

Locke, W. (2014). *Shifting Academic Careers: Implications for Enhancing Professionalism in Teaching and Supporting Learning*. York: The Higher Education Academy.

Macfarlane, B. (2011). 'The morphing of academic practice: unbundling and the rise of the para-academic', *Higher Education Quarterly*, 65(1): 59–73. DOI: http://dx.doi.org/10.1111/j.1468-2273.2010.00467.x

Macquarie University (2013). *Our University: A Framing of Futures*. Sydney: Macquarie University. www.mq.edu.au/our-university/pdf/Macquarie_University_A_Framing_of_Futures.pdf.

McInnis, C., Ramsden, P. and Maconachie, D. (2012). *A Handbook for Executive Leadership of Learning and Teaching in Higher Education*. Sydney: Office of Learning and Teaching. www.olt.gov.au/executive-leadership-learning-teaching-higher-education-2012.

QAA (2013). *Explaining Staff Teaching Qualifications: Guidance about Providing Information for Students*. Gloucester: Quality Assurance Agency.

Rowley, D. J. and Sherman, H. (2001). *From Strategy to Change: Implementing the Plan in Higher Education*. San Francisco: Jossey-Bass.

Shrives, L. (2012). 'From postgraduate certificates... to embedding UKPSF at all levels', *Educational Developments*, 13(3): 1–6, London: Staff and Educational Development Association.

Thornton, T. (2014). 'Professional recognition: promoting recognition through the Higher Education Academy in a UK higher education institution', *Tertiary Education and Management*, 20(3): 225–238. DOI: http://dx.doi.org/10.1080/13583883.2014.931453.

Turner, N., Oliver, M., McKenna, C., Hughes, J., Smith, H., Deepwell, F., & Shrives, L. (2013). *Measuring the Impact of the UK Professional Standards Framework for Teaching and Supporting Learning (UKPSF)*. York: The Higher Education Academy.

Zepke, N. (2014). 'What future for student engagement in neo-liberal times?', *Higher Education*, 1–12. Published online, DOI: http://dx.doi.org/10.1007/s10734-014-9797-y.

Chapter 18

Futures for academic development

David Baume and Celia Popovic

Summary

After an analytic history of academic development, the chapter offers a rationale for considering the future via scenarios. Scenario elements include the increasing power and ubiquity of computing; the need for play and creativity; individualised learning in mass higher education; a possible de-coupling of current higher education functions; the rise of just-in-time and lifelong education, training and CPD; the increased blurring of and collaboration between development functions; unpredictable disruptions and our responses; showing our cost-effectiveness; a stronger discipline focus; the further professionalising of teaching and development; the possible wider use of contracts for teaching and development; and futures for workshops. We conclude with suggestions on how we should conduct ourselves as developers.

Links to web sources referenced in this chapter can be found at www.seda.ac.uk/apad.

Origins

We are very grateful to Carole Baume, Liz Beaty and Eva Falk Nilsson (personal communications, 2015) for their contributions to this section on origins of academic development.

Academic development in higher education does not have its Declaration of Independence, its Magna Carta, the establishment of its United Nations, its defining starting moment, its creation myth. But we can see shapes, a sequence of stages, what Beaty calls the 'waves of change' that variously provoked and supported the origins of academic development, albeit that these waves overlap considerably.

These 'waves of change' include:

1 The interest of a few individuals in teaching, in specific teaching problems or issues.
2 Attempts to address these, sometimes based on or prompting investigation.

3   Local, and then institutional, and in time national, interest in teaching.
4   On a similar sequence of scales, interest in the improvement of teaching, some of this linked to concerns about teaching quality.
5   Some local, and then institutional and in time national, funding for improvements to teaching.
6   Also from very early days, research into higher education, again first individual, and then local and sometimes institutional and national, leading to published papers. The history of research into academic development is described in Chapter 12.
7   Monographs and books, some of which, crucially, offered practical guidance as well as reporting on research.
8   Interest in and development of the uses of technology in training, school teaching and then higher education was another early strand.
9   Attention to improving the educational practices of others, again on an increasing scale from local to institutional and in time national – this may be the starting point for the practice of academic development as we currently know it.

As well as the waves described above, all of which still apply, continuing propulsive forces include:

10   Changes to the nature and above all the scale of higher education.
11   Attendant changes in funding.
12   Attendant changes in the relationship between students and the university, considered below in the section on the student contract.

Many of the details, and indeed some elements of the big picture, will differ from country to country, and some also from institution to institution and between disciplines. This very partial and schematic account is included here to suggest tools for analysis, possibly also for planning.

In a little more detail, and as narrative rather than list:

Leaving little trace, there have probably always been individual teachers who had reservations about some aspects of their teaching, and sought to improve it – influenced perhaps by conversations with peers or students, or by ideas about, for example, primary education, secondary education or adult learning or by research into the psychology of learning, for example, by Skinner, Vygotsky, Rogers or Piaget. And there are still many such lone pioneers, although hopefully now they have access to our support, should we find them and should they wish it.

There were also individual pockets of concern about teaching. Some left little trace. But not all. Barbara Falk set up the University Teaching Project in Australia in 1962 (Lee et al., 2008). In Sweden, a starting point in 1965 was the national initiative by UKÄ, a civil service department under the Ministry of Education, which set up a commission called University Pedagogic Investigation, staffed by educational researchers, administrators, students, teacher training college staff and the Swedish Employers' Confederation. It supported departments, not individuals (Falk Nilsson, 2015, personal communication; Åkesson and Falk Nilsson, 2010). Chapter 11 shows this Swedish tradition of working with communities to be continuing.

The interest in teaching described above was sometimes accompanied by a research interest in teaching and learning in higher education, with the same motivations as any other form of disciplinary research; a wish to understand, to make sense, and also a hope that the research might be applicable to practice. (A very early piece of research, on the reliability of assessment, is Edgeworth [1890]. He found that assessment is not very reliable.) This pedagogic research continues, and continues to be influential, currently through ideas including deep and surface approaches to learning, constructive alignment and threshold concepts.

As a sufficient body of research was undertaken, this research was analysed and aggregated into scholarly monographs, often by the people who were undertaking at least some of the research described. In 1970 the Swedish commission published *University Pedagogics*, for use as a textbook for pedagogical courses for university teachers. Donald Bligh's *What's the Use of Lectures?* (2000), including a meta-analysis of research on lecturing, was first published in 1971. (Bligh concludes: 'Use lectures to convey information. Do not rely on them to promote thought, change attitudes, or develop behavioural skills if you can help it'.) (Bligh, 2000, p. 20). Bligh remains in print through successive editions, although his advice is still not universally followed. Ruth Beard's *Teaching and Learning in Higher Education* (Beard, 1979) was first published in 1972, and remains valuable. Significantly, both of these books comfortably join two functions; summarising research, and offering research-based practical guidance to those who teach in higher education. The tradition of this kind of book, offering explicitly research-informed guidance, has continued, including Cowan (1998), Knight (2002), Ramsden (2003) and Biggs and Tang (2011).

Then, in a crucial further stage, attempts began to be made to apply what was being learned about learning and teaching in higher education, not just to the practice of the researcher and perhaps their immediate colleagues, and not just through publication, but also more widely and systemically. The University Teaching Methods Unit at the University of London was established in the 1960s, Lewis Elton's Institute of Educational Technology at the University of Surrey in 1967. (The complex and evolving relationships between academic development and educational technology in higher education over the last 50 years or so provide a fascinating and continuing tale, as far as we know not yet written.)

The establishment of these and successive units and institutes, we would suggest, marks the emergence of academic development in higher education. The intention is no longer just to research practice and provide a base of information and guidance which can be used to improve practice. Additionally, the intention now is actively to improve, or to facilitate the improvement of, the practice of others. Indeed, the intention has gone much further, to improving programmes, departments, universities and indeed national higher education systems. A large academic and professional infrastructure has grown up, and continues to extend and change, of organisations and publications and events and qualifications, as described elsewhere in this book. Academic development has become a widespread (although not universal) and established (although not totally secure) function.

Another wave was the rise in the UK of new higher education institutions, Polytechnics, in the 1970s (Robinson, 1968), and in particular a national agency, the Council for National Academic Awards, which initially validated (approved) their degrees. In for the first time designing their own programmes, for external approval, the Polytechnics undertook much original academic development work, although not necessarily labeled as such, often being called course development.

There were and still are waves of technology and method. Slide-tape, where an audiotape triggered slide changes; programmed learning and the closely associated and optimistically named 'teaching machines'; Keller Plan/Personalised System of Instruction (PSI); and then distance learning, video, and more recently networking, virtual or managed learning environments, the flipped classroom, and on into near-ubiquitous personal computing and communication, Bring Your Own Device (BYOD) and mobile learning. Accounts of all of these can be found on the web, accounts more current as you read this than a reference written in May 2015 would be.

Another wave was and still is higher education policy changes, including dramatic increases in student numbers, and the Dearing report recommending training for higher education teachers (The Dearing Report, 1997).

Associated with policy changes were funding streams. Again in the UK, multi-million pound government-funded programmes, listed in Chapter 14, included Teaching More Students, the Teaching and Learning Technology Programme, the Teaching Quality Enhancement Fund and, the last of their kind for now anyway, the Centres for Excellence in Teaching and Learning. This funding fuelled and shaped the growth of academic development, as described in Chapter 14 on projects.

We explore below how some these and other waves may roll in, interact, and perhaps some of them recede.

Grant et al. (2009) provide a fascinating set of historical accounts.

Introduction – using scenarios

It makes little sense to talk about futures for academic development except in the context of futures for higher education. (It may make similarly little sense to talk about futures for higher education except in the context of futures for the world, but we have to keep the chapter at manageable length.)

It is difficult to make predictions, especially about the future. (Steincke, 1948)

Perhaps Steincke should have said, '... to make <u>accurate</u> predictions ...'. Despite this, there can still be value in thinking about the future. So, instead of predicting, with the attendant near-certainty of being mostly wrong, we shall consider a few possible scenarios for higher education in the world, and then explore their possible implications for academic development. As we think about scenarios for the future, it is worth remembering:

> We tend to overestimate the effect of a technology in the short run and underestimate the effect in the long run. (Amara, n.d.)

These scenarios and scenario elements are not all alternatives to each other. They point in different directions, and consider different issues, but some may run together. They are tools for thinking and planning. The actual future may be a little less startling if we have spent some time there, or in an approximation of it, in our heads.

Some implications for academic development, where these are not already obvious, will be drawn.

Ubiquitous and increasingly cheap and intelligent computing and communication

Put together Moore's Law (n.d.), which has held up well since around 1965 – it describes an exponential increase, a doubling, of the computing power in a device roughly every two years – with Hegel's observation that any quantitative change eventually becomes a qualitative change. Together, these suggest that the world in which higher education is immersed, and for which it is preparing students, will continue to change in its character and quality, very rapidly. The future will not just be more of the same, and we cannot predict the nature of the future by simple extrapolation. These changes will probably range in scale from myriad small changes to a few much more spectacular ones. If we add in Arthur Clarke's observation that any technology sufficiently advanced is indistinguishable from magic (Clarke, 2000), this suggests, rather pleasingly, that we need to prepare students and colleagues for a world which looks increasingly magical (adapted from Baume 2012).

Play and creativity

The sometimes desperate seriousness of the academic quest can militate against talk of magic. Creativity, play, wonder, are rarely part of the academic self-image. This is a shame. The straight-faced self-image is also inaccurate. The moment of discovery, whether as a researcher or as a learner – the moment when your view of a corner of the world, however small the corner, abruptly shifts to something that is, at least to you, new, that for however long makes better sense – this is a moment of almost magic. Before we revert to the slog of checking and testing and publishing ...

Implications for academic development?

- Show, in your work, that 'playful' isn't the opposite of 'serious'.
- Support and encourage colleagues to take a longer view, accepting that often they will be wrong about the detail.
- Remind colleagues from time to time that they are preparing students who will probably still be working in half a century, and hopefully living, and living well, awhile beyond that. Explore the implications of this for what and how we teach and assess, for how we want our graduates to be.

Individualised learning in mass higher education

The page you see when, as a registered user, you launch Amazon, is unique to you. The same is probably also true, for you and for students, when you and they log on to the University Virtual or Managed Learning Environment. This expectation – to be known and treated as an individual, even when you are part of, interacting with, a massive system – will only grow, and is moving rapidly from expectation to requirement. The student expects to have ready access to information about their recent progress, current timetable, forthcoming deadlines, course news that may affect them – a personalised student dashboard, if you will. A one-screen overview is useful, with the capacity to find more detail at the press of a finger or click of a mouse.

Implications for academic development?

- To what kinds of information do students want ready access? To what extent do they already have this access? What further work is needed? This is not just a technical or administrative matter – this is an educational matter, and therefore you have a locus in it.
- Repeat the previous questions for staff/faculty.

De-coupling/differentiation of current HE functions and roles

There may be increasing decoupling/differentiation of the current higher education functions, as suggested in the table below. Locke (2014) usefully analyses the increasing differentiation of roles at the level of the individual academic. There is no obvious reason why all the current higher education teaching functions should continue indefinitely to be provided by the same source; the university.

Working down Table 18.1: The library long ago removed the need for the teacher to be the only or even the primary source of knowledge. The online world has removed the teacher from their role as the gatekeeper to knowledge. MOOCs, textbooks and online courses mean that the teacher is no longer the

Table 18.1 Some university functions past, present and future

Function	University of Bologna, 1088 (adapted from 'University of Bologna', 2015)	Current University	Higher education, 20??
Provision of / access to content	Teachers, library	Teachers and library, perhaps / partly via VLE; WWW	WWW, partially curated by respected authorities (possibly accredited); increasingly adapted or created by students as part of their learning
Provision of learning activities	Teachers	Teachers, again partly via VLE; textbooks and sites	Learning activity providers (possibly accredited)
Provision of learning conversations	Teachers, peers within the University	Teachers; peers within and maybe beyond the University and across the world	Teachers and peers, within and beyond the University and across the world; learning facilitators (possibly accredited)
Encouraging and supporting student work	Teachers	Teachers	Teachers, peers as above, learning facilitators (possibly accredited)
Feedback	Teachers	Teachers, perhaps peers	Feedback providers, both human and machine (possibly accredited)
Assessment and accreditation	Teachers, the University	Teachers, the University	Assessment providers, both human and machine, and accrediting agencies

only possible source of learning activities. Teachers and peers remain valuable as sources of both learning conversations and, skipping a row, of feedback, although increasing student:staff ratios tend to reduce the amount of student:staff contact and staff time allocated to feedback. (Online forums can redress this to some extent, through shared feedback.)

The nature of student work has always varied spectacularly, in kind and in level, whatever the subject. There are two widely used accounts, taxonomies, of this. Bloom's (1969) venerable taxonomy of cognitive activity starts with knowledge, and progresses upward through comprehension, application and analysis to synthesis and evaluation. Biggs et al.'s (1982) SOLO taxonomy usefully complements Bloom. It considers rather the growing complexity and sophistication of students' use of ideas and information, from recall of isolated bits of knowledge, to increasingly sophisticated structuring and integration, and then going beyond what is known. Additionally, there is now – in the authors' view, a very welcome – emphasis on students as producers and co-producers of knowledge, rather than simply as learners of what is already known. The University of Lincoln provides a valuable and well-sourced guide to its work on students as producers ('Students as Producers', n.d.).

The assessment and accreditation functions may be the core of the university's role, and the very last to be lost by universities. The table above suggests the sequence in which university functions from 1088 to the present day and into the future may be lost. Assessment and accreditation, of course, provide the main reasons while the apparently more vulnerable functions – providing access to content, to learning activities, to learning conversations, encouraging and supporting student work and giving feedback – remain largely within the purview of the university. Assessment rules. The obvious way for a student to maximise their chances of success is to buy the complete package, the complete university experience. However, open learning with various degrees of student support and feedback; and perhaps the biggest current potential disruptor, the MOOC; suggest the scope for, and maybe the start of, the dislocation and differentiation of current university functions. This process is unlikely to stop now. Sharing a crowded lecture with hundreds of other students, watching on the big screen in the lecture room or the small screen on laptop or tablet, while accessing resources via the VLE, may come to feel less attractive than viewing online from a more comfortable or accessible place, interacting if watching live or pausing and reviewing and taking a bit more time for the activities if asynchronously. Definitions of contact start to blur.

Implications for academic development?

Universities, like most large organisations, are very good at continuing to do what they do, and reasonably good at fine-tuning to deal with modest new opportunities and challenges. Revolutions – not so much. One vital development role is horizon scanning, indeed looking beyond the horizon. Somewhere between simple linear extrapolation and apocalyptic or utopian science fiction lies an exciting and uncomfortable zone of possibilities, requiring at least some exploration. Academic development has a reconnaissance function, an intelligence function. Bring back interesting ideas from your reconnaissance, and discuss them with senior management and front-line staff. Become known as a source of interesting, if occasionally slightly wacky, ideas. Be ambitious for your university and its teaching. As suggested in the later sections of Chapter 10, and also in Chapter 16 – seek to lead innovation. Discover, over time, what kinds of ideas do and do not gain traction in particular parts of the university, indeed with particular individuals. Go with the ideas that do tend to gain traction, but do not give up on potentially important ones that don't. Optimal learning and development happen under conditions of mild discomfort, somewhere between complacency and terror.

Retired Vice Chancellor and previously academic development unit head Ingrid Moses (2012, p. 275) offers an invigorating account – '… I wanted the ADU [in my university] to be the research and development centre for higher education; a resource to be drawn upon by the university in its endeavours to meet strategic goals in teaching and learning and scholarship'.

Just-in-time and lifelong education and training and CPD

The idea of a degree as a full tank of intellectual fuel that will serve throughout a working life has long been absurd, and is becoming and will continue to become increasingly so, given the increasing rate of development of new knowledge and expertise, and, perhaps less widely acknowledged, the increasing rate of redundancy of old knowledge. Higher education probably has not got the relationship right between helping graduates to acquire on the one hand the knowledge and expertise and values to fit them for further study or immediate employment and on the other the passion and enthusiasm for, and high level of capability in, continuing to learn, qualities they will need throughout their lives. There is no reason why these two sets of qualities should be alternatives – passion and enthusiasm for, and capability in, learning, will lead to good learning now as well as in the more distant future.

Implications for academic development?

Continuing and just-in-time professional development require very responsive, needs-led rather than supply-led, flexible, educational provision. Academic developers know that this shift requires, not just new teaching and hence development techniques, but new models of curriculum and pedagogy. Developers can anticipate this, and experiment with their own approaches, so that they will be ready when the demand comes. Whichever cyclical model of learning you prefer (Kolb, 1984; Race, 2014), just-in-time will above all involved going round the cycle more rapidly.

So does lifelong learning imply the opposite – a long, contemplative learning process stretching over the years? Probably not. But there is a job to be done in helping learners – that is, everyone – including teachers and academic developers – to synthesise and integrate and interrogate their learning from whatever source, including full-time education and training as well as their continuing professional practice. Perhaps a portfolio is for life, not just for a degree?

Blurring of and collaboration between development functions

In Chapter 1, under the heading *Neighbours*, we provide a large but doubtless already incomplete list of the functions in universities which are also concerned with development; that is, with the improvement of student learning. We stressed the importance of collaboration amongst these various functions.

Implications for academic development?

Here we make three related but larger points, about regional and national organisations concerned with development in higher education.

First, the territory of development – what is happening in institutions – may be starting to diverge from the map, the organisations that represent these various functions. National organisations need to stay alive to these changes, rather than solidifying around earlier forms and functions. As an example – a large and successful national organisation, the Association for Education and Training/Teaching Technologies (AETT) in the UK, failed to adapt to changing circumstances and ceased to have an independent existence, folding into SEDA in 1996. (Its legacy lives on through its journal, now published by SEDA, now called *Innovations in Education and Teaching International*, now in its sixth decade.)

Second, just as it is important for the various development functions to co-operate within institutions, co-operation among the organisations is also important. An approximately biannual meeting of heads of UK development organisations, the informal Higher Education Development Community, has since 2008 tried to achieve this. In Australia in 2009 a broadly corresponding group of associations met to explore the feasibility of a regular Tertiary Education Associations Forum (Chalmers and Solomonides, personal communications, 2015). In Canada the first meeting of Heads of Centres was held in June 2014.

Third, a possible powerful focus for co-operation among associations would be continuing professional development and perhaps also accreditation. What all these development associations have in common – clearly, a commitment to the development, to the improvement, of higher education – may be more important than the particular routes through which they seek to achieve this development, this improvement. We return to this in a later section on the further professionalising of development.

Disruptions which will inform future practice in hard-to-predict ways

There will be disruptions – to the world, and hence to higher education, and hence to academic development.

Implications for academic development?

Time spent thinking about the future is only a very partial preparation for these disruptions, but still worth doing. Following and building on Lewin's (1936:169) sage advice that, 'There is nothing so practical as a good theory', we suggest that a reasonably well-founded pedagogy, and a similarly well-founded theoretical base for our academic development work, will be our best help when we get beyond the limits of available practical guidance; alongside a willingness to keep these theoretical bases under critical review.

Requirement for evidence of cost-effectiveness

Whatever the balance between private and public funding of higher education in different national systems, both private and public funders are likely to make increasing demands for evidence of the cost-effectiveness – to use an even less popular term, the efficiency – of higher education.

Implications for academic development?

We can try to make sure that cost-effectiveness and efficiency are described in appropriate and helpful ways, for example focusing on outcomes and return on investment rather than on simpler and less useful accounts of, for example, student satisfaction, or, even less helpful, input measures such as student:staff ratios. The advice in Chapter 10 on outcomes, monitoring and evaluation should help, and also the comments below on the nature of the student contract.

A stronger discipline focus

There is pressure for increased specialisation in higher education, whilst at the same time the world clearly needs people who can see the bigger picture, who can make links between specialisations, sub-specialisations and indeed micro-specialisations.

Implications for academic development?

The debate about the extent to which pedagogies variously are and should be generic and discipline specific is much too large to have, or even to review, here. A balanced and also defensible view says that (a) there are both common features and disciplinary differences in pedagogies, and (b) anyway many of the academics with whom we work often, with various degrees of base in evidence, emphasise the particular pedagogic needs of their disciplines. This being so, both the effectiveness and the credibility – linked factors – of academic development may be enhanced if some development work is undertaken by discipline specialists and in a way which acknowledges evidence-based disciplinary differences. A central development unit can provide valued support for such specialist, perhaps department-based, developers. Chapter 11, on communities, provides a rich analysis.

Further professionalising, of teaching and development

In the UK, the professionalising of teaching has reached the stage of absorption, hopefully not subversion (see *Responses to development initiatives* in Chapter 1).

We would guess that the pressures to professionalise university teaching will only increase and spread, albeit with some resistance. At the time of writing the Organisation for Economic Co-operation and Development (OECD) is developing a process to enable a comparison of generic and discipline-specific learning outcomes achieved by students in universities around the world ('Testing student and university performance globally: OECD's AHELO', 2014). A logical next step would be moves to standardise learning outcomes internationally, following the standardisation of awards as part of the Bologna process ('What is the Bologna Process?', n.d.). If widely adopted, this may become another driver for the professionalisation of teaching, as may moves to harmonise employment internationally. There is always a tension between the internationalising of standards and the maintenance of national or local appropriateness and autonomy. These tensions are probably best eased by finding a small essential core on which to agree – perhaps the overall purposes of the profession and some uncontentious necessary common capabilities and values – and then encouraging local (both geographic and disciplinary) specialisation.

The dynamics of professionalisation can be complex. The proportion of staff within a university who have gained professional accreditation is a tempting performance indicator, as explored in Chapter 3 on professionalism. However, most teaching staff in an institution have been teaching, there or elsewhere, for some time. How should a university seeking to maximise the proportion of its staff who are professionally accredited allocate its efforts? They will probably find it more economical to prioritise the accreditation of existing experienced staff over the training and development of new staff. The accreditation of existing staff may require perhaps 20 hours of the time of each faculty member to produce, with support, a hopefully evidence-informed and reflective portfolio or presentation, demonstrating their capability in teaching and mapped to the standards. A training and development process for new teaching staff, however efficient, is likely to require much more time.

The original intention of professionalising teaching was to improve teaching, and hence student learning. The results of a target-driven accreditation process may instead, in the short term at least, be to confirm existing teaching practices and to neglect the development needs of new staff, except perhaps for a day or two of induction into teaching, as many universities provided 20 or more years ago. Another illustration that progress is neither automatic nor steady. Chapter 3 explores in much more detail the nature and evolution of professionalism in both teaching and development.

It is difficult to see the pressures for the further professionalisation of developers. There is a defensive reason to professionalise, which can summed up as 'do it to yourself, well, before someone else does it to you badly'. But we strive to be more positive than that. A common development framework and approach across a growing number of development professions is appealing, as suggested above. This approach could focus on the mission, values and to some extent the capabilities that all developers share, whilst encouraging the recognition of specialist capabilities within the broad field of development, of which academic development is just a part. Also, as developers, we may feel more secure within a defined profession, with a qualification framework that provides a scaffold (or perhaps a climbing frame) rather than a cage for our initial and continuing development and accreditation, and thereby some justified element of professional confidence. We surely have to take our profession and ourselves seriously. And qualification, accreditation, in a sector – higher education – which qualifies and accredits people on an epic scale is surely a very appropriate way to show that we do take our profession seriously.

Implications for academic development?

Professionalising teaching provides many valuable roles for developers, roles which are clearly in line with the suggested overall mission of academic development to support and lead improvement in student learning. Developers should almost certainly encourage moves towards the professionalisation of teaching; of course doing whatever they can to ensure that professionalisation is done well. There was one near-miss in the otherwise reasonably smooth development of professional standards for university teaching in UK – the emergence of a proposed standard so incomprehensible that it would, and probably should, have wrecked progress towards accreditation had it been introduced. Vigilance is essential.

As for academic developers, our progress in adopting the trappings of professionalism started early but has been, as described in Chapter 3 on professionalism, slow. However, as SEDA-accredited developers, the authors are very aware of the advantages of development, accreditation and continuing professional development as developers. These include a public account of our capabilities, formally validated by our peers; the requirement for continued development and shared reflection thereon; and letters after our names, which we value. The nature of professional qualification, whether in teaching or development, is of course problematic. In Chapter 1, in a section called *Problems and solutions*, we suggest the predisposition of developers to act as well as analyse. SEDA may have learnt more about how to professionalise academic development by devising and launching a scheme, operating it and keeping it under review for, at the time of this writing, 20 years, than we would have learned by further years of pre-launch planning.

The student contract

The student joining a full-time course of higher education is making a large commitment. At a minimum they are committing a few years of their life, and a corresponding few years of income considerably reduced or forgone, obviously in the hope of a better and perhaps better-paid life afterwards. Beyond that, depending upon the particular higher education funding regime, they and/or their parents, partners, employers and government are also making a very substantial financial commitment. Despite this, the nature of the agreement between student and university is often unclear. There would be advantages to greater clarity. (The idea of a learning contract has a long history – see for example Baume and Brown [1992] and Brown and Baume [1992].).

The idea that students are paying for a degree is obviously unhelpful – the transaction is more complex than this. The idea, from gentler times, of students reading for a degree catches some of the reality. More direct and more helpful, perhaps, is the idea described by Kealey (2011) that students work for a degree, towards at least reasonably clearly defined ends. Beer's analogy (Beer in Anyangwe, 2011) – you pay for membership of the gymnasium, but you have to turn up, do the work, and sweat – catches it vividly.

Implications for academic development?

A key element of any contract or agreement between the student and their university would be an agreed account of the pedagogy. The view that students are paying for a degree, and expressed student wishes for increased class contact and more teaching, are all premised on an implicit pedagogy of the degree as a thing to be got, and of teaching as a way of delivering the degree that is to be got, of education as transfer of some kind of content. Developers have a considerable and valuable role in helping the university to articulate, perhaps to negotiate, and certainly to explain, pedagogy. A good account of pedagogy is likely to include the responsibilities of the students to work towards their degree and the responsibility of the university to support, prompt, challenge, etc. the students to do the necessary work; and to see the effectiveness of their work, to see any necessary changes to what the student should do, to understand what progress they are making towards their degree.

The development contract or agreement

Some of these ideas about the student contract might also inform the idea of a development contract or agreement, a clear and explicit agreement between the developer and the clients, and perhaps also the wider university where this would be useful. Such an agreement might address the needs and wishes of the client and the contribution of the developer; perhaps also when appropriate the overall goals and mission of the institution and the faculty, school or department or programme with which the developer is to work. Clarity and accountability might thereby be enhanced. The idea of an agreement is also considered in Chapter 5 on consultancy and Chapter 14 on projects. This development agreement would have some of the same features as the student contract, including a clear account of who will do and produce what, and to what end, and on what schedule, and with what resources, and how success will be judged. Of course such an agreement would be able to be renegotiated as circumstances change, as circumstances often do.

One value of such an agreement is that it acknowledges the expertise, the capability and the roles of the developer and the client. There has been concern about the legitimacy of the development role – expressed in the question, 'What right do we have to develop others'? Some of this debate has been rather confused. In particular, the idea that developing somehow shows a lack of respect for the expertise of those being developed is odd. Why should teaching someone – alongside our many other roles including consultant, facilitator, project manager, resource finder, colleague and critical friend – be seen as disrespecting them? Any good professional relationship involves both parties, whether teacher and student or developer and teacher, being clear about their expectations from the relationship; and about their own legitimacy, their expertise, their role in, expectations of and contribution to the relationship. Learning and its facilitation are joint ventures. Teacher and learner are also co-learners. Mutual respect is built in.

Respect and explicitness emerge from consideration of a development contract or agreement as powerful principles underpinning our practice as developers and the practice of teaching, and, beyond the scope of this book, many professional relationships.

Futures for workshops

Through most of the history of academic development to date, the staff/faculty development workshop has been a staple of the work of the developer. But the role of the workshop is probably both changing and fading. This is happening as we develop a more sophisticated understanding of what works and doesn't work in academic development, in particular the increasing emphasis on continuing change processes rather than isolated interventions. At the same time the demands on the time of everyone in universities continue to grow, and it becomes harder and harder to find a slot when enough people feel they can legitimately get together to attend a workshop. The introductory quotation to Chapter 11 provides one graphic account of why a whole academic development programme is, in the views of the participant, not working: The exciting ideas explored and developed during the programme did not survive the heat of objection or the chill of apathy on re-entry into the department.

There is still hope for the workshop. Webinars, typically short (sometimes just one hour) online events in which people can participate irrespective of geography as long as they have some form of computing device and a reasonable data connection, are growing in popularity in use. Even shorter courses, lasting just a few minutes per day, (rowellc, 2015; 'The 12 Apps of Christmas', 2014) are coming into use.

But instead of going through a large number of possible forms of workshops, it may be more appropriate, in a book optimistically titled *Advancing Practice in Academic Development*, to take a more analytic approach, and thereby offer tools for the construction of more effective, and possibly very different, sorts of workshops.

Let's go back to the distinction made in Chapter 1 between staff development, seeking to enhance the capabilities of staff; and educational development, seeking to improve educational systems and processes. We may feel that many workshops have historically been staff development workshops. The pedagogic model underpinning staff development workshops, in its purest form, is the pedagogy underpinning many forms of teaching. This pedagogy says that participants, students, will, in the class or workshop, be taught the ideas, the facts, the methods, whatever is the content of the class or workshop. They will then be able to go away and apply this to their own practice. The difficulty with this pedagogy, of course, is that application and implementation are often much more difficult than simply absorbing new information and ideas.

But of course the best workshops were never like this, never just about transmitting content. In the best workshops, participants have ample time to explore the implications for their own practice of the ideas being presented (Rust, 1998). Such a workshop requires the facilitator not to obsess about getting through all the material. A good workshop is more like an educational development event. It provides time, intellectual, even physical space, and support and challenge, from the facilitator and from peers to develop and test ideas which can then be taken back into practice in a well-developed, perhaps even approaching practice-ready, form. The awful, 'And now let's, oh dear, we've only got three minutes left, sorry, I talked too much as usual, anyway, let's spend the last three minutes before you fill in the feedback sheet planning what we'll do next', instead becomes the core of the workshop. Vital parts of the action planning will be deciding who to talk to next, through what channels to work, perhaps which elements are crucial and which negotiable, on the path to implementation. If they do not have complete authority – and, in a university, as Noble and Pym (1970) explore in still recognisable ways, who does? – each participant will need to become, at least in a few respects, an academic developer, supporting and influencing the work of others.

At the same time, of course, information and skills are being learned. The best workshops will probably always be in this sense academic development events. And perhaps this is how we rescue the workshop, if we want to do so, if we can find an appropriate word to describe it. In such a workshop, teams of people work together to plan how to advance their practice. This suggests an advantage to working in existing groupings, again as described in Chapter 11, although the many advantages of working for a couple of hours with colleagues from other disciplines, chief among them the discovery of very different ideas, are lost.

Workshops are typically synchronous, irrespective of geography. This need not be the case. They could take place, probably online, over a defined period – a day, even a week. The asynchronous workshop will provide a different experience. Interaction will be slower, perhaps more reflective, perhaps more considered. At longer durations, such events probably merge into online forums.

Workshops are typically designed either as online or as face-to-face. As the reliability and quality of communication links improves, this distinction become steadily less important. Videoconferencing over a high-quality link is almost like being there, only with much less travel and much better coffee. Sophisticated online meeting spaces also allow for the presentation and sharing of content, alongside speech with or without video, with a running commentary as text or as Twitter with a hashtag for the event.

Bumpy experiences with technology, and the short but still finite learning curve associated with any new technology, can be off-putting. Developers need to work with technical colleagues to minimise these bumps, and allow and support the necessary learning. We do not need to be experts, but we do need to be at least fluent, whilst not forgetting our early discomforts and difficulties. Dealing with difficulties is part of the skill of any professional.

The classic workshop started with a pre-published set of intended learning outcomes, which formed a kind of contract between facilitators and participants. Another possibility is to negotiate the intended learning outcomes, before or at the start of the session. If, following the discussion above, the workshop is to be an academic development rather than a staff/faculty development workshop, the outcomes will no longer primarily be learning outcomes. 'Participants will be able to…'. They will be just outcomes, or outputs: 'By the end of this workshop we will have drafted and critically reviewed an implementation plan to increase the amount, quality and usefulness and feedback to students in module X, including an account of who else we will need to persuade and how we will start to do so'.

It may be that the word *workshop* has been contaminated, and that another term is needed. But this has to be more than a change of name. We need to find a way to describe accurately what development process will be undertaken; how we developers will lead, facilitate, support, whatever is required, it. Maybe they are just development sessions, as part of the change process? (Similarly, a lot of difficulties about methods for teaching students and names for teaching sessions – lecture, seminar, tutorial – could be solved by simply describing every session as a class, and then deciding what would be the most appropriate activities to undertake in that class.)

A cross-institutional role

Because we can see both the breadth and the depth of the institution, academic developers can help to articulate and integrate together, or at any rate help to achieve consistency between, some of the goals and activities of different stakeholders in different locations within the institution.

Appropriate confidence

We need confidently and courteously to assert and apply what we know, from experience and from research, to the development and implementation of policy and strategy and practice. We work for the most part in academic institutions, institutions that value the production and use of scholarly knowledge. We need to be scholarly, valuing and contributing to the scholarships of academic development and of teaching and learning. Here lies part of our strength, if we choose to assert it. This suggests that, contrary to Manathunga (2006, p. 26), we do not need to 'sacrifice our claims to being an *authority* on teaching and learning'; although, as discussed in an earlier section of this chapter on the development contract or agreement, we should of course treat all colleagues with appropriate respect. This is explored further in Chapter 15 on managing a unit.

We also need – again confidently and courteously, and from the position of scholarly strength suggested above – to speak reasoned truth to power, accepting the realities of the institution above and around us described in Chapter 16. We usually need to be invited in – but we should enter with confidence and courtesy.

Research questions

Chapter 12 provides valuable guidance on how to research academic development. What should we be researching? Two obvious at least partial gaps in our knowledge as academic developers are (i) why universities and individual faculty adopt the teaching and learning regimes (Trowler and Cooper, 2002) that they do, and (ii) what factors, including but not limited to the work of academic developers, lead to changes in those regimes? This latter receives some consideration in Chapter 4 on CPD, and some clues are emerging from work on informal learning (see for example Knight, Baume, Tait and Yorke, 2007; *IJAD*, 2015). But we still have much to learn.

Devolution and redundancy

The improvement of academic practice will proceed more rapidly and more deeply if every department and programme is committed to and skilled at development, and if every member of the institution is also, to some extent of least, a developer. Whatever we do as developers, we are, or should be, trying to do ourselves out of a job. That's fine – there is always more for us to do.

Predictions

We wrote earlier in this chapter about the inadvisability of prediction, and opted instead for the comparative safety of scenarios. But we cannot resist making a few predictions, couched here in terms of elements that may feature in the 2020 or so version of this book.

The title, or an overarching theme, may be 'Integrating Development in Higher Education'. We have discussed in Chapter 1 of the current book the myriad development functions in higher education. Hopefully a big story in five years' time will be how these functions are working much more closely together, at the same time as advancing their specialisations. Hopefully another big story will be enhanced co-operation among the development associations.

Use of Artificial Intelligence should merit a chapter. Tutorial conversations with an AI, as part of the educational mix, will help learners – whether students or teachers or developers – engage with ideas and practices in more active and individually appropriate ways. The learner will know they are working with an AI. Once the 'Robotutor' headlines have faded, higher education will have another tool. Through learner and tutor contributions, these systems will learn and improve. The AI should also be able to give some feedback on written work. This should go beyond recognising key concepts and also levels of activity (Bloom, 1969). It may involve using Biggs SOLO taxonomy or later versions thereof to discuss with the student the structure and complexity of the work (Biggs and Collis, 1982), the use and linkage of information and concepts. The interesting issue in AI is not how it can replace us, but how we can best work with it.

Another chapter or two may be about the integration of development, into the role of everyone in the institution and into the processes and structures of the institution. Quality is dynamic. Today's 'good' becomes tomorrow's 'OK' and next year's 'not satisfactory'. Development, enhancement and improvement have to be continuing and distributed processes, towards a common and embraced overall goal; such as, we suggest, improving student learning, a concept which will always need considerable unpacking and will itself continue to evolve.

We are confident that chapters or sections will review further substantial progress made on most or all of the trends in educational development that Gibbs (2013) identifies.

The book itself may be available for sale, as journal issues now often are, chapter by chapter, as indeed may this current volume. The editors of the book, keen that the overall coherence that they have worked so hard to embed into the book will be appreciated by readers, will no doubt seek to link chapters, as we have done here, through much cross-referring. It will be intriguing to see how individual chapter sales affect the writing and editing and marketing of the book.

As the book will also be available as an e-book, the issues of updating, of links and perhaps also of content, will be harder and harder to ignore. Hopefully the book will again be backed by a website, at least containing the links in the text.

We look forward to reading it.

Concluding comments on advancing practice in academic development

We each have to find – or, better, with our colleagues, to make – our own way as an academic developer, depending on, among many other things, our history and background, our current contexts, and our aspirations. We hope we have suggested some useful principles to lean on, and some rich examples to inspire. You will need to interpret for yourself most, if not all, of the advice and examples in this book.

How to be, and continue to improve as, an academic developer? We suggest, addressing individual developers and development units, and at a minimum, a list, hopefully whose backing is to be found in the book, for you to add to:

- Be strategic
- Be principled
- Be pragmatic
- Be scholarly
- Be professional
- Be collaborative
- Be explicit
- Be playful
- Be exemplary
- Be courageous
- Be confident
- Be versatile
- Enjoy it!

References

Åkesson, E. and Falk Nilsson, E. (2010). *Framväxten av den pedagogiska utbildningen för universitetets lärare. Berättelser ur ett lundaperspektiv.* [*The development of pedagogical courses for university teachers. Stories from a Lund-perspective*]. Lund: Lund University.

Amara, R., (n.d.). http://en.wikipedia.org/wiki/Roy_Amara, viewed 24 April 2015.

Baume, D. and Brown, S. (1992). *Learning Contracts One; A Theoretical Perspective.* SCED Paper 72. Birmingham: SCED.

Baume, D. (2012). Prepare for Magic | David Baume's Blog on WordPress.com. Retrieved 27 April 2015 from http://davidbaume.com/2012/05/09/prepare-for-magic/.

Beard, R. (1979). *Teaching and Learning in Higher Education.* Harmondsworth: Penguin.

Beer, J. in Anyangwe, E. (2011). 'Are students the consumers of higher education? Live chat best bits'. *The Guardian.* Retrieved from www.theguardian.com/higher-education-network/blog/2011/dec/14/marketisation-best-bits.

Biggs, J. B. and Collis, K. F. (1982). *Evaluating the Quality of Learning: The SOLO Taxonomy: Structure of the Observed Learning Outcome.* New York: Academic Press.

Biggs, J. B. and Tang, C. (2011). *Teaching for Quality Learning at University: What the Student Does*. United Kingdom: Society for Research into Higher Education.

Bligh, D. A. (2000). *What's the Use of Lectures?: First U.S. Edition of the Classic Work on Lecturing*. San Francisco: Jossey-Bass Publishers.

Bloom, B. S. (1969). *Taxonomy of Educational Objectives: The Classification of Educational Goals*. United Kingdom: Longman Group.

Brown, S. and Baume, D. (1992). *Learning Contracts Two: Some Practical Examples*. SCED Paper 73. Birmingham: SCED.

Clarke, Arthur C. (reprinted 2000). *Profiles of the Future. London: Orion*.

Cowan, J. (1998). *On Becoming an Innovative University Teacher: Reflection in Action*. Buckingham, Society for Research into Higher Education and Open University Press.

The Dearing Report (1997). Higher Education in the learning society, London: Her Majesty's Stationery Office 1997.

Edgeworth, F. Y. (1890). 'The Element of Chance in Competitive Examinations', *Journal of the Royal Statistical Society*, 53(3): 460–475 and 53(4): 644–663, quoted in Rowntree, D. (1996). *Assessing students – how shall we know them?* London: Harper and Row.

Gibbs, G. (2013). 'Reflections on the changing nature of educational development', *International Journal for Academic Development*, 18(1): 4–14.

Grant, B., Lee, A., Clegg, S., Manathunga, C., Barrow, M., Kandlbinder, P., Brailsford, I., Gosling, D. and Hicks, M. (2009). 'Why history? Why now? Multiple accounts of the emergence of academic development', *International Journal for Academic Development*, 14(1): 83–86.

International Journal for Academic Development, 2015(2), Special Issue: Social networks and informal learning: implications for academic development.

Kealey, T. (2011, February). *A new model for universities?* Paper presented at The Crisis in the University?, Cumberland Lodge, Windsor Great Park.

Knight, P. (2002). *Being A Teacher In Higher Education*. Philadelphia, PA: Society for Research into Higher Education and Open University Press.

Knight, P., Baume, D., Tait, J. and Yorke, M. (2007). 'Enhancing part-time teaching in higher education: a challenge for institutional policy and practice', *Higher Education Quarterly*, 61(4): 420–438.

Kolb, D. A. (1984). *Experimental learning: experience as the source of learning and development*. United States: Prentice Hall.

Lee, A. and Kandlbinder, P. (2008) (eds.). 'Making a place: an oral history of academic development in Australia'. HERDSA.

Lewin, K. (1951). D. Cartwright (ed.) Field theory in social science, selected theoretical papers. New York: Harper & Row.

Locke, W. (2014). 'Shifting academic careers: implications for enhancing professionalism in teaching and supporting learning'. York: Higher Education Academy. Retrieved from www.heacademy.ac.uk/sites/default/files/resources/shifting_academic_careers_FINAL.pdf.

Manathunga, C. (2006). 'Doing educational development ambivalently: post-colonial approaches to educational development?', *International Journal for Academic Development*, 11: 19–29.

Moore's Law. (n.d.). Retrieved 17 April 2015 from www.mooreslaw.org.

Moses, I. (2012). 'Views from a former vice-chancellor', *International Journal for Academic Development*, 17(3): 275–277.

Noble, T. and Pym, B. (1970). 'Collegial authority and the receding locus of power', *The British Journal of Sociology*, 21(4): 431–445.

Race, P. (2014). *Making Learning Happen: A Guide for Post-compulsory Education.* Thousand Oaks, CA: SAGE Publications.

Ramsden, P. (2003). *Learning to Teach in Higher Education.* London: RoutledgeFalmer.

Robinson, E. E. (1968). *New Polytechnics A Radical Policy For Higher Education.* London: Penguin.

rowellc. (2015). Reflections on the 12 Apps of Christmas at Regent's University London. Retrieved 23 June 2015 from https://totallyrewired.wordpress.com/2015/04/22/reflections-on-the-12-apps-of-christmas-at-regents-university-london/.

Rust, C. (1998). 'The impact of educational development workshops on teachers' practice', *International Journal for Academic Development,* 3(1): 72–80.

Steincke, K. K. (1984). *Goodbye and Thanks.* Denmark.

Students as Producers. (n.d.). Retrieved 11 May 2015 from http://studentasproducer.lincoln.ac.uk/.

Testing student and university performance globally: OECD's AHELO. (2014). Retrieved 11 May 2015 from www.oecd.org/edu/skills-beyond-school/testingstudentanduniversityperformancegloballyoecdsahelo.htm.

The 12 Apps of Christmas. (2014). Retrieved 23 June 2015 from https://the12appsofchristmas.wordpress.com/.

Trowler, P. and Cooper, A. (2002). 'Teaching and learning regimes: implicit theories and recurrent practices in the enhancement of teaching and learning through educational development programmes', *Higher Education Research & Development,* 21(3): 221–240.

What is the Bologna Process? (n.d.). Retrieved 24 June 2015 from www.eua.be/eua-work-and-policy-area/building-the-european-higher-education-area/bologna-basics.aspx.

Index